Better Homes and Gardens®
Do-It-Yourself
HOME REPAIRS

© Copyright 1985 by Meredith Corporation, Des Moines, Iowa.
All Rights Reserved. Printed in the United States of America.
First Edition. Printing Number and Year: 10 9 8   95 94 93
Library of Congress Catalog Card Number: 84-63046
ISBN: 0-696-01520-X

BETTER HOMES AND GARDENS® BOOKS

Editor: Gerald M. Knox
Art Director: Ernest Shelton
Managing Editor: David A. Kirchner
Copy and Production Editors: Marsha Jahns,
Mary Helen Schiltz, Carl Voss, David A. Walsh

Associate Art Directors: Linda Ford Vermie,
Neoma Alt West, Randall Yontz
Assistant Art Directors: Faith Berven,
Harijs Priekulis, Tom Wegner
Senior Graphic Designers: Alisann Dixon,
Lynda Haupert, Lyne Neymeyer
Graphic Designers: Mike Burns, Mike Eagleton,
Deb Miner, Stan Sams, Darla Whipple-Frain

Vice President, Editorial Director: Doris Eby
Group Editorial Services Director: Duane L. Gregg

Senior Vice President, General Manager: Fred Stines
Director of Publishing: Robert B. Nelson
Vice President, Retail Marketing: Jamie Martin
Vice President, Direct Marketing: Arthur Heydendael

Do-It-Yourself Home Repairs
Editors: Larry Clayton, Jim Harrold, Carl Voss
Copy and Production Editor: Carl Voss
Graphic Designers: Mike Burns, Harijs Priekulis, Tom Wegner
Contributing Writers: Greg Erickson, Gary Havens,
David A. Kirchner, James A. Hufnagel
Technical Consultants: George Granseth, Al Roux,
Don Wipperman, Jim Downing, Ron Tesdell, Jim Heger,
Kenn Spahr
Drawings: Carson Ode

INTRODUCTION

Ah, the joys of owning a home. Even if you're still buying a home, as most of us are, it's a great feeling to know that at least some of the money you spend on shelter is building equity in your property.

But unlike an apartment building, there's no maintenance man to come around and fix the sticking door, mend the torn screen, replace the float bowl in your toilet, or add a dimmer switch in your living room. If you want any if these jobs done, you'll have to do them yourself or hire someone else to do the repairs. And who really wants to go through the frustration of finding a competent jack-of-all-trades and pray he or she will come at the appointed time and not gouge your budget (or a favorite antique)?

For a lot less frustration, you probably can get professional results by making the repair yourself. Have confidence! There is no great mystery to making home repairs—the right tools, some good instruction, and a little patience can carry you through the projects found in this book.

The five major sections in the book help you tackle repair problems you're likely to encounter around your house and offer you ideas to implement improvments to your home.

The first section helps you get started with the woodworking tools, materials, and techniques used in basic carpentry. The second section continues working with wood and discusses building cabinets and shelves for your home.

In the wiring section, you can learn anything from how to replace a lamp plug to adding a ground fault circuit interrupter. And between the first and last plumbing pages, you can learn everything from repairing leaky faucets to adding bathroom fixtures to your home.

Finally, the household repairs section walks you through those nagging malfunctions that sometimes take the joy out of homeownership.

CONTENTS

BASIC PLUMBING 200

HOUSEHOLD REPAIRS 274

INDEX 314

BASIC CARPENTRY

Ever watch a magician pull a rabbit from a hat? If so, you know that there's more to the trick than a few magic words and a wave of the wand. That "more" is a knowledge of the *basics* of illusion, the *right equipment,* and *lots of practice.*

These same elements can make you into a pretty fair home carpenter, too. That's because nothing is intrinsically difficult about carpentry, no matter whether you're building a birdhouse or a room addition. With a knowledge of the basics of carpentry, the right equipment, and practice, you should be able to take on almost any project and do it well.

That's not to say, however, that after digesting the material in this book, you'll be able to conquer every carpentry challenge. You won't. What the book will do is provide you with a good foundation on which you can build your carpentry expertise.

Because getting off to a good start is important with any hobby, we begin with a section titled "Start Out Right." In it we talk about the importance of setting up shop and how to do it, the basic tools you'll need, and the many materials and hardware items you'll encounter as you begin your carpentry career.

Then it's on to the real tricks all carpenters use to pull off their magic acts—*techniques.* You'll learn how to measure, cut, drill, fasten, shape, smooth, and finish—the techniques common to all carpentry projects. In addition, a short section tells how to keep your tools razor-sharp.

So that you can put your newfound knowledge to work, we've included several projects in this section. In it you not only will come across the basic box (and several things you can do with it), but also find out how to hang shelves on walls, and how to frame or furr-out walls as well as how to install drywall.

And you'll be relieved to know that you can complete all of the projects featured here without having to resort to using expensive power tools or any tricky joinery techniques.

Likewise, none of the projects requires that you have a permit from any municipality or an after-completion inspection by building officials. If you decide to take on other, larger-scale projects such as adding to an existing structure or making other structural changes, check with local officials as to their requirements.

A word about safety: As with any other do-it-yourself activity, THINK SAFETY is the watchword with carpentry. Be especially watchful of how you use the carpentry tools whose purpose it is to cut. They don't discriminate. For more information on this important topic, please turn to and carefully read page 15.

STARTING OUT RIGHT

Why spend 20 pages of a book talking about how to get your carpentry career off to a good start? Because it's the best way we could think of to introduce you to this wide, wide world you're about to enter.

In it you'll discover a myriad of products and materials. You'll also encounter some pros and sales help who assume you are familiar with the things they deal in each day. The only way to keep confusion to a minimum is to be prepared by reading this section.

Because one of your first concerns probably will be where to do your carpentry projects, that's where this chapter begins. As you'll see, your shop can be in any number of places.

Then we discuss the tools you'll need—both power and hand tools. You may be surprised at how few you actually need to complete most projects.

After this, you'll learn about how to select and handle the many materials you'll come in contact with, as well as the potpourri of hardware items you'll see at most building materials outlets.

Setting Up Your Home Workshop

No matter what the hobby a person involves himself with, having an area set aside especially for that pursuit makes good sense. And carpentry is certainly no exception. You need a convenient, comfortable, well-organized place to work and to store all the tools and other paraphernalia you'll accumulate as you continue doing various carpentry projects.

Your carpentry headquarters can be in any number of places around your home, can be large or small, and can be basic or elaborate. But have one you must—and the sooner the better.

Locating Your Work Center

Where you locate your workshop depends on available space and your needs. Basements, garages, seldom-used rooms, even closets and attics are all candidates. But if you have a basement, look there first, as it has several distinct advantages over any other area. It's off the beaten path, so you needn't worry too much about disrupting family activities as you work. In most homes it's also one of the few areas with sizable amounts of unused space—an important factor especially if you are eventually planning to equip the shop with stationary power tools. And, basements offer a comfortable environment to work in—moderately warm in winter, pleasantly cool in summer.

Not all basements will work, however. Access and dampness can be problems. Obviously, if you can't get materials in and out, or if you can't control dampness by waterproofing the walls or dehumidifying the area, you'll have to look elsewhere.

Planning Pointers

Once you've decided on your shop's location, you need to spend some time planning how to equip it. The workshop shown below illustrates many of the items you'll want to include in yours, space permitting. Also keep the following pointers in mind as you plan.
• Because a workbench is the activity hub of every workshop, selecting one that's right for your situation is an important first consideration. Full-size workbenches typically measure 6 to 8 feet long, 24 to 36 inches deep, and 40 to 42 inches high. Obviously, however, not all shops can contain a bench of these dimensions. Likewise, not all people will find the heights listed comfortable. So you may *(continued)*

Planning Pointers *(contd.)*

have to do some tailoring. Measure from the floor to your hipbone to determine your best work surface height.

Whether you buy or build the bench is up to you. Commercially made ones range from simple steel and particleboard arrangements to elaborate versions that would satisfy even the most dedicated cabinetmaker.

If you elect to build your own, use building materials and fasteners that will yield a strong, stable work surface. We've included plans for a couple of well-designed benches here—one full-size one, and a closet-size version —both of which can be knocked together in a weekend or less.

• Be sure to provide for plenty of storage, both for your tools and for the many containers and other supplies that otherwise will quickly clutter up the area. Use perforated hardboard racks to store small hand tools within easy reach, and get yourself an inexpensive organizer for keeping all those nails, bolts, screws, and other hardware items in their place. Store power tools and flammable liquids in locked cabinets, if possible, or another *safe* place.

• Arrange for adequate shop lighting. You'll want one or more lights for general illumination as well as more intense task lighting for those workshop operations that demand it.

• Run at least one 20-amp electrical circuit with ground fault circuit protection to the shop to provide power for your power tools and lighting needs. Large shops should have separate circuits for tools and lights. Position electrical outlets strategically around the workshop so that power is never far away.

• To ensure adequate ventilation, install an exhaust fan capable of

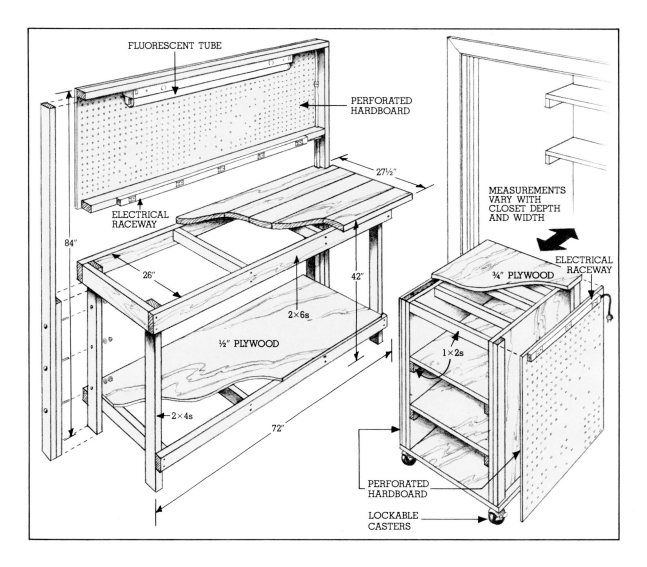

FLUORESCENT TUBE

PERFORATED HARDBOARD

27½"

ELECTRICAL RACEWAY

84"

26"

42"

2×6s

½" PLYWOOD

2×4s

72"

MEASUREMENTS VARY WITH CLOSET DEPTH AND WIDTH

ELECTRICAL RACEWAY

¾" PLYWOOD

1×2s

PERFORATED HARDBOARD

LOCKABLE CASTERS

changing the air in the shop every four minutes. The number of cubic feet (length x width x height) in your shop determines the size fan needed.

• To warn against fire, you'll want a smoke detector as well as a good-size ABC-rated fire extinguisher. Also, have a first-aid kit handy to deal with injuries if they occur.

• To facilitate cleanup, have a broom and dustpan or a shop vacuum on hand. And don't forget to get yourself a metal trash container with a tight-fitting lid to safely house the many wastes that will result from your carpentry projects.

• To support bulky sheet goods and lengths of lumber while they're being measured and cut, you'll need a couple of sawhorses. We show three different possibilities here. If space is at a premium in your shop, consider buying the hinged metal leg horses or the metal bracket type, both of which you can break down for easy storage. Otherwise, you may prefer to build your own entirely from wood.

• You'll want to have some way to conveniently carry your tools from place to place as you work. The tool caddy shown here has plenty of room for many tools at one time. It's deep enough to hold a few power tools, and long enough to accommodate a crosscut saw or ripsaw and a carpenter's level. Holes drilled through the shelf provide grab-it-quick storage for a hammer, screwdrivers, and other hand tools.

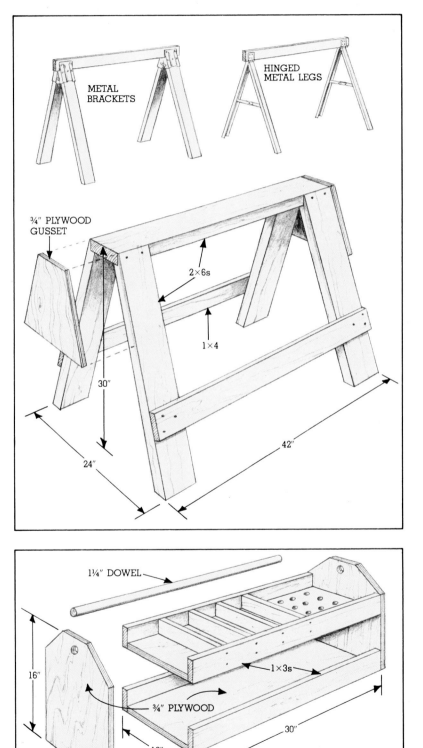

Buy the Basic Tools

For many home carpenters, purchasing tools is a never-ending process. A tool exists for every conceivable need. But as a beginning carpenter, you don't need all the "extras." Instead, concentrate on assembling a few key tools—those shown and discussed here and on the following three pages—then add to this core group others as the need arises. (Note: When tool shopping, buy the best you can afford. Good-quality tools, properly used and cared for, often last a lifetime.)

Hand Tools

1 Few if any carpentry tools see more action than the *flexible steel tape,* so make it one of your first purchases. A 12-footer with a lock-button and plastic coating on the tape itself offers adequate measuring flexibility.

2 Use a *framing square* to square almost anything, to check stud spacings quickly, even to mark rafter and stair stringer cuts.

3 Square up smaller pieces and mark 45-degree angles with a *combination square.* Look for one with a built-in level and scriber.

4 Duplicate angles of from 0 to 180 degrees with a *T bevel.*

5 Plumb and level large projects with a *carpenter's level.* Buy a 24- or 28-inch model.

6 Mark cutoff lines and make pilot holes with an *awl.*

7 Snap long, straight lines with a *chalk line reel.* This tool also doubles as a plumb bob to establish true vertical lines.

8 A 26-inch, 8-point crosscut *handsaw* will handle most general-purpose cutting chores.

9 To make perfect miter joints, you need a *backsaw* and *miter box.*

10 And to cut curves and straight lines easily in tight places, use a *keyhole saw* with its narrow, tapered blade.

11 Cut intricate curves in thin materials with a *coping saw.*

12 *Wood chisels* enable you to shape mortises, cut and smooth wood joints, and do other specialized cutting work. Look for ones with metal-capped handles.

13 And don't be without a retractable-blade *utility knife* for cutting chores that require a razor-sharp blade.

14 For driving and removing nails and other fasteners, buy a 16-ounce *curved-claw hammer.*

15 And to sink the heads of finishing nails below the surface of the work, use a *nail set.* Purchase several sizes.

16, 17 You'll need a set of *slotted* and *Phillips-tipped screwdrivers* or a *ratchet-action screwdriver* with several tips for driving and removing screws.

18 To fasten nuts, bolts, and lag screws, buy a pair of 10-inch *adjustable-end wrenches.*

19 If you don't have a pair of *slip-joint pliers,* add them to your tool collection right away.

20 For holding about-to-be-sawed, -drilled, or -joined members, invest in several *C clamps* of varying sizes. Later, you may want to add pipe and miter clamps, too.

21 For good results when planing with the grain, purchase a *jack plane.*

22 A *block plane's* specialty is planing across grain.

23 The triangular teeth of a *rasp* remove wood in a hurry. Look also at the rasp-like forming tools available. These have replaceable blades.

24 *Wood files* smooth edges and do other light smoothing duty. The best purchase here is a coarse, half-round, double-cut file.

25 And purchase an *oilstone* for various tool-sharpening needs.

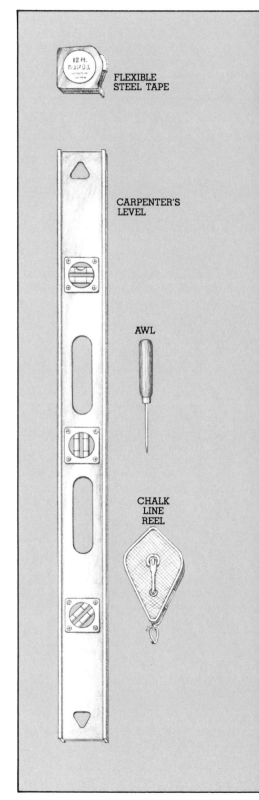

FLEXIBLE STEEL TAPE

CARPENTER'S LEVEL

AWL

CHALK LINE REEL

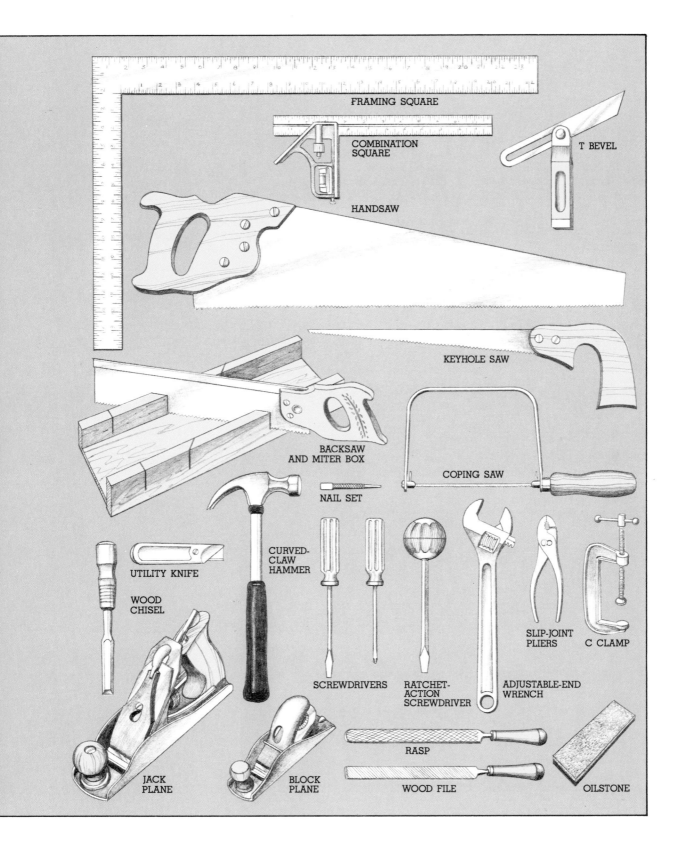

FRAMING SQUARE

COMBINATION
SQUARE

T BEVEL

HANDSAW

KEYHOLE SAW

BACKSAW
AND MITER BOX

COPING SAW

NAIL SET

CURVED-
CLAW
HAMMER

UTILITY KNIFE

WOOD
CHISEL

SLIP-JOINT
PLIERS

C CLAMP

SCREWDRIVERS

RATCHET-
ACTION
SCREWDRIVER

ADJUSTABLE-END
WRENCH

JACK
PLANE

BLOCK
PLANE

RASP

WOOD FILE

OILSTONE

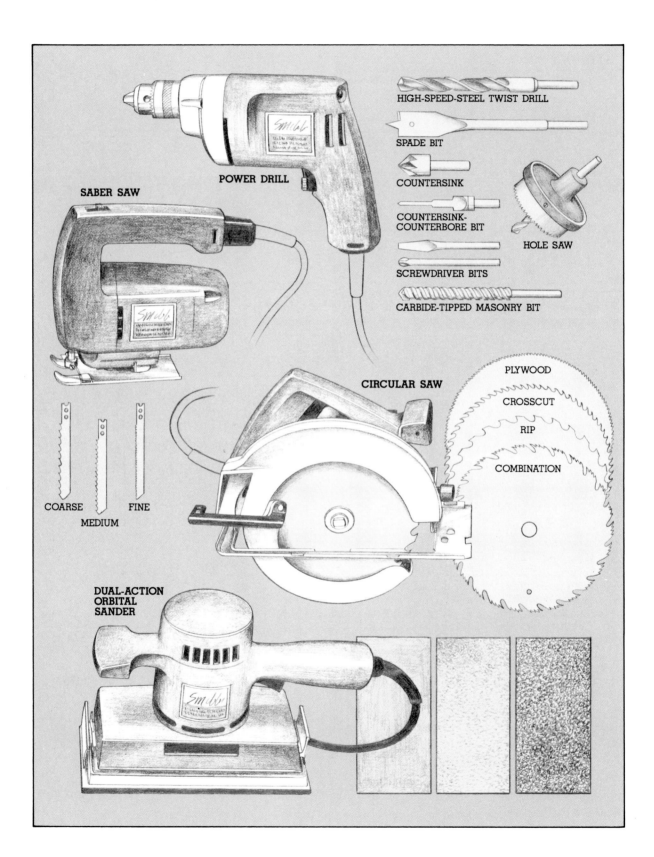

HIGH-SPEED-STEEL TWIST DRILL

SPADE BIT

COUNTERSINK

COUNTERSINK-COUNTERBORE BIT

SCREWDRIVER BITS

CARBIDE-TIPPED MASONRY BIT

HOLE SAW

POWER DRILL

SABER SAW

CIRCULAR SAW

PLYWOOD

CROSSCUT

RIP

COMBINATION

COARSE

MEDIUM

FINE

DUAL-ACTION ORBITAL SANDER

Affordable Power Tools

You may not associate power tools with the basic tool kit; but if you think in terms of the convenience and speed that power drills, saber saws, circular saws, and dual-action orbital sanders bring to the home workshop, you really can't afford to be without them. Following is a rundown on each member of this power tool quartet.

Power drills come in three sizes—¼ inch, ⅜ inch, and ½ inch. These fractions describe the maximum diameter of bit shafts the drills can accept. The ⅜-inch model, because it's sturdy enough to handle all but the heaviest types of work, is your best bet. Make sure the one you choose has a reverse switch and a variable-speed trigger. Both features come in handy if you use your drill as a screwdriver.

As you can see, a power drill can drive a variety of bits. With *high-speed-steel twist drills* you can bore up to ½-inch holes in wood or metal. To make ¼- to 1½-inch-diameter holes in wood, get a set of *spade bits.* And if you have a need for even larger holes—up to 2½ inches—purchase a *hole-saw* set or an *adjustable hole saw. Carbide-tipped masonry bits,* not surprisingly, find their way through masonry and concrete surfaces. *Countersinks* and *countersink-counterbore bits* make form-fitting holes for screws. And *screwdriver bits* will speedily transform your reversible drill into a power screwdriver.

No tool in the carpenter's workshop can claim the versatility of the portable *saber saw.* This little giant can crosscut, rip, angle cut, bevel, even cut holes and scrolls in almost any material. Just put in the correct blade for the job, and you're off and running.

You can select from dozens of blades to cut through a variety of materials. As a general rule, though, the fewer number of teeth the blade has, the faster and rougher the cut will be. The more teeth per inch, the slower and smoother the result.

Circular saws can make many of the same cuts its saber saw counterpart can, only faster.

When shopping for one of these, look for a 7¼-inch model with an automatic blade guard, a saw blade depth adjustment, an adjustable baseplate so you can make bevels, and a ripping fence accessory.

The saw you buy probably will come with a *combination blade,* which means it's designed for both across-the-grain and with-the-grain cuts. You may later want to buy a different blade for each of these two types of cuts—*crosscut* and *ripping.* And for making clean cuts in sheet goods, get yourself a *plywood* blade. You may want to invest in tungsten-carbide-tipped blades rather than less-expensive but short-lived standard blades.

A dual-action *orbital sander* makes quick work of almost any sanding job. In its orbital mode, it removes excess material fairly quickly. Then with the flip of a switch, the action changes to straight-line sanding, the perfect motion for finish sanding.

So you'll be prepared for any sanding eventuality, you should lay in a supply of coated abrasives. Your selection should include several sheets in varying degrees of coarseness—coarse, medium, and fine. (Note: The larger the grit number, the finer the texture of the abrasive. For example, 150-grit is *fine,* whereas 60 is *coarse.*) For most of your sanding needs, aluminum oxide abrasive is probably your best bet, all things considered.

Tool Safety Tips

Experienced home carpenters know that tool safety is a blend of exercising common sense and following certain guidelines when working in and around the shop. To make all of your experiences with tools happy ones, keep in mind the following:

- Use tools *only* for the jobs they were designed to do. If a tool came with an instruction manual, take the time to read it to find out what it will do and will not do.
- Check on the condition of a tool before using it. A dull cutting edge or a loose-fitting hammer handle, for example, spells trouble. Also inspect the cord of a power tool to make sure it's not frayed.
- Don't work with tools if you're tired, in a bad mood, or in a big hurry.
- Wear goggles whenever the operation you are performing could result in eye injury.
- The safety mechanisms on power tools are there for your protection. Do not tamper with or remove them from the tool.
- Don't wear loose-fitting clothes or dangly jewelry while you are using tools, especially power tools.
- Keep children and others at a safe distance while you're using any tool. And before letting children use a tool, instruct them on how to operate it.
- Before servicing or adjusting a power tool, unplug it and allow moving parts to come to a standstill.

Selecting and Handling Materials

Choosing and Buying Lumber

As a home carpenter, you will be buying lots of lumber for various projects. And although you needn't become a lumber "expert," smart buymanship requires that you know what's available, when to use what type and size lumber, and how to order this most basic of all building materials. After reading this and the next three pages, you'll know the basics.

Begin by realizing three things about lumber. First, there are only two basic types—*softwoods* and *hardwoods*. Second, keep in mind that both types have a set of *nominal* dimensions (what you order) and a set of *actual* dimensions

(what you get after the lumber is milled and dried). And third, remember that both softwoods and hardwoods have different grading systems, which we explain on pages 18–19.

Now, take a look at the chart, opposite. It classifies lumber into five groupings, then lists common uses for each, as well as nominal and actual dimensions of various-size members.

Because of the array of lumber thicknesses and widths, lumberyard and home center personnel use the *board foot* to measure and price the amount of wood in a given piece. (As shown below at left, a board foot is defined as the wood equivalent of a piece 12 inches square and 1 inch thick.) For most of your needs, though,

just specify a piece's length in linear feet and the yard will compute the cost.

When lumber shopping, come prepared with a list detailing your needs. To order, state the quantity, thickness, width, length, grade and species—for example, four 2″ × 4″ × 8′ No. 2 fir. And after placing your order at the desk, walk out into the yard to see firsthand what you're getting. If you spot any of the defects shown below at right and if they'll seriously interfere with how you intend to use the lumber, ask for replacements. And to prevent some of these problems from occurring once the goods are in your hands, follow the handling and storage advice given on page 23. *(continued)*

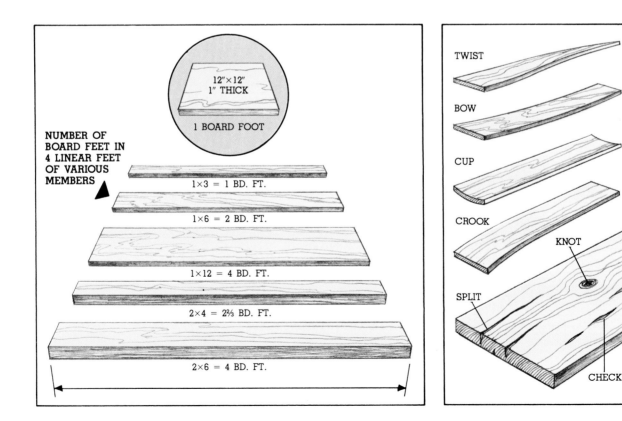

12″×12″
1″ THICK

1 BOARD FOOT

NUMBER OF
BOARD FEET IN
4 LINEAR FEET
OF VARIOUS
MEMBERS ▲

1×3 = 1 BD. FT.

1×6 = 2 BD. FT.

1×12 = 4 BD. FT.

2×4 = 2⅔ BD. FT.

2×6 = 4 BD. FT.

TWIST

BOW

CUP

CROOK

KNOT

SPLIT

CHECK

Lumber Selector

Type		Common Uses	Nominal Sizes	Actual Sizes
Strips		Furring for wall-paneling material (drywall, hardboard, plywood) and ceiling material (drywall, composition tiles); trim; shims; spacers; blocking; bridging; stakes; forms; crates; battens; light-duty frames; edging; latticework.	1 × 2 1 × 3	¾ × 1½ ¾ × 2½
Finish Lumber: Boards	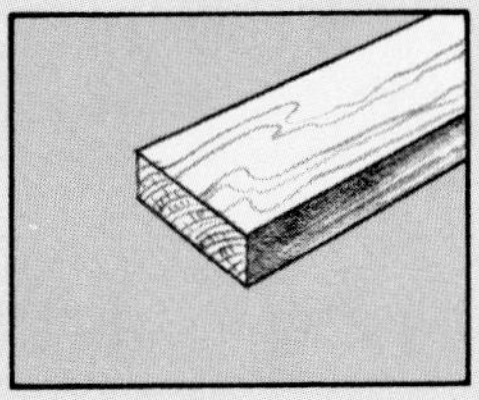	Interior paneling; exterior sheathing; structural framing and finishing; exterior siding and soffits; subflooring and flooring; decking; fencing; walks; interior and exterior trim; fascias; casing; valances; shelving; cabinets; closet lining; furniture; built-ins.	1 × 4 1 × 6 1 × 8 1 × 10 1 × 12	¾ × 3½ ¾ × 5½ ¾ × 7¼ ¾ × 9¼ ¾ × 11¼
Tongue and Groove		Subflooring; flooring; exterior sheathing; exterior siding; decorative interior wall treatments.	1 × 4 1 × 6 1 × 8 1 × 10 1 × 12	Actual sizes vary from mill to mill.
Shiplap		Exterior sheathing and siding, decking; underlayment; subflooring; roof sheathing; decorative interior wall treatments.	1 × 4 1 × 6 1 × 8	¾ × 3⅛ ¾ × 5⅛ ¾ × 6⅞
Dimension Lumber		Structural framing (wall studs, ceiling and floor joists, rafters, headers, top and soleplates); structural finishing; forming; exterior decking and fencing; walks; benches; screeds; stair components (stringers, steps); boxed columns.	2 × 2 2 × 3 2 × 4 2 × 6 2 × 8 2 × 10 2 × 12	1½ × 1½ 1½ × 2½ 1½ × 3½ 1½ × 5½ 1½ × 7¼ 1½ × 9¼ 1½ × 11¼
Posts	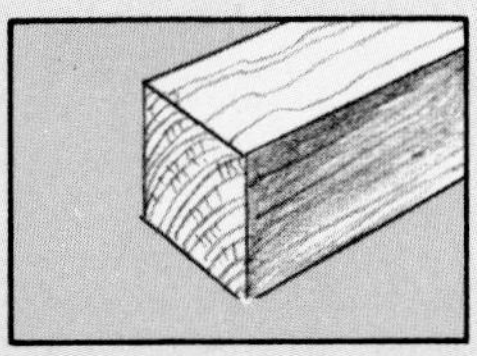	Heavy-duty structural framing; support columns; fencing; decking; turning material for wood lathes; building material for architectural and decorative interest.	4 × 4 6 × 6	3½ × 3½ 5½ × 5½
Timbers	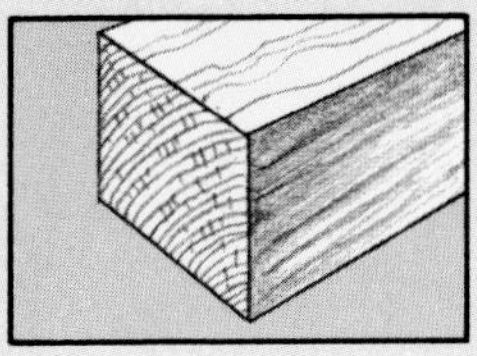	Heavy-duty structural framing; support columns; building material for architectural and decorative interest.	Rough-sawn; sizes vary.	Actual sizes vary slightly up or down from nominal sizes.

Choosing Softwoods

At this point, you may not know one softwood from another. (The chart below compares the most commonly available species.) But don't let that bother you a great deal because unless you're framing a major structural component that will bear great weight, such as a ceiling joist, you can't make a serious mistake when buying softwoods.

You can also take comfort in knowing that many building material home centers and lumberyards, because they bulk-buy lumber to achieve greater savings, stock only a few species. As a result, you may find you can actually do very little selecting in most cases. You may have only one or two species to choose from. However, you will be asked what grade lumber you want, which in large part depends on the nature of your project.

Admittedly, softwood lumber grading is tricky at first. That's partially because several grading systems exist. But in general, you'll be on safe footing if you think in terms of two overall grade classifications: *select* and *common*. Use select lumber *(B and Better, C,* and *D)* for showy projects such as cabinetry where good appearance is a vital consideration. For all other projects, common lumber *(Nos. 1, 2, 3,* and *4)* will do nicely. Not surprisingly, the better the grade —that is, the more defect-free— the more you will pay.

Talk over your project with sales personnel, too; often, they can suggest the best buy for your particular need.

Softwood Selector

Species	Characteristics	Common Uses	Additional Information
Cedar, Cypress	Lightweight but good flex strength; easy to work with; take nails well; highly resistant to rot; no preservative needed for exterior use; cedar has a sweet aroma.	Trim; paneling; decks; fencing; posts; chests; closet lining (aromatic cedar); shingles (cedar).	Cedar 1×4s, 1×6s, and 1×8s usually come with one smooth-cut face, one rough-cut face. Cedar is commonly available in the North; cypress, in the South.
Fir, Pine, Spruce, Hemlock	Easy to work with; finish well; good strength; weights vary; resist shrinking.	House framing; paneling; trim; interior furniture; decking; fencing; sheathing; general utility.	Spruce also is known as "white wood." You can use these species almost interchangeably in small projects. Apply a preservative if used outdoors. All will split if carelessly nailed near ends of boards; drill pilot holes or blunt nail ends to prevent this. This classification includes southern (yellow) pine, which is very yellow in color, strong, but also brittle. Nails may not "seat" well in this wood.
Treated Lumber	*Pressure treated:* Heavy and strong; usually greenish in color; tends to shrink; can be painted, stained, or left to weather naturally; highly resistant to rot. *Creosote-* or *penta-treated:* Solution applied only to surface; not as rot-resistant.	Outdoor projects of any kind: soffits, fascias, decking, fencing, posts.	Use gloves to protect your hands against splinters, which sting and burn. Never use scraps from this chemical-laden wood in your fireplace or wood-burning stove.
Redwood	Lightweight; fairly strong but brittle; can snap under enough pressure; highly resistant to decay; no preservative needed; cuts cleanly and easily, but splits easily, too; weathers quickly.	Trim; paneling; decks; fencing; fascias; outdoor furniture; house siding.	For posts and near-ground structural members, *heartwood* is best. For all other projects, save money by using *garden-grade* redwood. Drill pilot holes before nailing to avoid splitting.

Choosing Hardwoods

You can readily buy all kinds of papers, vinyls, and laminated plastics that *look* like hardwood, but nothing quite measures up to the real thing.

Unfortunately, genuine hardwoods are an increasingly scarce commodity. The demand for their unique aesthetic and structural qualities—some of which you'll find listed in the chart below—far outstrips the amount of lumber produced by these slow-growing deciduous trees. The result: You pay a premium price for most hardwood lumber or settle for a man-made facsimile.

Hardwood lumber, unlike softwoods, is milled to make use of virtually every splinter. So instead of the standard sizes softwoods come in, hardwoods are sold in pieces of varying lengths and widths, usually from ½ to 2 inches thick (nominal size). Individual boards generally are smooth-surfaced on two sides (S2S), and are priced at so much per board foot (see page 16).

Hardwood grading differs from softwoods, too—it's based primarily on the amount of clear surface area on the board. Heading the list is *FAS Grade* (Firsts and Seconds), which is the most knot-free, followed by *Select Grade, No. 1 Common,* and *No. 2 Common.*

Most lumberyards can't afford to maintain an extensive inventory of hardwood lumber, and generally stock only a limited assortment of a few species such as birch, mahogany, or oak. For the best selection, try to find a yard that specializes in hardwoods. You'll be astounded at the exotic species they stock or can special-order.

Hardwood Selector

Species	Characteristics	Common Uses	Additional Information
Ash	Heavy; strong; hard; rigid; works well with tools; holds nails and screws well but is prone to splits.	Formed parts of furniture; cabinets; millwork; baseball bats; implement handles.	Ash has a grain pattern similar to oak, but wilder and more yellow.
Cherry	Heavy; strong; hard; rigid; difficult to work with hand tools; resistant to shrinking and warping; fine grained; sands very smooth.	Fine furniture; cabinets; gun stocks.	Cherry is also known as fruitwood. Because of its scarcity, it is expensive.
Mahogany	Durable; easily worked; resistant to shrinking, warping, and swelling; fine grained; finishes well.	Fine furniture; cabinets; millwork; moldings; plywood veneers.	Genuine (Honduras) mahogany has a more pronounced grain than Philippine (lauan) mahogany.
Maple and Birch	Heavy; strong; hard; rigid; difficult to work with hand tools; resistant to shrinking and warping; fine grained; finish well.	Furniture; cabinets; millwork; moldings; flooring; inlays; veneers; butcher blocks.	Maple and birch have similar characteristics, although birch is somewhat softer and less expensive.
Oak	Heavy; strong; hard; rigid; difficult to work with hand tools; resistant to swelling; open grained; finishes well.	Fine furniture; cabinets; millwork; interior trim; flooring; stair rails.	Red oak is coarse grained and has a pink cast, and white oak is more decay resistant and has a yellow cast.
Poplar	Lightweight and soft for a hardwood; quite easy to work; fine grained; paints well.	Furniture; cabinets; trim.	Poplar is gray-white in color with slight green streaks. It has some tendency to fuzz when sanded.
Walnut	Strong; hard; durable; works well with either hand or power tools; resistant to warping, shrinking, and swelling; fine grained.	Fine furniture; cabinets; millwork; paneling veneers; gun stocks.	Tropical walnut has a coarser, more porous grain than native North American walnut.

Choosing and Buying Sheet Goods

To fashion many of the large components of a cabinet or shelving unit in the "old days," cabinetmakers had no alternative other than edge-joining narrow widths of lumber—an exacting and time-consuming task. Then along came plywood and the other sheet goods. Today, it's difficult to find a project that doesn't use one or more of these useful products. They save valuable time; are widely available, easy to work, and inexpensive compared to their lumber equivalent; and come in quite an array of thicknesses and panel sizes.

The chart below summarizes your sheet goods material options. Note that we've included a couple of items you might not expect to see in a chart of this type—*wood veneer* and *glass*. Wood veneer—actually a thin slice of real wood—allows craftsmen to finish the raw edges of plywood and other sheet goods and to use less-expensive sheet goods as a core material. Some of it comes with an adhesive backing; other types require contact cement.

We've listed three types of glass in the chart—sheet and plate glass and mirror tiles. When ordering glass for your project, jot down the exact size sheets you need and have a glass company do the cutting for you. And be sure to have the edges ground and polished.

Before ordering plywood, particleboard, or hardboard, develop a cutting diagram of the various pieces you need, as discussed on page 94. This is especially important if you're working with hardwood plywood, which can cost $60 or more per sheet. You can't afford to waste any.

What's What in Cabinetmaking Sheet Goods

Material	Grades and Common Types	Thickness (in inches)	Common Panel Sizes (in feet)	Typical Uses
Plywood	Softwood plywood A-A; A-B; A-C A-D	¼; ⅜; ½; ⅝; ¾	2x4; 4x4; 4x8	Projects in which appearance of one or both sides matters—cabinets, drawer fronts, bookcases, built-ins, shelves, tabletops
	MDO	⅜; ¾	4x8	Projects requiring an extra-smooth painting surface—tabletops, cabinets
	Hardwood plywood A-2 (good both sides)	⅛; ¼; ⅜; ½; ¾	2x4; 4x8	Fine furniture and cabinetmaking; decorative wall panels
	G1S (good one side)	⅛; ¼	4x8	
Wood Veneer Available in oak, birch, mahogany, walnut, ash, and others	Strips Slabs	$\frac{1}{32}$ $\frac{1}{64}$	13/16" wide 8"x2'; 3'x8'	Finishing exposed edges; veneer work
Particleboard		⅜; ½; ⅝; ¾	2x4; 4x4; 4x8	Core material for laminated furniture and countertops
Hardboard	Standard; tempered (moisture resistant)	⅛; ¼	2x4; 4x4; 4x8	Underlayment; drawer bottoms and partitions; cabinet backs
Glass	Sheet	⅛; 3/16; ¼	Per order	Cabinet doors
	Plate	⅛; ¼; ⅜; ½	Per order	Shelving
	Mirror tiles	⅛	12"x12"	Cabinet liners

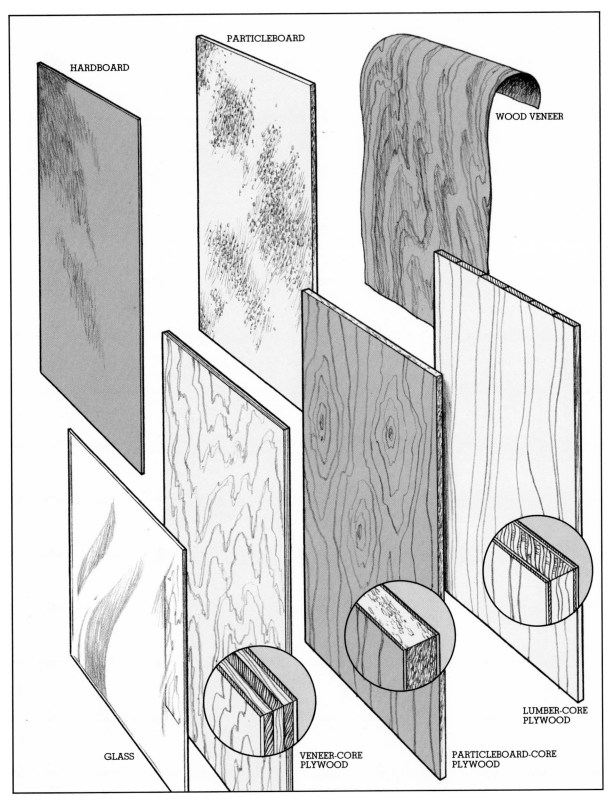

HARDBOARD

PARTICLEBOARD

WOOD VENEER

GLASS

VENEER-CORE
PLYWOOD

PARTICLEBOARD-CORE
PLYWOOD

LUMBER-CORE
PLYWOOD

Selecting and Ordering Moldings

If you could buy something that would add an instant decorative touch to your carpentry work, conceal unsightly seams and mistakes at the same time, and maybe even protect against damage from accidental nicks and bumps, would you?

Before you say that no such miracle material exists, take a look at the sketch and chart at right. They show and discuss more than a dozen moldings, all of which can serve you well in one or more of the above-mentioned ways. You'll find all of these moldings and more at most lumber and millwork outlets, in styles that range from ornate and traditional to sleek and contemporary. And if you can't find a stock molding that suits your needs, some shops will mill shapes to your order. (This is often the only way to duplicate intricate moldings in older homes.)

Most moldings, which you can purchase in random lengths from 3 to 20 feet, are made of softwood, usually pine. A few of the most popular sizes and types, though, come in selected hardwoods—usually mahogany, oak, and birch. You can purchase softwood moldings unfinished or, if you're working with prefinished paneling or doors, prefinished to match.

To estimate your needs, make a list of each piece of molding and round each measurement up to the next larger foot. Doing this will ensure that you don't come up short of material.

When ordering, keep in mind that you can save money if you'll settle for random lengths purchased on a so-much-per-hundred-linear-feet basis rather than insisting on pieces of a specific length. And if you'll be painting the molding, you can save even more by ordering finger-jointed moldings—short pieces that have been joined end to end.

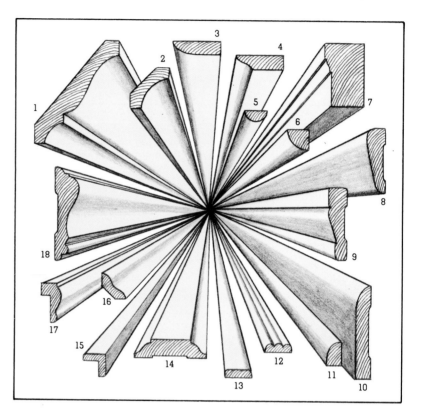

Molding Selector	
Common Types	**Typical Uses**
1, 2 Crown, Cove	Trim and conceal joint between walls and ceilings.
3, 4 Stop	Attaches to faces of door jambs to limit door swing. Holds inside sash of double-hung windows in place.
5 Half round	Serves as screen bead, shelf edging, and battens.
6 Quarter round	Serves as base shoe and inside corner guard.
7, 8, 9 Brick mold, Casing	Trim around openings for interior (casing) and exterior (brick mold) windows and doors.
10, 11 Baseboard, Base shoe	Trim and protect walls along wall-floor line.
12, 13 Screen bead	Covers seams where screen material fastens to frames. Finishes edges of shelves.
14 Batten	Conceals vertical or horizontal panel seams.
15, 16 Outside, Inside corner guard	Conceal seams and protect areas where walls or different wall finishes meet at corners.
17 Plycap	Conceals plywood edges. Caps top of wainscoting.
18 Chair rail	Protects walls from damage from chair backs. Hides seams where different wall materials meet.

Handling and Storing Materials

When you drive out through the exit gate of a building materials dealer with your materials, the assumption is that you're leaving with the correct amount of everything you ordered and that you're satisfied with its condition. Some suppliers even have you sign the purchase ticket to this effect. So from that moment on, keeping the materials in good condition becomes your responsibility. To keep from damaging your purchases, follow these tips as you handle and store your goods.

• To ensure a safe, uneventful trip home, make sure all materials are well secured to your vehicle with rope or baling twine. For large purchases, or if your car can't safely transport building materials, you can (for a charge) arrange to have the supplier truck the goods to your home.

• When transporting or unloading sheet goods, try to have a helper on hand. If that's not possible, grab hold of the panel as shown in the drawing inset below (one hand near the center of each long edge) then pick it up and wrestle it to its destination. Take care that you don't damage the edges or scratch the surface of the panels. And keep in mind that drywall, because it's thin, heavy, and brittle, can snap under its own weight.

• Store all materials in a cool, dry place, off the floor. Moisture can distort lumber, delaminate some plywoods, and render drywall useless.

• If possible (often it isn't), store sheet goods flat. If lack of space prevents this, stand them on one of their long edges, as nearly vertical as you can.

• Store lumber flat, and weight it down at each end and in the center to prevent warping and other distortions. Weighting down is especially important if you purchased wood with high moisture content.

• To keep excess building materials from cluttering up your shop, you may want to build a storage rack (the one shown below is easy to construct and occupies a minimum of space).

Selecting Hardware

Nails

If you've always thought of nails as plain-Jane fasteners, the sketch below may surprise you. It shows a grouping of commonly sold types—each one carefully engineered for a specific use.

Both *common nails* and the thinner-shank *box nail* excel at construction-type work (use commons for heavy jobs, box nails for lighter work). Use *roofing nails,* which have wide, thin heads, to hold down composition roofing.

Casing nails, finishing nails, and *brads* can tackle heavy-, medium-, and light-duty finish work, respectively. For a neat appearance, you should countersink them, then fill the depressions.

Ring-shank and *spiral nails* are designed to achieve a firm grip in wood. Specially hardened *masonry nails* can penetrate mortar joints and concrete. The protruding top head of *double-headed nails* allows quick dismantling of temporary work. *Corrugated fasteners* are used mainly for strengthening wood joints.

To determine the size nail you need, keep in mind that generally you want one long enough to go two-thirds through the material you're nailing into. Once you've determined the correct length, refer to the size chart below. Many, though not all, nails still are sold by the antiquated "penny" system, so if you need 3½-inch common nails, for example, ask for so many 16-penny common nails. You can buy nails either in bulk or already boxed.

For most projects, you'll be using uncoated steel nails, though they are available in several other metals as well. For outdoor use, buy galvanized steel nails. One other coating deserves mention, too. So-called *cement-coated nails* have an adhesive coating that actually bonds to wood fibers under the heat and friction of driving. Use these when superior holding power is a must.

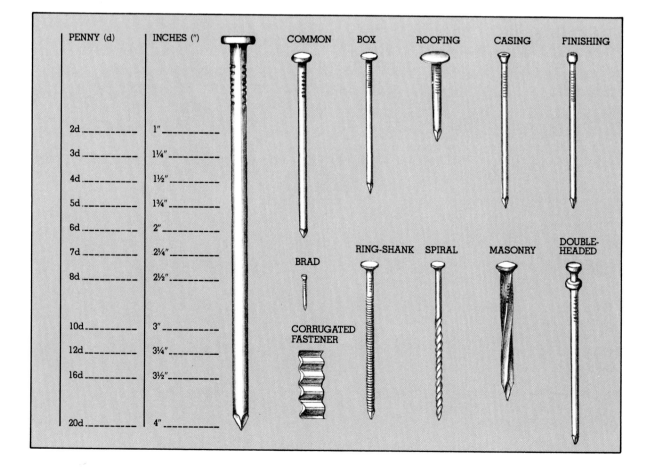

PENNY (d)	INCHES (")
2d ————	1" ————
3d ————	1¼" ————
4d ————	1½" ————
5d ————	1¾" ————
6d ————	2" ————
7d ————	2¼" ————
8d ————	2½" ————
10d ————	3" ————
12d ————	3¼" ————
16d ————	3½" ————
20d ————	4" ————

COMMON · BOX · ROOFING · CASING · FINISHING

BRAD · RING-SHANK · SPIRAL · MASONRY · DOUBLE-HEADED

CORRUGATED FASTENER

Screws and Bolts

For the few seconds they take to drive, nails do a remarkable holding job. Yet for the extra time involved in driving a screw into the same material, you get an even tighter hold, a neater appearance, and another plus—the option of disassembly.

The sketch below shows, among other items, the two broad types of screws you'll run across—*wood screws* and *metal screws*. Wood screws, the type you'll be using most often for carpentry work, come with various head shapes *(flathead, ovalhead,* and *roundhead)* and slot configurations *(single slot* and *Phillips).* And they are available in plated steel and brass. Use flatheads when the screw must be flush with the surface, ovalheads for decorative ac-

cent, and roundheads for more utilitarian tasks. *Flat* and *trim washers* protect against marring wood surfaces.

As with nails, the right size screw for the job should go two-thirds through the member you're fastening to. When ordering wood screws, specify the *length* (from ¼ to 5 inches), *gauge* or shank diameter (No. 0, which is about ¹⁄₁₆ inch, to No. 24, about ⅜ inch), *head type,* and material. The larger a screw's gauge (that is, the thicker its shank), the greater its holding power.

Use *lag screws* for heavy framing jobs and *hanger screws* for hanging heavy objects. To order lag screws, specify *diameter* (from ¼ to 1 inch) and *length* (from 1 to 16 inches).

Machine and *carriage bolts,* both of which usually are zinc-

plated to resist corrosion, handle all kinds of heavy fastening jobs. Which type you use isn't critical.

When ordering bolts, specify the *diameter, length,* and the *type* (machine or carriage). Add about ¾ inch to the combined thicknesses of the materials to be joined to determine the correct length. The diameter you need depends on the strength required of the fastener. Carriage bolts are available in diameters ranging from ¼ to ¾ inch and lengths from ¾ to 20 inches. With machine bolts, choose from diameters of ¼ to 1 inch and lengths of ½ to 30 inches.

For information about two specialized hollow-wall bolts—toggle bolts and hollow-wall anchors—see page 53.

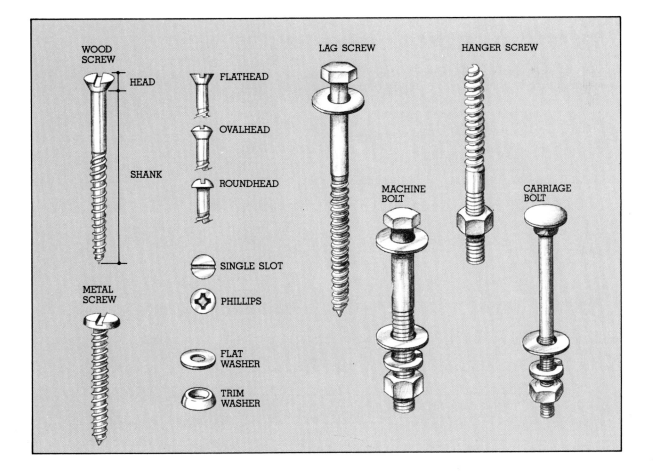

Miscellaneous Hardware

The grouping shown on these pages represents just a few of your specialized hardware options. The best way to get a feel for the multitude of items available is to spend some time in the hardware section of any building materials outlet. There you'll find a product designed for every conceivable carpentry need.

Shelf Supports

Aluminum shelf standards and brackets, your most attractive and versatile choices, come in a wide range of sizes and finishes. A lip on the front edge of each bracket holds shelves in place.

Less attractive but quite functional, bent-metal *Z brackets* and *utility shelf brackets* support shelves in a fixed arrangement. With utility brackets, fasten the longer leg to the wall. Fasten both types to walls with nails or screws.

When closed, *folding steel brackets* hug the wall. But when locked in their open position, they provide firm support for shelves or work surfaces that need periodic setup and dismantling.

Metal Plates and Framing Fasteners

Whenever you want to beef up an otherwise weak wood joint, reach for one of the four plates shown below. And for heavy framing jobs—stud walls, joists, rafters, and so forth—you may want to consider using framing fasteners, one of which (a *joist hanger*) is shown. *Mending plates* reinforce end-to-end butt joints; *T plates* handle end-to-edge joints. *Flat corner irons* strengthen corner joints by attaching to the face of the material. *Corner braces* do the same thing, but attach to edge surfaces.

Door and Cabinet Hardware

Most full-size doors, and some smaller ones, too, hang on the classic *butt hinge. Continuous hinges* flush-mount on cabinets and chests, combining great strength with a slim, finished look. *Strap* and *T hinges* often appear on gates and trunk lids.

You'll run into three basic types of cabinet hinges, too. You can use *offset hinges* on lipped, overlay, or flush doors, and *pivot hinges* for doors that completely overlap the frame. For cabinet doors set flush with the frame, choose a surface-mounted *decorative hinge* or the already-mentioned butt hinge.

To open your cabinet doors, fit them with *knobs* or *pulls,* available in myriad sizes and styles. *Roller* or *magnetic catches* keep them closed (if you use self-closing hinges, these aren't necessary).

And to keep drawers on track, you'll need *drawer slides,* either side- or bottom-mounted. The ones shown opposite use nylon rollers and ball bearings in side-mounted tracks.

Adhesives

Although not "hardware" as such, adhesives do play an important role in many fastening jobs. Lay in a supply of *wood glue* for general-purpose interior work and *epoxy* or *waterproof resin glue* for exterior jobs. You may also want several tubes of *panel adhesive* if you'll be installing drywall or paneling.

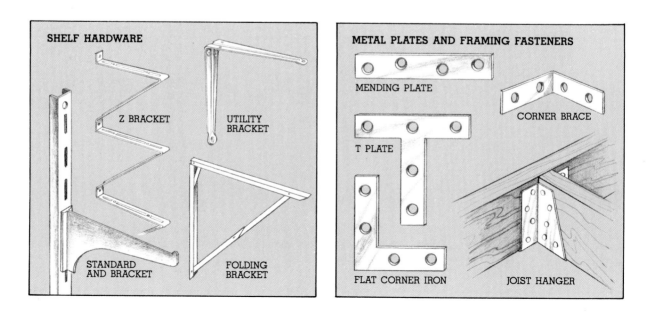

SHELF HARDWARE — Z BRACKET, UTILITY BRACKET, STANDARD AND BRACKET, FOLDING BRACKET

METAL PLATES AND FRAMING FASTENERS — MENDING PLATE, T PLATE, FLAT CORNER IRON, CORNER BRACE, JOIST HANGER

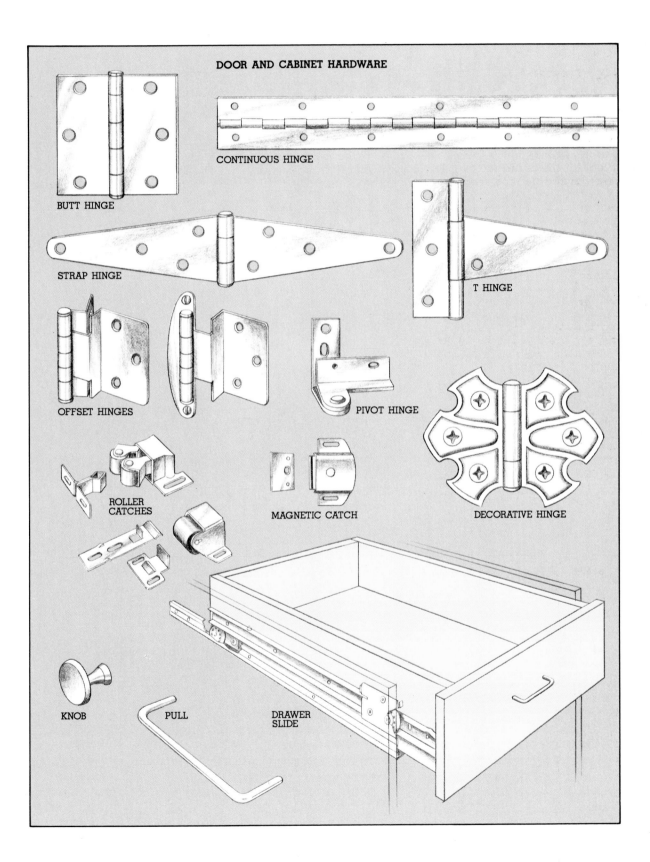

DOOR AND CABINET HARDWARE

CONTINUOUS HINGE

BUTT HINGE

STRAP HINGE

T HINGE

OFFSET HINGES

PIVOT HINGE

DECORATIVE HINGE

ROLLER CATCHES

MAGNETIC CATCH

KNOB

PULL

DRAWER SLIDE

MASTER THESE BASIC TECHNIQUES

If you can't quite envision yourself as a capable home carpenter, try this. Think of each of the techniques presented in this chapter as a building block. And each project you tackle as nothing more than several of the blocks stacked up. That's all any carpentry project is—no matter how simple or elaborate.

But also realize that just knowing how to do something is quite different from doing it well. What we provide here are the techniques. The rest is up to you, and that means practice, practice, and more practice.

Note that we've arranged the techniques so the order coincides with the sequence in which you'd do them when working on a project.

We open with a survey of measuring techniques, the mastery of which is imperative if you hope to achieve good results. Then it's on to cutting, drilling, fastening, shaping, smoothing, and finishing techniques.

And because it's nearly impossible to do satisfactory work with dull tools, there's a brief section on tool sharpening.

Measuring Techniques

Square the Work

Have you ever very painstakingly marked a material for cutting, carefully followed your cutoff line, and still wound up with a piece that didn't fit correctly? You probably made the mistake of beginning your measurement from an edge that wasn't *square*—at a 90-degree angle to an adjoining edge. Follow our tips for starting out square (and staying that way), and you won't make that mistake again.

1 Check board ends for square by positioning a combination square or try square with the body or handle firmly against a factory edge. (For more accuracy use a framing square.) If the end isn't square, mark a line along the outside edge of the square's blade.

2 To determine whether adjoining members are square, lay a framing square up against both members where the two meet. If the tongue and blade of the square rest neatly against the members, all is well.

3 No framing square handy? Then just call back some of your high school geometry and lay out the two sides of a 3-4-5 triangle at the test corner, using whatever units are convenient. If the corner is square, the diagonal joining the sides will measure five units.

See the detail for a third equally satisfactory way to check a project for square. This technique involves measuring diagonally between opposite corners. If your layout is square, both measurements will be the same.

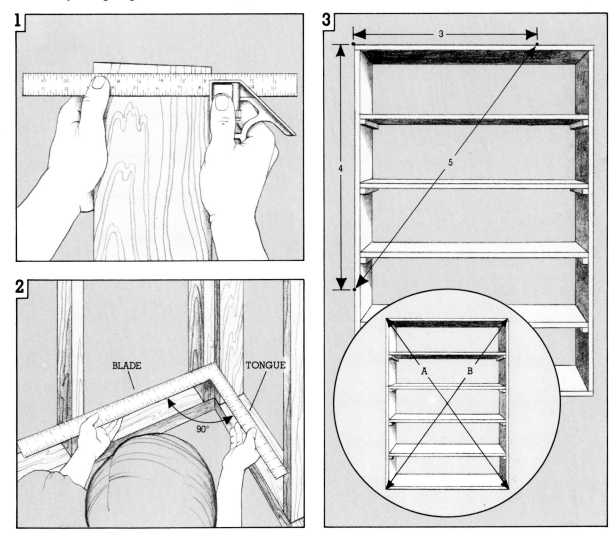

Mark with Care

How important are accurate measurements? VERY! Just ask a building contractor who has just miscut a rafter, or a cabinetmaker who suddenly realizes that a drawer opening is a glaring ⅛ inch too wide. To these pros, and to you, too, being off on a measurement means lost time and money—not to mention plenty of irritation.

When an experienced carpenter makes a measuring mistake, it's generally because he's in a hurry. The same holds true of a beginning woodworker. So, especially when you're just starting out, *take your time* and adopt the policy, "Measure twice, then cut once."

Also, no matter what measuring device you use to position your marks, learn to read it accurately. Many a board has met its ruin because someone couldn't distinguish a ¼ inch from a ⅛ inch.

And once you have made a measurement, jot it down on a piece of paper or a wood scrap. This way you can refer to it later, eliminating the need to remeasure.

Last but not least, use a sharp instrument for marking. A sharp No. 2 pencil works well, as does a scratch awl or a knife. Shy away from flat carpenter's pencils; their bulky size can cause you to make mistakes.

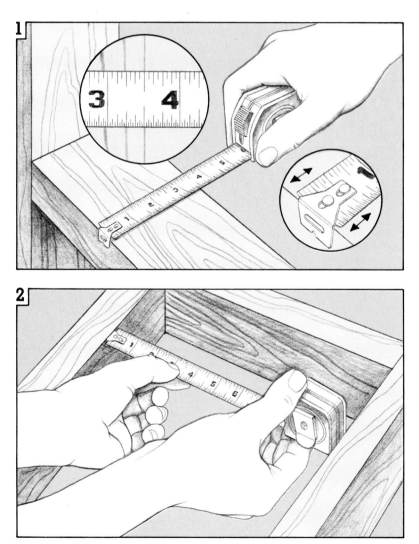

1 By far the most versatile measuring device, the steel measuring tape does lots of measuring and marking jobs well. Here, it's taking an outside measurement. Note how the hook at the end of the tape slides out to compensate for its own thickness. Note, too, that along the bottom of the first several inches, each inch is divided into thirty-seconds to facilitate extra-fine measurements.

2 Here's the same tape, this time taking an inside measurement. Simply add the length of the tape case (it's marked on the side of the tool) to the length of the extended blade and you have the total inside dimension. Some newer models do the math for you and give readings through a small window on the case top.

3 Marking, as you can imagine, involves just as much care as does measuring. Mark all your cutoffs with a V so you know precisely where to draw the line. And to ensure pinpoint accuracy, place the point of your pencil at the V, slide the square up to it, then strike your line. (To extend 45- or 90-

degree angle lines across most board widths, you'll find a combination square the ideal tool. For longer line segments, use a framing square or a straightedge.)

4 Need to mark a cutoff line along the length of a board or a piece of plywood? For a fast but slightly rough line, use your ever-handy measuring tape. Lock the blade at the dimension you want, angle a pencil into the notched clip, and pull it firmly toward you as shown.

For sheet goods, first mark the cutoff line at both ends of the sheet, then snap a chalk line between the two marks. Or make your marks, then use a straightedge to complete the line.

5 Whenever you cut any material, the saw blade reduces some of it to sawdust. Because of this, you must allow for the narrow opening in the blade's wake—called the *kerf*—when making your measurements. Otherwise, you could end up short $1/16$ inch or more, depending on the kerf's width. If you're making just one cut, account for the kerf by identifying the scrap side of the cutoff line (by X-ing it as shown) so there's no confusion later about which side of the line to cut from. For multiple cuts along a board or on sheet goods, allow for the width of the saw kerf between the kerf lines.

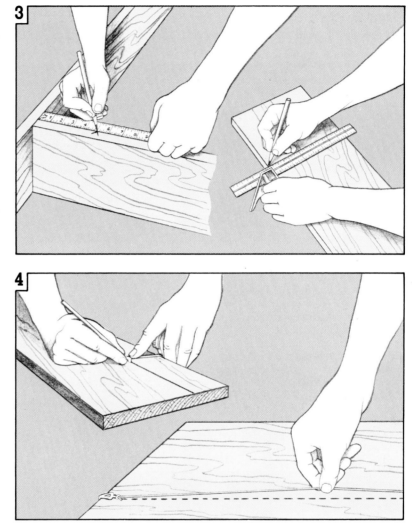

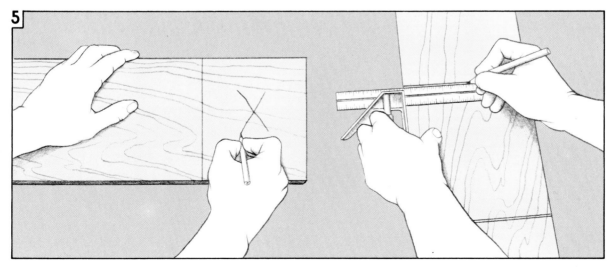

Keep Projects Plumb and Level

Ask any three carpenters how to drive a nail correctly, the best way to cut roof rafters, install a pre-hung door, or almost any other carpentry-related question, and you'll probably get three different answers. That's because in carpentry, there often are several "right" ways to do something. But one thing these pros all agree on: the importance of making sure that projects are square, which we discuss beginning on page 29, plumb, and level.

In case you're not familiar with what plumb and level mean, a surface is plumb when it is vertical, and level when it is horizontal.

To understand the importance of plumb and level, just consider what happens if you don't bother checking for them. The results are predictably unsatisfactory—walls lean, shelves slope or tilt, newly installed doors bind in their frames, to name just a few maladies.

As you're about to discover, checking for plumb and level is neither difficult nor time-consuming. So don't sacrifice the appearance and function of a project for the few seconds it takes to make these vital checks.

1 To check most projects for plumb, hold a carpenter's level against one face of the vertical surface—a partition wall in this instance—and note the position of the air bubble in the appropriate glass vial. If it comes to rest between the two guide marks printed on the vial, you know the wall, for instance, is plumb. If it doesn't, tap the project toward the direction needed to achieve plumb.

Vertical members must be plumb in two directions, so you'll need to repeat this procedure on a sur-

face adjacent to the one you just checked.

2 On occasion you may need to locate a point on the floor directly below a point on the ceiling, as when determining the placement of the top plate and soleplate for a wall, for example. A level would not help here, as you have no surface to support it on. Instead, use a plumb bob—a pointed weight suspended on a line.

Simply attach a line to the overhead reference point so the bob falls just short of the floor. When the bob comes to rest, mark its position with intersecting lines. In the case of a wall, you'd repeat the procedure several times.

3 You can check most projects for level by simply setting your carpenter's level atop the member —here, we're leveling a closet shelf—and raising or lowering the member until the level's bubble rests between the register marks. Then mark the member's position for later reference.

4 A member must be level from *front to back* as well as from *side to side*, so be sure that you make this check, too.

In quarters too tight for a carpenter's level, use a torpedo level if you have one or the level on your combination square.

5 Sometimes, you'll need to establish level over a long distance where there's no convenient support for a carpenter's level, as when cutting fence posts or deck supports to size. Here, go with the versatile line level.

To set up a line level, fasten a heavy string to your reference post and pull it taut to the post you want to level. With the line level hung midway between the posts, mark the post for cutting at the height where the line is level.

Cutting Techniques

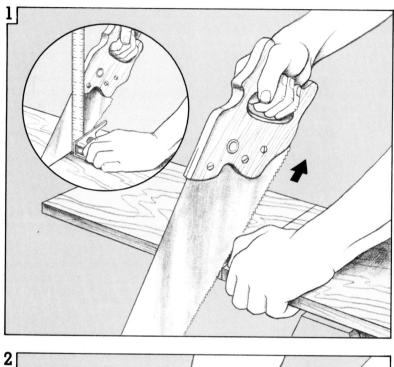

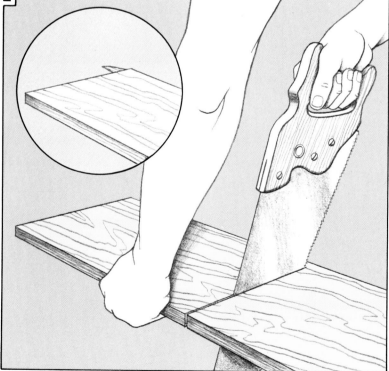

Making Rips and Crosscuts

Though from time to time you'll need to make the specialty cuts shown on pages 36–39, the vast majority of your cutting chores will involve either crosscuts (cuts across the grain of a material) or rips (cuts parallel to the grain).

On these two pages we've included some pointers that will enable you to make both types of cuts in a variety of materials with both hand- and power saws—and be proud of the results when you've finished. Many of the techniques you'll learn about here apply also to the more advanced cuts we'll show you on the following pages.

(Note: When cutting sheet goods that have a "good side," as paneling and some other panels do, you must guard against splintering them. To do this, cut with the material good face up if you're using a handsaw, good face down for saber and circular saws.)

1 To make a crosscut in narrow goods with a handsaw, start by setting the blade's heel end (nearest the handle) at a 45-degree angle to the work on the scrap side of the cutoff line. To make sure the blade doesn't stray from this position as you begin your cut, use the knuckle of your thumb as a guide. Pull the saw back toward you several times to start the cut. Don't force the blade—just let the weight of the saw do the work while you guide it. Then begin sawing, using a "rocking" motion, with a steeper blade-to-material angle at the beginning of the downstroke, and a slightly less acute angle at its completion. Periodically, check your work with a square to ensure that the saw blade stays perpendicular to the board.

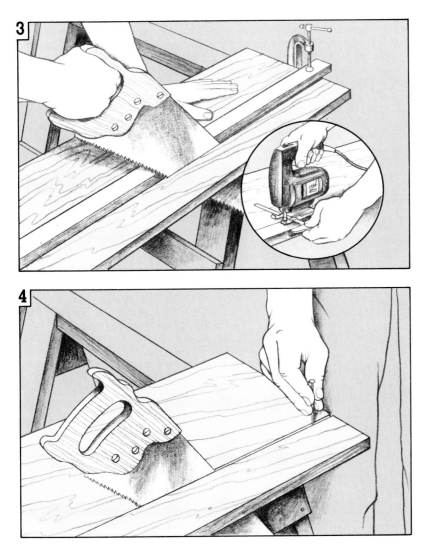

2 When you near the end of the cut, be sure to support the scrap piece of wood with slight upward pressure from your free hand. This keeps the piece from snapping (and splintering).

3 When ripping lumber or sheet goods, your main concern should be getting a straight cut along the entire length. To guarantee this, clamp a straight board or straight-edge to the work to guide the saw. If the cutoff line is close to the edge of the material, you can accomplish the same thing with an edge-guide attachment fitted to a saber or circular saw.

4 Because of the length of many rip cuts, saw blades tend to bind, especially near the end of the cut. If binding occurs, wedge a nail or a screwdriver into the kerf to keep it open, and give adequate support to the scrap piece.

5 Sheet goods are best cut with a circular saw that is fitted with a plywood-cutting blade. For this the trick is not so much one of cutting the material as it is supporting it properly. Here is one easy solution to this problem. Cut the sheet on a flat floor surface, supporting its entire length with 2×4s. Notice the two 2×4s on each side of the panel; they completely stabilize both halves during cutting.

Making Angle, Bevel, and Coped Cuts

From time to time, we've all marveled at the carpentry skill displayed in the joinery of a custom cabinet or hutch adorned with a variety of moldings; in a picture frame with its well-tailored, tight-fitting mitered corners; or in a seemingly seamless joint between two pieces of base-board molding. But you know something? At the root of all

this carpentry excellence is the ability to make accurate angle cuts, bevel cuts, and coped cuts—the three shown on these two pages.

Before getting into the techniques for making the cuts, let's briefly discuss what each is. When you make a cut *at an angle through the width* of a member, you've got an *angle cut*. A *bevel cut*, on the other hand, is one made *at an angle through the thickness* of a member. And *coped cuts* are those made to shape a member so it conforms to the shape of an ad-

joining member. (Note: When two members that have been angle cut or bevel cut at the same angle meet to form a corner, the joint is a *miter*.)

1 To make angle or bevel cuts in narrow stock the easy way, use a miter box—essentially a jig for holding the saw at the proper angle to the work.

Before placing the piece in the miter box, support it on a scrap of 1x4 or some other suitable material. This allows you to saw completely through the work without cutting into the bottom of the miter box. Position the member against the back of the miter box as it will be when in use, then use a backsaw to make the cut, holding the work against the back of the box with your free hand.

If there's any trick at all to using a miter box, it's not in the technique of cutting, but in correctly measuring and marking for the cut. To make sure you don't cut the piece too short or angle it the wrong way, draw a rough sketch of how the pieces will fit together before you begin.

2 As handy as a miter box is for making cuts through narrow stock, it just can't accommodate material much wider than a few inches. For angle cuts on material too wide to fit in a miter box, you can improvise a saw guide that will be just as accurate.

The first step is to set a T bevel to the desired angle and then to transfer that angle to the material. Now select a piece of 1x material with an edge you know is straight (or a straightedge) and C-clamp it along the cutting line as a saw guide.

To use a handsaw, clamp the guide close to the cutoff line. If you're using a circular or saber saw, offset the guide to position the saw blade alongside the cutoff line. To do this, measure the distance between the blade and the edge of the baseplate, and clamp the saw guide this distance from the cutoff line.

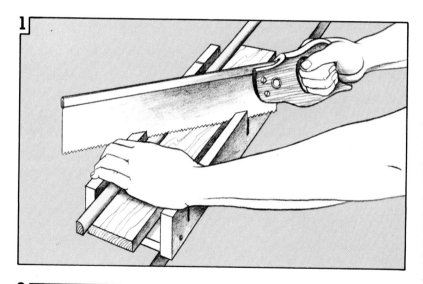

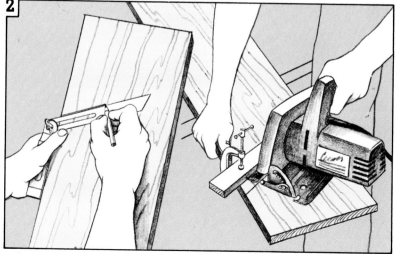

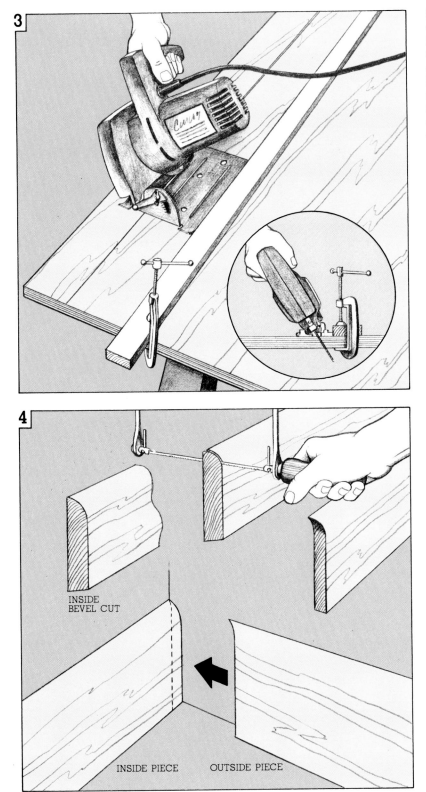

3 To make a bevel cut through wide stock, first use a straightedge to mark the cutting line on the face of the material. Then mark the exact angle of the bevel on the beginning edge. Now, with the saw unplugged (use either a saber saw or a circular saw), loosen the wing nut on the baseplate and adjust the plate-to-blade position to duplicate that angle. To double-check your work, place a correctly set T bevel between the bottom of the baseplate and the blade to verify the angle. Tighten the baseplate in this position, and make the cut by guiding the saw blade along the surface cutoff line.

4 When you're working with decorative moldings, it's sometimes hard to get a perfectly matched inside corner—especially if the corners aren't square to begin with. That's when it's useful to know how to cope an inside corner joint.

Start by cutting the "inside" piece of molding at a 90-degree angle so it butts against the adjacent wall. To cope the "outside" piece, first make an inside 45-degree bevel cut, as shown. Then use a coping saw to cut away the excess wood along the molding's profile. Back cut slightly to avoid a gap if the walls aren't perfectly square.

INSIDE
BEVEL CUT

INSIDE PIECE   OUTSIDE PIECE

Making Inside and Contour Cuts

Sometimes a carpentry project will throw you a curve—a cut you have to make from the center of your material, or an irregularly shaped cut. But don't be intimidated in the least. Neither inside nor contour cuts are difficult to make, though they do require some time and care.

1 The technique you use to start an inside cut depends on the material to be cut and the type of saw you're using. With lumber and most sheet goods, you have a couple of options. One way is to drill a starter hole at each corner of the piece to be cut away, as close as possible to the cutting lines. The other involves making a pocket cut with a saber or circular saw. To do this, first tip the saw forward on its baseplate as shown. Then start the saw and slowly lower the blade into the wood along the cutoff line. (You may want to practice this technique on a piece of scrap before making your finish cut. It takes some getting used to.)

Starting inside cuts in drywall is even easier. Just put the tip of a keyhole saw on one of the cutoff lines, and punch the saw's handle with the heel of your hand.

2 One advantage to inside cutting with a saber saw is that you *can* maneuver around corners easily and quickly. Don't try to turn the saw at a 90-degree angle, though. Instead, use the following two-step procedure for cutting corners perfectly square.

On your first approach to a corner, cut just up to the intersecting cutoff line. Now carefully back up the saw about 2 inches and cut a gentle curve through the scrap material over to that adjacent cutoff line. Continue in this manner, supporting the scrap material as you cut, until the scrap piece is free. Now you can easily finish trimming the corners with four short, straight cuts.

3 To make short work of most contour cuts, use a saber saw; its narrow blade lets you make curves and circles that are as smooth and perfect as you're able to draw them.

To make the decorative scallops on a window valance, for example, first clamp the board to a workbench or other firm surface, making sure nothing blocks the blade's path.

Before beginning the cut, allow the saw to reach full operating speed. Then as you make the cut, guide the saw slowly, without forcing the blade. If the saw begins to bog down or overheat, you're cutting too fast. Remember to support the scrap material as you reach the end of each cut to prevent it from breaking off.

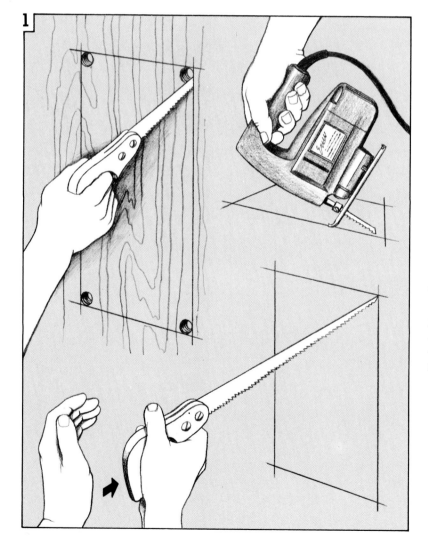

4 For intricate cutting or scrollwork jobs in narrow stock, you may want to use a coping saw. With one of these, you can approach the cut from an edge or from inside the material. To do the latter, just remove the blade from the saw frame and reinstall it through a starter hole.

For better control when making especially delicate cuts, fit the blade on the saw frame so the teeth are angled toward the handle. This enables the saw to cut on the backstroke. Blade holders conveniently let you turn the blade in different directions independent of the position of the frame.

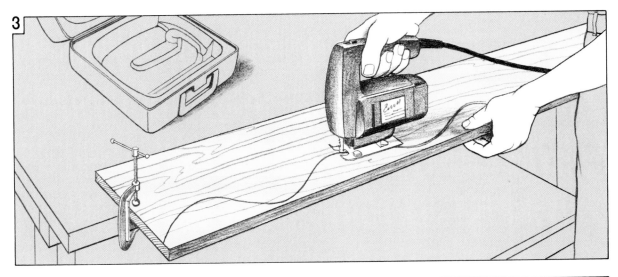

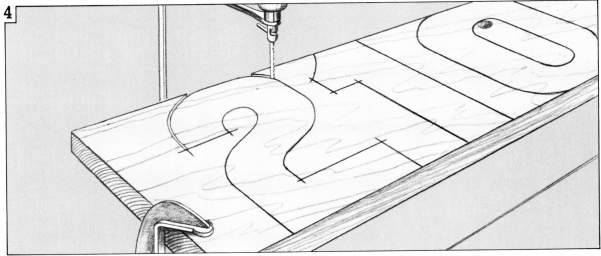

How To Use Chisels

Used to be, you could tell a true woodworking craftsman by his skill with a set of chisels. Few hand tools are as simple and, in experienced hands, as versatile. Today, routers do most of the work that once fell to chisels. Even so, there remain plenty of mortising, dadoing, and notching jobs for which chisels are ideally suited.

Whenever you pick up a chisel, keep your hands behind the cutting face of the blade and work the chisel away from your body. And since it takes both hands to operate a chisel, always clamp or anchor the material you're cutting. Finally, save yourself wasted effort and ruined materials by keeping your chisels sharp (see the tips on page 63).

1 All of your care in executing a chisel cut is wasted unless you've marked accurately for the cut to begin with. When preparing to cut a mortise for a butt hinge, for example, use the actual hinge as your template. Position it correctly on the edge of the door and mark

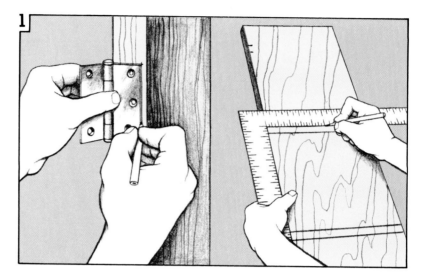

its perimeter with a sharp pencil. Also be sure to mark the "open" end of the mortise with the thickness of the hinge to indicate the depth of the cut.

When laying out dado cuts across the width of shelf uprights, marking square and straight are your watchwords. Hold a carpenter's framing square against a factory edge of the upright to square your marks, and outline the top and bottom of the cut.

2 To prevent the wood grain from splintering at the edges of chisel cuts, break the surface fibers along your cutting outline by scor-

ing the wood with a simple utility knife to a depth of approximately ⅛ inch.

For deeper dado cuts, bring your circular saw into play. Adjust the blade to the depth of your dado and cut against a clamp-on guide to ensure that you stay on your outline mark.

3 Now hold the chisel with the beveled face of its blade facing the direction of your cut and at the angle shown. Always cut in the direction in which the wood's grain runs to the edge of the board. If you don't, the chisel can follow, descending the grain lines,

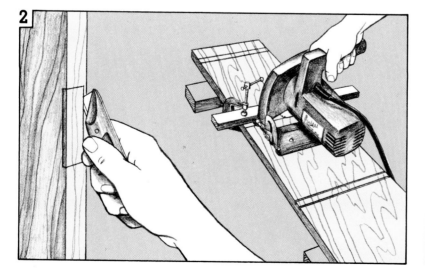

and gouge deeper than you intend. With your free hand, use a wooden-headed mallet to drive the chisel to the depth of the mortise, making several "notches" across its width.

4 To complete a dado cut after sawing to depth along its top and bottom, chisel out the wood between the cuts. Firmly tap the chisel with the palm of your hand. Start at an edge and hold the chisel at a slight upward angle as shown.

After you've removed a wedge of wood that extends to the center of the dado, do the same from the opposite edge. Now with the chisel bevel still faceup carefully remove the remaining wood, guiding the chisel with your hand wrapped around the blade shank as shown.

5 It's hard to remove wood for a deep mortise cut with only a chisel. Even when there's enough handle clearance to maneuver the blade to the bottom of the mortise, you run a great risk of splitting the wood.

In situations like this, your cut will be easier and more accurate if you begin by drilling a series of overlapping holes within the scored outline of your mortise. If possible, choose a bit diameter the

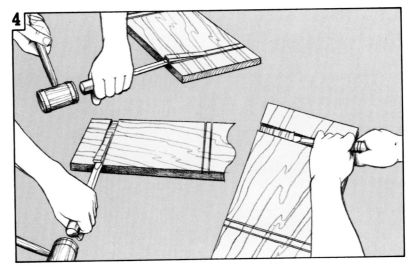

same size as the width of your mortise. To avoid drilling too deep, use the improvised depth gauge shown on page 42.

Finish the cut with a chisel, driving it with a mallet if necessary. Remember to hold the chisel with its beveled face toward the inside of the mortise.

6 Cutting a hefty notch from a 2x4 would be hard work for an unaided chisel, but becomes considerably easier with the help of a circular saw.

After marking for the notch, including its depth, adjust your saw blade to cut to this depth. Now

make cuts at the top and bottom of the notch, and fill in with closely spaced cuts across the entire width of the notch.

Finish the cut by positioning the chisel blade at your depth-of-cut mark with the beveled edge facing toward the face of the notch and driving it with a mallet. Again, begin cutting at a slight upward angle that becomes more horizontal as you chip away more of the wood.

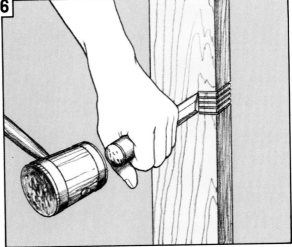

Drilling Techniques

Things were different before the advent of the electric drill. If a carpenter wanted to bore a small hole into or through a material, he'd reach for a hand drill or a push drill. And for larger holes, he'd pull his trusty brace down off the tool rack and fit it with the appropriate bit for the job.

But the electric drill has changed all that. This one tool has, to a great extent, made all other boring tools obsolete. Just insert the correct bit in its chuck (see page 14 for some of your bit options), and it will do any job any of the other drills can, but a great deal faster. Following are some techniques you should find helpful as you use this jack-of-all-trades boring machine.

1 Because drill bits cut using a rotary motion, they tend to skate away from their intended location when you begin boring holes. To prevent this (and keep the bit from marring the surface of your work), make a shallow pilot hole with an awl or some other sharp-pointed object. In softwoods, a gentle tap with the palm of your hand will do the job. But with hardwoods, you'll probably need to tap the awl with a hammer.

With this done, grip the drill with both hands and center the bit in the pilot hole. Apply firm pressure and begin drilling. If you have a variable-speed drill, bring it up to full power gradually.

2 In most instances, you'll want the holes you drill to be perpendicular to the work. Though you can guarantee this by buying a drill press or an attachment that approximates a small drill press, you can achieve good results—less expen-

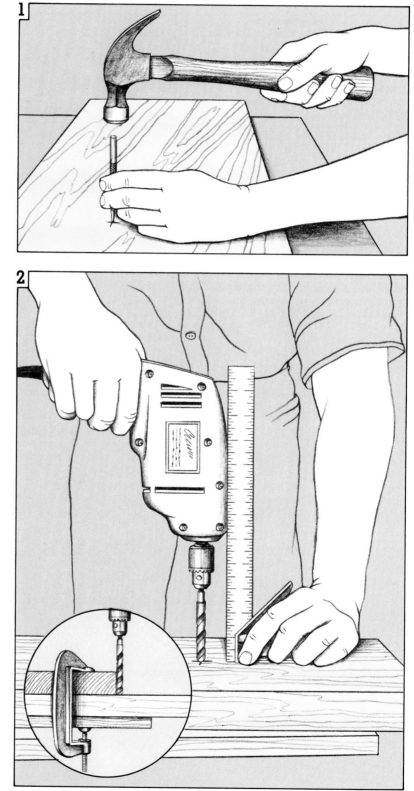

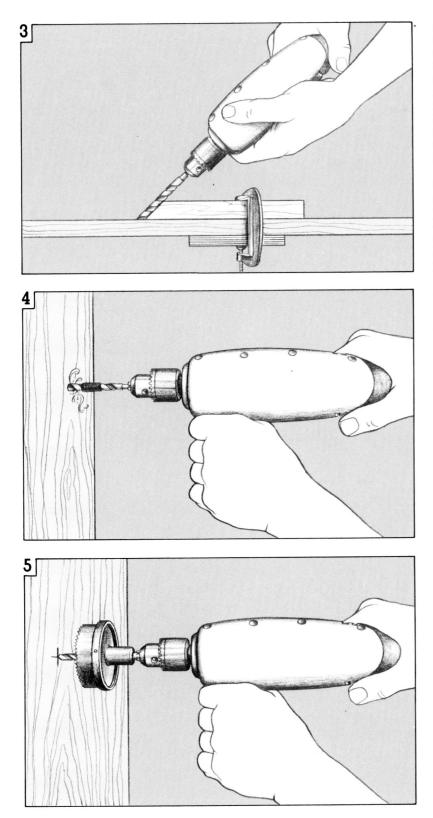

sively—by checking the bit for square as it enters the material. To do this, hold the body of a combination square (or the handle of a try square) firmly against your material, aligning the drill against the blade as shown. If your drill has a tapered body, you can check the bit for square by placing the edge of a piece of scrap lumber next to the bit.

3 Sometimes you'll *want* your bit to enter the material at an angle, in which case maintaining that angle becomes the real trick. Fashioning a jig will help simplify things a lot. Begin by cutting the edge of a piece of scrap lumber to the desired angle of your hole (see page 36 for how to make bevel cuts). Now C-clamp the scrap to the surface of your material so it aligns the tip of the bit exactly on your center mark. Carefully guide the bit into the material, keeping its sides in contact with the edge of the guide.

For steep angles, angle your pilot hole to prevent the bit from skating out when you begin drilling the hole.

4 For situations in which you want to drill one or more holes to a certain depth, simply wrap masking or electrical tape around your drill bit so the bottom edge of the tape contacts the surface of the material at the desired depth. Drill with gentle pressure, and carefully back the bit out of the hole as soon as the tape touches the material's surface.

5 When using a hole saw to bore large-diameter holes, make a pilot hole on your center mark to guide the starter bit. And to ensure that the underside of your material doesn't splinter when the bit penetrates it, place a piece of scrap stock underneath. Here again, keep your drill perpendicular to the material. (*continued*)

Drilling Techniques *(continued)*

6 Another technique for preventing the back side of your material from splintering involves drilling through the material until just the tip of the bit penetrates the back side. Then carefully back the bit out of the hole and finish drilling from the other side, using the pilot hole you've just made.

7 When you drill deep holes in thick material, wood chips will build up in the hole, clogging the bit and causing it to bind. To minimize this problem, feed the bit into the wood slowly, and back the bit out of the hole frequently with the drill's motor still running. This brings the trapped wood particles to the surface.

If you're working with extremely sappy wood, shavings may clog the bit's flutes. If this happens, let the motor stop and then use the tip of a nail to scrape them out.

8 When you use wood screws to fasten two pieces of material together, especially hardwoods, always provide adequate clearance for the screw, to ensure easy driving and to avoid splits. Here's one way to proceed.

First, drill a hole partway through the top material to accommodate the screw shank. Next, drill a deeper pilot hole for the screw threads, using a smaller-diameter bit. And if you plan to *countersink* the screwhead (see page 49 for more on this), use a countersink bit to make a shallow depression at the top of the shank clearance hole.

9 Though the technique discussed for sketch 8 will work, it is time-consuming. With a combination countersink/counterbore bit, you can cut your work in half. Available in sizes for most common wood screws, these bits prepare the way for screws in one simple operation. Just select the proper size bit for the screw you'll be driving, and

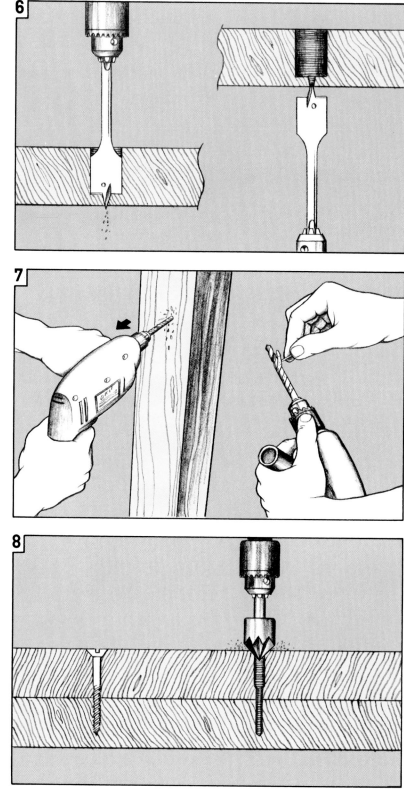

drill the hole. If you want the screwhead flush with the surface, drill to the top of the bit's scored area. To counterbore the screwhead, drill deeper.

10 Measuring and marking for a hole often can be more time-consuming than the actual drilling. So if a project calls for drilling holes in exactly the same location in several pieces of lumber, try this highly accurate, work-reducing technique. Align the edges of your pieces, stack them in a bundle no thicker than the length of your drill bit, and C-clamp them together. Now center-mark the top surface, make a pilot hole, and drill through all the pieces. Use a piece of scrap stock beneath your stack or finish your hole from the underside to avoid splintering the bottom piece.

11 If the job calls for many holes, you can save a great deal of time by building a jig. With one of these, once you've done the initial setup, you can drill any number of accurately placed holes as fast as you can feed the material into position. The jig's bottom platform prevents splintering.

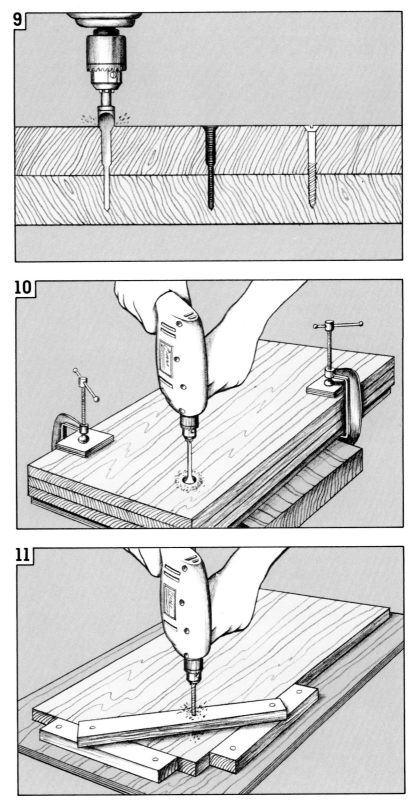

Fastening Techniques

How To Drive and Pull Nails

If you've ever watched an experienced carpenter wield a hammer, you've probably marveled at the speed he can fasten together the components of a large project. Impressive, yes, but for your purposes, speed isn't what counts. What does is your ability to drive and remove nails without hurting yourself or damaging the materials. And to do that requires only two things: a knowledge of a few basic techniques, and *plenty* of practice.

1 To make sure that the hammer strikes the nail—not your fingers—and that the hammer's blow will drive the nail squarely into the work, grasp the nail near its head and the hammer near the end of the handle. *Keep your eye on the nail* as you swing the hammer downward, and let the weight of the hammer's head do the driving. If you must drive a nail near the end of a material (especially lumber), blunt its point with a hammer. The blunted point will punch through the wood fibers and thereby reduce the chance of splitting the material.

2 The last blow from the hammer should push the head of most nails flush with the surface of the wood. (The convex shape of the hammer's face should allow you to do this without marring the surface of the material.) With finishing or casing nails, though, you'll want to drive the heads below the surface. Use a nail set and fill the hole with wood putty later.

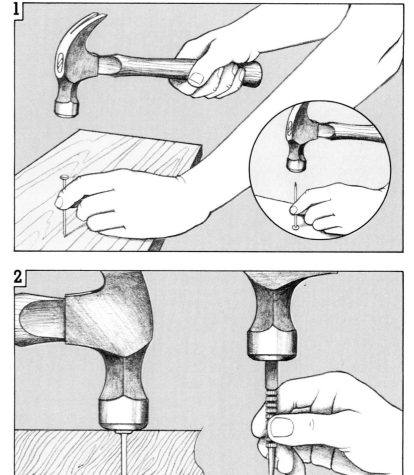

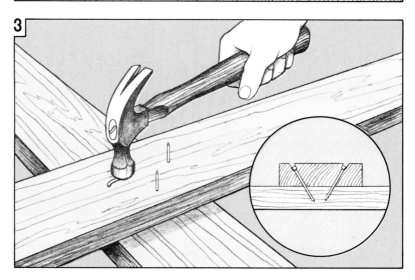

3 For maximum holding power in rough projects, use nails about an inch longer than the thickness of the pieces you're fastening. Drive the nails, then turn the members over and *clinch* (bend) the exposed portion of the nails in the direction of the grain so they're nearly flush with the surface. For showier projects or in situations where you can't get at the back side of the material, drive pairs of nails in at an angle.

4 For best results when fastening a thin sheet of material to thicker stock, nail through the thinner one into the thicker.

5 When driving several nails along the length of a board, stagger them so you don't split the board.

6 With some materials, especially hardwood lumber and moldings, you'll have to drill pilot holes before driving the nails to avoid splitting. Make the pilot holes slightly smaller than the diameter of the nails.

7 From time to time, you'll strike a glancing blow or encounter a knot while driving a nail, both of which may bend the nail. When this happens, remove the deformed nail and start again with a new one. To keep from marring the surface of the material and for better leverage, place a piece of scrap material beside the nail, slip the hammer's claw beneath the nailhead, and pull back on the handle. With long nails, you may have to substitute a thicker piece of scrap once you get the nail partway out.

8 How you remove nails that have been driven flush with the surface depends on the situation. If you're lucky enough to have access to the back side of the joined materials, first strike the joint *(continued)*

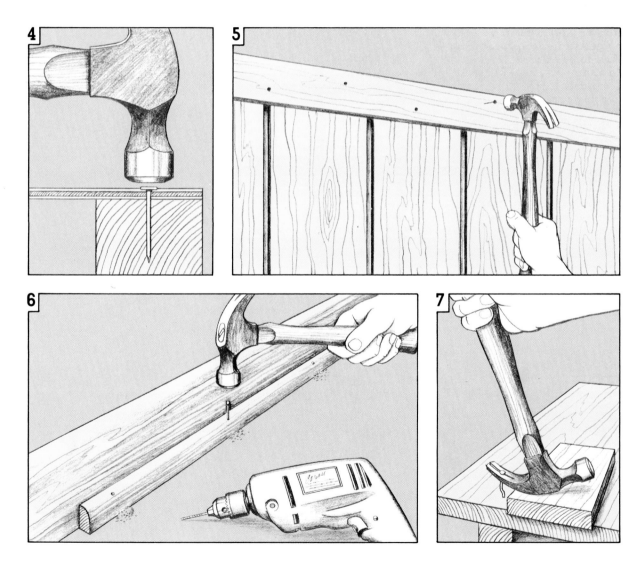

How To Drive and Pull Nails *(continued)*

from behind, then hammer the members back together again from the front side. This should pop the nailheads out far enough for you to get hold of them with a hammer.

9 No access from behind? Then try tapping the V-shaped claw of a pry bar (it's thinner than the claw of a hammer) underneath the nail's head. Then pry the nail up far enough so you can get the head of a hammer claw under-

neath the nailhead. This technique will leave its mark on the surface of the wood, but often you have no other option.

10 Sometimes, as in this situation, you can "disjoin" two nailed-together members by sawing through the nails. Then when you have separated the members, pound the nails from the back side with a hammer and a nail set to gain access to the nailheads.

11 Removing moldings intact is a difficult chore that requires care and patience. Because the nails holding them in place have been

sunk and the cavities filled, your best bet is to first drive the nails deeper into the stock, using a hammer and nail set. Then slip or force a prybar under the molding near each nail, and rock the bar back and forth to free the molding.

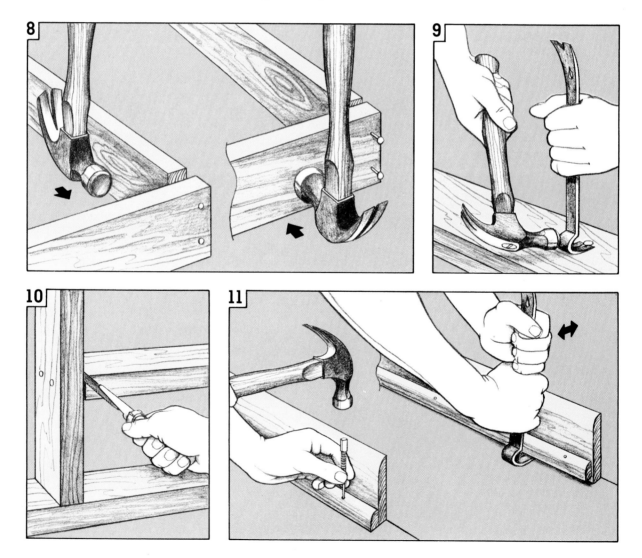

How To Drive and Remove Screws

It's not difficult to see why screws do such a good job of fastening materials. The many threads along the shank of every wood screw grip the wood fibers of the members being joined and, when the screw has been driven home, exert tremendous pressure against the screwhead.

Unfortunately, the same characteristics that make screws the super fastener they are can cause you problems when driving and removing them. Here, we tell you how to minimize such hassles.

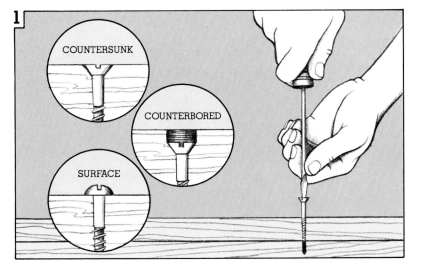

1 Once you've decided on where a screw will go, drill an appropriately sized pilot hole in one of the two ways shown on page 44. (Note that depending on the need, the screwhead can rest on top of, flush with, or below the surface.) Then select the correct screwdriver for the screw you're driving (it should fill the slot completely for maximum torque). Set the screw in the pilot hole, and with one hand on the screwdriver's handle and the other steadying its blade in the screw's slot, slowly turn the screwdriver clockwise. Apply only moderate pressure at first.

2 If the going gets tough, exert pressure on the screwdriver with the palm of one hand and turn it with the other. And if you still can't drive the screw all the way home, remove it and drill a slightly larger pilot hole or lubricate the threads with candle wax or soap and try again.

3 Driving lots of screws (or even just a few large ones) by hand can tire you out in a hurry. To cut down on fatigue and to speed the whole operation, drive the screws with an electric drill and a screwdriver bit. Make sure the bit is firmly seated in the screw slot before beginning, and don't drive the screw too quickly. If you damage the screw's slot, you may be able to salvage the screw by deepening its slot with a hacksaw.

4 Faced with a hole that's too big for the screw you're driving? Insert a toothpick, a sliver of wood, or a bit of steel wool into the hole. Tightening down the screw will force the filler material against the wall of the hole and hold the screw tight.

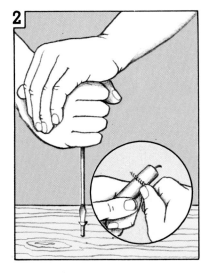

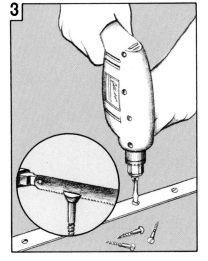

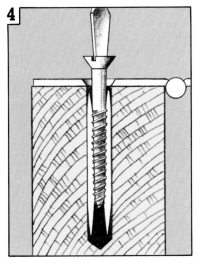

How To Tighten and Loosen Bolts

Nails and screws depend on friction between the fastener and the wood to do their job. Not so with bolts, however. When you tighten a nut on a bolt, you're actually "clamping" adjoining members together, and in the process creating the sturdiest of all joints.

On this page we limit our discussion to techniques involving machine and carriage bolts—the heavyweights.

1 For machine bolts, which have threads running the length of the shank, first slip a flat washer onto the bolt, then slide the bolt through the hole. Put another flat washer, then a lock washer over the bolt, and follow these with a nut. (The flat washers keep the nut and the bolthead from biting into the wood; the lock washer prevents the nut from loosening.)

To draw the nut down onto the bolt, you'll need two wrenches; one to steady the nut, the other to turn the bolt's head.

2 To tighten down a machine bolt in hard-to-get-at places or when you have countersunk the bolt's head, you will need a socket wrench, possibly with an extension to reach into the recess. (Again, steady the nut by using a second wrench.)

3 To tighten a carriage bolt, simply insert it into the hole and tap its head flush with the surface. Then slip a flat washer, a lock washer, and a nut onto the bolt and turn the nut clockwise. The shoulder under the bolt's head keeps the bolt from spinning as the nut is tightened from the other side. The lock washer should keep the bolt from working loose. But if you want to make absolutely sure of it, thread another nut onto the bolt, snug it up against the first nut, then "jam" the two together using the action depicted by the arrows.

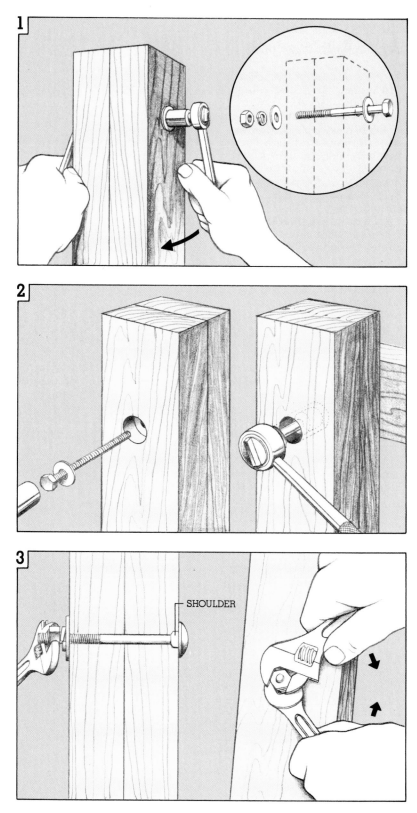

SHOULDER

Using Glues and Adhesives

Today's glues and adhesives are incredibly strong, easy to work with, and durable. So it's no wonder that amateur and professional carpenters alike depend on these "super" fasteners for so many of their needs. The two types discussed here—wood glues and panel adhesives— involve different application techniques, both of which we explain.

1 For best results with wood glues, first check the members to be joined for a snug fit. Then apply a thin, even coat to both surfaces.

2 Now fit the members together and secure the joint with clamps or a weight until the glue sets up. Keep the following in mind when using clamps.
• Protect the good surfaces by placing scrap material between the clamp jaws and the project.
• Use as many clamps as you need to make sure that the glue-coated surfaces will remain in contact.
• Apply just enough clamping pressure to create a tight seal without distorting the wood.
• Recheck the fit after tightening the clamps, and make any necessary adjustments.
• Wipe off any glue that flows from between the clamped members. (A few tiny droplets of glue along the edges of the seam is a good sign that you've used enough but not too much.)

3 Unlike wood glues, panel adhesives don't require clamping. Instead, you follow this four-step procedure. (1) Lay a bead of adhesive on one of the surfaces to be joined. (2) Press that surface against the mating surface. (3) Pull the materials apart slightly. (4) And after waiting the time specified on the adhesive tube, press the materials back together again.

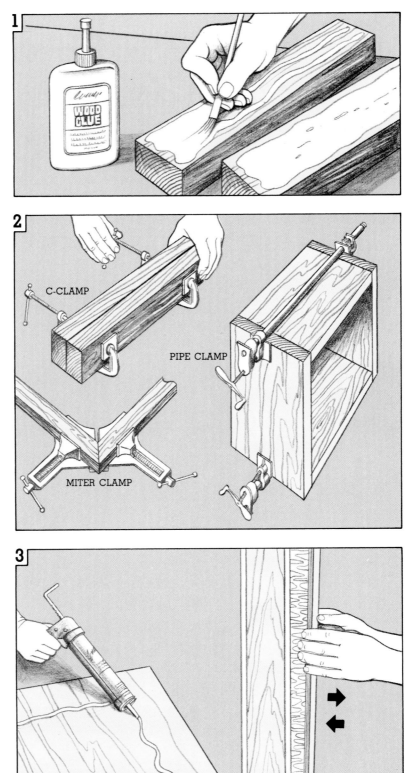

How To Hang Things on Walls

Obviously, when you hang an item on a wall, you want it to stay put. And that means you must use the correct fastener for the job. Which one you choose depends on two factors: the weight of the object to be hung, and what—if anything—is behind the wall.

1 With lightweight items, often just driving a small nail at an angle provides adequate support. For pictures and other similar wall ornaments, you'll be best off with a steel picture hanger such as the one shown here. Or if holes in walls are frowned-on where you live, a gummed hanger may be your only answer.

2 Whenever it is possible, secure medium- and heavyweight items to wall studs. To locate one of them, rap on the wall at various spots with your hand. The spaces between studs will respond with a hollow sound. A solid "thunk" indicates that you've found a stud. Or if you have walls made of drywall, you can use a magnetic stud finder to quickly locate the nailheads holding the material to the studs.

3 Tying into a single stud will give more than enough support for most items, even heavy ones. However, with large or bulky objects such as kitchen cabinets and the like, you may need to span several studs and nail a support ledger to them. To locate adjacent studs, measure over 16 inches and you should find one. (Occasionally, however, studs are placed on 24-inch centers.) To confirm this, drive a small nail through the wall material.

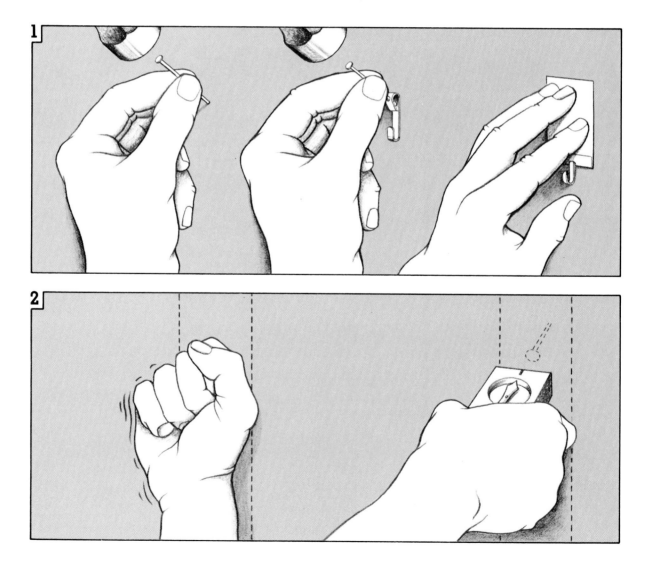

4 What if a stud isn't where you need it? Then reach for a *hollow-wall anchor, Molly bolt,* or a *toggle bolt.* You'll find both available in a wide range of sizes; the larger the fastener, the greater its strength.

To install a hollow-wall anchor first bore a hole through the wall material that's large enough to accommodate the anchor's shank. Insert the anchor into the hole, tap its barbed flange into the wall material, and then turn the bolt clockwise till tight. As you tighten the bolt, the anchor's slotted flange collapses and grips the back side of the wall material.

Toggle bolts function in much the same way as do hollow-wall anchors, but they mount different-ly. First drill a hole through the wall—this one big enough to ac-commodate the folded-up wings of the toggle. Remove the bolt from the spring-loaded wings; slip it through a washer and then through the object to be hung. Re-attach the wings and push them all the way through the hole in the wall. As the wings move past the back side of the drywall, they'll spring out. When this hap-pens, pull out on the fastener and at the same time, tighten the bolt.

5 Hanging things on brick, block, or stone walls isn't difficult to man-age if you follow the procedures here. First, drill an appropriately sized hole into the masonry, pref-erably into the mortar between units, using a masonry bit. Then drive a lead, fiber, or plastic an-chor into the hole with a hammer. Now, slip a lag screw through a washer, through a hole in the ob-ject you want to hang, and into the anchor. Drive the screw with a wrench. As you do so, the anchor will expand and grab the interior surface of the hole.

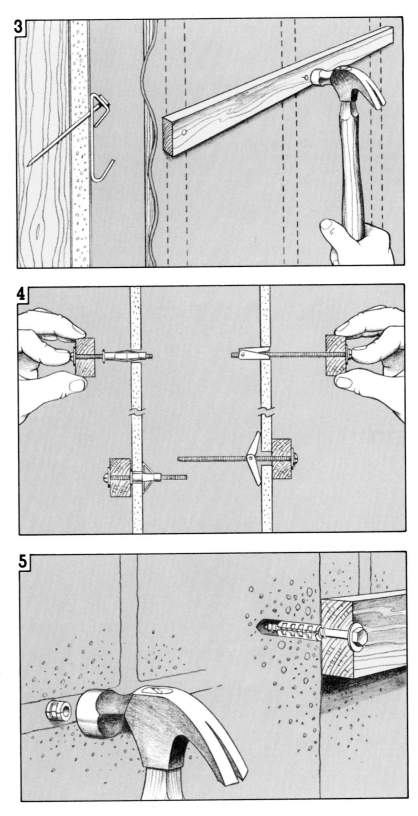

Shaping Techniques

Beveling edges and corners, planing down binding doors, trueing the edges and ends of lumber or sheet goods—you can do all these things and more once you learn how to use the various wood-shaping tools at your disposal. For most shaping jobs, three types of tools will see you through: planes, surface-forming tools, and rasps and wood files. If there's a secret to using any of them, it's keeping them clean and sharp.

However, even the sharpest shaping tools are no match for a board that's irreparably twisted, bowed, cupped, or warped (see page 16 for how to spot these defects). So, always inspect your material for flaws first, and if you find a serious one, don't waste your time and your patience trying to shape it away.

1 When smoothing almost any surface, a carpenter's framing square becomes as important as the tool you'll use to do the actual work.

To determine what needs to be done to the material to true it, first position the blade of the square along a straight, lengthwise edge and highlight the high spots with a pencil line.

Then lay the square on edge on the face of the material, and again record any unevenness with a pencil line. (You can use this same two-step procedure to shape an edge if you're sure the end of a material is true.)

2 If you need to remove lots of wood from the edge of a material, use either a jack plane or a surface-forming tool. When using either, keep these things in mind.
• First, since it takes both hands to operate the tool, clamp your work in a bench vise.
• Note the direction of the grain, and plane only in that direction.
• To avoid nicking corners, apply greatest pressure to the knob of the tool at the beginning of your cut, and to its heel at the cut's completion.
• If you plane off anything but a continuous, even-thickness shaving, a plane is either dull or adjusted for too thick of a cut, or you're planing against the grain.

Note the technique shown here for keeping a plane square to a narrow board edge. Grip a square-cornered block of wood against the bottom of the plane as shown here. Guide it firmly against the face of the board as you cut to prevent the plane from tilting on the board's edge.

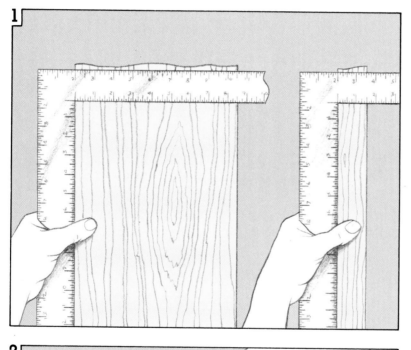

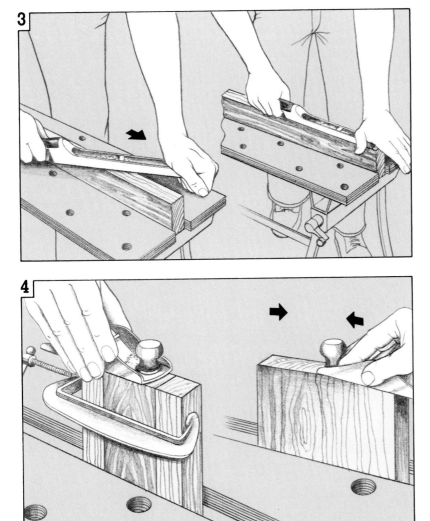

3 Surface-forming tools, also commonly known as serrated rasps, come in a variety of plane- and file-shapes and sizes. The plane-like tool shown here works much like the jack plane. How you use it differs, however. You can't adjust it for depth of cut, but you can regulate the amount of material it removes by the way you position it against the material.

For rough-cutting applications, hold the tool at a 45° angle to the work as you move it along the edge. Shavings will curl up through the serrations without clogging the holes. For a smoother result, hold the tool parallel to the board's edge.

4 Shaping end grain requires both a different tool and differing techniques from those used for shaping edges. Note, too, that you must follow the procedures outlined here to keep from splintering the ends—a frequent problem whenever shaping end grain.

For narrow stock, C-clamp pieces of scrap material at both ends and plane across the end in a single direction.

Use a three-step procedure with wider stock. Begin by planing from each end only to the center. Then finish by planing off the hump in the middle, being careful not to plane all the way to the edges.

5 Wood files and rasps come into their own when you need to shape small edges or curves that planes and surface-forming tools just can't reach.

For finishing-touch shaping in which you don't need to remove a lot of material, you may operate a file one-handed, as shown here. Where you have more wood to remove, use your free hand to apply downward pressure on the toe end of the file.

Always be sure to keep your file perpendicular to the stock, and push its full length diagonally across the work, lifting it clear on the backstroke. Periodically, use a square to check your filed edge for flatness.

Smoothing Techniques

Smoothing a piece of wood is a lot like retouching a photograph: both are fine for removing minor imperfections. But if you need to go much beneath the surface—$\frac{1}{16}$ inch or more—you should do more cutting or shaping.

For best results when using sandpaper (technically called "coated abrasives") start with a "coarse" or "medium" grade, depending on the surface's condition, then finish with "fine." As mentioned earlier, aluminum oxide abrasive is the best all-around type for most carpentry needs.

1 The simplest and best way to hand-sand a surface is with a sanding block—either the commercial variety shown here or one you can improvise by wrapping a piece of abrasive around a wooden block. Sanding with a block is less tiring than using only the palm of your hand on the paper, and it equalizes sanding pressure over a larger area for more uniform results.

When you are preparing a sanding block, tear—don't cut—abrasive sheets to size: Abrasives dull blades fast! And check that the bottom of your block is clean and smooth. Any debris trapped between the block and the paper can tear the abrasive or mar your work.

Use a sanding block only in the direction of the wood's grain. Abrasives work by tearing the surface fibers of the wood, and sanding across the grain or in a circular motion can leave hard-to-remove blemishes. If you're using the right grade of paper, light back-and-forth strokes normally are all you'll need.

2 When you need to smooth the surface of a small item, try rubbing the surface to be smoothed against a full sheet of abrasive held flat with your free hand.

Frequently inspect the surface of the work to monitor your progress, and wipe the surface with a clean cloth to prevent the abrasive from clogging quickly. When the paper finally does fill up, clean it with a few sharp raps against your workbench.

3 Because the edges of wood products are susceptible to nicks and splinters, it's a good idea to blunt them with a light sanding. Use gentle pressure and a rhythmic rocking motion. Be careful not to move the block side-to-side; the torn edge of the abrasive might catch a splinter and tear the wood.

A molded rubber sanding block like the one shown is ideal for this purpose because its base "gives" slightly under pressure. You can

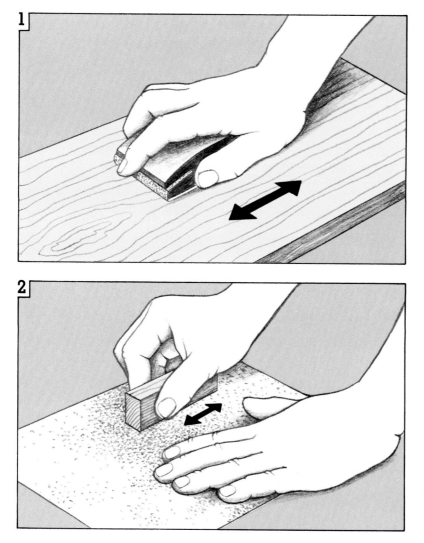

accomplish the same thing with a hard plastic or an improvised sanding block if you line the base with a thin layer of cork before wrapping sandpaper around it.

4 Smoothing the surfaces of round stock such as stair rails and chair spindles is both awkward and time-consuming. And if you use only fingertip pressure on a small square of sandpaper, the end result will be less than satisfactory.

To make this operation easier —and to achieve a better end product—use the shoeshine technique shown. Here, a cloth-backed abrasive is your best choice.

5 When smoothing wood in tight quarters, you often can get the job done with a sheet of abrasive and a little ingenuity, as in the two examples shown here.

Occasionally, you'll want to smooth two surfaces where they meet at an inside corner—neatly and quickly. A creased sheet of abrasive wrapped around a sharp-cornered block of wood is made to order.

Likewise, a strip torn from a full sheet of sandpaper and wrapped around your finger is ideal for smoothing the inside edges of circles and other small cutouts.

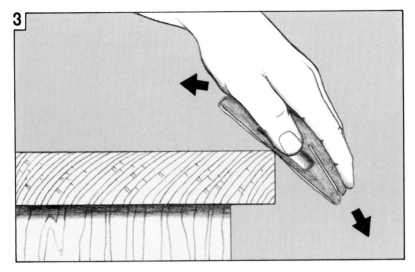

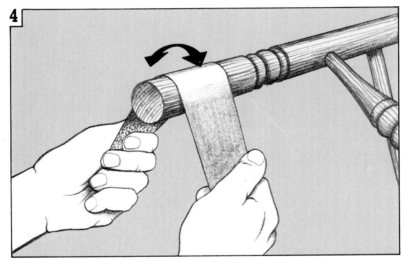

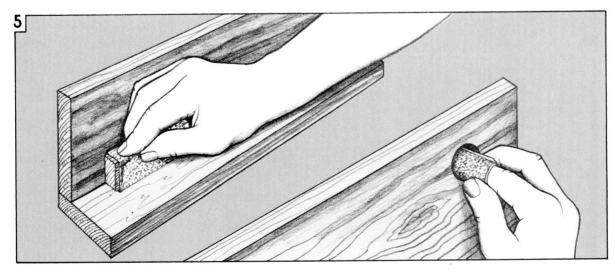

Finishing Techniques

Fill or Hide Imperfections

Often, especially near the end of a long, drawn-out carpentry project, you may be tempted to cut a few corners and slap on a finish without doing the prep work so necessary to achieve a professional-looking result. If you find yourself in this situation—and you will—remember this: No finish surface is any better than what's underneath. And in some cases, it's worse.

How you prepare your project for the finish coat depends on the type of wood you're working with and the type finish you plan to apply. If you've opted for a paint finish, simply fill any voids in the material with water putty, and after letting the putty dry, sand the surface smooth.

Preparing for a clear finish isn't quite that quick and easy. First, conceal all exposed plywood edges with wood veneer tape or screen bead molding. Then, if you're working with oak or one of the other open-grained woods, apply a *filler stain, filler sealer,* or *filler mixed with stain* to close the wood cells.

Follow this with a coat or two of sealer—shellac or "sanding sealer" works well here—to keep the stain or filler from being attacked by the varnish. Be sure to sand after each coat with very-fine grit abrasive.

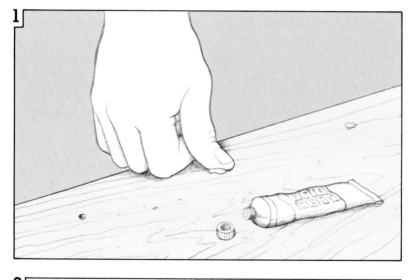

1 To fill voids in wood you plan to paint, such as nail holes and counterbored screw holes, a plastic dough-type filler is a good choice. Simply tamp a small amount of it into the hole with your thumb. As the solvent in the dough evaporates, the filler will harden and become sandable.

For very deep or large voids, apply two or three layers of filler, letting each dry completely before filling further. Let your final layer overfill the void slightly to allow for the putty's tendency to shrink as it dries, and to leave a base for sanding.

2 Water-mix putties excel at filling shallow depressions over a large surface area. (Again, use this type of filler only on projects you'll be painting.) By mixing in a little more water (or a little more powder), you can achieve just the right spreading consistency. One caution, however: Water-mix putty sets up quickly, so don't mix more than you'll be able to use in 10 or 15 minutes.

To blend in a knot with its surrounding wood, mix the putty to a pastelike consistency and apply it with a putty knife. Force the mixture into all cracks, feather the edges of the patch to the surrounding wood, and sand smooth when dry.

To fill the voids on plywood edges (or to level the end grain of

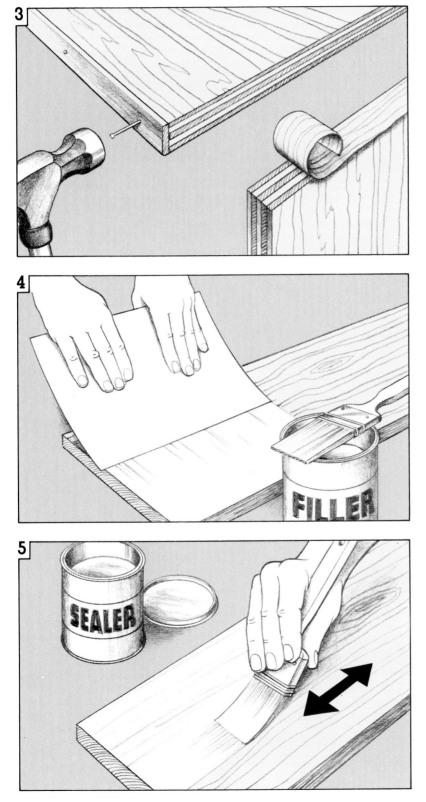

boards), mix the putty to a slightly thinner consistency. When it's completely dry, sand with a sanding block. For a really smooth surface, apply a thin second layer of filler.

3 If you plan to clear-finish the project, you'll want to finish the edges of plywood in either of the ways shown here. To conceal an edge with *wood veneer tape,* simply cut a length of it with scissors and apply it to the plywood's edges with contact adhesive (some self-adhesive types are applied with a hot iron). Purchase tape that is wider than the material is thick and that matches the veneer of the plywood. Trim the excess tape from the edge with a sharp chisel or pocket knife.

You also can hide unsightly plywood edges with inexpensive *screen bead molding.* To do this, butt the molding to the plywood edges (preferably using glue), and nail it in place with finishing brads. Sink nailheads below the surface. Don't fill the voids yet; you'll do this with color-matched wood putty after staining the project.

4 When you want a glassy smooth finish on fir, oak, or other open-grained woods, don't waste your time trying to sand the surface smooth. Instead, tame pronounced wood grain with *paste wood filler.*

Use a clean, dry brush to work the filler into the surface from all directions. After 10 to 15 minutes, level the filler by dragging a piece of cardboard across the wood grain. Finally, when the filler is almost dry, carefully drag the surface again—this time with the wood grain.

5 After filling or staining, apply a coat or two of shellac thinned with denatured alcohol, or sanding sealer.

Using a clean, dry brush, work it into the wood from several directions, but always finish brushing with the grain, using long, even strokes.

Apply the Finish Coat

A correctly applied paint or clear finish does two important things: It beautifies and protects. And providing you've prepared the wood surface with care, this last step in the finishing process can be one of the most satisfying parts of your project.

Unless you've been making a furniture-grade item, you'll probably go with a paint finish. In this case, first apply a water- or solvent-based prim-er to the bare wood—one that's compatible with the topcoat you plan to apply. Primers prepare the wood to accept the topcoat and serve to fill the wood pores. Allow the primer to dry, sand the surface with very-fine abrasive, and lay on one or more coats of paint.

For showy projects that have a beautifully grained wood you want to highlight, choose one of the many clear finishes available as your protector/beautifier. If you want to darken or lighten the wood's color, stain or bleach it first, then seal the surface with a sealer. With open-grained woods, you may want to apply a filler stain (see page 58), then a sealer. Whatever method you use, allow each coat to dry thoroughly and sand smooth with very-fine abrasive. Complete the project by applying two or more coats of varnish or hand-rubbed oil.

1 Painting with a brush is a familiar task, but perhaps not so familiar that a few work-saving tips aren't in order.

Begin applying paint to wood surfaces with short strokes across the wood grain, laying down paint in both directions. Don't bear down too hard on the bristles. Finish painting with longer, sweeping strokes in one direction only—this time with the wood grain. Just use the tips of the bristles to level the paint.

This two-step technique ensures complete coverage of the surface. This technique is useful for applying varnishes, too.

2 Professional painters have had years of practice to perfect the technique of freehand painting; they can guide a sash brush along razor-thin lines with hardly a second thought. For the rest of us, however, some judiciously placed masking tape can bring about equally satisfying results.

To cut-in wall surfaces around woodwork, use tape to conceal all adjacent wood surfaces, butting it against the wall.

3 Now work your brush all the way into corners (you needn't worry about spilling over onto the wood).

Masking windows and woodwork can save you hours of tedious cleanup. Just be sure to remove the tape while the paint is still tacky; otherwise, you risk leaving a ragged edge where the tape meets the walls, as well as difficult-to-remove tape.

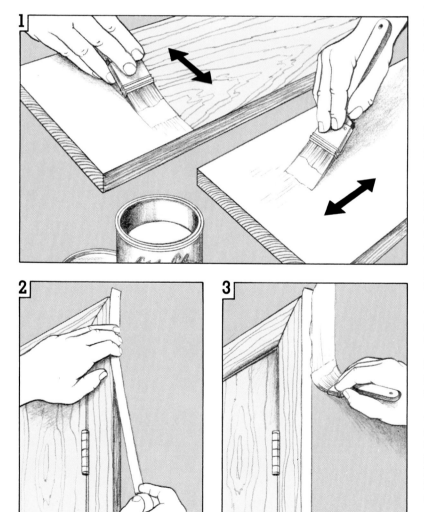

4 For painting large areas, a roller is the tool to use—and this is how to use it to achieve complete, uniform coverage. Load the roller with paint and begin applying it in a large "M" shape. Start with an upward stroke, increasing pressure to squeeze out more paint as you go. Cross-roll with horizontal strokes to level the paint and to fill in between your diagonal strokes.

5 Spray-painting with an aerosol can is fast and easy, but potentially messy. Minimize the mess by masking off adjacent areas with newspaper. Or, when spraying small objects, improvise a paint-ing booth from cardboard and clear plastic. To avoid breathing airborne paint, always wear a painter's mask.

6 Stains can beautify almost any wood, and are among the easiest finishing products to use—just brush them on, then wipe them off.

Use a clean, dry brush to apply stain in the direction of the wood grain. Let it stand for a few minutes, then simply wipe it off with a clean rag. To achieve a darker hue, let the stain stand longer before wiping, or apply a second coat. If you've already gone too dark, you can rub off some of the pigment with a cloth moistened in the thinner recommended for the stain you're using.

7 Any wood finish you apply in successive coats will look better and last longer if you lightly abrade the surface between coats. Whether you're between coats of paint, coats of varnish, or a sealer coat and a lacquer, a light smoothing with very-fine abrasive gives the next coat an acceptable surface to cling to and makes it easier to see where you've been as you apply the next coat.

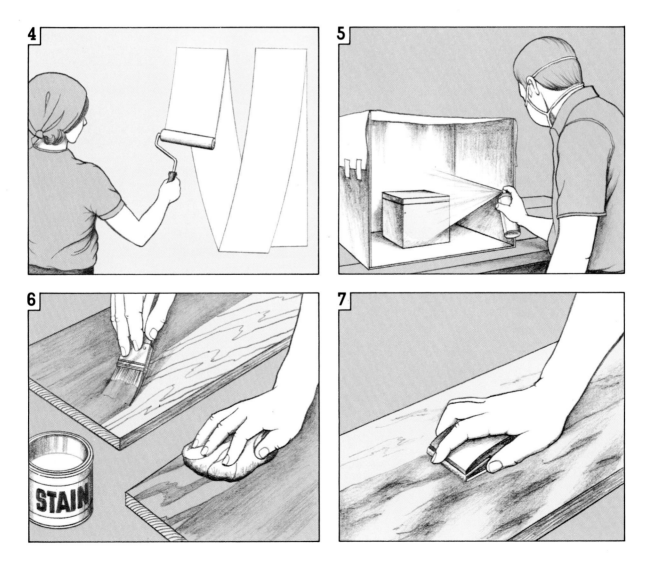

Tool-Sharpening Techniques

A do-it-yourselfer of our acquaintance once observed that working with a dull tool is a lot like trying to roller skate uphill with the wind in your face. How true! But if you heed the sharpening advice on these pages, you needn't fight uphill battles against balky tools.

When a tool dulls, your sharpening goal is to remove any nicks and burrs and to restore the cutting edge to its original factory angle. Usually, you can do this by giving it a touch-up.

But in the case of saw blades, after several touch-ups, the teeth will need *setting*—rebending the blade's teeth to the proper angle. This kind of work—and the sharpening of circular saw blades—is best left to a sharpening service.

As easy as it is to restore most cutting edges, some-times it's better to replace a worn-out tool than to resharpen it. Unless you have top-quality drill bits, for example, you may want to buy a new bit rather than take time to sharpen the old one.

1 Sharpen the blades of pocket- and small utility knives (but never sawtooth or serrated blades) with a two-grit whetstone. Hold the blade at a 30-degree angle to the surface of the stone, and in such a way that the blade travels over the stone at a slight diagonal. Wet the stone with a few drops of honing oil, then stroke the blade across the surface, rocking it from heel to blade tip. Turn blade over and stroke in the opposite direction the same number of strokes.

2 Dull plane irons respond well to touch-up sharpening with a whetstone, too. Remove the iron from the plane and use the following two-step procedure.

First hone the beveled edge of the plane iron with back-and-forth strokes on the whetstone. Try to maintain the factory-set angle—approximately 30 degrees. Now turn the iron over, lay it flat on the whetstone, and move it in a circular motion to remove burrs that may have formed on the flat side.

3 You hone chisels in exactly the same way as plane irons (see opposite page). But when their tips become badly nicked or blunted, file them first.

Lock the chisel in a bench vise as shown, and file off the worn cutting edge with a file held perpendicular to the chisel.

4 Now restore the cutting edge by holding the file at the angle of the chisel's bevel and slowly filing diagonally across the bevel.

5 When you seem to be sawing harder and cutting less with a

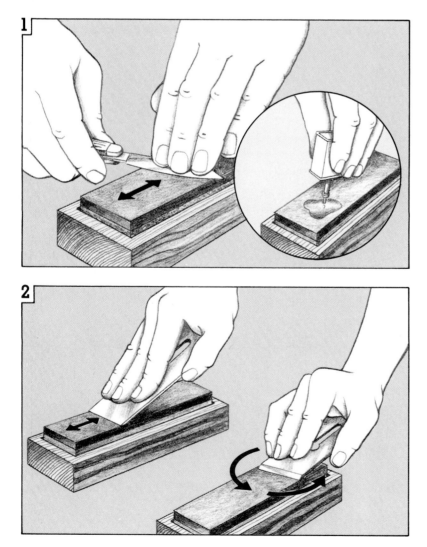

handsaw, it's time for some touch-up sharpening. Clamp the saw in a bench vise so the blade's teeth are about ⅛ inch above the scraps, and run a flat file across the points of the teeth until you've made small "plateaus" on the tips. Now select a small triangular file and use one of the following two procedures.

For crosscut saws, begin at the tip and place the triangular file in the *gullet* (valley) to the left of the first tooth that's set toward you. Seat the file against the bevel of the tooth (it will be at a 60-degree angle to the saw) and file until you've removed half of the neighboring plateaus you made earlier. Hold the file at both ends, and keep it perfectly level. Now skip the next gullet, file again, and continue in this manner.

When you reach the handle, reverse the saw in the vise and resume filing in the first gullet to the right of the tip-most tooth set toward you (the first gullet you skipped on the other side). File away the remaining plateau halves on each side of the gullet, and file alternate gullets until you reach the handle.

Sharpen ripsaws in the same manner, except keep the file perpendicular to the saw blade. File the teeth set toward you, reverse the saw, and complete filing.

6 Sharpening a twist drill bit requires a bench grinder with a tool rest to help you maintain the precise 59-degree angle with the grinding wheel. Holding the bit at the proper angle, slowly guide the leading edge of one of the cutting lips into the wheel. Upon contact, rotate the bit clockwise, slightly raising the chuck end of the bit and moving it to the left. This tricky maneuver grinds the heel of the bit's lip at a slightly greater angle so only the lip's leading edge cuts. Repeat this procedure with the opposite cutting lip.

Sharpening a spade bit is easier. Just touch up the shoulders with a flat file, holding it at the angle of the bevel—about 8 degrees.

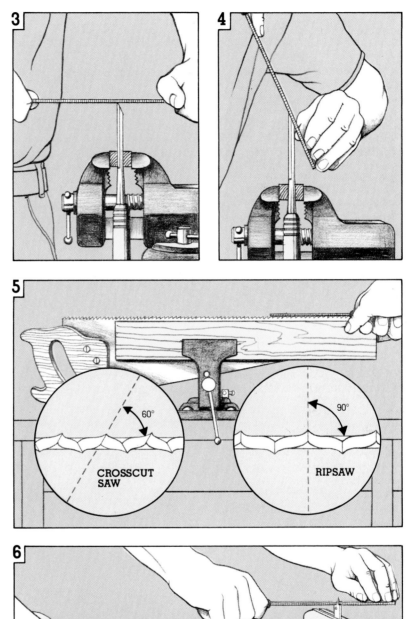

Framing Walls

If you could look at the 2×4 framework behind most finished residential walls, you would discover a rather simple construction. Upright members (called studs) butt against horizontal members (plates) at top and bottom. But building such a wall, whether to finish off a basement or some other room, doesn't just happen. It requires some thoughtful planning and know-how.

You must examine the situation at hand before determining the wall assembly method that's right for you. If the floor and ceiling are nearly level, *preassembly* makes good sense. If, on the other hand, the wall and ceiling are uneven, opt for *building a wall in place* (see page 67). With the first method you build the wall on the floor, then raise it; with the latter, you custom-cut each stud to fit and nail it to top and bottom plates already in place.

Whichever way you go, try to position the wall perpendicular to or directly beneath the ceiling joists so you have a sturdy surface to attach the wall to.

Preassembling on the Floor

1 Begin by deciding on the wall's location. Then, lay a framing square against an existing wall as shown, and have a helper hold one end of a chalk line against the outside corner of the square while you extend the line's other end along the square's blade to the desired wall length. Pull the line taut, reach in toward the middle of the line, and snap it.

2 Now you're ready to secure the nailer plate, which, though not ab-

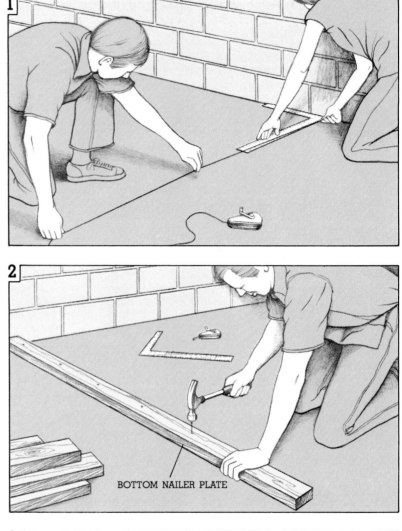

BOTTOM NAILER PLATE

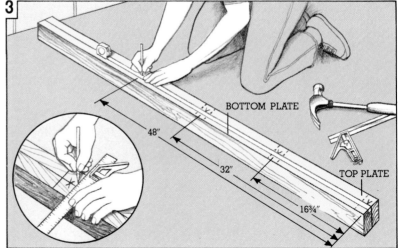

BOTTOM PLATE

48″

32″

16¾″

TOP PLATE

solutely necessary, provides the firmest possible hold on a concrete floor for preassembled walls. Cut a 2×4 to size, align it with the chalk line, and drive concrete nails through the plate and into the floor. (For long walls, cut additional 2×4s to the needed length and butt them end to end before securing them.) To make nailing easier, drill pilot holes through the 2×4s and on into the concrete using a carbide-tipped bit.

3 Cut the bottom and top plates, and mark stud locations on them as shown here. Place the plates on edge alongside of one another and mark the center of the first stud location ¾ inch in from the end. Now hook your tape on the end of the plates and extend the blade down along the members. Place stud center marks at 16¾ inches, 32 inches, 48 inches, and every 16 inches thereafter. Then, using your center marks as a reference, and a framing square, mark the studs' outlines.

4 To obtain stud lengths for the wall, measure the distance from the bottom of the joists to the top of your nailer plate at several points along the proposed wall. Subtract 3 inches from the shortest distance (to account for the top and bottom plates), and cut all studs to that dimension. Since the wall may only touch the ceiling joists at one location, you can expect to do some shimming.

5 If you weren't able to position the wall below or perpendicular to the floor joists, glue and nail blocking between the joists as shown here. Ideally, you should use the same size material your joists are made of, usually 2×8s. Space the blocking 16 to 20 inches apart to provide plenty of support.

6 Working on a flat surface, lay the studs on edge between the top and bottom plates. It helps to have something solid, such as a block *(continued)*

Preassembling *(continued)*

wall or the nailer plate, to nail against while assembling the wall.

For speed, nail one plate at a time to the studs. Drive two 16-penny common nails into each end of each stud. Since hammer blows tend to knock studs out of alignment, continually double-check your work while nailing. Keep the studs' edges flush with the plates' edges, and if any of your 2×4s are twisted or bowed, replace them. If you don't, these deformities will detract from the looks of the finished product.

7 Now comes the fun part— raising the wall! Try to have a helper on hand, especially for lengthy walls. The framework you've assembled is both heavy and bulky. Begin by resting the bottom plate against the nailer plate, then tip the wall into position. If the wall won't quite clear the joists, tap the top and bottom plates alternately with your hammer until the edges of the bottom plate flush up with those of the bottom nailer plate, and the top plate appears roughly straight up and down.

8 If, on the other hand, the wall is a bit short, drive shims between the two bottom plates as shown. Have your helper steady the framework while you drive the shims. (Remember to shim both sides to balance out the load of the structure and to prevent it from tilting.)

9 Once the wall is snug, nail the bottom plate to the nailer plate with 10-penny common nails, angling them for the best possible hold. Check the framework for plumb, in two directions, with a level. If adjustments are needed, take the level away and tap the framework into position. Check for plumb again, then go ahead and nail the top plate to the joists.

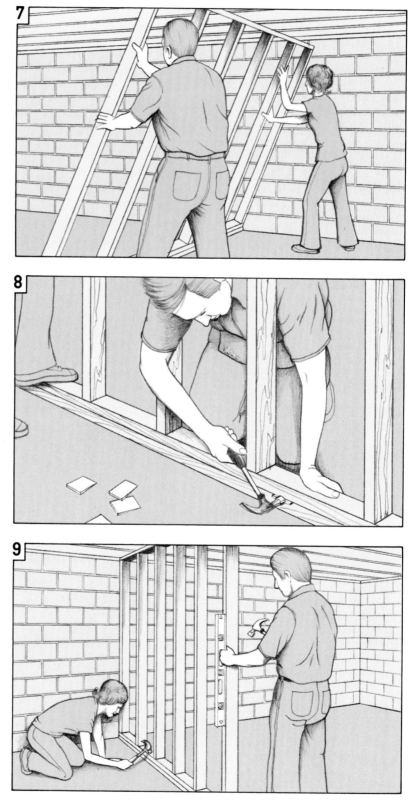

Building a Wall in Place

By building a wall in place, you not only eliminate one of two bottom plates found in preassembling, you also sidestep having to shim.

1 Start by cutting the top and bottom plates the desired length, then marking stud locations (see page 64). Though spacing is the same used in preassembly, place marks here on the plates' faces for effective alignment while toenailing. Now nail the top plate to the joists as shown here. You'll need a helper to hold the plate against the joists while you nail. And don't forget to wear protective goggles while hammering.

2 Next, have your helper dangle a plumb bob from the end of the top plate and at two or three points along one edge of it. Or if you're working alone, dangle the bob from a nail driven into the edge of the top plate. Mark the exact location of the plumb bob on the floor. Connect the marks by penciling a line along a straightedge or by snapping a chalk line. Secure the bottom plate to the floor as explained on page 64.

3 With both top and bottom plates installed, measure each stud length. Add $\frac{1}{16}$ inch for a snug fit, then cut the studs. Tap each stud into place.

4 To secure the studs, drive nails at a 45-degree angle through the end of a stud and into the plate as in the sketch on page 68. Don't worry if the first nail you drive moves the stud. The second nail, *(continued)*

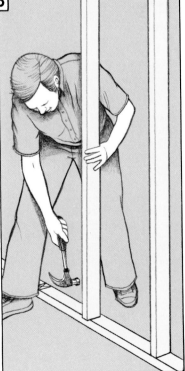

Building a Wall
in Place *(continued)*

driven in from the other side, should drive it back. For extra strength, drive in a third nail down through the edge.

If the stud won't line up, try knocking it with a baby sledge. Or cut a spacer the appropriate length and place it between the last secured stud and the one you're about to install. Still another way would be to drill holes at an angle through the stud first. This eliminates the shifting.

Framing Corners and Intersecting Walls

If your project calls for building two or more walls that connect to each other, you need to know how to join the wall sections together properly. This involves making sure the walls are square with each other and providing a nailing surface for the wall material that will later dress the framework.

Here, we show three ways to get the job done. In situation 1, the extra stud offers a nailing surface for finish materials and buttresses the corner as well. To tie two walls together using this framing arrangement, drive 16-penny common nails through the extra stud and into the end stud of the adjoining wall, clinching the nails for a firm grip (see page 47.)

In situation 2, several foot-long 2×4 scraps (use three in a standard 8-foot high wall) serve as spacers between two full-length studs placed at the end of one wall. Tie the wall sections together with 16-penny common nails.

Situation 3 shows what the framing should look like when two walls intersect. Nail three studs together and to the plates at the point of intersection. Then center the intersecting wall between the two outside faces of the three studs, square the corners, and nail the wall into place.

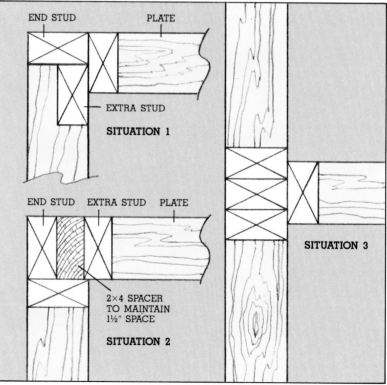

END STUD   PLATE

EXTRA STUD

SITUATION 1

END STUD   EXTRA STUD   PLATE

2×4 SPACER
TO MAINTAIN
1½" SPACE

SITUATION 2

SITUATION 3

Roughing-In an Opening

If your wall-building plans include a door opening, but you're a little unclear about how to do the framing, the information on this page should help you.

To begin with, find out from your supplier the rough opening dimensions for the size and type of door you want. Normally, hinge-type doors come in 18-, 20-, 24-, 26-, 28-, 30-, 32-, 34-, and 36-inch widths; door heights remain standard at 6 feet 8 inches. Another way to find the needed dimen-sions is to add 2½ inches to the door width (to allow for the side jambs and shims), and 2 inches to the door height (to allow for the head jamb, shims, and carpeting or other flooring that goes beneath the door).

Once you know the size of your opening, build the wall as described on pages 64–68, only this time include the rough opening members shown below.

Trimmers (vertical 2×4s found at each side of the opening and attached to a stud or another trimmer) provide solid, unbending support for the door that will hang from them.

The *header* (two 2×6s with a ½-inch plywood spacer sandwiched in between) spans the top of the opening, providing a rigid defense against bowing that results from a door's weight or any overhead load. (For openings less than 3 feet wide, replace the 2×6s with 2×4s placed on edge.)

Cripples (short lengths of 2×4s between the header and the top plate) help maintain a 16-inch stud spacing for nailing on sheet goods, and distribute the weight equally from above.

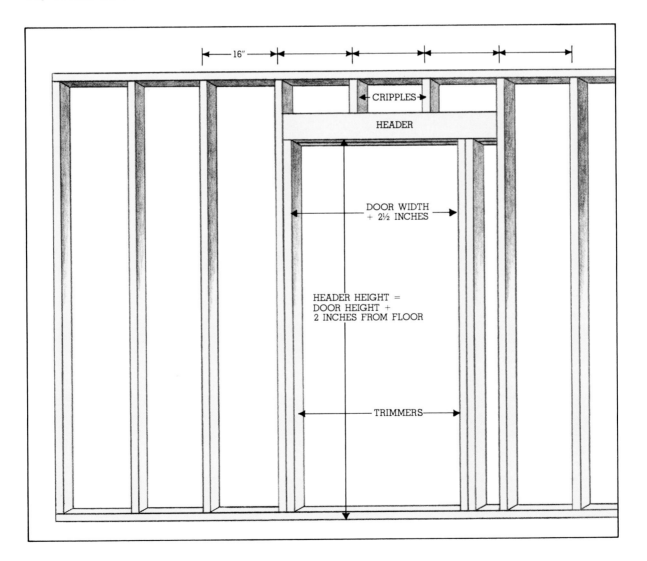

Other Framing Situations

Though there's no substitute for experience in carpentry when confronted with a new framing situation, using ready-made solutions such as those shown here can save you lots of time and trouble.

1 For framing-in a soil stack, rely on the chase construction below. Measure, cut, and preassemble three wall sections that consist of short top and bottom plates and two studs. Placing 2×4 cross members at 2-foot intervals between the studs further solidifies the chase. Now raise and secure each section to the floor, ceiling, and adjoining framing.

2 To frame-in a steel I-beam or a triple 2×12 beam in a basement, follow this procedure. Hang horizontal 2×4 rails along the length of the beam from the ceiling joists via notched 2×4 vertical supports. Tie the sides together and ensure consistent spacing with 2×2s of equal length. If you are fortunate enough to have a helper, build the framework on the floor, then lift and nail it in place.

3 Another familiar framing situation, the closet may look complicated, but it's really not. It's just a short wall with an opening (see page 69) joined at a typically framed corner (see page 68) to a shorter wall with no opening. Note that the header is simply a pair of 2×4s turned on edge and sandwiching a length of ½-inch plywood. You can use 2×4s no matter how wide the closet opening.

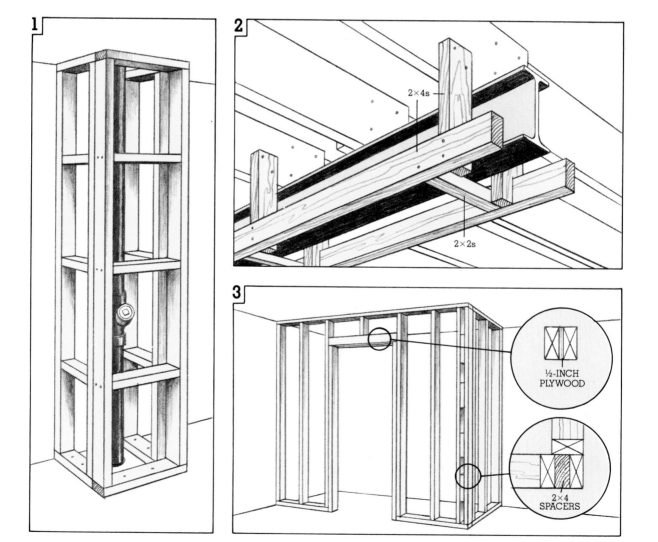

1

2
2×4s
2×2s

3
½-INCH PLYWOOD
2×4 SPACERS

Furring Out Walls

On pages 64–70 we take a thorough look at how to build stud walls. Here we discuss an alternative. Furring out a wall (see the typical layout below) is especially appropriate in those situations in which you can't afford to sacrifice the room stud walls require. But 1×2 or 1×3 furring strips have more going for them than being able to save you valuable space. They're also easier to work with and less expensive than studs.

To find out what's involved in readying a wall for paneling, drywall, or other material requiring a solid, plumb backing, turn the page.

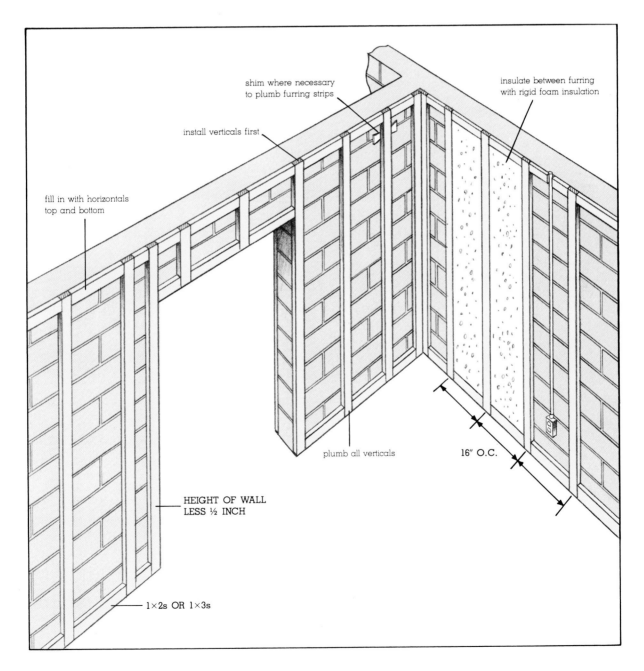

shim where necessary
to plumb furring strips

install verticals first

insulate between furring
with rigid foam insulation

fill in with horizontals
top and bottom

plumb all verticals

16" O.C.

HEIGHT OF WALL
LESS ½ INCH

1×2s OR 1×3s

Furring Out Walls *(continued)*

1 Start by marking the vertical furring strip locations. One easy way to do this is to position a sheet of the desired wall material in the corner of the room, plumb it, and strike a line down along its outside edge. Using the line as a guide, and 16 inches as your center-to-center measurement, mark the location of the other vertical strips along that wall.

Now, measure and cut each strip (one at a time) to fit between the floor and ceiling. (If yours is a basement construction, subtract ¼ inch from each measurement—the distance you will want your wall to be above the floor as a safeguard against flooding and settling.)

Next, apply a wavy ¼-inch bead of panel adhesive down one side of the furring strip as shown in this sketch. Now raise and center the strip on the line, pressing it firmly into place to help spread the adhesive.

2 Pull the strip back off the wall and prop it against the back of a chair or the wall. Doing this helps the adhesive dry more quickly. After the amount of time that is specified on the label of the product you're using), again press the strip into place.

3 Using your carpenter's level, plumb the furring strip as shown in the sketch. Double-check the 16-inch spacing, too. (If any adhesive makes contact with and sticks to your level, be sure to wipe it off immediately with a rag dampened in mineral spirits.)

4,5 Now check the strip for plumb as shown. If all is well, secure the vertical strips to the wall with common nails (for wood frame walls) or specially hardened ma-sonry nails (for concrete or masonry walls). If, however, some glaring irregularities exist, which you can discover by holding a straight 2×4 perpendicular to the wall after installing the furring, drive pairs of shims (wherever necessary) as shown behind the strips.

6 Drive the fastener through the strip and shims, and into the existing wall (into studs or mortar joints wherever possible). Do the same to all remaining strips. If going into a masonry wall, you'll be best off driving the masonry nails with a baby sledge.

7 After installing all the vertical strips, begin work on the horizontals. For these, measure between the vertical strips at the top and bottom. Apply adhesive, shim, if necessary, and install as already described.

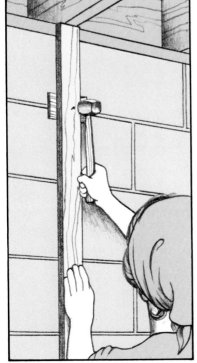

Installing Drywall

Drywall is a do-it-yourself dream material. It is easy to handle, cut, and hang; doesn't cost much; and covers lots of territory fast. Below and on the following pages we tell and show you how to hang and finish drywall like the pros do it.

Before actually hanging the drywall, however, study the sketch below. It gives the drywalling rules of thumb that will save you time and trouble. Then, make sure you have a sturdy backing of stud walls or furring strips on which to hang the drywall. For information on both of these, see pages 64–73. And if you plan to insulate, or do any plumbing or electrical work, do it now. Be sure to use a vapor barrier to protect against moisture.

And lastly, determine your drywall and other material needs. To do this, first multiply the *length* by the *width* of each wall or ceiling to find the number of *square feet* to be covered. From this number subtract the square footage of all door and window openings, then add 10 percent to the remainder for waste allowance. Now divide this figure by the number of square feet in each sheet.

You'll also need one 5-gallon container of premixed joint compound, a 250-foot roll of joint tape, and 5 pounds of 1½-inch ring-shank nails for each 500 square feet of surface. For outside corners, order *corner bead*.

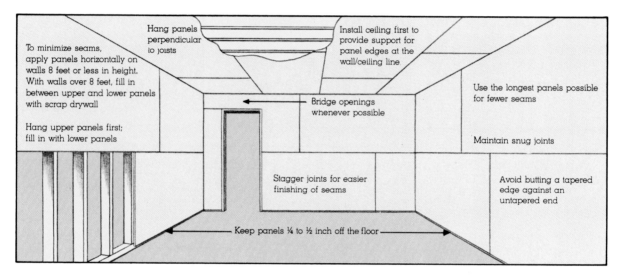

To minimize seams, apply panels horizontally on walls 8 feet or less in height. With walls over 8 feet, fill in between upper and lower panels with scrap drywall

Hang upper panels first; fill in with lower panels

Hang panels perpendicular to joists

Install ceiling first to provide support for panel edges at the wall/ceiling line

Bridge openings whenever possible

Use the longest panels possible for fewer seams

Maintain snug joints

Stagger joints for easier finishing of seams

Avoid butting a tapered edge against an untapered end

Keep panels ¼ to ½ inch off the floor

Measuring and Cutting

When cutting drywall to fit, the pieces should rest snugly against their neighbors, with measuring and cutting errors not exceeding ¼ inch. This is especially true for corners that are out of square, electrical outlets, and pipes, all of which require custom-made pieces.

1 Most generally, it's best to cut drywall on the floor. After making sure there aren't any stray nails, drywall scraps, or other objects

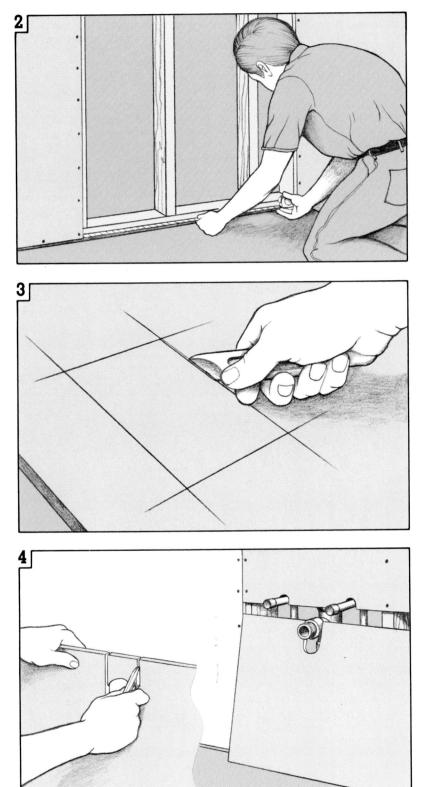

beneath the panel, press a straightedge firmly against the cutoff marks. Now, score along the cut line with a utility knife, severing the top layer of paper and slicing into the gypsum core. Next, lift the panel onto its edge, snap the cut segment back and cut the backing still connecting the two pieces.

2 If you need only to determine the cutoff height of a panel, measure the distance from the floor to the ceiling at the panel's left and right edges, and subtract ¼ inch from the shorter distance.

To determine the correct cutoff width of a corner panel, measure the distance from the last panel at the top and bottom to the corner. Transfer these markings to the panel, then make your cut.

3 To cut around an outlet box, measure the distance from the box's edges to the edge of the last panel. Then measure the distance from the box's top and bottom to the floor minus ¼ inch. Transfer these onto the face of your panel, extend the lines from the marks until you've outlined the box, then make the cut, using a utility knife or drywall saw.

4 A different kind of surgery awaits you when cutting around plumbing pipes. First, mark and cut out the needed holes in a piece of drywall, using a hole saw. Then, cut the panel into two sections so you can slip them around the pipes for a snug fit.

Hanging the Panels

1 Here are three *effective* drywall fastening patterns. Note that with ceiling panels, you should drive nails at 12-inch intervals around the perimeter, and double-nail every 12 inches along each joist. Why double-nail? Even if one of each pair pops, the other will keep the panel from sagging. (Always use ring-shank nails to secure the panels; 1½ inchers with ½-inch drywall, 1⅜-inch ones with ⅝-inch material.)

When hanging wall panels, you have two ways to go. If you use only nails, drive one every 7 inches around the border, and double-nail every 16 inches along each stud. If, however, you use adhesive and nails, run a bead of adhesive along each stud the panel will cover, except the two at its borders, making sure to keep it at least 6 inches from the panel's edges. Then position the panel and drive nails at 7-inch intervals along the border. If the panel bows, drive one nail into each intermediate stud or furring strip midway between the panel's ends or edges.

(Note: Drive perimeter nails ⅜ inch in from the panel's edges.)

2 As you can see here, there are several ways to drive a drywall nail—but only one correct one. Driving the nail flush will cause problems when you try to conceal it with compound and texture. If you drive the nail too deep and tear the cardboard facing, the nail won't hold the panel to its backing.

But if you manage to just barely dimple the drywall with the last hammer blow, neither of these problems will occur.

3 To install ceiling panels, start in a corner and against one side of the room and work out from there, keeping panels perpendicular to the joists. When placing a panel, try supporting one end of it with

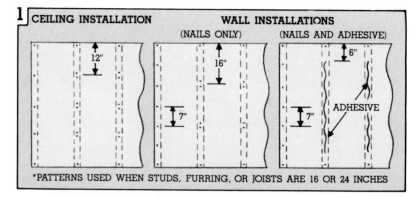

CEILING INSTALLATION   WALL INSTALLATIONS

(NAILS ONLY)   (NAILS AND ADHESIVE)

12"   16"   6"

ADHESIVE

7"   7"

*PATTERNS USED WHEN STUDS, FURRING, OR JOISTS ARE 16 OR 24 INCHES

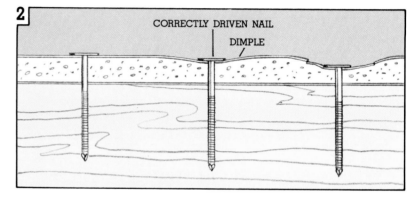

CORRECTLY DRIVEN NAIL

DIMPLE

DRYWALL HOIST

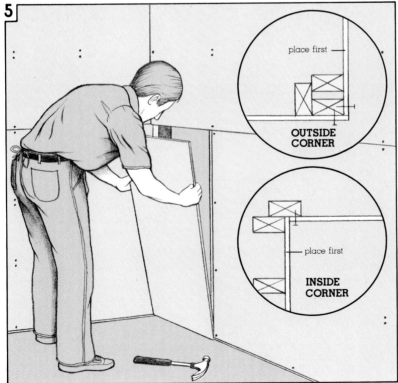

your head, leaving your hands free to hold and drive nails. Have a helper support the other end. When nailing, drive nails around the panel's perimeter first, then fill in between as shown in sketch 1. If you're working alone, consider renting a special drywall lifter like the one in the detail.

4 Once the ceiling panels are in place, begin work on the walls, installing the upper panels first. (It's a good idea to start a few nails into the drywall before lifting the panel into place.) Make sure those panels butt firmly against the ceiling before nailing. As shown in the detail, keep nails that are driven into the upper panels at least 7 inches from the ceiling corner. If the end of a wall panel fails to fall midway across a nailing member, trim it with a straightedge and utility knife so that it does.

When installing the lower wall panels, fit them firmly against the upper panels—tapered edge to tapered edge—raising them with a wooden wedge as shown. Remember, too, to maintain a ¼- to ½-inch spacing along the floor.

5 You'll probably have to cut filler pieces to finish any drywall job. To do this, simply measure and trim each piece to size, making sure that it has at least two nailing members to support it. Now insert the pieces—cut edges against the corner.

Taping and Texturing

There are no two ways about it: Taping drywall seams and corners is an art. Even some professionals can't do an adequate job of taping every time. But given the guidelines described here, and with some care and practice, you should end up with a wall that looks professionally done.

Naturally, the more you practice, the better you'll get. So if you're just beginning, work on some scrap drywall first. And when you do begin taping the real thing, start in an inconspicuous area—a closet would be great.

In most cases, three coats of compound will give satisfactory results. Let each coat fully dry for 24 hours before spreading another. (Humid weather, however, can extend the normal drying time.) Note: You can buy a 90-minute quick-set joint compound from some drywall suppliers, but unless you are exceptionally speedy you needn't bother with it.

Once taping is complete, texture the ceiling and walls, in that order, to disguise any imperfections that remain. You can blow-on texture materials of various kinds with a rented texture gun and hopper, or roll them on using a paint roller.

1 Before applying compound to tapered wall or ceiling joints, make sure adjoining panels are flush with one another. Then, using a 4- to 6-inch-wide drywall knife held at a 45-degree angle to the wall surface, spread an even *bed coat* of compound over the joint depression as shown.

If you're working with an end joint, spread a thin layer over it, being careful not to build up a

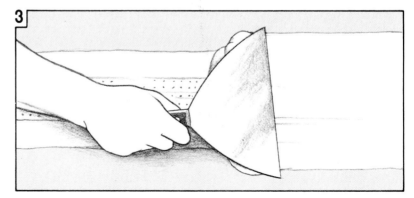

TAPERED JOINT

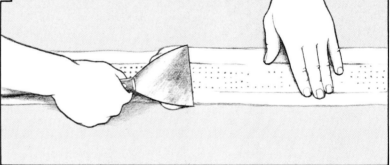

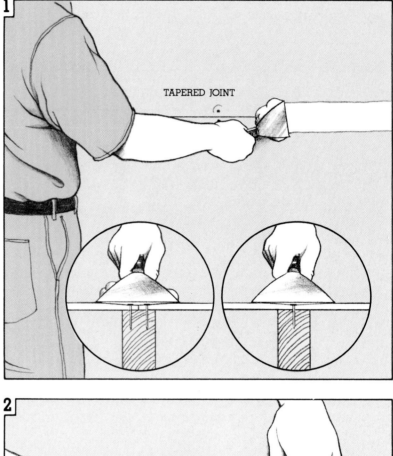

noticeable mound that later would require extensive feathering and sanding.

To conceal nailheads, pass over them several times—until the depression fills completely with drywall compound.

2 Immediately after applying the bed coat to a joint, center a length of drywall tape over the joint and press the tape firmly against the filled joint with your hands. Then, using one hand to hold the tape, further embed the tape by pressing it (but not too hard) with a taping blade. If bubbles form beneath the tape, peel it off and apply more compound; then press the tape back against the joint. Do the same, too, if wrinkles occur.

3 After the bed coat dries, load a 10-inch-wide drywall knife with compound and apply a topping coat over the joints. Feather out the material to about 6 or 7 inches on each side of the joints in order to

blend the compound in with the surrounding surface.

For end joints, feather out 7 to 9 inches on each side; for nail dimples, apply another coat to fill the shrinkage cracks of the first coat.

In all cases, apply additional skim coats over the second coat if needed. Then, once the final coat dries, smooth the surface using 80- or 100-grit open coat sandpaper or a dampened sponge.

4 With outside corners, you have a slightly different operation. To protect and conceal the raw drywall edges that meet at an angle, cut a strip of corner bead the appropriate length, using tin snips. Fit the strip over the corner, then fasten it to the wall one side at a time. Drive nails at 10-inch intervals through the nail holes on each side of the strip and across from one another.

Next, apply a bed coat of compound over the corner bead with a 4-inch knife angled away from the

corner. Allow one side of the blade to ride on the bead; the other side on the wall. Spread the compound 3 to 4 inches on each side of the bead's nose until the depressions underneath are filled and smooth. Wipe up any excess and let dry.

Later apply a second coat, feathering the edges 7 to 9 inches from the corner with a 10-inch knife. Add another coat(s) if needed, let dry, and sand or sponge.

5 For inside corners, begin by applying a bed coat, first down one side, then the other, with a taping knife. Cut a piece of joint tape to the correct length, fold it, then insert it by hand as shown here. With your knife angled away from the corner, wipe down each side, applying enough pressure to embed the tape. Let the compound dry. Apply another coat (and a third one if necessary) to further feather the compound. After the final coat dries, sand or sponge the surface smooth.

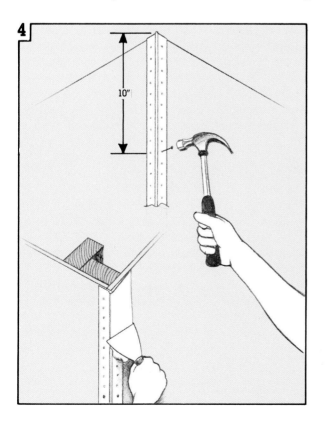

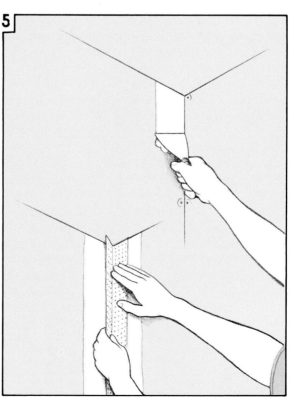

CABINETS & SHELVES

Most people assume that being able to fashion good-looking shelving and cabinetry projects is the exclusive domain of the professional cabinetmaker. But that's simply not the case. Sure, a professional has the advantage of many years of experience and a thorough knowledge of his trade—both big pluses.

But if you're willing to invest some time and effort in learning the art of cabinetmaking, we're sure you can achieve results that will please you and anyone else who views your handiwork. Not only that, but we'll also guarantee you that you'll get a lot of satisfaction from a job well done—and save a considerable amount of money by building your own units rather than purchasing manufactured ones or hiring out the work.

It would take a book many times larger than this one to explain all of the nuances of the cabinetmaker's trade. But that's not our goal—just as it's probably not yours to learn them all.

In this book we concentrate on the basics—those things you need to know to achieve good results, whether you're taking on an easy-to-construct shelving unit or a more demanding project such as a bank of kitchen cabinets. Every effort has been made not to overwhelm you with optional information.

We turn immediately to the first major section, "Materials and Hardware." Basically an awareness and buymanship chapter, this is where you'll learn about choosing and buying the various items needed to build your projects. Included is information on millwork lumber, moldings, and sheet goods as well as countertop and finishing materials, manufactured cabinet and shelving components, and last but not least, hardware.

Once you know what's what in materials and hardware, you can then set about developing your project plan. On pages 82-95, in the "Planning Guidelines" section, we walk you through the entire planning process. We help you decide what size, shape, and style of unit is best for you, show you your various construction options and the typical dimensions for several types of projects, and teach you how to draw your plan on graph paper, as well as make materials lists and cutting diagrams.

After you've charted your course by developing a plan, you're ready for the next section, "The ABC's of Cabinet Construction." Here, we take you step by step through the cabinet-building process, starting with assembling the cabinet shell, then on to adding the face frame, adding shelves, building and installing doors and drawers, applying a paint or clear finish, installing the cabinet itself, installing countertops, and working with plastic laminate.

You'll learn how to make a variety of basic cuts with circular and table saws and a router. In addition, we explain several ways to join cabinet and shelving members together, as well as the role clamping plays in quality construction.

PLANNING GUIDELINES

Regardless of the pursuit, having a plan always pays off—even if you have to alter it along the way. At the very least, you know where you are headed. That's why we spend the next 13 pages showing you what to consider in developing your "project blueprint."

We begin by exploring some of the questions you must answer at the outset of a project, such as what type of unit do you need, will it be a utility item or a piece of furniture, and what style should it be.

Then we turn to the construction options you have with both shelving and cabinets. You'll read about the various types of shelving and shelf support systems, and see charts that will help you determine shelf spans and spacing between shelves. In addition, you'll learn how wall and base cabinets go together, and be exposed to the various cabinet front possibilities, door/drawer style options, common cabinet configurations, and typical cabinet dimensions.

And to help you actually visualize your plan, we show you how to make graph paper drawings and cutting diagrams, as well as how to develop your cutting and materials lists.

First Things First

When architects and design consultants begin working with a client, they start by asking questions designed to find out if the client knows where he or she is headed with the project being considered. Not surprisingly, sometimes the end result differs entirely from what the client originally envisioned.

While you probably don't need an architect's help with your shelving and cabinet needs, you can still pick up valuable tips by considering the following:

What Are Your Needs?

Need more space to house space-consuming items that always seem to be piling up around your place? If so, a few wall-hung shelves or a floor-to-ceiling 2x4 and plywood shelving unit should provide the space quickly and inexpensively.

For dressier storage and display space, consider a freestanding or wall-hung open shelving unit or even a wallful of storage. And if you want a unit with closed storage and the good looks of fine furniture, a cabinet is an excellent choice.

Should the Unit Be Movable or Built In?

Each type has advantages. Many people prefer to build projects they can take with them if they move. With this approach, even large, whole-wall units can be dismantled, if necessary. Built-ins, on the other hand, appear more integrated in the overall room design.

What Materials Should You Use?

Obviously, you want to choose the least expensive material that will do the job. With purely practical units in areas of the home not generally seen by outsiders, shop-grade materials make good economic sense.

Showy projects require better grade materials that, not surprisingly, are more expensive. You can cut project costs somewhat by using lesser-grade goods for parts not exposed to view.

When deciding on materials for furniture-quality units, make sure they complement those used in nearby pieces. For example, if you have an oak dining table and want to build a complementary hutch for the same room, use oak again. This way not only would the grain in the new addition be similar, but your chances of matching finishes would greatly improve.

Finally, keep in mind that the materials you choose will give a certain style to the project. The three examples here point this out very clearly. While nearly identical structurally, visually they're quite different.

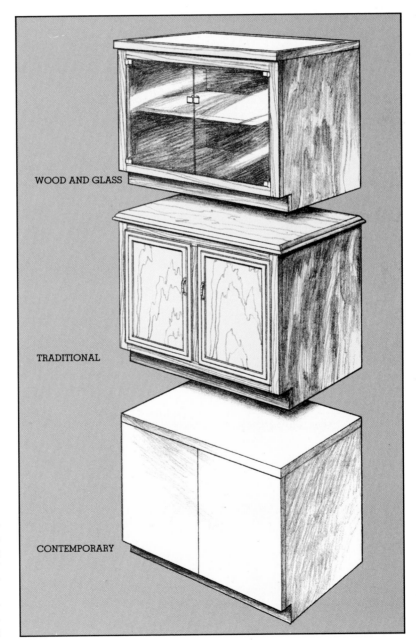

WOOD AND GLASS

TRADITIONAL

CONTEMPORARY

Know Your Construction Options

Shelving

Maybe you need a purely practical place to stash some stuff. Or perhaps it's an attractive showcase for collectibles, knickknacks, or books you want. Whatever your requirements, building a shelving unit is a relatively quick, inexpensive way to satisfy them. And you needn't be a woodworking wizard to produce some dazzling effects of your own—even the first time.

The sketch below classifies shelving into four different categories—*wall-mounted open shelving, floor-to-ceiling open shelving, freestanding enclosed shelving, and stack-* *able shelving.* Of course, many variations exist within each category. Which you choose depends on your storage and style needs at the time of construction.

Another choice you'll have to make is whether you want *fixed* or *adjustable* shelves. Many people prefer the flexibility afforded by the

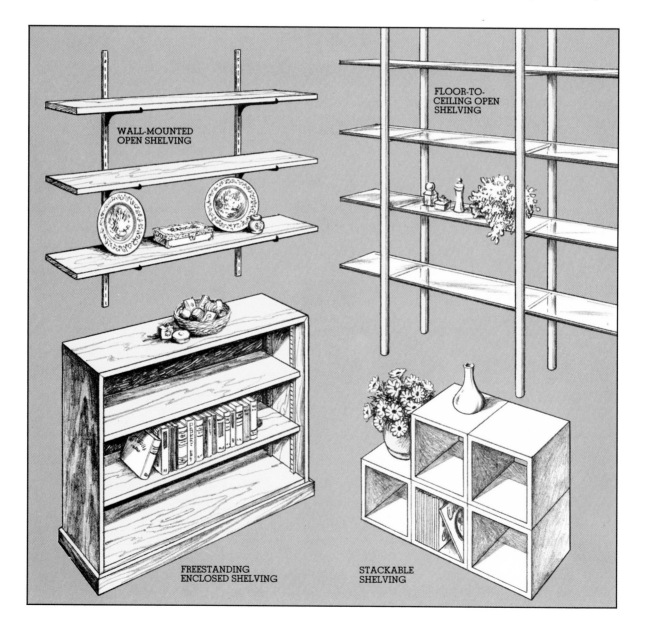

WALL-MOUNTED
OPEN SHELVING

FLOOR-TO-
CEILING OPEN
SHELVING

FREESTANDING
ENCLOSED SHELVING

STACKABLE
SHELVING

latter. The sketch below shows several ways to build either type.

For the shelves themselves, choose from plywood, particleboard, solid lumber, acrylic, or glass. Refer to the Shelving Spans and Shelf Spacing charts at right for help in determining the optimum distance horizontally between shelving supports and vertically between shelves. For items not listed, allow an inch or more clearance between the top of the object and the next higher shelf.

Shelving Spans

Material Used	Maximum Span
¾-inch plywood	36"
¾-inch particleboard	28"
1x12 lumber	24"
2x10 or 2x12 lumber	48-56"
½-inch acrylic	22"
⅜-inch glass	18"
(Assumes shelves fully loaded with books)	

Shelf Spacing

Item	Space Required
Paperback books	8"
Hardback books	11"
Oversized hardbacks	15"
Catalog-format books	15½"
Record albums	13¼"
Cassette tapes	5"
Circular slide trays	9¾"

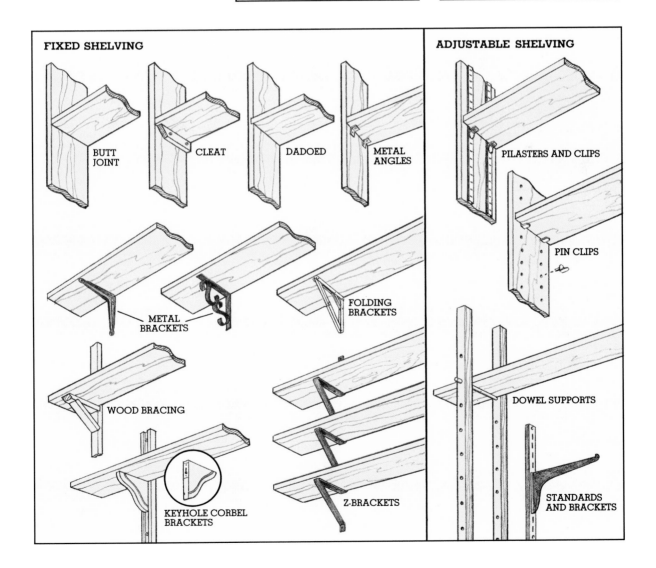

FIXED SHELVING

BUTT JOINT
CLEAT
DADOED
METAL ANGLES
METAL BRACKETS
FOLDING BRACKETS
WOOD BRACING
KEYHOLE CORBEL BRACKETS
Z-BRACKETS

ADJUSTABLE SHELVING

PILASTERS AND CLIPS
PIN CLIPS
DOWEL SUPPORTS
STANDARDS AND BRACKETS

Cabinets

Cabinetmakers know it. So do architects and others in the building field. But if you've never built a cabinet before, you may not realize that you needn't be a master craftsman to fashion a good-looking, solidly built project yourself.

On the next six pages, we show you some of the options you have when building kitchen cabinets and vanities. And even if the project you have in mind is more furniture oriented—a hutch, dresser, end table, or desk, for example—you'll find the information quite helpful.

The Carcass

Behind every good-looking cabinet front you'll find a *carcass,* or frame, made of edge-joined stock, plywood, or framing lumber sheathed with plywood. As you can see at right, we've chosen to use plywood panels.

Though we show two anatomies for you to study—a *base cabinet* and a *wall cabinet*—there aren't many differences in the way they're constructed. In each case, ¾-inch plywood panels form the perimeter of the cabinet, ¼-inch plywood encloses it at the back, and a dowel-joined face frame of solid lumber ties the unit together at the front and serves as the frame for doors and drawers.

Note that the base cabinet rests on a frame that creates necessary *toe space* at the front of the cabinet. The notch in the front frame member allows the notched side panels to fit flush against the unit and hide the exposed plywood edge for a finished appearance. The *ledger* at the back of the cabinet provides a solid surface through which screws are driven to anchor the unit to the wall.

With wall cabinets you don't need a base, but you will need a ledger at the top and bottom, again as a surface for securing the unit to the wall.

For more about constructing cabinet carcasses, see pages 96-99.

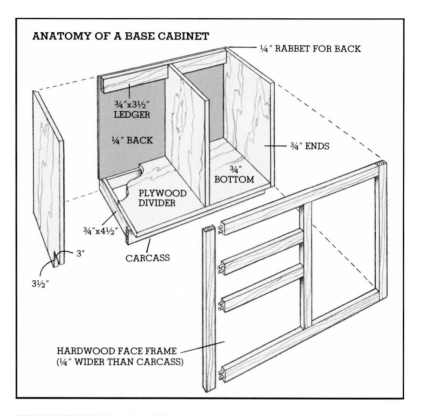

ANATOMY OF A BASE CABINET

¼" RABBET FOR BACK
¾"x3½" LEDGER
¼" BACK
¾" ENDS
¾" BOTTOM
PLYWOOD DIVIDER
¾"x4½"
3"
3½"
CARCASS
HARDWOOD FACE FRAME (¼" WIDER THAN CARCASS)

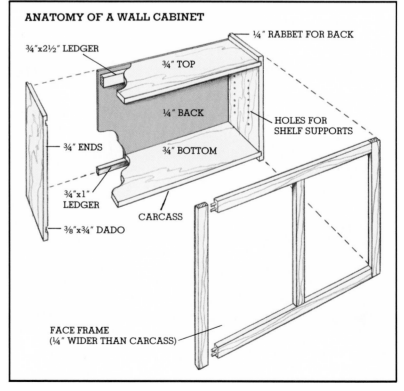

ANATOMY OF A WALL CABINET

¾"x2½" LEDGER
¼" RABBET FOR BACK
¾" TOP
¼" BACK
HOLES FOR SHELF SUPPORTS
¾" ENDS
¾" BOTTOM
¾"x1" LEDGER
⅜"x¾" DADO
CARCASS
FACE FRAME (¼" WIDER THAN CARCASS)

Planning guidelines **87**

Cabinet Front Possibilities

You add personality to a cabinet when you fit it with doors and drawers. In shaping this personality, there are several things to consider.

First, choose the *type* doors and drawers you want—*lipped, flush,* or *overlay*. (Whichever you choose, we'll show you the hinging options.) Select a *style—traditional* or *contemporary*—and the *configuration* of the cabinet—how many doors and drawers and in what arrangement. All of these considerations are explained on this and the following four pages.

Lipped Doors and Drawers

As the name implies, this construction features doors and drawers with rabbeted edges overlapping each edge of the opening. Typically, the doors and drawer fronts are cut ½ inch wider and longer than the opening, then rabbeted so that the lip rests flush with the face frame.

Offset hinges, with or without a butterfly (a flange), secure the doors to the face frame. The self-closing type is best.

The exploded-view drawing of the drawer below reveals a ¾-inch drawer front, ½-inch sides and back, and a ¼-inch bottom that fits into dadoes in the front and sides.

The back sits atop the bottom and between the rabbeted sides. Here, as in the other constructions, we show metal slides being used, mainly because they offer durability and ease of operation. Note, also, that the front is rabbeted to accept the sides and metal slides and still overlap the face frame.

You must construct the drawer no less than 1 inch narrower than the face frame opening to make way for the drawer slides, and ¼ inch shorter than the height of the opening. Drawer depth, however, is a matter of personal preference.

(continued)

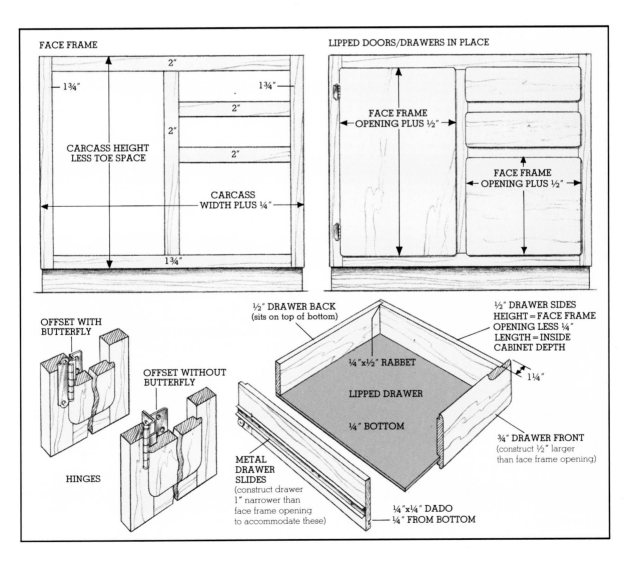

Cabinet Front
Possibilities *(continued)*

Flush Doors and Drawers

If your tastes lean toward the contemporary, you'll probably be interested in flush doors and drawers. (Flush here means flush with the face frame surface.) Be advised, though, that these are the most difficult of the three hinged door options to position in the frame opening.

In the sketch at right, we show two face frame situations from which to choose. If you prefer uniform spacing around the doors and drawers, construct the face frame as shown in the first example. Otherwise, you can dispense with the bottom portion of the face frame and cut the doors and drawers so they cover the bottom shelf of the cabinet.

To the right of each of the face frames, note that we've included formulas for determining the correct dimensions of doors and drawers. What you'll end up with is about a $1/16$-inch space between the door or drawer and the face frame.

NOTE: If using plastic laminate as a finish material, be sure to factor in its thickness.

With flush doors, you have several hinge options. Which you decide on depends on what look you want. Choose from butt, invisible (both shown here), decorative, inset, and concealed hinges. You can learn how to install all of them on pages 104-105. Butt and decorative hinges are the easiest to install; invisible, the most difficult. Many prefer concealed hinges because they are unobtrusive and self-closing.

Flush drawers go together in very much the same way lipped doors do. Note, though, that instead of having a rabbeted drawer front, flush drawers have two front members: one that fits between the rabbeted sides, and another that screws onto the drawer. One advantage of this construction is that if you decide to change the looks of your cabinets, you can simply screw another drawer front to the drawer. Too, only the front piece needs to be of cabinet-quality stock.

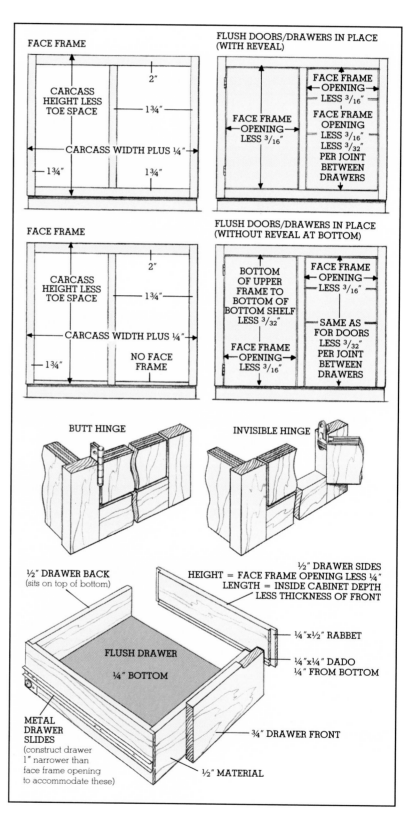

An overwhelming majority of kitchen and vanity cabinets commercially produced, and many of the custom-made ones, have *overlay* doors and drawers. Why? They offer clean, good looks and allow for more adjustment flexibility during installation. Even if your measurements are slightly off, you can still achieve professional-looking results by making minor adjustments.

Another type, the *full-overlay*, completely covers the face frame. Though not nearly as easy to install as the overlay, they, too, give cabinets a crisp, well-ordered appearance. For help with determining the dimensions of the door and drawer fronts, refer to the sketch at right.

For hinging these doors, several options exist. With full-overlay doors, choose from pivot (shown), offset, and concealed hinges. If you decide on overlay doors, self-closing or concealed hinges (shown) are best. For installation pointers for all of these types, see pages 106-107.

Drawers with overlay fronts are constructed much the same way as those with flush fronts. (See the exploded-view drawing at right for details.) The only real difference is the size you cut the drawer fronts.

Glass or Plastic Hinged Doors

Sometimes you want the items stored in a cabinet to be seen, as in a hutch or even wall-mounted kitchen cabinets. For situations like these, or if you just want something a bit different from what everyone else has, plastic or glass doors are a logical choice. You can combine either with a wood frame, and hang the door as discussed on pages 87-89, or let the doors stand alone as is done on page 90.

If you prefer the look of flush doors, size them so there's a ⅛-inch clearance all around. With overlay doors, plan for a ¼-inch overlap of the face frame. *(continued)*

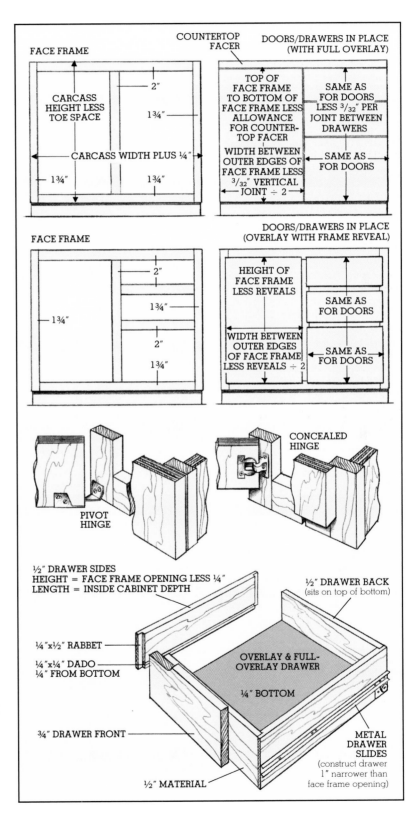

Cabinet Front
Possibilities *(continued)*

Note the hinges used with each of these types of doors. The hinge holding the flush door in place does so with pressure that's exerted by setscrews. After you mount two of these hinges to the cabinet, fit the glass or plastic into the hinges' channels.

Unlike the hinge just discussed, the one used with the overlap door requires that you have holes cut in the glass to accept the barrel portion of the hinge. Before ordering glass or plastic doors, read the instructions accompanying the hinges to

find the location of the holes. It's usually advisable to have these holes cut by a supplier who does this sort of thing regularly.

Sliding Doors

Rather than being supported by a pair of hinges, sliding cabinet doors glide in or on channels fastened to or recessed into the cabinet's top and bottom shelves. Their drawback is that you only have access to one side of the cabinet at a time.

The sketch below depicts two typical sliding door situations. In the first example, the cabinet's face frame neatly conceals the aluminum track in which the doors travel.

Here, the track is fastened to spacer blocks that are attached to the cabinet's top and bottom shelves, but if you'd rather, you can recess the track into dadoes cut into the cabinet. The doors for this installation should be $1/16$ inch shorter than the distance between the top of the upper track and the top of the lower one. Also, make each door $1/2$ inch wider than half of the distance between the inner edges of the cabinet sides.

If you choose vinyl splines, as in the second example, size the doors according to the guidelines below.

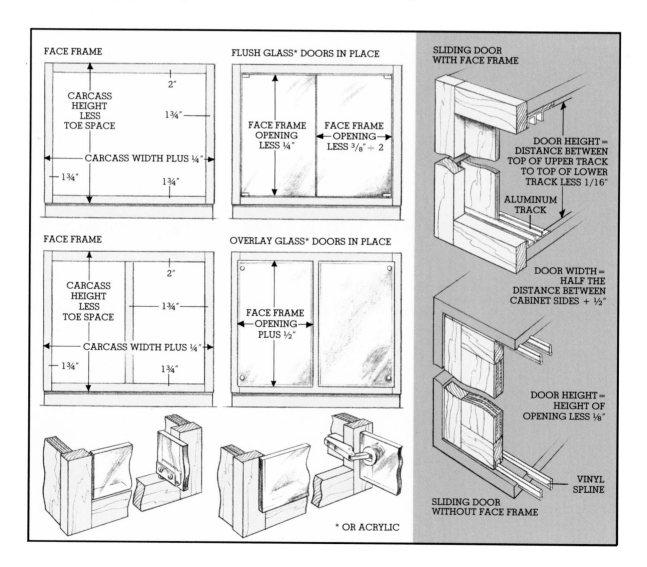

FACE FRAME

CARCASS HEIGHT LESS TOE SPACE

2"

1¾"

CARCASS WIDTH PLUS ¼"

1¾"

1¾"

FACE FRAME

CARCASS HEIGHT LESS TOE SPACE

2"

1¾"

CARCASS WIDTH PLUS ¼"

1¾"

1¾"

FLUSH GLASS* DOORS IN PLACE

FACE FRAME OPENING LESS ¼"

FACE FRAME OPENING LESS ³⁄₈" ÷ 2

OVERLAY GLASS* DOORS IN PLACE

FACE FRAME OPENING PLUS ½"

* OR ACRYLIC

SLIDING DOOR WITH FACE FRAME

DOOR HEIGHT = DISTANCE BETWEEN TOP OF UPPER TRACK TO TOP OF LOWER TRACK LESS 1/16"

ALUMINUM TRACK

DOOR WIDTH = HALF THE DISTANCE BETWEEN CABINET SIDES + ½"

DOOR HEIGHT = HEIGHT OF OPENING LESS ⅛"

VINYL SPLINE

SLIDING DOOR WITHOUT FACE FRAME

Door/Drawer Style Options

As you can see in the sketch at right, there's no shortage of cabinet door and drawer styles from which to select. Actually, hundreds of variations exist; however, they all fall into one of two categories—*slab* or *frame and panel.*

If you decide on the slab type, use ¾-inch panels to ensure adequate stability. Thinner stock doesn't hold up to the rigors doors and drawers are subject to. Glass doors are the only exception to this; typically, they're ¼ inch thick. As for styling slab doors and drawers, you can leave them plain, rout designs into them, or add moldings to their surface (see sketch). The style of the drawers should match the style of the doors.

With frame and panel doors, the frame supplies the needed strength, so you can go with thinner panels, fabric, or other inserts. Generally, these are set into rabbets cut into the back side of the frame. Be sure to style the drawer fronts so they're compatible with the doors; realize, though, that they'll have to be solid rather than frame and panel.

Common Cabinet Configurations

How you divide up the space in your cabinet depends on its size and intended use. Cabinets up to 24 inches wide generally have one door and sometimes a drawer or false drawer front above it, or a bank of drawers, and no doors. With cabinets wider than 24 inches, you can select a couple of doors, a door and a bank of drawers, or any of several other combinations.

An important reminder—be sure to keep doors and drawers in vertical and horizontal alignment. Doing this will yield a cabinet that's as eye-catching as it is functional.

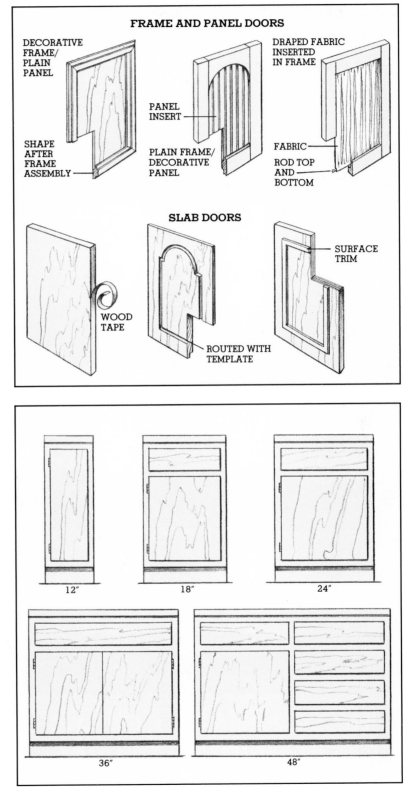

Typical Dimensions

Before you can commit your cabinetry plan to paper, which we advise you to do on pages 94-95, you need to decide on the unit's overall dimensions. While you have some flexibility here, you'll want to stay fairly close to the standard dimensions found on these two pages. Experience has shown that they work well in most situations.

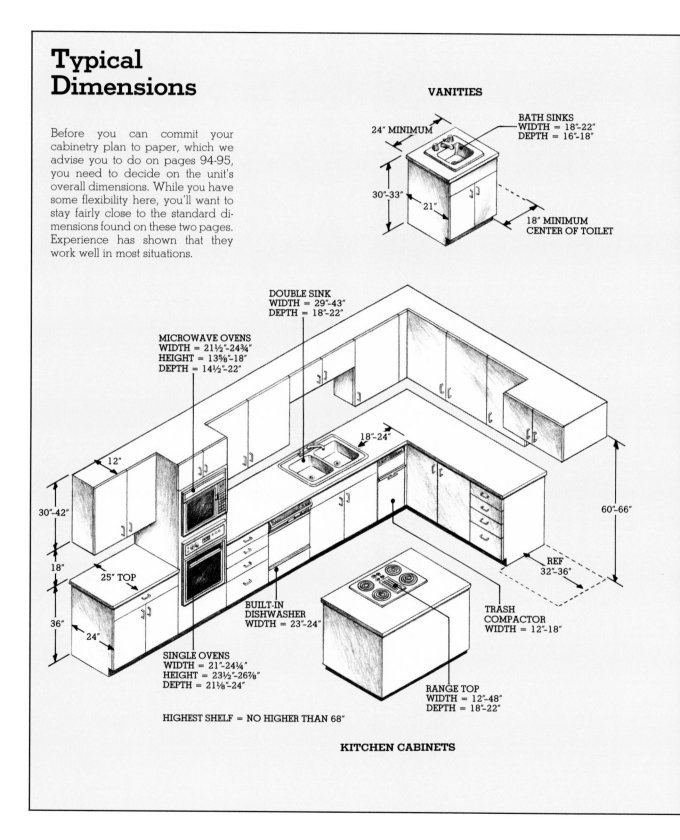

VANITIES

24″ MINIMUM

BATH SINKS
WIDTH = 18″-22″
DEPTH = 16″-18″

30″-33″

21″

18″ MINIMUM
CENTER OF TOILET

DOUBLE SINK
WIDTH = 29″-43″
DEPTH = 18″-22″

MICROWAVE OVENS
WIDTH = 21½″-24¾″
HEIGHT = 13⅝″-18″
DEPTH = 14½″-22″

18″-24″

12″

30″-42″

18″

25″ TOP

36″

24″

60″-66″

REF
32″-36″

SINGLE OVENS
WIDTH = 21″-24¼″
HEIGHT = 23½″-26⅞″
DEPTH = 21⅛″-24″

BUILT-IN
DISHWASHER
WIDTH = 23″-24″

TRASH
COMPACTOR
WIDTH = 12″-18″

RANGE TOP
WIDTH = 12″-48″
DEPTH = 18″-22″

HIGHEST SHELF = NO HIGHER THAN 68″

KITCHEN CABINETS

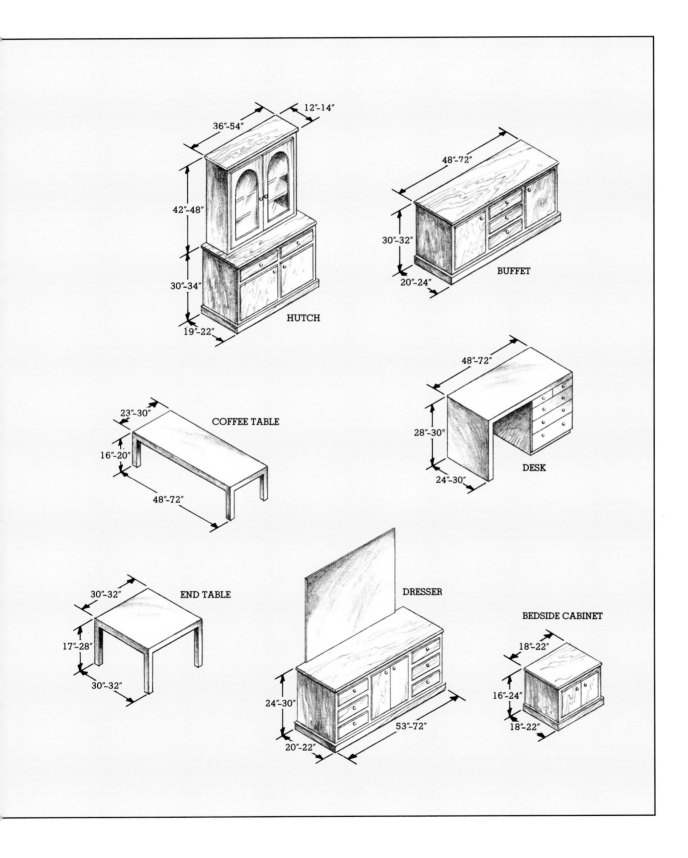

12"–14"

36"–54"

42"–48"

30"–34"

19"–22"

HUTCH

48"–72"

30"–32"

20"–24"

BUFFET

23"–30"

COFFEE TABLE

16"–20"

48"–72"

48"–72"

28"–30"

24"–30"

DESK

30"–32"

END TABLE

17"–28"

30"–32"

DRESSER

BEDSIDE CABINET

18"–22"

24"–30"

16"–24"

53"–72"

18"–22"

20"–22"

Commit Your Plan to Paper

Without a road map, finding your way around in an unfamiliar city is almost impossible. So is building a cabinet without a detailed plan in front of you. Even professional cabinetmakers take the time necessary to dimension all of a cabinet's components before making the first cut. Why? Because even minor measurement or cutting errors will detract from the looks of a project—and cost money.

Committing your plan to paper involves several things. First, using graph paper, draw three *scaled sketches* of your project—a front view, an end view, and a top view—noting the dimensions of each member. Draw detailed sketches of any areas with construction oddities. Recheck all of the dimensions for accuracy. (The drawings below and on the following page are for a vanity cabinet that measures 38 inches wide, 22 inches deep, and 30 inches high.)

Next, make a *cutting list* like the one we made for this project. Notice that the list is divided by the type of lumber used—¾-inch hardwood, ¾-inch framing lumber, ¾-inch plywood, and ¼-inch plywood. A further breakdown of the materials needed under each type of lumber helps categorize the components of each subassembly. For best results, discipline yourself to be specific.

Then make the *cutting diagrams* of the various components using graph paper. Doing this will help you determine how much of each material you need to buy. Remem-

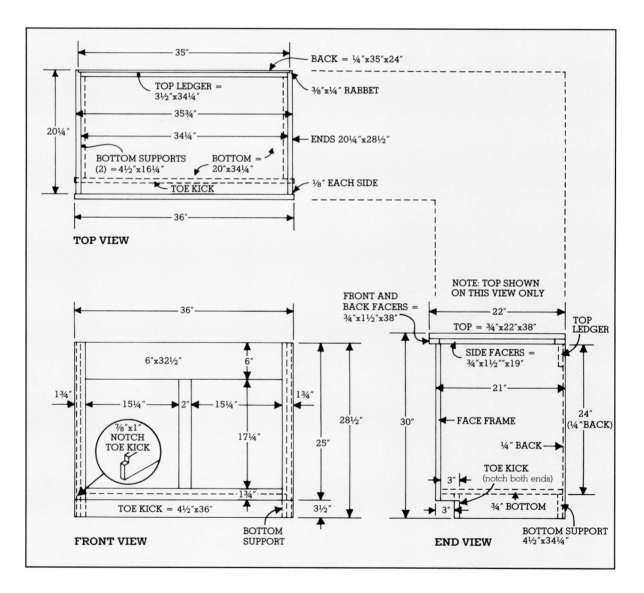

ber to consider grain direction when positioning members on plywood panels. You will want the grain of the side panels, for example, to be running the same direction. Also, when laying out any of the components, be sure to figure in the amount of material that will be lost to the saw blade.

Finally, you'll need a *materials list* to take to your materials supplier. Jot down your lumber needs as well as the miscellaneous items such as hinges, nails, etc. You also may find it helpful to take your sketches and cutting list with you.

Cutting List

¾″ Hardwood
Face Frame	6″x32½″
	2″x17¼″
	1¾″x32½″
	1¾″x25″
	1¾″x25″
Toe Kick	4½″x36″

¾″ Framing Lumber
Top Ledger	3½″x34¼″
Bottom Support	4½″x34¼″
Side Supports	4½″x16¼″
	4½″x16¼″

¾″ Plywood
Ends	20¼″x28½″
	20¼″x28½″
Top	22″x38″
Bottom	20″x34¼″
Doors	15¾″x17¾″
	15¾″x17¾″
Front Facer	1½″x38″
Back Facer	1½″x38″
Side Facers	1½″x19″
	1½″x19″

¼″ Plywood
Back	24″x35″

Materials List

1 Piece Hardwood ¾″x7″x8′
1 Piece Framing Lumber ¾″x5″x9′
1 Sheet Plywood 48″x96″x¾″
1 Sheet Plywood 24″x48″x¼″
2 Pairs Self-Closing Hinges
2 Pulls
Nails
Glue
Stain
Sealer
Plastic Laminate
Contact Cement

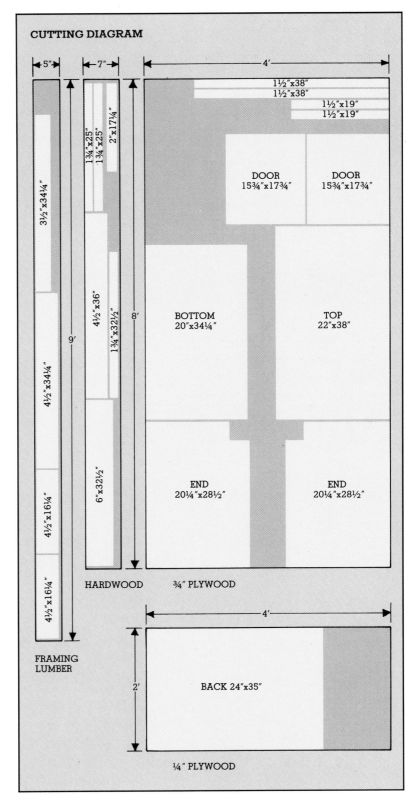

CUTTING DIAGRAM

FRAMING LUMBER

HARDWOOD   ¾″ PLYWOOD

¼″ PLYWOOD

THE ABC's OF CABINET CONSTRUCTION

Earlier in this book, you learned about the materials and hardware available for making cabinets and shelves. In the last chapter, we walked you through the steps involved in planning your project.

Now comes the exciting part—assembling and finishing your project. As you're about to find out, cabinet construction is a process that's not nearly as complex as you might have thought. We begin by showing you how to assemble the cabinet shell, or *carcass,* and how to fasten the face frame to it.

Next, you'll read about three ways to install shelves and learn how to install hinged and sliding doors, as well as drawers and false cabinet fronts.

Applying a finish to the project—either paint or a clear finish—comes next, followed by instructions on cabinet installation.

And because no base cabinet is complete without a countertop, we conclude the chapter by showing you how to install several different types of tops.

The cabinets we show in various stages of construction in this chapter are the popular kitchen/vanity type.

Assembling the Cabinet Shell

Base Cabinets

1 Start by cutting the base pieces to the sizes specified in your plan. (For help with planning your project and committing that plan to paper, refer to the "Planning Guidelines" chapter beginning on page 82.) Then, with your material on a flat surface, join the members using woodworkers' glue and 6d or 8d finishing nails. Be sure to align the sides with the notched front piece as shown in sketch 1.

Now, using a framing square, check the base for square. If it's a bit off, nudge it into position with your hammer. If it's way off, recheck your measurements. You might have to do some trimming.

2 Cut the cabinet sides to size, notch the front edge of each so it will fit over the notch in the front base member, and rabbet the back edge of each side to accommodate the cabinet back. (For information on how to make rabbet cuts, see the cutting and joining techniques beginning on page 118.) Glue and nail the sides to the base.

To ensure a good bond, tip the unit on its back and clamp the sides and base together, using a pair of pipe clamps and a couple of pieces of scrap wood to equalize the pressure being exerted.

3 After allowing the glue to set up for the time specified on the container label, remove the clamps and return the cabinet to its upright position. Then cut the bottom shelf to size and test-fit it between the cabinet sides. Be sure to position the shelf so it is flush with the front of the sides. If it fits correctly, run a wavy bead of glue along the top edge of the base members, set the shelf in place, and secure it with finishing nails. *(continued)*

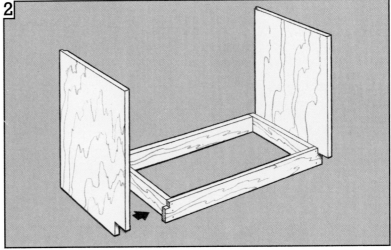

Base Cabinets *(continued)*

4 Before cutting the ledger, double-check its length by measuring the distance between the inside edges of the cabinet sides. (Cutting the ledger to this dimension ensures a square opening for the cabinet back to fit into.) Now, position the ledger between the sides as shown and drill pilot holes through the sides and into the ledger. Remove the ledger to apply glue, then secure it by driving in finishing nails.

5 (If the unit you are building has shelves supported by stopped dadoes, insert them into the cabinet shell now; you can't do it after the back goes on.) Cut the cabinet back to size, then prior to positioning it, drive several finishing nails partway through it near the edges. Now lay a bead of adhesive in the rabbet on both sides and secure the back.

6 If your plan includes one or more vertical dividers to compartmentalize space within the cabinet, cut the panel(s) so its front edge aligns with the cabinet sides and bottom shelf, and its top edge aligns with the side panels' top edges. And don't forget to cut a notch at the top back edge so the divider will fit in around the ledger.

Where you position the divider(s) depends on the configuration of the interior space of the cabinet. If yours will have two doors and no drawers, fasten the divider midway between the sides. But if you've opted for a door and a bank of drawers, you'll want it off-center enough so that when the face frame is attached, the divider will serve as the surface for the drawer slide.

Run a bead of glue along the back and bottom edges of the divider and nail it into place from the back and bottom of the cabinet. If you prefer, you can fit the divider in place at this point and secure it after you've attached the face frame (see page 100).

If your cabinet has shelves supported by full dadoes, insert and secure them now.

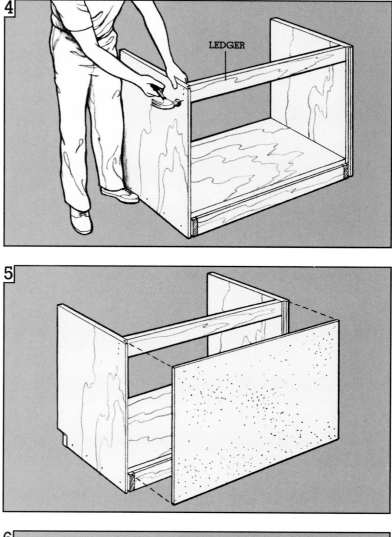

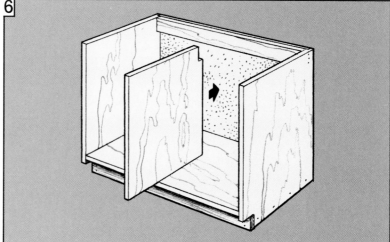

Wall Cabinets

1 Start by cutting the top, bottom, and sides to the size specified in your project plan. (For help with planning your project, see the "Planning Guidelines" chapter beginning on page 82. And for information on making various cuts, refer to the cutting and joining techniques, beginning on page 118.) Don't forget to rabbet the back edge of each side to accept the cab-inet back and to cut dadoes for the top and bottom shelves. You may also want to cut grooves or drill holes in the sides at this time if you plan to support shelves with recessed pilasters or shelf clips (see pages 101-102).

Now, glue and nail the frame together. To ensure a good, tight fit, use a couple of pipe clamps and wood scraps to apply pressure to the unit. (See the glue container to determine the proper curing time.)

2 Cut top and bottom ledgers to length, then glue and nail them to the cabinet as shown.

3 Cut the cabinet back to size, then lay the shell facedown, and glue and nail the back as shown.

4 Cut any dividers to size, notch the top back edge to fit around the top ledger, and glue and nail in place. Use a square to confirm that the divider is square with the shelves.

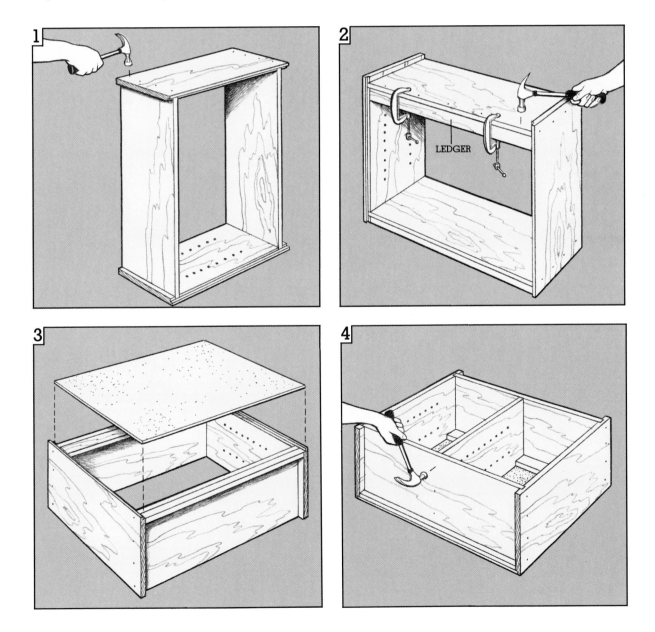

Attaching the Face Frame

1 With the cabinet on its back, apply glue and spread it along the front edge of the sides and top and bottom shelves.

2 If you joined the face frame members with dowels (discussed on page 131) or preassembled the face frame using butt or lap joints, apply glue to the back side of the face frame, then position and nail the frame to the cabinet every eight inches with 6d finishing nails. (The top of the upper face frame member should align with the top of the sides; the top of the lower member, with the top of the bottom shelf. On cabinets with sliding doors, the top of the lower member should be flush with the top of the track.) Clamp the face frame to the cabinet (see pages 130-131).

3 If you nail on the members separately, secure the side members first, then clamp the rails between the sides and nail the members together. Now, clamp the face frame to the cabinet (see pages 130-131).

4 Recess the nails on the face frame and elsewhere on the cabinet.

Adding Shelves to Cabinets

Basically, you have four major shelf support options to consider when building cabinets. With adjustable shelves, choose from pilasters and clips, and pins or dowels that fit into dowel holes. If you want fixed shelves, you need to decide between ledgers and butt joints.

On pages 101-103, we show you how to install all but the butt-joint shelving. With the latter type, simply decide where on the uprights to locate the shelves, then either cut dadoes for the shelves to slip into or butt the shelves directly against the surface of the sides. (If you choose this method, install the shelves while you're assembling the shell—see pages 97-99.)

Keep in mind that if you decide on plywood or particleboard shelves for your unit, you'll need to cover their front edges and sometimes their end edges in one of the three ways shown in the top sketch. *Wood filler* works well if you plan to paint the shelves. For clear-finished cabinets or shelving units, use either *wood molding* or *wood edge tape*.

Fastening Shelf Cleats to a Cabinet Shell

1 Make a mark (on either upright) at each point where you want the *top* of a shelf. Then, using a combination square as shown, strike a line at each point.

2 Now, hold each cleat in position with one hand and drill a pair of holes through the cleat and into the upright. Glue and nail each cleat in place. Repeat this same procedure for the other upright.

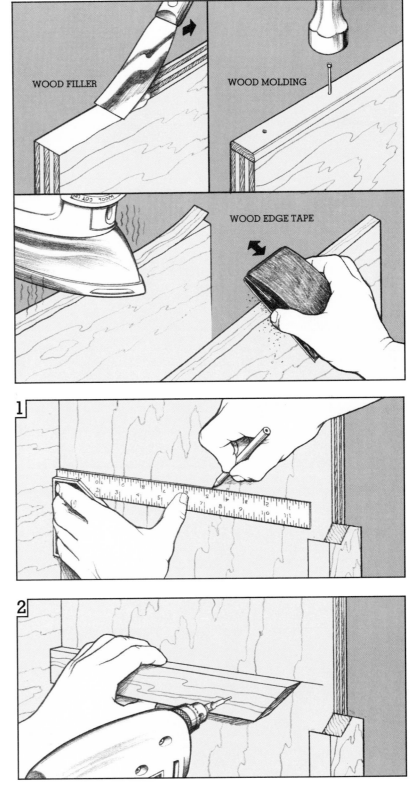

WOOD FILLER

WOOD MOLDING

WOOD EDGE TAPE

Adding Shelves to Cabinets *(continued)*

Fastening Pilasters to a Cabinet Shell

1 Measure the distance between the top of the bottom shelf and the bottom of the top shelf (or the top edge of the cabinet side). Now lay a pair of pilasters side by side, with the numbers and hash marks lined up, and mark the cutoff line. Cut them to length with a hacksaw. Use either of these as a pattern to cut enough pilasters to satisfy your needs, again making sure that the numbers and hash marks line up. (The numbers and hash marks will help you correctly position the clips used to support the shelves.)

2 (If your unit has recessed pilasters, you can skip this step, as you would already have made the dado cuts in the cabinet sides.) Now, mark the location of the pilasters. Make a light pencil mark near the top and bottom of the cabinet sides, and if you have mid-support, also on the back side of the middle face frame stile. (In most situations, you'll want the pilasters that support the ends of the shelves positioned about an inch in from the front and back edges of the shelves.) Connect your marks, using one of the pilasters as a straightedge.

3 If your unit has recessed pilasters, place each strip into a recess and mark the location of the screws that will hold it in place. For flush-mount situations, align the pilaster with the guideline you made and mark the location of the screw holes. Now, drill pilot holes for the screws.

4 Finish this part of the job by repositioning the pilasters and driving screws to secure them. Just snug the screws down; you don't want to strip any threads.

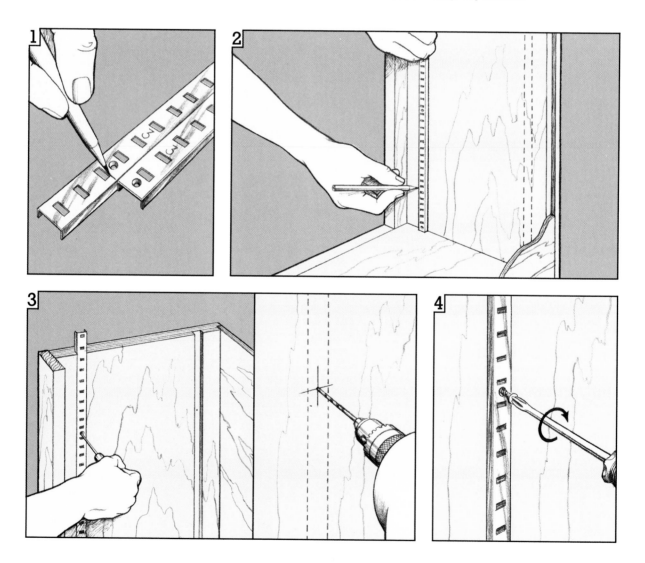

Drilling Holes for Shelf Clips or Dowels

1 Start by determining where to locate the holes. Generally, they should be positioned about one inch in from the front and back edges of the shelves. If you don't have too many holes to drill, you can first draw vertical lines to indicate the vertical center of each row of holes. Then, using a square, mark the horizontal center of each hole as shown. Finish by drilling each hole as shown.

Notice the piece of electrical tape wrapped around the drill bit; it allows you to drill all of the holes to a uniform depth. (See sketches 2 and 3 for an easy way to accomplish the same thing.)

2 Here's a nifty solution when you're faced with having to drill a large number of holes for a cabinet or shelving unit. First, cut a piece of perforated hardboard—the type with ¼-inch-diameter holes—the same width as that of the side members and almost as high. Position it as shown and use it as a guide to cut the holes. (To avoid mix-ups, mark the top of the guide.) Here again, you'll want the holes positioned about one inch in from the front and back edges of the shelves. Electrical tape wrapped around the drill bit helps you gauge hole depth.

Once you have finished boring all the holes in one side, simply move the template to the other side of the cabinet and bore through the same holes as before. (Be sure to keep the template in the same position when you move it; otherwise, the holes won't line up correctly.)

3 If your cabinet or shelving unit has one or more vertical dividers, your procedure is similar to that shown in sketch 2, with one important exception. When you drill holes in a divider, you must offset the holes as shown to keep from boring all the way through it.

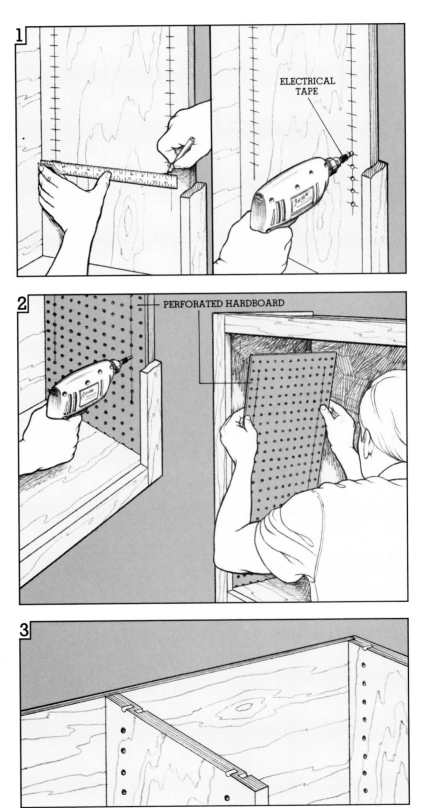

Adding Hinged Doors to Cabinets

Most hinge manufacturers assume that the consumer knows how to install their hinges, so they don't include instructions in the package. Usually, the package contains only a *pair* of hinges and enough screws to fasten the hinges in place.

What we try to here through page 108 is fill a void we think exists by explaining how to install several different types of hinges, pulls, and catches.

Lipped Doors

Offset Hinges

With the door facedown, measure in an equal distance from its top and bottom and make a mark (A).

Align the hinges with your marks as shown (B), mark the location of the screws, drill pilot holes, and secure the hinges with the screws.

Now center the door over the opening, mark for and drill pilot holes (C), then hang the doors. (With lipped doors, offset hinges are your only alternative.)

Flush Doors

Butt, Decorative, and Inset Hinges

Start by measuring in an equal distance from the top and bottom of the door (usually the width of the hinge). Then, position the hinge, mark for and drill pilot holes, and fasten the hinges to the doors (A).

Center the door in the opening and rest it on a couple of nails to effect equal spacing at top and bottom. (You may have to recess one of the hinge leaves to get equal side-to-side spacing.) Mark the top and bottom of the hinge as shown (B). (With decorative hinges, just mark the location of the screw holes.)

Remove the door, chisel out a recess if necessary (C), align the hinge with the marks, and mark for and drill pilot holes in the stile (D).

Finish by hanging the door.

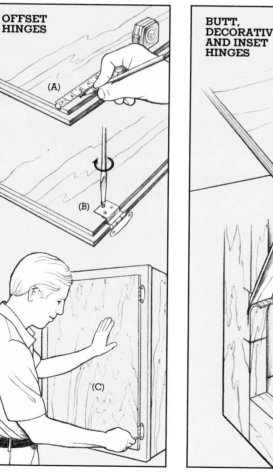

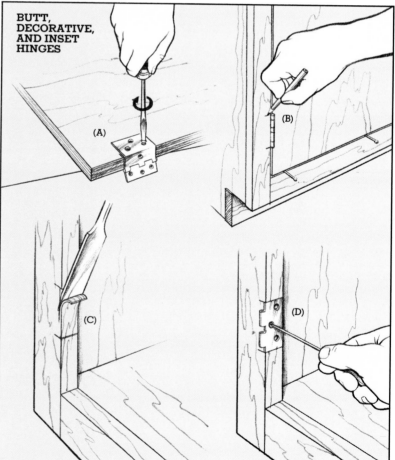

Invisible Hinges

Measure in an equal distance from the top and bottom of the door (usually the width of the hinge's leaves or about two inches) and make light marks on the face and edge of the door as shown at right (A).

Now, center the door in the opening, using nails to achieve equal top-to-bottom spacing (B). Make a corresponding mark on the stile. Be accurate; even small errors can cause big positioning problems.

Position the template as shown on both the door and stile and, using an awl, mark the drill holes (C).

Next, drill holes deep enough to accept the hinge leaves (D). Chisel out any wood left by the drilling.

Finally, drill pilot holes for the screws and mount the hinge to the door and then to the stile (E).

Concealed Hinges

(Before installing this type of hinge, mount it on scrap to avoid positioning errors. Also ask your supplier to see the manufacturer's catalog for installation particulars.)

With the door facedown, measure in two inches from its top and bottom and make light pencil marks as shown (A). Then, using a square, extend the lines out onto the back side of the door (about 2 inches).

Now, make a template as a guide for cutting the recess for the hinge's cup. (You'll be cutting the recess with a router fitted with a guide bushing.) To do this bore a hole the diameter of the cup—plus the thickness of the bushing—in a piece of wood with a spade bit or hole saw. Position the template so it is the exact distance in from the edge of the door as specified in the manufacturer's catalog and is centered over your guide mark (B). Now rout out the material to the correct depth.

Next, make a mark on the cabinet shell at the same distance from the top and bottom as for the hinge (plus clearance) (C), then fasten the hinge to its baseplate and mark the baseplate position as shown (D).

Fasten the baseplate to the cabinet and the hinge to the door (E), then mount and adjust the door to fit the opening.

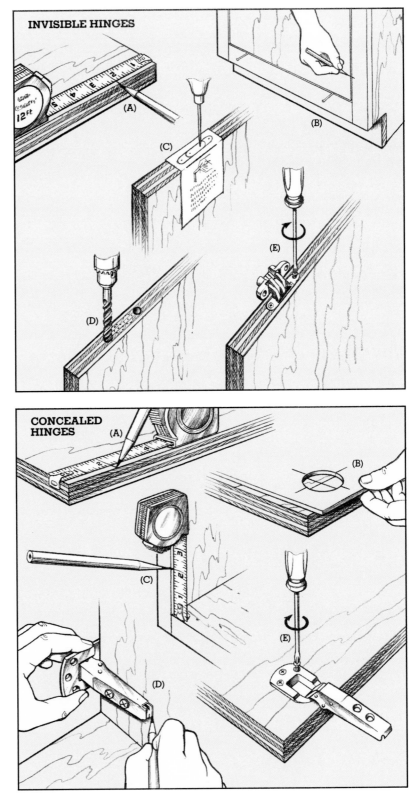

Adding Hinges to Cabinet Doors *(cont.)*

Overlay Doors

Inset and Self-Closing Hinges

With the door facedown, measure in about two inches from its top and bottom and make guide marks. Then, fasten the hinges to the doors with the screws provided (A).

Now, position the door as it will be when hung and make guide marks on the stile (B). (For overlay-with-reveal doors, first make guide marks as shown in the detail to ensure the correct reveal at each side and at top and bottom.)

Carefully align the hinges with the guide marks on the stile, mark the location of the screw holes (C), drill pilot holes, and secure the door to the frame, adjusting the hinges as necessary for a good fit.

Pivot Hinges

Start by making a pair of cuts the thickness of the hinge leaf on the hinge side of the doors with a table saw (A). Practice on scrap first to avoid cutting mistakes.

Secure the hinges to the door with screws (B), then position the door against the face frame and mark the location of the hinges on the stile (C). Finish the installation by mounting the door to the face frame (D) and adjusting, if necessary.

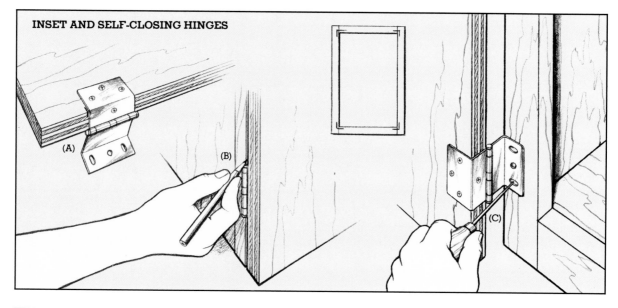

INSET AND SELF-CLOSING HINGES

(A)   (B)   (C)

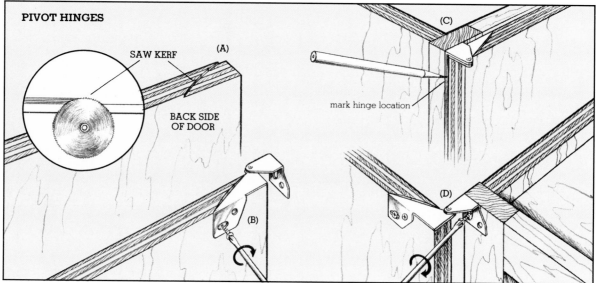

PIVOT HINGES

SAW KERF   (A)

BACK SIDE OF DOOR

(B)

(C)

mark hinge location

(D)

Concealed Hinges

(When you purchase this type of hinge, ask your supplier to show you the manufacturer's catalog describing your hinge; it contains essential mounting information you can't get elsewhere. Also, to avoid positioning errors, mount the hinge on scrap before installing it on the door itself.)

Measure in an equal distance from the top and bottom of the door (usually about two inches) and mark the location of the hinges as shown at right. Extend the marks on the back side of the door about two inches (A).

Make a template as described on page 105 under "concealed hinges" and cut the hinge cup recesses to the correct depth (B).

Fasten the hinges to the door with screws (C) and position the door against the face frame. Mark the location of the hinges on the stile (D), then with the door opened, fasten the hinges to the stile (E); adjust if needed.

Glass and Plastic Doors

Flush Glass Doors

To mount the hinge shown at right, drill a pair of holes near the edge of the top rail and one near the edge of the bottom one (make them deep enough to accept the sleeves and bullet catch).

Then, fit the sleeves and catch into the holes and tap them into place with a hammer and block of scrap wood.

Slip the hinges into the sleeves, fit the doors into the hinges' channels, adjust the doors so they clear the face frame, and tighten the holding screws on the hinges.

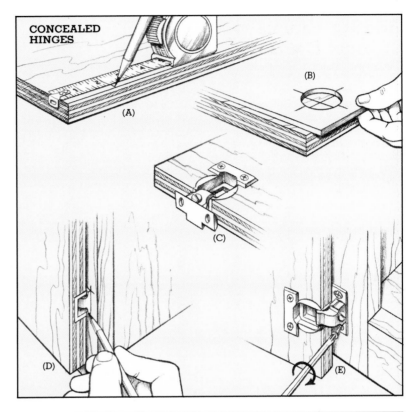

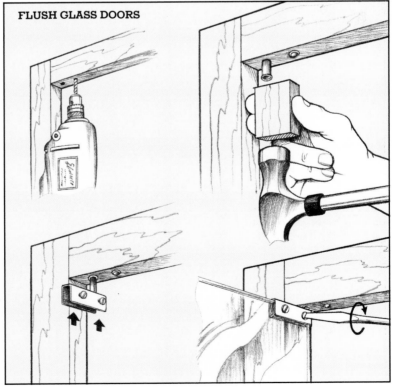

Adding Hinges to Cabinet Doors *(cont.)*

Overlay Glass Doors

(When purchasing this type of hinge, have your supplier show you the mounting instructions in the product catalog; it contains information you need to install the hinge. Also, it's best to have the holes in the doors cut professionally.)

Start by positioning each door as it will be when hung and make marks on the cabinet that align with the horizontal center of the holes in the door (A). Now, fasten the hinges to the baseplates, align the hinges with the guide marks, and mark the location of the baseplates (B).

Fasten the baseplates to the cabinet and the hinges to the door with screws. Connect the hinges to the baseplates and adjust the door (C).

Installing Catches and Pulls

Fastening these hardware items to cabinets isn't difficult, but there are a few general rules you need to be aware of before beginning. First, you should locate the catch as close as possible to the handle or pull to avoid undue pressure on the hardware. Second, the latch portion of the catch mounts on the cabinet; the strike, on the door. And third, the position of the pull itself is determined by the position of the cabinet it's being installed on. Typically, with base cabinets, you'll find them near the top of the door; with upper cabinets, near the bottom.

1 To mount typical pulls, drill the required number of holes where desired, position the pull, and secure with screws. (Fit the continuous pulls, as shown, onto the door and screw in place. Trim the door first to allow for the pull's thickness.)

2 Mount catches by screwing the latch to the cabinet, then positioning the strike and securing it to the door.

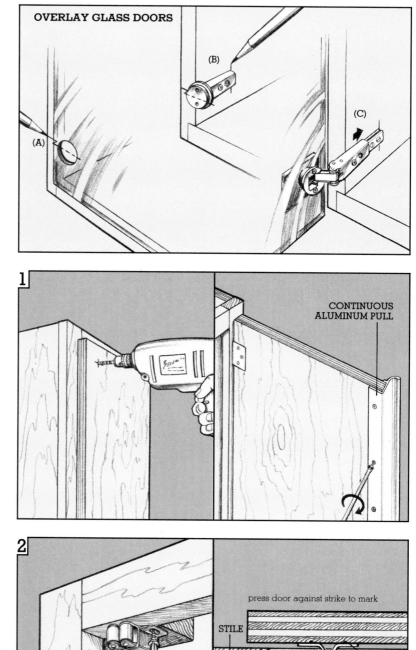

OVERLAY GLASS DOORS

(A) (B) (C)

CONTINUOUS ALUMINUM PULL

press door against strike to mark

STILE

SHARP MARKING POINTS

VIEW FROM BELOW

Adding Sliding Doors to Cabinets

1 Start by cutting the doors to the size specified in your plan (see page 90). Then, if you're using aluminum or plastic track, cut two lengths of it and screw them to the cabinet's top and bottom panels. Remember, the track with the deeper channels goes on top; the shallower channels, at the bottom. If your cabinet has a face frame, fit the track against its back side. If not, position it about ¼ inch in from the cabinet's front edge. (On cabinets with face frames, you'll need to put a spacer block above the top track so the track's bottom edge will be flush with the bottom of the face frame.)

If you've opted for a vinyl spline-type track, you already will have cut the grooves for the splines, so just press them into the recesses. If you find the going tough, tap them gently with a hammer.

2 Now, if you're dealing with thin doors, bore a hole through each door. These serve as your pulls. For thicker doors, drill holes partway through the material (see the package directions for correct size and depth of the holes). Locate the holes about ¾ inch in from the outside edge of the doors and center them vertically. Then, friction-fit the pulls into their holes.

Lastly, fit the door panels—the rear one first, the front one last—into their channels, top edge first. Lift up on them until the bottom edge clears the lower track. They should then drop into the channel.

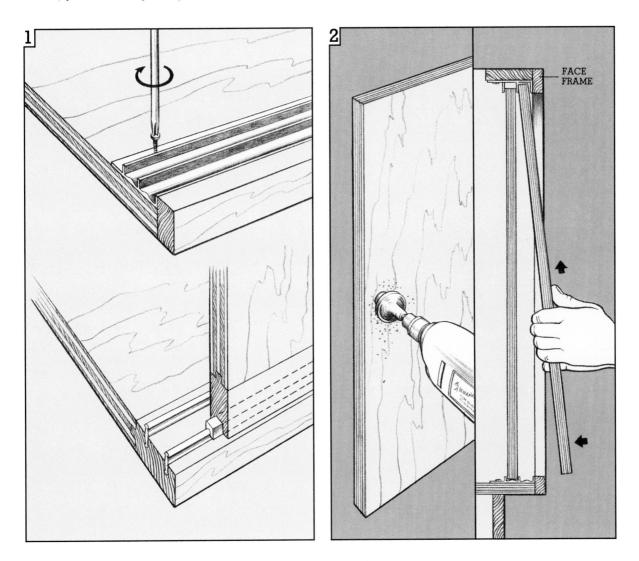

FACE FRAME

Adding Drawers to Cabinets

In the planning section, we showed you how to fit a cabinet's drawers together (see pages 87-89). The emphasis here, however, is on correctly positioning the drawer in the opening. We'll show two ways to do this—side-mounted metal slides and side-mounted wooden ones.

Before installing the metal type, be sure to read the directions that accompany the slide. They all mount somewhat differently. Also, if your unit has flush drawers, you'll have to put a piece of scrap at the back of the cabinet to stop the drawers flush with the front of the face frame.

Side-Mount Metal Slides

1 If you're installing this type of metal slide, position the drawer part of the slide so that the front of it butts against the back side of the drawer front, and the flange on the other end aligns with the bottom of the side of the drawer. Secure the flanged end with a screw. Now, move the front of the slide up or down so the slide is parallel to the drawer side. Drive a screw in the hole provided to secure it. Finish screwing the slide to the side. Repeat this for the other slide.

2 To install the mating part of the metal slide, position it as shown, with a piece of plastic laminate below the slide to provide clearance. If you're installing a bank of drawers without rails between them, lay plastic laminate on the top edge of the drawer below the one you're installing. (In most instances, you'll first need to nail a filler strip to the cabinet side to serve as a nailing surface for the drawer slide.)

Now, secure the slide's front end by driving a screw into the face frame. Using a torpedo level, level the slide's other end and secure it with screws.

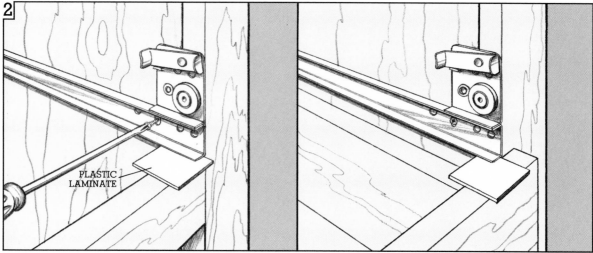

PLASTIC LAMINATE

Side-Mount Wooden Slides

1 First, mark the location of the two cleats you'll be attaching to each side. Center them vertically, and so that they are parallel with the drawer, being sure to allow enough room between them to accept the cleat that will be nailed to the cabinet. Run a bead of glue along each mark, then position and nail the cleats with brads or small finishing nails.

2 Now, fit the drawer into the opening and place a nail near each edge of the drawer, as shown, to provide clearance. Using a pencil, mark the location of the cleats you will be attaching to the cabinet. (If you're dealing with a bank of drawers not separated by face frames, set the nails on top of the drawer beneath the one you're installing.)

Using a framing square, extend the guide marks, then using glue and brads or small finishing nails, secure the cleats.

Attaching False Fronts to Cabinets

In some cabinet situations, when you need to hide a plumbing fixture from view, you'll want to install a false front, which is nothing more than a door or drawer look-alike that doesn't open or pull out. The instructions below and the sketch at right show you how to do this.

Cut the false front to the size specified in your plan. Then, cut a couple of scrap blocks and drill a pilot hole near each end of each one. Secure the blocks to the back side of the face frame as shown with glue and screws, then position the front and drive screws through the blocks into the front's back side.

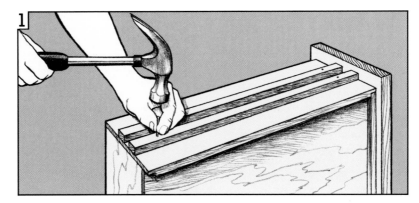

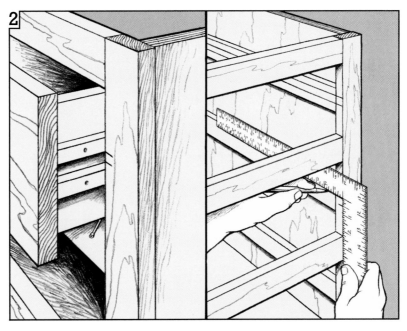

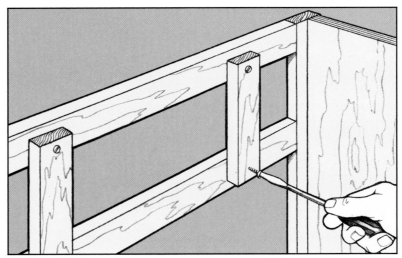

Installing Cabinets

A neat-looking cabinet installation requires that you hang or position your unit so it is plumb and level. But that's not the only prerequisite. You also must be concerned with securing it adequately to the wall and floor or ceiling. In the illustrations below, we show you how to achieve both of these marks of good cabinetry. (Since custom cabinets—especially banks of them—weigh plenty, you'll need an assistant or two for this part of the project.)

1 Start by marking the outline of the unit(s) on the floor and walls, using a framing square and a chalk line. Doing this allows you to spot potential positioning problems prior to the actual installation. Also locate the wall studs that run behind the cabinet(s) and mark their location with a chalk line. Extend the lines far enough that you can still see them when the cabinets are raised into place.

2 Now, move the cabinet(s) into the desired position. If you're installing a bank of cabinets similar to the situation shown in sketch 1, start with the upper cabinets first, and work from the corner outward. If yours are wall-hung cabinets, it helps to nail a ledger strip to the wall along the line defining the bottom of the cabinets before hoisting them up.

Again, if you are hanging wall-hung units, you'll find it easier to make the face frames of adjoining cabinets flush with each other if you join as many cabinets as you can manage before positioning them. To do this, lay the units on their back and clamp their face frames together. Then drill pilot holes through the edges of the face frame members, and screw them together.

3 Have your assistant check the cabinets for plumb and level while you shim as necessary.

4 Drill pilot holes through the ledger(s) and into the studs, then drive good-size screws to secure the unit to the wall. To provide even more stability, screw or nail the unit to the floor or ceiling (or bulkhead).

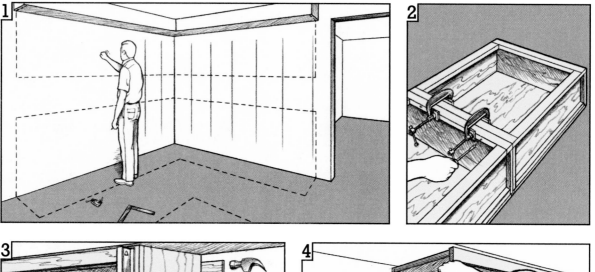

Installing Countertops

Today, you have several countertop options, (see pages 20-21), and with most, the installation procedures vary only slightly. With site-built countertops, you first build the top and then fasten it to the cabinet. If your plans include plastic laminate as the surface material, apply it at the same time you're building the top. Ceramic tiles and other such materials go on after the top has been fastened to the cabinet.

For all other types, though, the finish material is in place when you purchase the top, so all that remains is to fasten it to the cabinet. On this through page 117, we take you step by step through each option.

Site-Built Tops

1 Cut a piece of ¾-inch particle-board or plywood to the size specified in your plan. (If one end of your cabinet fits up against a wall, as the one shown here does, the top should overlap the other end and the front by one inch. If both ends butt against walls, cut the top flush with both ends and overlap the front by one inch. And for cabinets whose ends don't butt against walls, allow 1-inch overlap at both ends and the front.) Test-fit the top and make adjustments to compensate for irregularities.

2 Now, turn the top upside-down and glue and nail 1x2s (or ¾-inch particleboard or plywood strips) around its perimeter as shown. (For more stability, install bracing at the top of the cabinet.)

3 Steps 3-8 apply to plastic laminate installations. *(continued)*

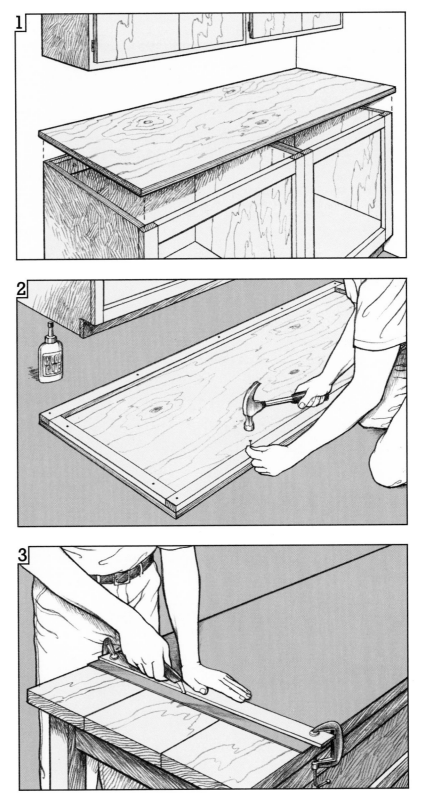

Installing Countertops *(cont.)*

Cut the banding strips for the edges of the countertop.

You can cut plastic laminate two ways, depending on the tools you have at your disposal. Some professional installers start by measuring the size of the piece that they'll need (allowing a ½-inch overlap in all instances). Then, they lay a straight-edge along the cutoff line and score the face of the laminate with a carbide-tipped cutting tool similar to the one shown at right. To finish the cut, they snap the laminate toward the scored line.

You also can cut laminate with several types of electric saws. To do this, first score the face of the laminate with an awl or other sharp-pointed object, then saw along the scored line with a saber, circular, or table saw and a fine-toothed blade.

To make inside cuts, use a drill to make an opening large enough to enable you to insert the saw blade, then finish the cut with the saw. (To prevent plastic laminate from stress cracking, you must radius inside corners at least ¼ inch.)

4 Before adhering the banding to the top's edges (or any laminate to any surface), you must prepare the surface correctly. With new surfaces, make sure you fill all voids with wood putty, then after allowing the putty to dry, sand the entire surface smooth. With already-finished surfaces, remove paint or other finish by sanding, then repeat the procedure for new surfaces.

Now, apply contact cement to both the core material and the back side of the laminate, allow the cement to dry, then *carefully* position the laminate so it overlaps the top and bottom of the edge. To ensure maximum adhesion of the contact cement, use a hammer and wood block or a rubber mallet to make sure the cemented surfaces meet. Sand the excess laminate with a belt sander, being careful not to burn it.

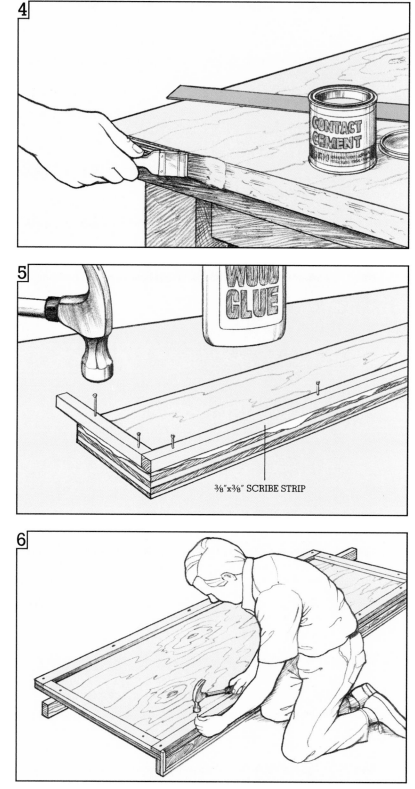

⅜"x⅜" SCRIBE STRIP

5 If you plan to have a laminated backsplash and/or endsplashes, cut a 4-inch-wide piece of ¾-inch particleboard or plywood to the length needed. With glue and brads driven partway in, attach a ⅜x⅜-inch *scribe strip* flush with the top edge of the splash. (Brads should be pulled out later.) Now, cover the face of the splash with laminate and sand off the excess as described in step 4. Then, laminate the top edge of the splash (and the ends, if applicable), and trim the back but not the front edge.

6 Run a bead of glue along the bottom edge of the splash, let the glue get tacky, position the splash on the countertop, and nail the two together as shown on page 114.

7 Cut the countertop laminate to the size needed (be sure to allow excess on all sides) and apply contact cement to the back side of the laminate and the countertop surface. Allow the cement to dry. Now, lay kraft or waxed paper on the counter surface, position the laminate, and remove the paper gradually. Tap the surface with a hammer and wooden block or a rubber mallet to ensure a good bond.

8 After tapping the laminate, begin trimming the excess. If you have a router, use it and a laminate-cutting bit. If not, you can get satisfactory results with a double-cut hand file. A 7-degree bevel is standard. If you're using a router, be sure to keep it moving as you work. Otherwise, you'll burn the surface.

9 Lift the countertop onto the cabinet and check it for a good fit. If you see gaps between the top and the wall, use a compass or a pencil to follow the contour of the wall. Trim away excess with a block plane. Recheck the fit, then run a bead of glue around the top edge of the cabinet. Position the top, and from underneath, secure it to the cabinet with corner braces. (If you plan to set a sink or lavatory into the countertop, position the fixture template, then make the cutout with a saber saw.)

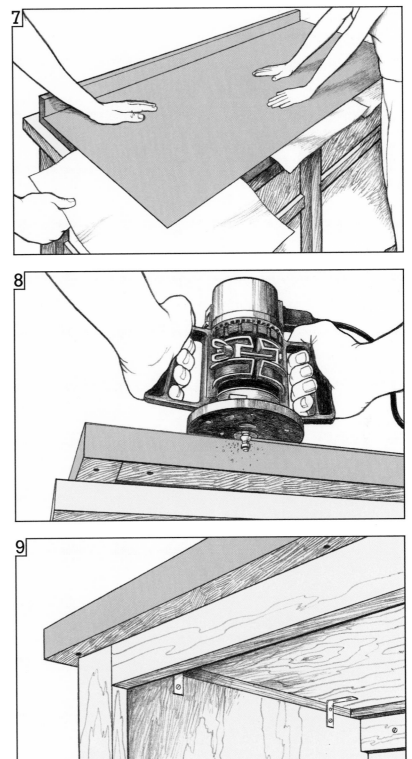

Installing Countertops *(cont.)*

Post-Formed Tops

1 Start by setting the top on the cabinet. It should overlap the cabinet uniformly at the front. If it doesn't or if you can see gaps between the countertop and the wall it butts against, lay a pencil up against the wall and make a scribe line. Then, using a saber saw, block plane, or a coping saw, cut along the line. (If you're installing a two-piece top, you'll have to make sure the pieces fit together at the correct angle and that they rest flush against the wall.)

2 To join a two-piece post-formed countertop, set both pieces onto the cabinet (after you have test-fit them). Then, apply a bead of glue to one of the mating surfaces, and from underneath, partially tighten the bolts or other connecting devices that came with the product. Now, check the surface of the counter at the joint line. Both pieces should be on the same plane. If one is higher than the other, use a hammer and wooden block to move them into alignment. When you're satisfied, tighten down the bolts.

3 There are a couple of ways to secure a post-formed top to cabinets. If you used wood bracing for additional support of the top, you can drive screws through the bracing and into the countertop's underside. Or you can make the connection with metal corner braces.

    To fasten a countertop to an unreinforced cabinet, screw metal corner braces to the ledger at the rear of the cabinet and to the back side of the face frame as well as to the countertop. Three or four braces at the front and back will normally be sufficient.

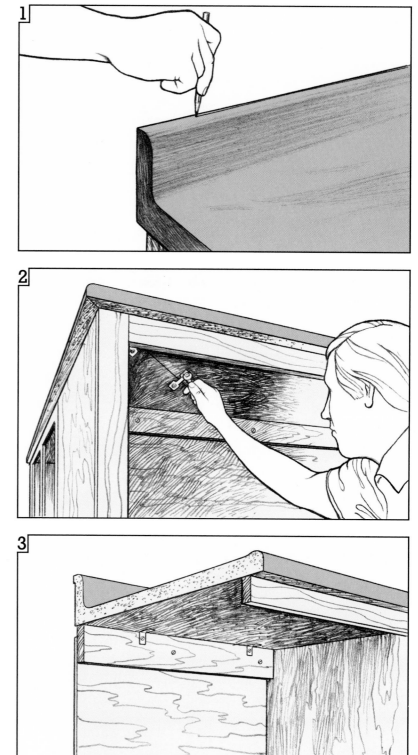

Cultured and Natural Marble Tops

1 Both of these products are ready to install right out of their package. And you install both in exactly the same way. Start by test-fitting the top. It should extend about one inch beyond the front edge of the cabinet and one inch beyond the cabinet sides if they're exposed. (Top should be flush if sides are not exposed.) If the fit isn't correct, cut the cultured tops to fit along the edge that won't show; with natural marble, it's best to have your supplier recut it.

Run a bead of panel adhesive along the top edge of the cabinet and allow it to set up briefly.

2 Lift the counter into position and weight it down with some heavy objects. Finish the project by installing the sink or lavatory and/or faucets.

High-Density Plastic Tops

1A First glue and nail 1x2s to the top edge of the cabinet. Then position the top. (It should extend one inch beyond the front and all exposed sides. Also, allow ⅛ inch between the counter and walls.) Make any needed cuts with a circular saw. Mark the location of any cutouts, such as for a sink. With the top adequately supported, partially cut the opening with a router; allow a ⅜-inch radius at the corners.

2A Now, carefully move the top into position, finish cutting the opening, then have an assistant lift up the top while you apply panel adhesive to the 1x2s as shown.

If you're joining two sections, position them ½ inch apart on the cabinet, lay a ¼-inch bead of silicone caulk between them, and then slide the sections together to form a tight joint.

Press the top into place and weight it with some heavy objects. Round off the corners with fine sandpaper. Trim the front edge, if desired, by applying a 1-inch-wide strip of the same material. Then, glue the backsplash to the wall.

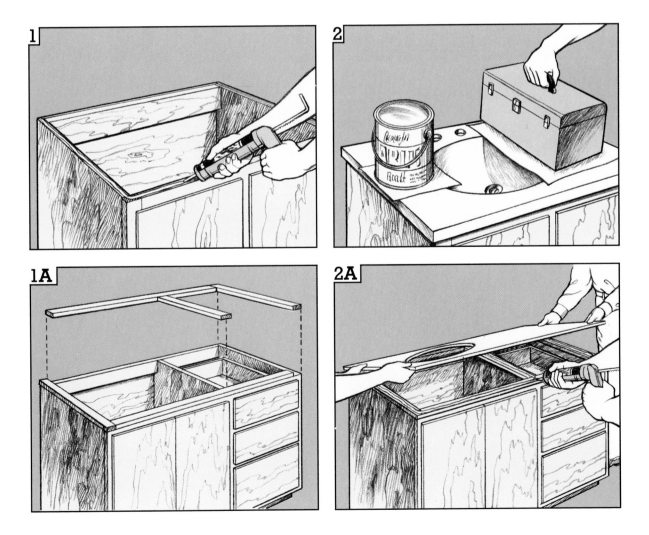

Making the Basic Cuts

Making Cuts with A Circular Saw

Many people think that building a cabinet or shelving unit first requires a major investment in tools. Not so! Though not the ideal tool for making cabinets and shelving units, a portable circular saw will perform well if you're patient and have a good straightedge.

When using a circular saw, keep these points in mind:
• **Always stand to one side of the work to avoid serious injury from kickback.**
• **Raise the guard when first making a cut so it doesn't catch on the workpiece edge.**
• **For best looks, face the good side of the workpiece down when cutting.**
• **Keep plenty of slack in the cord so it doesn't hang up.**
• **Prevent binding and ensure a straight cut by using a guide.**
• **If the saw should bind, release the switch immediately.**
Rip and angle cutting are shown on pages 35-37.

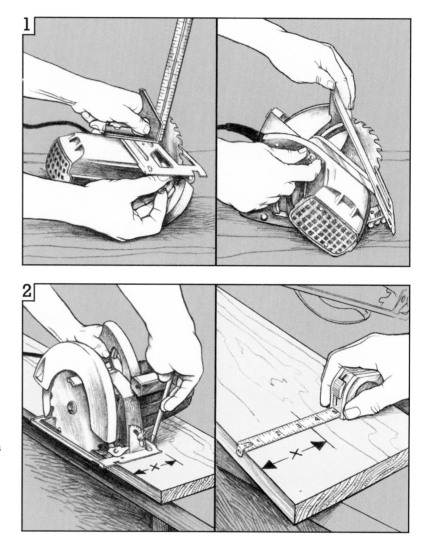

Crosscutting

1 To check a blade set perpendicular to the base, **unplug the saw** and use a combination square as shown here; to check lesser angles, go with a T-bevel. If you need to adjust the angle, loosen the wing nut on the bevel scale and turn the base to the desired angle. Then tighten the nut.

Now is also the time to check and, if necessary, adjust the blade depth. To do this, rest the saw on the edge of the work and loosen the appropriate locking mechanism. Raise or lower the base until the blade extends below the workpiece by ⅛ to ¼ inch. Tighten the wing nut.

2 To determine how far to clamp your straightedge guide from the intended cutoff line, hold the saw against the workpiece edge as shown above and mark the location of the edge of the saw base. Next, measure the distance between the workpiece edge and the mark. This distance varies depending on the blade you use.

3 To make the cut, position the saw firmly against the straightedge, then enter the work. To prevent the wood from splintering, have a helper support the scrap end of the work.

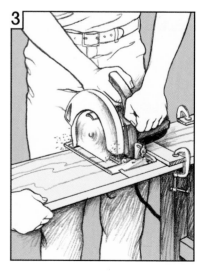

Dadoing and Grooving

Using a square, draw two parallel lines that define the borders of the channel to be cut. Clamp a straightedge at the appropriate distance from one of the borders (see sketch 2, opposite). Keep in mind, however, that the saw kerf should run along the inside edge of the channel. Now, **with the saw unplugged,** adjust the saw blade to the desired dado depth (⅓ to ½ the thickness of the goods). Plug in the saw and begin your cut along the straightedge.

Next, move your straightedge and make a cut along the other cutting line.

Plow out the remaining material by making additional passes with the saw. Finish by removing burrs or rough spots with a chisel.

Rabbeting

Measure in from the edge of the workpiece the width of the rabbet you desire and mark the location of your cut line. Set up a straightedge (see sketch 2, opposite), keeping the kerf on the waste side of the line. Now, **with the saw unplugged,** adjust the saw blade to match the rabbet depth (see sketch 1, opposite), plug in the saw, and proceed with the cut.

Working toward the edge, freehand the remaining number of saw passes needed to clean the rabbet out. Remove any rough spots along the rabbet with a chisel.

Note in part 2 how to rabbet narrow stock, a procedure that's a bit more involved. Here you need to frame in the workpiece with a jig made from scrap of the same thickness. This provides support for the saw base, offering you more control over the saw. Continue, following the instructions above for rabbeting wider material.

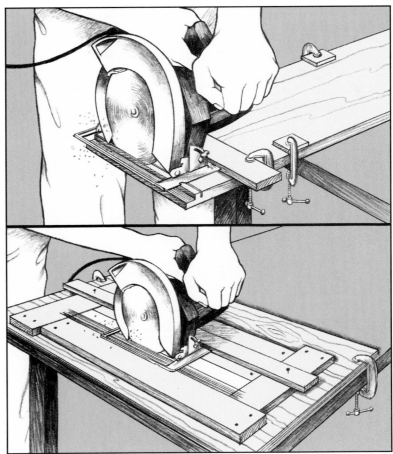

Making Cuts With a Table Saw

Measuring mistakes aside, cutting errors occur for two reasons: either the tool doing the cutting wanders from its intended path, or the workpiece moves around too much during the cut. With a table saw, such control problems are minor.

The table saw is a stationary power tool; it can't move around like the hand-held circular saw. And with the aid of the rip fence, miter gauge (standard accessories), and other aids shown below, you can feed material (good side up) into the blade, and it will come out as precisely cut as can be expected.

A table saw's other virtues include its versatility—it

can make all the cuts required of the cabinetmaker—and its ease of adjustment.

Keep in mind, however, that this tool demands your utmost respect. In addition to the general safety tips covered on page 15, avoid injury by heeding the specific table saw tips listed below and in your operator's manual:
• **Always stand to one side of the blade while sawing.**
• **Keep your fingers at least 6 inches away from the blade during the saw's operation.**
• **Never remove the guard apparatus unless it interferes with the cut.**
• **Avoid making freehand cuts; instead, use the proper guides and saw helps for each cut.**

Crosscutting

1 Before making a cut, **unplug the saw** and, using a combination square, check to see if the blade is

square to the table. If it isn't, turn the *tilt handwheel* (located under the table surface) and recheck for square. Then crank the *elevation handwheel* so the blade extends ⅛ inch above the workpiece.

Now adjust the miter gauge to zero and plug in the saw. With the workpiece on the table and against the miter gauge, align the cut line with the saw blade so that the kerf ends up on the scrap side of the line. Turn on the saw and slowly feed the workpiece into the blade.

When cutting long lengths, as shown below, screw a 1x facing strip onto the miter gauge to steady the work and have an assistant support the stock's dangling end.

2 For crosscutting identical lengths of material, clamp a length of scrap onto the *front end* of the rip fence, space the fence and block from the blade the length you want your pieces, and begin cutting. Or use a stop rod (see lower left sketch).

(continued)

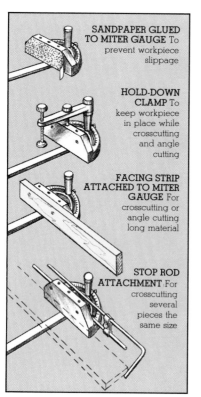

SANDPAPER GLUED TO MITER GAUGE To prevent workpiece slippage

HOLD-DOWN CLAMP To keep workpiece in place while crosscutting and angle cutting

FACING STRIP ATTACHED TO MITER GAUGE For crosscutting or angle cutting long material

STOP ROD ATTACHMENT For crosscutting several pieces the same size

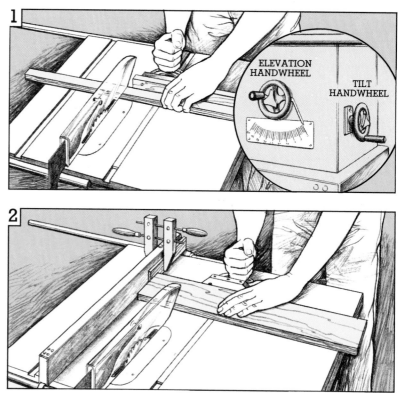

ELEVATION HANDWHEEL

TILT HANDWHEEL

Crosscutting *(continued)*

3 When cutting fairly wide cabinet components, such as doors or cabinet sides, begin by removing the rip fence from the saw table and locking the miter gauge at zero. Now reverse the miter gauge in the groove and place the workpiece firmly against it. Align the cut line with the blade and start the saw.

When you're halfway through the cut, stop the saw. Slide the miter gauge out of the back end of the groove and into the front and finish the cut as shown.

Rip Cutting

1 With the saw unplugged, adjust the rip fence at the necessary distance from the saw blade. To do this, use a measuring tape as shown to measure from the saw's *inside* teeth to the fence at both the front and back of the blade. This ensures having a parallel fence, which is important not only for accuracy but for safety, too. (If your blade needs adjusting, see sketch 1, page 120.)

Next, clamp featherboards to the table and fence; these hold the workpiece snugly in place during the cut.

Now plug in the saw, flick on the switch, and begin sawing, slowly feeding the material into the blade. For long stock, have someone support the material as it comes off the saw table at the other end or construct a stand that will do the same thing. **To prevent your hands from getting dangerously close to the blade, use a push stick to finish the cut.**

2 In cases where you need to reduce material to less than 2 inches wide, **pull the plug** and remove the guard and antikickback apparatus. Then follow the ripping procedure shown in sketch 1. *(continued)*

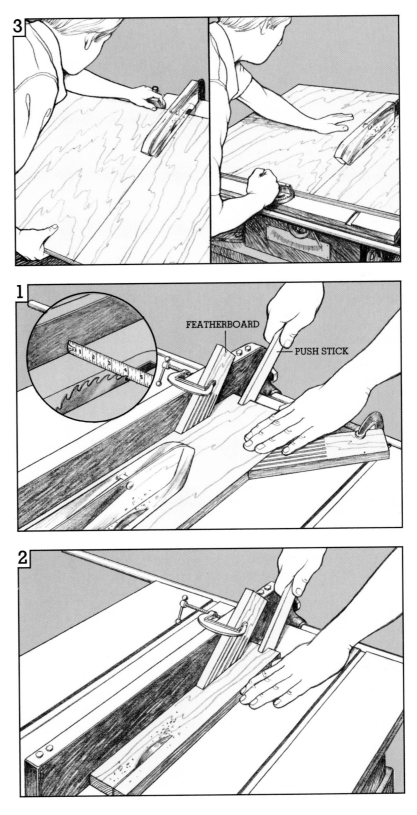

Rip Cutting *(continued)*

3 If rip cutting sheets of plywood, first **unplug the saw** and adjust the fence to the desired width (see detail in sketch 1). Then plug in the saw and have someone stand to one side to assist you in positioning the sheet on the table and against the fence as shown. (Don't put too much pressure on the fence, however; this could move it and result in a bad cut or cause the workpiece to bind.) Now, have your assistant flip on the switch underneath the sheet and begin sawing. **WARNING: If the blade binds during the cut, turn off the saw immediately.**

As you continue to feed the sheet, instruct your assistant to stand behind the saw to support that portion of the workpiece leaving the table.

Angle Cutting

1 Cut along the angled cut line scribed on the workpiece (see the detail in sketch 1), then adjust the miter gauge to the desired angle. (If you need to adjust the blade, see the copy that accompanies sketch 1, page 120.)

Now place the workpiece against the miter gauge, sliding it along until the cut line aligns with the blade. Remember to keep the kerf (the void created by a cutting saw blade) on the scrap end of the stock.

With the workpiece held firmly to the miter gauge, begin your cut.

2 For angle cutting large pieces of material, reverse the miter gauge in the channel and secure a facing strip to it. Adjust the gauge and align as shown in sketch 2, then plug in the saw and start sawing.

Once you've cut halfway through the material, turn the saw off and return the miter gauge to its normal place at the front of the table. Now complete the cut.

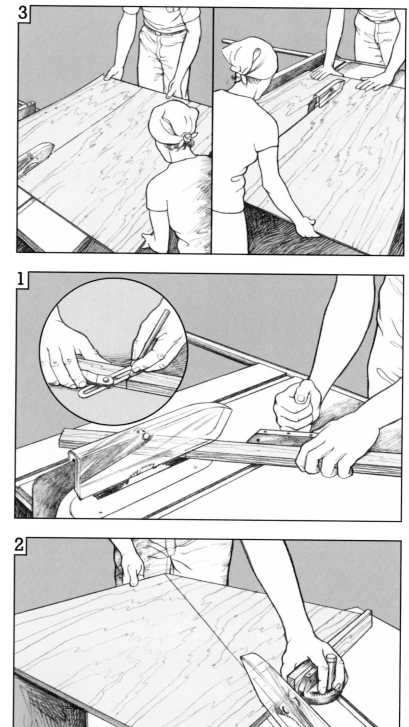

Beveling

1 After you know the degree of bevel you want, adjust a T-bevel accordingly. Then, hold this tool against the saw blade and table. Turn the tilt handwheel until the correct bevel angle is duplicated (see the detail in sketch 1, page 120). **NOTE: Before making any adjustment on the saw, pull the plug. Also, make sure the blade guard and spreader are tilted to match the angle of the blade.**

You may have to temporarily raise the blade to check for the proper blade angle and then later lower it to ⅛ inch above the thickness of the workpiece (see sketch 1, page 120).

2 If you're cutting across the grain, slip the miter gauge into the right-hand channel and lock the setting at zero. Placing the workpiece against the gauge, sight along the cut line until the blade and workpiece are in alignment. When you're satisfied, turn on the saw and ease the workpiece into the blade.

If making a bevel rip, as in the second example, position the rip fence with the stock held alongside it until the cut line agrees with the blade. Lock the fence in place and check to see if the front and back of the blade are equidistant from the fence. If they are, proceed as you would for any rip cut.

3 To bevel edges of a solid door for a raised panel look, start by fastening a wide, straight piece of 1 x stock to the full length of your rip fence. This prevents the workpiece from wobbling during the cut.

Next, draw the cut line, letting the width of the groove the panel is to fit into guide you in determining the width of the panel's edge (see detail in sketch 3). Allow a ⅛-inch difference between the raised and beveled portions of the panel. Now adjust the fence, remove the guard (since it interferes), clamp a featherboard to the table, and begin your cut.

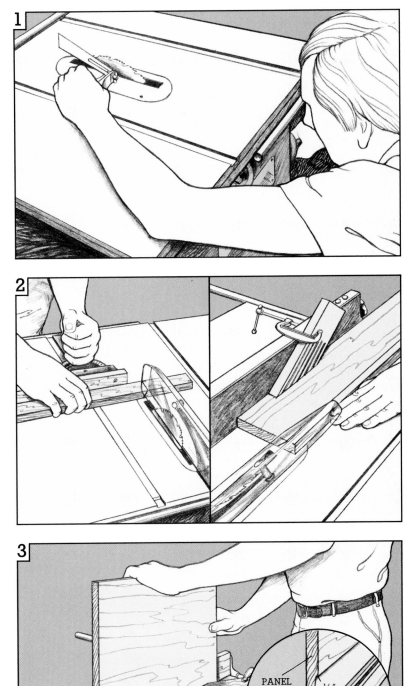

Dadoing and Grooving

1 Prepare for the dado by **pulling the plug** and replacing whatever blade you have on the saw with a dado cutter of the proper width. (Refer to the instructions that came with the cutter for help with this.) Also, replace the regular table insert with the special dado insert. (Purchase this item when you purchase the dado blade.) Now adjust the dado cutter to the depth of cut marked on the workpiece.

If handling long stock, attach a facing strip to the miter gauge and have an assistant support the stock during the actual cutting.

Also, since the guard and spreader would only get in the way, remove them from the table.

As a final preparation, adjust the rip fence and accompanying scrap to serve as a stop, moving it to the right with each successive dado.

For a blind dado, clamp a stop block the appropriate distance along the other end of the fence as in the detail.

2 For cutting grooves, install and adjust the dado cutter as explained in step 1. Clamp on featherboards as needed, align the cut line on the leading edge and surface of the workpiece with the blade, and tighten the lock on the rip fence. Begin sawing.

For grooving along an edge, as with the door frame member shown at right, simply attach a featherboard to the table, adjust the dado cutter and fence, and begin cutting. **WARNING: Because this can be close-in work, use a push stick to keep hands away from the cutter.**

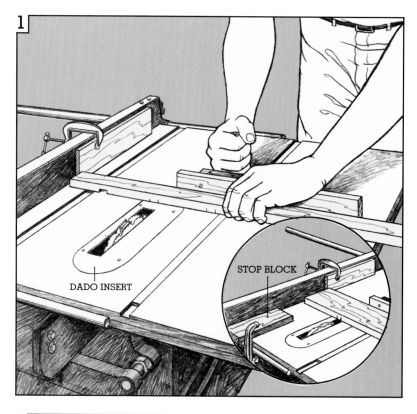

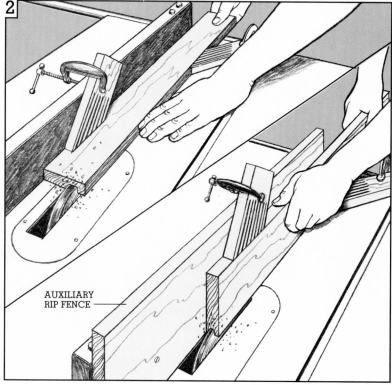

Cutting Rabbets

1 If your project plans call for a rabbet, you'll be happy to know you don't need a dado cutter on your table saw to achieve the desired effect. As shown, a sharp combination blade will produce as good a rabbet as you'll want, though it requires you to make two cuts instead of one.

Prepare for the first cut by laying the workpiece flat on the saw table. Then, check the blade for square and adjust the depth. Now slide the rip fence (with attached wood scrap) over and adjust it so that the kerf is on the waste edge of the cut line. Clamp a featherboard as in sketch 1 and run the piece through.

Make the second cut by holding the workpiece vertically to the rip fence. Be sure to make any blade depth and rip fence adjustments needed to align this cut line, and begin sawing the rabbet.

If, on the other hand, you use a dado cutter, simply add the number of chippers needed to arrive at the correct rabbet width, **unplug the saw and insert and adjust the cutter,** and proceed with the cut.

2 If cutting a rabbet that's considerably wider than it is deep, as when with a half-lap joint, again, use a dado cutter. With the workpiece against the miter gauge, align its cut line with the cutter and slide the fence over. When the fence is flush to the workpiece end and parallel to the dado cutter, lock it in place.

Now plug in the saw and start sawing. Make as many passes as necessary to remove the waste material, shifting the workpiece farther away from the fence with each pass.

3 To rabbet a workpiece using a dado cutter (right), **unplug the saw** and slide the rip fence (with an auxiliary fence attached) the desired distance from the blade and lock it. With the blade on the scrap side of the cut line, adjust the cutter depth. Plug in the saw and begin making your cut.

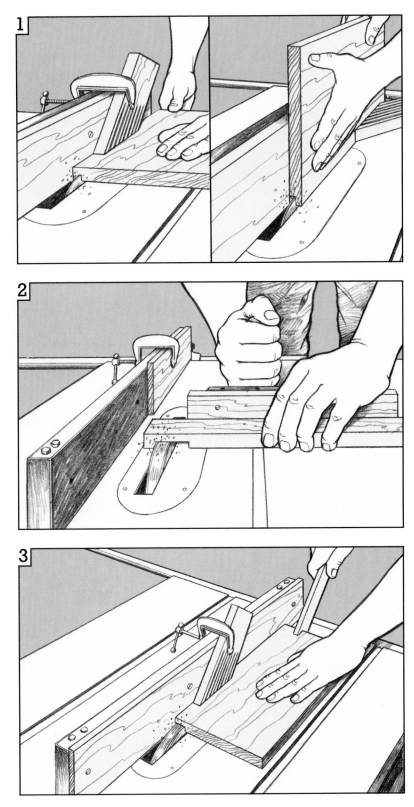

Router Work

Though you can use circular and table saws to dado and rabbet, be assured that the router performs these tasks best. Add to this the router's ability to fashion a fancy edge or decorate a surface, as well as trim laminate (see pages 116-117), and you'll agree there's no other tool quite like it.)

If you're a first-time user, acquaint yourself with the tool while practicing on scrap. You'll note immediately how the router jerks slightly in a counterclockwise direction when it first makes contact with the workpiece. This errant tendency doesn't have to be the rule, however, especially when there are so many guiding attachments available (several of which we show here). There are even inexpensive router tables available to which you mount the router underneath. Not only do these provide a smooth, flat work surface, but they also have adjustable fences for consistent, accurate cuts.

Keep in mind, though, that like other power tools, the router deserves your deepest respect. Aside from the safety and use tips on page 15, look over those in your owner's manual and below for the best possible results:
• Wait until the bit reaches full speed before routing.
• Hold the router with both hands while operating it.
• Keep the router base flat on the work surface.
• For best control, use guides whenever possible.

Dadoing, Grooving, And Edging

1 Once you've **unplugged the router** and secured the bit of your choice in the router's chuck, adjust the bit depth. To do this, place the router on a flat surface and loosen

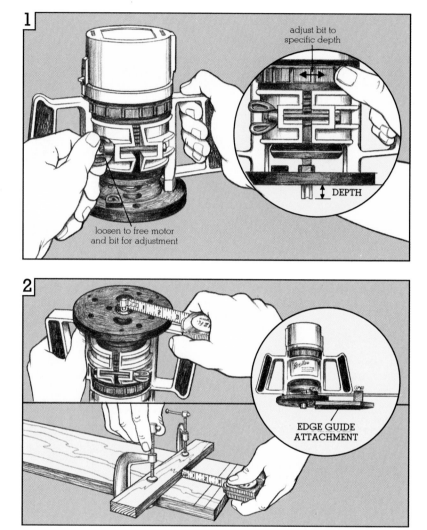

the router base around the motor. On most models this involves turning a wing nut and adjusting the depth gauge—usually a calibrated ring or rotating drum—until the bit and subbase are even. (See sketch 1, above.) At this point, set the gauge at zero.

Now, position the router on the edge of a table and lower the bit to the desired depth. (Manufacturers advise making router bit adjustments and cuts in ⅛-inch increments.)

If your router doesn't have a depth gauge, place it on the edge of the workpiece and go by the depth of the cut line. Now secure the base by tightening the wing nut.

2 Next, establish your straightedge location by taking a measurement from the edge of the bit to the outside edge of the subbase as shown above in sketch 2, part 2.

Mark on the workpiece where you want the outside edge of the cut. Then measure out from this line using the above measurement and clamp your straightedge here.

An alternative to this is to buy the versatile edge guide attachment (see detail, sketch 2) that rides along the workpiece edge during the cut.
(continued)

Dadoing, Grooving, and Edging *(continued)*

3 At right, we introduce you to related setup procedures that permit you to expand the uses of your tool.

To rout a blind dado, as shown in part 1 at right, clamp a straightedge the appropriate distance from the cut line. Then, clamp a stop block perpendicular to the straightedge the same distance beyond where you want the dado to end.

For grooving the edge of a narrow piece of stock, as shown in part 2, provide a flat, work surface for the router by sandwiching the stock between two lengths of 2x stock. Then attach a router guide attachment, adjusting it to the proper width.

When trimming inside or outside edges, as shown in part 3, simply use a bit with a pilot as your guide.

For best results, operate the router from left to right and counterclockwise around corners (see detail in sketch 3). If routing all four edges of a square or rectangular workpiece, reduce splintering by routing across the grain first, then with the grain.

Because of the bit size, depth of cut, and differences in workpiece hardness, expect the rate of travel to vary from cut to cut. **Don't force the tool or you'll slow the action of the bit and tear into the wood; on the other hand, go too slow and the high-speed bit could blemish the routed edges with burn marks.**

Adding Surface Designs

To route distinctive designs onto the face of cabinet doors with a router, start by tracing and cutting out a template of your design from plywood and clamp it to the workpiece. Allow room for the guide bushing (see detail A at right).

Then, **with the router unplugged,** attach the guide bushing. Adjust the bit to the desired depth, plug the tool in, and begin routing along the inside template edge.

Using an accessory as in detail B will help you achieve the same end result.

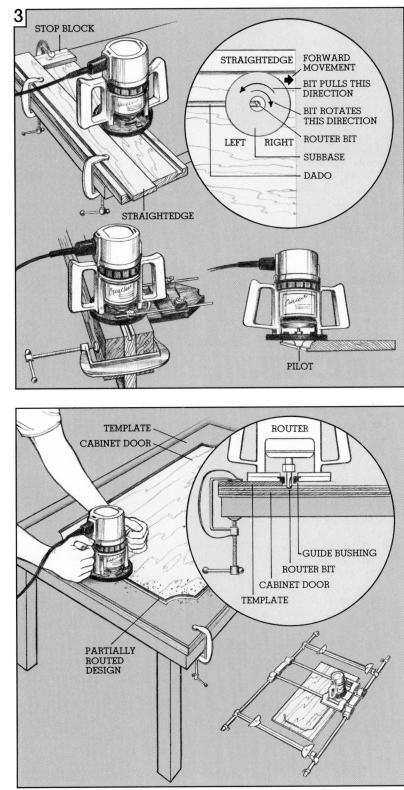

Making Simple, Strong Joints

Strong, good-looking wood joints have long been the hallmark of skilled carpenters and cabinetmakers. That's because these pros realize how important good joinery is to the end product.

Here, we show you several different ways to successfully join two pieces of wood at an angle, none of which requires cabinetmaker expertise. Before you make your joints, though, be sure to review the material beginning on page 46. It tells you how to work with the fasteners you'll be using.

To form a *butt joint,* position the end of one member against the face or edge of another member. Though not one of the strongest in and of itself, when reinforced by any one of the methods shown here, butt joints yield satisfactory results for many projects in which appearance isn't a prime factor.

Lap joints offer greater strength than butt joints and, at least in the second and third examples shown, better looks. To make an *overlap* joint, simply lay one of the members atop the other and nail or screw it in place with at least two screws or nails driven as shown.

For a *full-lap* joint, cut a recess into one member that's as deep as

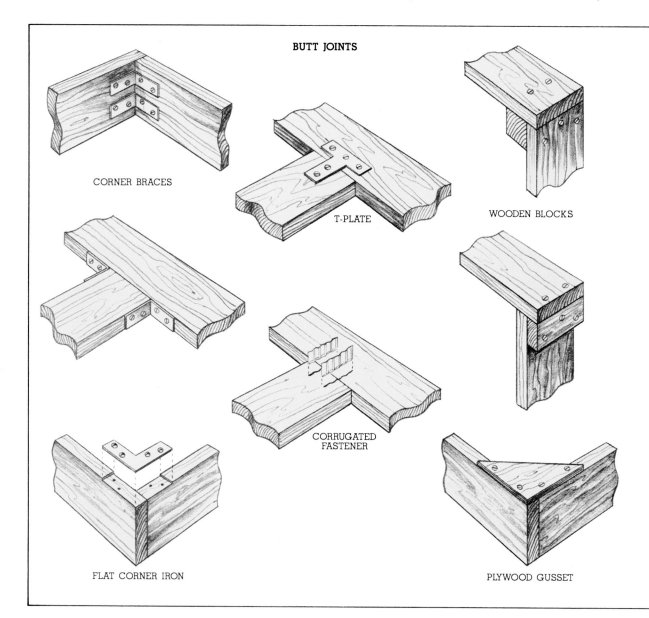

BUTT JOINTS

CORNER BRACES

T-PLATE

WOODEN BLOCKS

CORRUGATED FASTENER

FLAT CORNER IRON

PLYWOOD GUSSET

the second piece is thick. Then spread glue on the mating surfaces, position the members, and clamp until the glue dries. To fashion a *half-lap*, the strongest of the lap joints, cut a recess into each of the members that's as wide as and half as deep as each piece is thick. Glue and clamp the pieces together.

Though not quite as easy to make as butt and lap joints, *dadoes* are both attractive and strong. First, cut a recess in one of the members—no more than one-third that member's thickness and as wide as the other member. (See pages 40-41 for hand chiseling techniques and pages 119, 124, and 127 for dado techniques with power tools.) Again, apply glue and clamp until the glue sets.

For a perfectly concealed joint, a *miter* is your best bet. Begin by cutting the members to be joined at the same angle (usually 45°)—see pages 36, 37, and 122 for how to do this—then glue and nail the members together. Note in examples 2 and 3 how you can use wooden splines and dowels to strengthen the joint. With these you eliminate the need for a metal fastener while achieving a cleaner, all-wood look. Be sure, however, to make the spline grooves and dowel holes slightly deeper than the splines and dowels in order to accommodate the glue.

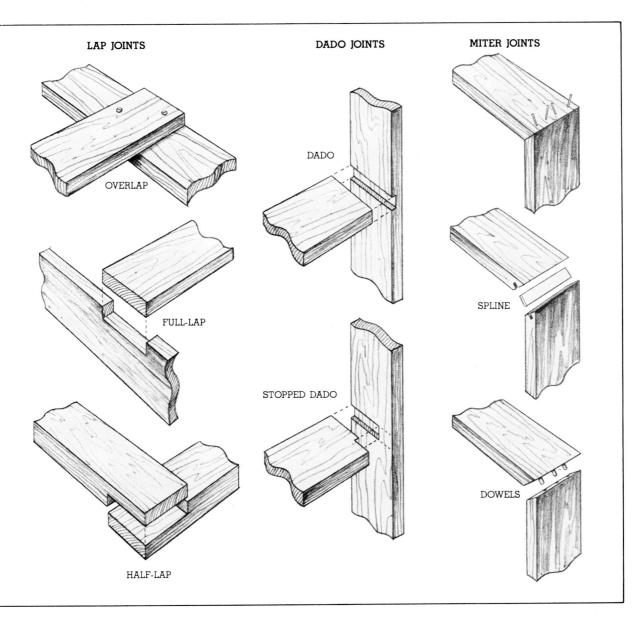

LAP JOINTS

OVERLAP

FULL-LAP

HALF-LAP

DADO JOINTS

DADO

STOPPED DADO

MITER JOINTS

SPLINE

DOWELS

Joining with Nails and Glue or Screws and Glue

1 When joining with nails and glue, start by applying a bead of wood-worker's glue evenly along the contact surface of one of the members.

For best results, use a brush or stick to spread the glue into a thin layer over the entire contact area. If dealing with end grain, which absorbs the glue, as in the plywood example at right, coat both of the joining members. Be sure to allow the glue to get tacky.

2 Fit the glued members together and secure them with clamps. If you're using pipe or C-clamps, slip in scrap wood between the clamp jaws and work to protect the work surface. After testing the joints for square, drill pilot holes and drive your nails.

To maintain snug corner joints, such as with face and door frame constructions, drill diagonal holes, then toenail members together as shown in sketch 2.

After driving your nails, go back and set them with a nail set. To ensure a strong glue bond throughout the contact area, remove the small scrap pieces between the clamp jaws and workpiece and insert a single long piece such as a 2x4 placed on edge.

3 When joining with screws and glue, first position and clamp the members together as you would when nailing. Then use a countersink/counterbore bit to drill the appropriate number of pilot holes. (Note in the detail at right how the desired finished look determines the depth of the holes.) Now, apply glue to one or both mating surfaces, allow it to get tacky, and drive the screws. Clamping here is optional.

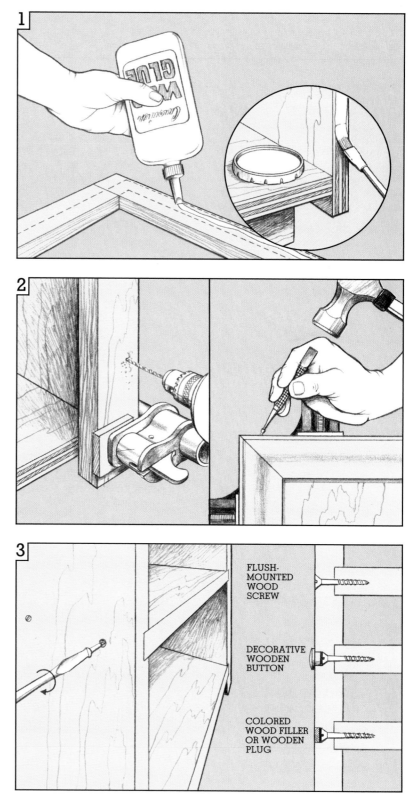

FLUSH-MOUNTED WOOD SCREW

DECORATIVE WOODEN BUTTON

COLORED WOOD FILLER OR WOODEN PLUG

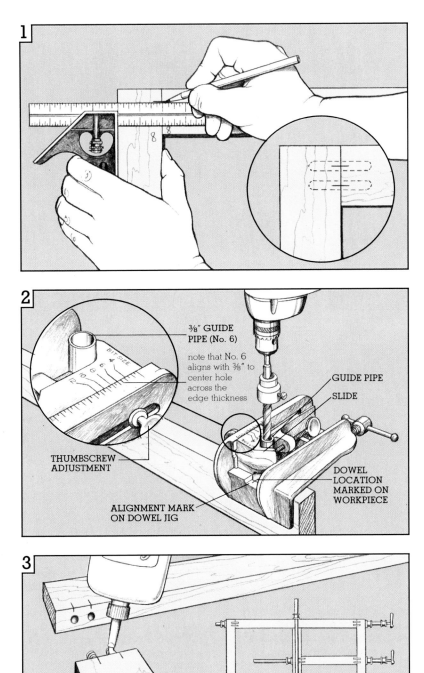

Joining with Dowels and Glue

1 First dry-fit the pieces using clamps. If you have a dowel jig like the one shown in sketch 2, place a combination square against the work at each joint location. Now strike two lines one-third of the way in from the appropriate frame edges to mark dowel locations, as shown.

To avoid a situation where the pieces refuse to fit together due to protruding dowels, plan your assembly so that the perimeter pieces are joined last. Also, it's a good idea to number the joining members of each joint in their order of assembly.

2 Select the dowel size you feel will do the job. Three ideally suited for face frames are $1/4$-, $5/16$-, and $3/8$-inch dowels. With any of these, you'll need to cut 2-inch lengths from dowel rods the right diameter, or buy a bag of dowels that have a spiral groove for holding more glue and beveled ends for easy joining.

Now, with the model dowel jig shown at left, secure the proper pipelike guide in the slide. Adjust the slide until the notch indicating your dowel's diameter on the slide aligns with the notch on the jig scale indicating one-half the thickness of the workpiece. This permits centering the dowel holes.

Next, locate the jig over one of the marks made on the workpiece and clamp it in place. Tighten the depth gauge on the drill bit allowing the bit to pass through the guide pipe and bore a 1-inch-deep hole. Now begin drilling. Other brands of dowel jigs operate somewhat differently. If you have one of them, refer to their package instructions.

3 Apply glue to the dowels and tap them into the holes. Assemble and clamp the members together, squaring all corners. After the glue begins to set up, go back and lightly scrape off any excess that oozed from between the joints. After waiting the prescribed time for the glue to cure, finish the job by sanding each joint smooth with a belt sander.

BASIC WIRING

How do you feel about working with electricity? Many otherwise intrepid do-it-yourselfers would rather cozy up to a deadly snake. "Sure," they say, "the power's supposed to be off, but what if it's not? And couldn't a simple mistake set the house on fire?"

Electricity's mighty energy most certainly deserves respect, but then so does gasoline. Pour a few gallons into a car with bad brakes, get behind the wheel, and you're headed for trouble.

Neglecting your home's wiring can be every bit as devastating. Faulty electrical equipment claims thousands of lives and homes every year, in too many cases because someone didn't bother to make a simple repair.

To help clear away any phobias or misunderstandings you might have about electrical principles, this section begins with a series of visual analogies that represent how household wiring works and how two vital safety systems protect against fire and shock. These drawings

also introduce you to the primary electrical colors—black, white, and green—that enable you to decipher exactly what's going on at any point in your home's network of wires.

Next, we turn to those all-important repair jobs. Most of us feel some trepidation every time we remove the wall plate from a receptacle or drop a light fixture from the ceiling, but you needn't worry about shock as long as you observe these two cardinal rules:
- **Always shut off power to the circuit you'll be working on, or the entire house if you're not sure which fuse or breaker controls the circuit.**
- **Double-check with a testing device to be absolutely sure the circuit is dead.**

To help you remember, we've red-lettered power-off jobs and other important safety information. When you see red, proceed with caution.

After you begin to understand how your home's electrical system works and have successfully completed a few repair jobs, you'll probably begin to think of some improvements you'll like to make. We show you how to add circuits and make other improvements.

Try a few improvements and you'll discover just what a joy electrical work can be. Compared to carpentry, lawn-keeping, painting, and other around-the-house chores, wiring projects involve a minimum of time, trouble, and mess. In fact, most of the work takes place in your head—while you figure out what's to be done —and with your feet—as you travel to the service panel to cut and restore the power.

One big reason electrical jobs go so quickly lies with the highly modular components you'll learn about in our final major section, Electrical Basics and Procedures. It tells how to select the right equipment and how to interconnect all the elements correctly.

When you shop for wiring materials, look for the same UL symbol you've seen on appliances and other items. This means the equipment has been examined for safety defects by Underwriters Laboratories, an independent testing organization. Using products that are not UL-listed may violate your local electrical code and possibly your home's fire insurance contract.

Incidentally, insurance policies typically say nothing one way or the other about fires caused by owner-installed wiring, but if you're thinking about taking on a major project, it's worth checking your policy's fine print.

Of course the best insurance against insurance hassles and the tragedies that cause them is to do the work right to begin with, and this, in electrical parlance, means working strictly "to code."

Working to Code

As you may already know, local and, in some cases, state laws, known as "codes," mandate what wiring materials you can use in your home and how they're to be installed. Ignoring these statutes not only risks a fine and an order to do the work over again, it also jeopardizes your family's safety.

Fortunately, modern codes are almost as standardized as the components you'll be working with. Credit for this goes to the National Fire Protection Association, a nonprofit, industry-wide agency that publishes the *National Electrical Code* (NEC).

The NEC is a voluminous "bible" of rules and regulations that covers just about any conceivable electrical situation. Although not law itself, the NEC serves as a model on which virtually all local codes are based. Some communities have simply adopted the national code as their own. Others are slightly more restrictive, but none permit practices that would be in violation of the national code.

The procedures shown in this book represent the editors' understanding of the 1984 NEC. (It's updated every three years.) If you're contemplating a major wiring job, check into both the NEC and local ordinances before you begin.

Technical bookstores often carry copies of the *National Electrical Code,* or write to the National Fire Protection Association, Batterymarch Park, Quincy, MA 02269. Canadian residents can obtain a copy of the Canadian Electrical Code by writing to the Canadian Standards Association, 178 Rexdale Blvd., Rexdale, Ontario, Canada, M9W 1P8.

Realize, too, that if you're planning to extend an existing circuit or add a new one, you may need to apply to your community's building department for a permit, and arrange to have the work inspected before it's put into service. Local officials can tell you about this and whether you'll need a licensed electrician to "sign off" the job.

GETTING TO KNOW YOUR SYSTEM

Electrical energy, as you undoubtedly know, flows into and through your home via a network of wires. You've probably never seen most of these wires, though. They're wrapped with insulation, sometimes clad in metal, and usually concealed inside walls, floors, and ceilings.

Even if you could get a good look at a live, bare wire, you wouldn't see any action. That's because electricity consists of invisible particles of matter, called *electrons*, moving at the speed of light.

Electrons always flow in circles, known as *circuits*. To trace their route through one of your home's circuits, follow the trucks along the special sort of freeway illustrated here.

It all begins at your power supplier's generating plant, which pumps out charged electrons, illustrated by the

black loads of the trucks. Overhead or underground wires bring power from the utility company's lines to your home's *service entrance,* then through a *meter* that keeps track of your household consumption.

Next, traffic proceeds to the *service panel,* which directs the flow to a series of circuits such as this simplified example. (Fuses or circuit breakers here stop traffic instantly if an accident occurs in any circuit. More about these on pages 136 and 140-143.)

Now the freeway narrows to two lanes, corresponding to the two wires needed for a single 120-volt circuit. One of them is typically covered in black insulation, identifying it as "hot" with charged traffic. The other wire always wears white insulation, signifying that it carries no charge.

Every potential exit from an electrical circuit is called an

outlet, regardless of whether it consists of a *receptacle, switch,* or *light.* At our first exit, a receptacle outlet, electron traffic passes right on by because nothing is plugged in and turned on. But the moment you hook in an electrical device, charged electrons flow into it and do their work, as shown at the second receptacle. In the process, the electrons "dump" their charges. Now they begin a return trip back to the service panel.

Notice, too, what's happening down the road. Here charged electrons are being halted by a light switch in its off position. Flip on the switch, and the energy flow begins.

Back at the service panel, all empty, uncharged electrons return to the power company, or to the earth via a *ground.* More about this vital safety element on page 137.

ANATOMY OF A CIRCUIT

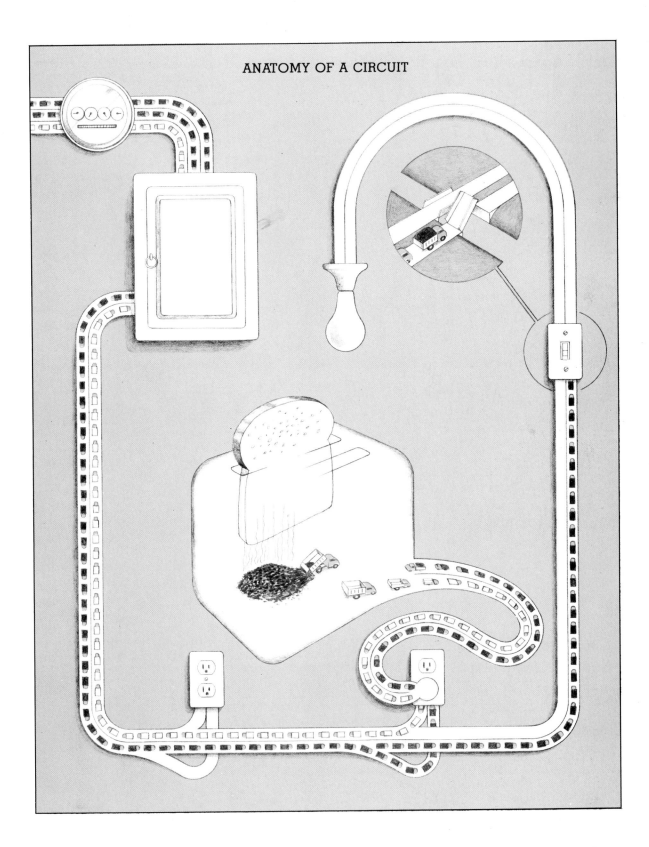

Fuses or Breakers Protect Against Fire

The freeway illustrated on the preceding page shows how traffic normally flows through an electrical circuit, but what if an accident occurs?

First, let's consider a head-on collision between our circuit's two "lanes." The result would be a *short circuit,* such as the one shown in sketch A. When a short occurs, traffic instantaneously piles up, and electricity's energy could touch off a fire.

That's why every properly wired household circuit includes a *fuse* or *circuit breaker* at the service panel. Either of these devices serves as a traffic cop. If a pileup occurs, it almost immediately shuts down the entire circuit.

Fuses and breakers also stop traffic if the circuit becomes *overloaded* with more current than it can handle. In this situation (see sketch B) there would be no head-on collision, but too much traffic would generate excess heat that might start a fire. For additional information about circuit breakers, fuses, shorts, and overloads, see pages 140-143.

Amps x Volts = Watts

The key to making good use of this very important electrical equation lies in your understanding of the terms used in it, so let's start there.

Amps represents the number of electrons flowing through a conductor. (This rate of flow can vary considerably, depending on the demand.) *Voltage* is the load of potential energy being carried by the electrons. And *wattage* measures the total energy consumed.

In our example (sketch C) we show two roadways on which trucks (electrons) are traveling. Both of these freeways have 120 volts of potential energy, so why is the low road twice as busy as the high road? Because one customer is using twice as much energy (wattage) as the other.

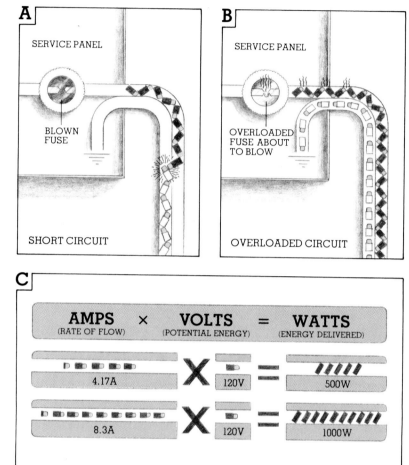

One way to measure the amperage of our freeway circuit would be to count the number of trucks going by a certain point in one second. You'd have to be a fast counter because one amp stands for billions and billions of electrons. This is why the amps x volts = watts formula was devised.

Using it, you can compute the amount of energy required to operate any appliance or other item on a circuit. Smaller electrical devices, such as light bulbs, are commonly rated according to the wattage they draw. Bigger power users, such as appliances, often are given amp ratings. To convert from watts to amps, simply divide the wattage by the voltage.

To show how helpful the formula can be, let's look at an example. Suppose you are thinking about buying an air conditioner rated at 9 amps and want to know if an existing circuit can handle it.

First check the circuit's fuse or breaker for its amp rating. In most cases this will be 15. Next, add up the wattages of every electrical "customer" on the circuit. Let's say the total is 600. Dividing this by the circuit's voltage tells you how many amps the circuit is already drawing. At 120 volts it would amount to 5 amps.

Now add this to the newcomer's demand — 5+9 — and you get 14, one amp less than the circuit's capacity.

Grounding Protects Against Shock

Head-on collisions and traffic jams aren't the only types of freeway incidents, nor are short circuits and overloads the only things that can go wrong with electrical traffic.

Examine drawing A, which shows an ungrounded circuit, and you'll see what can happen when some of our electron trucks get off at an other-than-normal exit, a situation that can occur inside a faulty motor, fixture, receptacle, or switch.

In this case a small amount of current is leaking, but because there's no collision, the fuse or breaker back at the service panel won't shut off the circuit. Some traffic, in effect, is stalled.

But electricity likes to keep moving. Pulled by the earth's magnetic force, it always seeks the shortest possible route to the ground. This means that if you are in contact with the earth and touch a device that's leaking current, all the stalled electrons will detour through your body.

Electrical shocks can amount to anything from a slight tingle to a fatal jolt, depending on how much current is leaking and how well you're grounded. If you happen to be touching a water pipe, or standing on a wet lawn, you could be seriously hurt or killed.

That is why today's codes, Underwriters Laboratories, and common sense require that all equipment using substantial amounts of current be *grounded* with a third "lane" that safely detours stray current to the earth.

In drawing B we've represented the grounding path in green, the color commonly used in wiring diagrams. Some of the grounds in your home may well be covered in green or green and yellow insulation, although grounding wires needn't be insulated at all. Many are bare, and if the wires that run through your walls are metal-clad, the metal itself may be serving as the ground lane.

The important thing about any ground is that it follow an unbroken path to the earth. You're probably familiar with the three-blade plugs that most major appliances have. The third, rounded blade carries the ground and fits into a corresponding slot in newer receptacles. The receptacle itself and often the box that houses it are in turn grounded back to the service panel. (Note: Only metallic boxes are grounded; nonmetallic boxes needn't be. Power tools with "double-insulated" plastic housings don't require grounding, either.)

(With older, two-slot receptacles, you may or may not get a safe ground with a special *adapter*. That depends on whether the receptacle and its box are grounded. To learn whether yours are, see page 149.)

Back at the service panel, the grounding wire for each circuit is connected to a *bus bar*, as are all the white neutral wires. A *system ground wire* then ties the bus bar to a metal water pipe, or a metal rod driven into the earth.

Why ground the white wires? This protects you and your home's electrical system against the enormous surge of current that might occur if the utility company's lines become short-circuited or are hit by lightning.

A newer code provision calls for another safety device in certain circuits. It's called a *ground fault circuit interrupter*. To learn what it does and how to install one, see pages 164 and 165.

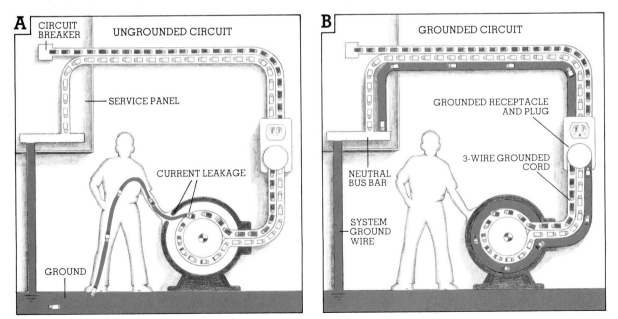

A — CIRCUIT BREAKER — UNGROUNDED CIRCUIT — SERVICE PANEL — CURRENT LEAKAGE — GROUND

B — GROUNDED CIRCUIT — GROUNDED RECEPTACLE AND PLUG — 3-WIRE GROUNDED CORD — NEUTRAL BUS BAR — SYSTEM GROUND WIRE

TOOLS FOR ELECTRICAL WORK

You don't need an arsenal of specialized equipment to do the electrical projects in this book. In fact, for most repair jobs, you can get by with just a couple of screwdrivers, two or three pairs of pliers, and one or two of the testing devices shown here. For improvements, you need to add a few more items.

Long-nose and *linemen's pliers* are musts. The first help you curl wires into the loops needed for many electrical connections. Linemen's pliers handle heavier cutting and twisting jobs. *Side-cutting pliers* are handy when you have to snip wires in tight places.

A *utility knife* slices through insulation, drywall, and almost anything else that calls for a cutting edge. A *combination tool* does a variety of tasks—cuts and strips wires, sizes and cuts off screws, crimps connectors, and more. If your wiring is protected by cartridge-type fuses, a plastic *fuse puller* lets

you remove them without danger of electrical shock.

With testers, you have some options. The *continuity* type has a small battery and bulb so you can test switches, sockets, and fuses, but only with the power off. A *neon tester*, on the other hand, lights up only when current is flowing. It tells you whether an outlet is live and hooked up properly.

You'll need one of each of these, or you can invest in an inexpensive *voltmeter* instead. This one works with the power on or off, and also measures how much voltage you have at an outlet. If you'll be installing a number of new receptacles, you might also want a *receptacle analyzer*. Plug it in and indicator lights warn you of faulty connections. You can learn the same things with a neon tester or voltmeter, but it takes more time.

Thinking about running some new wiring? Regardless of how

you plan to do it, you'll probably need an *electric drill*, a *spade bit*, and maybe a *bit extension* to lengthen the bit's reach.

If codes permit nonmetallic sheathed cable in your area, use a *cable ripper* to cut open the plastic sheath quickly. This one also strips insulation from conductors. For conduit, you'll need a *tubing cutter* or a hacksaw, a *bender*, and a *fish tape* to pull wires through the run. With a pair of tapes, you can also sneak cables through finished walls and ceilings.

Some codes require soldered connections in house wiring, and low-voltage installations also are usually soldered. A *soldering gun* and a spool of rosin-core *solder* do this job.

Most of the gear shown here packs easily into a *tool pouch*. Electrical work keeps you on the move, and you'll appreciate the convenience of having anything you might need at your hip.

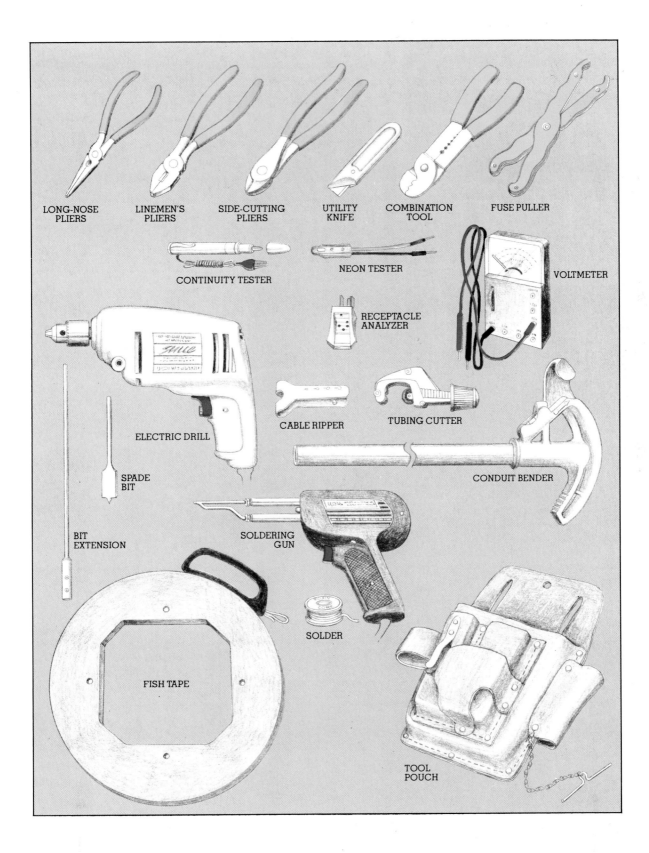

LONG-NOSE PLIERS

LINEMEN'S PLIERS

SIDE-CUTTING PLIERS

UTILITY KNIFE

COMBINATION TOOL

FUSE PULLER

CONTINUITY TESTER

NEON TESTER

VOLTMETER

RECEPTACLE ANALYZER

ELECTRIC DRILL

CABLE RIPPER

TUBING CUTTER

CONDUIT BENDER

SPADE BIT

BIT EXTENSION

SOLDERING GUN

SOLDER

FISH TAPE

TOOL POUCH

SOLVING ELECTRICAL PROBLEMS

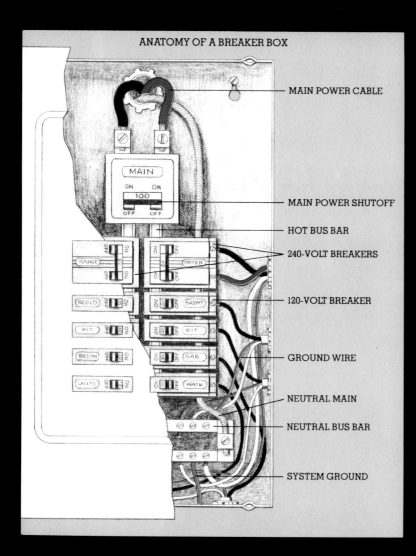

ANATOMY OF A BREAKER BOX

MAIN POWER CABLE

MAIN POWER SHUTOFF

HOT BUS BAR

240-VOLT BREAKERS

120-VOLT BREAKER

GROUND WIRE

NEUTRAL MAIN

NEUTRAL BUS BAR

SYSTEM GROUND

Most electrical projects begin at a service panel such as the breaker box shown at left, or the fuse box on page 142. When a short or an overload shuts down power to a circuit, this is where you go to restore the flow. It's also where you cut off power to a circuit *before* beginning a project.

Power from the meter arrives, in this instance, via those big black and red *main power cables* at the top. They connect to the *main power shutoff.* Turning off this breaker *does not* de-energize the main power cables, but everything else in the panel will be dead.

Note, too, that the main shutoff and the breakers labeled *range* and *dryer* are bigger than the others, and have two hot wires connected to them. These handle 240-volt circuits.

Single hot wire, 120-volt breakers protect individual branch circuits. Each of these devices snaps onto a *hot bus bar,* then is connected to its circuit by a black wire. White wires for each circuit and a bare copper *ground wire* tie into the *neutral bus bar.* Also connected to the neutral bus bar are a *neutral main* and a *system ground,* for reasons explained on page 137.

Troubleshooting Tripped Circuit Breakers

Think of a circuit breaker as a heat-sensing, spring-loaded switch. The cutaway drawings at right show one of these sensitive devices in its normal and tripped states.

When the *toggle* is in its "on" position, current flows through a set of *contacts* held together by a *spring* and *lever*. These are kept in tension by a *bimetal strip*, which is part of the circuit's current flow.

Typically, if something goes awry in the circuit—either a short or an overload—the bimetal heats up, bends, and the spring separates the contacts.

Once current stops, the bimetal cools and tries to straighten again, but it's not strong enough to stretch the spring, so the contacts remain open until the toggle is manually reset.

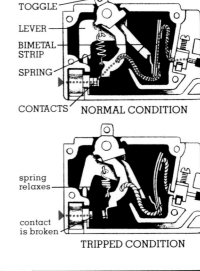

TOGGLE
LEVER
BIMETAL STRIP
SPRING
CONTACTS   NORMAL CONDITION

spring relaxes

contact is broken

TRIPPED CONDITION

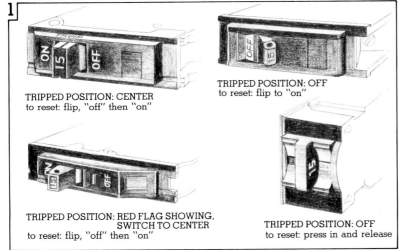

TRIPPED POSITION: CENTER
to reset: flip, "off" then "on"

TRIPPED POSITION: OFF
to reset: flip to "on"

TRIPPED POSITION: RED FLAG SHOWING, SWITCH TO CENTER
to reset: flip, "off" then "on"

TRIPPED POSITION: OFF
to reset: press in and release

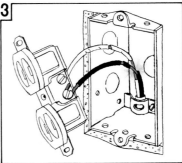

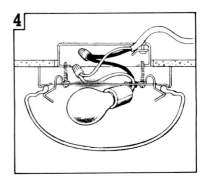

1 A tripped breaker may identify itself in any of the four ways shown above. To find out whether the problem that caused the outage has corrected itself, reset the breaker. Don't worry about shock or fire. If there's still a short or overload, the breaker will snap itself off again.

Overloads are easy to relieve. Usually you only need to unplug or turn off one of the circuit's bigger electricity users.

If that doesn't help, suspect a short. To locate one, systematically unplug items until the breaker holds. A defective plug, cord, or lamp socket may be the culprit (see pages 144-147).

2 Short circuits can occur in outlet boxes, too. Here, a wire has pulled loose from the switch and shorted out against the box.

3 Frayed or cracked insulation can expose a wire and cause a short. The solution: Wrap it with several layers of electrical tape.

4 High-wattage bulbs in a light fixture can melt insulation and produce a short. Never use bulbs larger than those for which the fixture is rated. More about troubleshooting light fixtures on pages 150-153.

Troubleshooting Blown Fuses

If yours is an older home that hasn't been rewired, chances are its electrical "heart" is a fuse box rather than the breaker box illustrated on page 140. Fuses and circuit breakers serve exactly the same purpose, but instead of tripping as a breaker does, a fuse "blows" when there's too much current in its circuit. Then you must eliminate the short or overload (see page 141), remove the blown fuse, and screw in or plug in a new one.

Refer to the anatomy drawing below and note that once again power comes in via a couple of *main power cables*. (In a house with no 240-volt equipment, there may be only one of these.)

Next, current flows through a main disconnect, in this case a *pullout block* that holds a pair of *cartridge fuses.*

Next in line are a series of *plug fuses* that protect the black "hot" wires of branch circuits. Unscrewing one of these (handle it only by the rim) disconnects its circuit.

1 Peer closely through the window of a plug fuse and you'll see a strip of metal through which current flows. The intense heat of a short or an overload causes this strip to melt, disconnecting the circuit.

Often just looking at a plug fuse can tell you whether a short or an overload caused it to blow. A short circuit explodes the strip, blackening the fuse window. An overload, on the other hand, usually leaves the the window clear.

2 Cartridge fuses, such as those you might find on the back of a main or 240-volt pullout, can't be checked visually. To determine whether one has blown, either install a new one or check the old one with a continuity tester as shown. The bulb will light if the fuse is good.

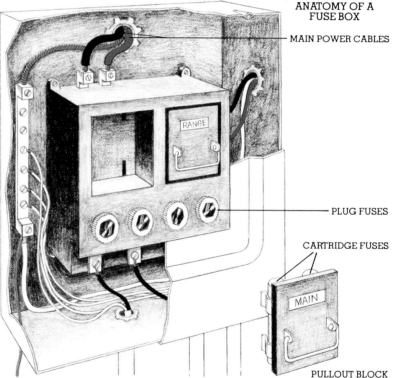

ANATOMY OF A FUSE BOX

MAIN POWER CABLES

RANGE

PLUG FUSES

CARTRIDGE FUSES

MAIN

PULLOUT BLOCK

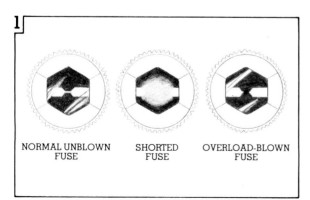

1

NORMAL UNBLOWN FUSE

SHORTED FUSE

OVERLOAD-BLOWN FUSE

2

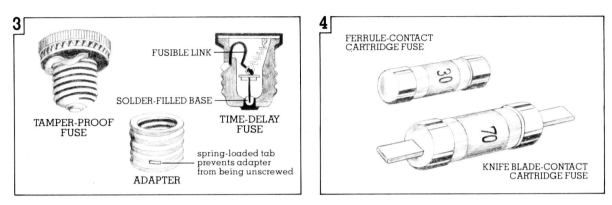

3

FUSIBLE LINK

SOLDER-FILLED BASE

TAMPER-PROOF
FUSE

TIME-DELAY
FUSE

spring-loaded tab
prevents adapter
from being unscrewed

ADAPTER

4

FERRULE-CONTACT
CARTRIDGE FUSE

KNIFE BLADE-CONTACT
CARTRIDGE FUSE

3 Ordinary plug fuses are interchangeable, regardless of their amperage ratings. **So if you have a chronically overloaded circuit, you might be tempted to install a "bigger" fuse. Don't do it. Wiring that gets more current than it was designed to handle heats up and can catch fire.**

Tamperproof fuses make it impossible for you or anyone else to "over-fuse" a circuit. Each comes with a threaded *adapter* that fits permanently into the box. The adapter accepts only a fuse of the proper rating.

Another problem with ordinary plug fuses is that they can be blown by even the momentary overload that often happens when an electric motor starts up. A *time-delay* fuse waits a second or so. If the overload continues, its *solder-filled* base melts and shuts down the circuit. A short blows the *fusible link*, just as it would in any other fuse.

4 Circuits rated at 30 to 60 amps typically use *ferrule-contact* cartridge fuses. *Knife blade-contact* fuses handle 70 amps or more. Both must be handled with extreme caution. Touching either end of a live one could give you a potentially deadly shock.

5 For safety, keep a plastic *fuse puller* with your spare fuses, and use it as shown at right. Note, too, that the ends of a cartridge fuse get hot, so don't touch them even after you've pulled the fuse.

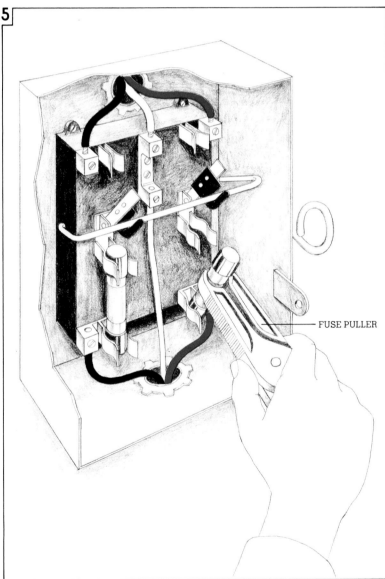

5

FUSE PULLER

Replacing Plugs, Cords, and Lamp Sockets

Have you ever been zapped by an electrical shock? If so, it probably came from a faulty plug, cord, or lamp socket. These pose the most common shock and fire hazards.

Fortunately, they're also far and away the easiest to repair. Master just a few basics and you can make short work of any potential short circuit.

Plugs get stepped on, bumped against, and yanked out by their cords. Even properly handled ones eventually wear out. So glance at any plug before you use it. If it shows signs of damage, replace it immediately.

The drawing at right shows some of the plug variations you'll encounter. *Round-cord* and *flat-cord* plugs are suitable for lamps, radios, and other low-amperage users. Newer lamp and extension cord plugs are *polarized,* with one blade wider than the other. To learn why, see page 194.

Heaters, irons, and similar appliances pull more current and require heftier plugs; *240-volt* equipment calls for special blade configurations.

Cords vary, too. *Zip cord,* the most common, should be used only for light duty. Twisted cords have two layers of insulation. *Heater cords* are triple-insulated, as is the *heavy-duty*, three-wire type required to ground appliances and other equipment. The *240-volt cords* have three fatter wires.

Lamp sockets come with a variety of different switching mechanisms. Most have brass-plated shells.

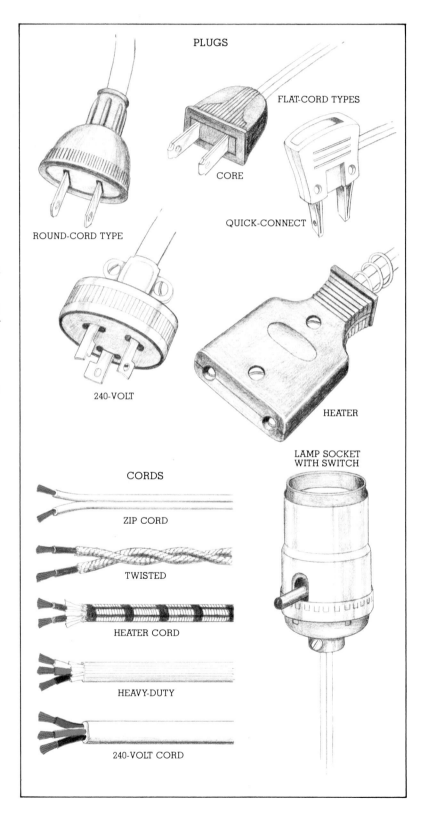

PLUGS

FLAT-CORD TYPES

CORE

ROUND-CORD TYPE

QUICK-CONNECT

240-VOLT

HEATER

LAMP SOCKET WITH SWITCH

CORDS

ZIP CORD

TWISTED

HEATER CORD

HEAVY-DUTY

240-VOLT CORD

Replacing Plugs

Round-Cord Plugs

1 Begin by snipping off the old plug, slipping a new one onto the cord, and stripping away insulation as shown. (For stripping techniques, see pages 196-197.)

2 Now tie the "Underwriters knot" so that tugging the cord can't loosen the electrical connections you'll be making. Always try to protect connections from stress.

3 Twist the wire strands tight with your fingers. Then, with a pair of long-nose pliers, shape clockwise hooks like these.

4 As you tighten the screws, tuck in any stray strands. If the screws differ, attach the black or ribbed wire to the brass one.

5 Finally, check to be sure all wires and strands are neatly inside the plug's shell, then slip on the cardboard cover.

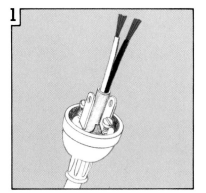

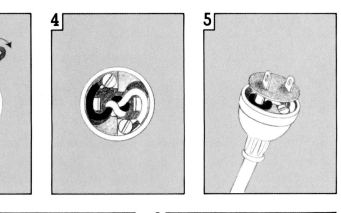

Flat-Cord Plugs

Flat-cord plugs connect in a variety of ways. Some require the same procedure shown above. Others have a core that you attach the wires to, then snap into a shell, as depicted here. Still another core type bites into unstripped cord, such as the quick-connect plug on page 146 does.

1 First slip the shell onto the cord, peel apart the wires, and strip away about half an inch of insulation. (More about stripping wires on pages 196-197.)

2 Twist the strands and form clockwise hooks big enough to wrap three-fourths of the way around each screw.

3 Slip the wires under the plug's screws, then tighten the screws to secure the connection.

4 Now just snap the core into the shell. With practice, the entire job takes only minutes. *(continued)*

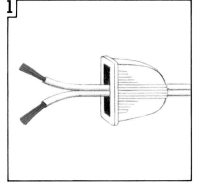
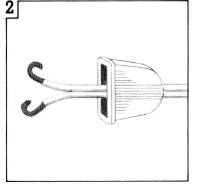

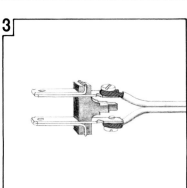
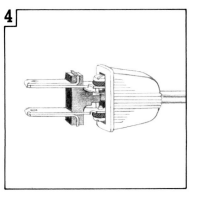

Replacing Plugs *(continued)*

Quick-Connect Plugs

Keep a few quick-connect plugs on hand and you'll never again be tempted to put off replacing a faulty or questionable plug. Installing one takes about as long as changing a light bulb, and the only tool you need is a sharp knife or pair of scissors.

1 Snip off the old plug. Lift the lever on top of the new plug and insert the zip cord at the side.

2 Closing the lever pierces and holds the wire. It's that easy.

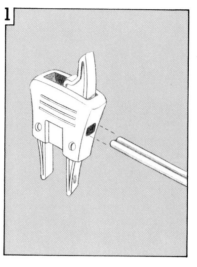

240-Volt Plugs

Really just an oversized round-wire plug with an extra blade, a 240-volt plug installs in much the same way. You don't have to tie an Underwriters knot, however. A steel clamp grips the cord.

1 Slide the plug onto the cord and strip the three wires as shown. Twist the strands tightly together and form hooks.

2 Attach the black and red wires to brass-colored terminals, and the green one to the silver-colored screw. Tuck everything into place, tighten the cord clamp, and slip on the cardboard cover.

Heater Plugs

Wall plugs for heaters, irons, and other "hot" appliances typically are molded to the cord. To replace the plug, it's best to replace the cord as well. You may or may not be able to replace the female plug at the cord's other end, depending on whether it comes apart.

1 If your plug is like the one shown at right, it will pull apart. Note how the spring relieves strain on the cord.

2 If the plug has a brass terminal, connect the black wire to it, the white to the silver one. Clips tie the plug to the heater blades.

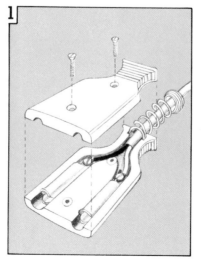

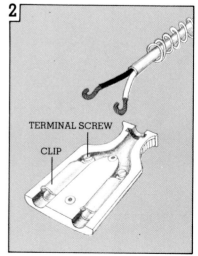
TERMINAL SCREW

CLIP

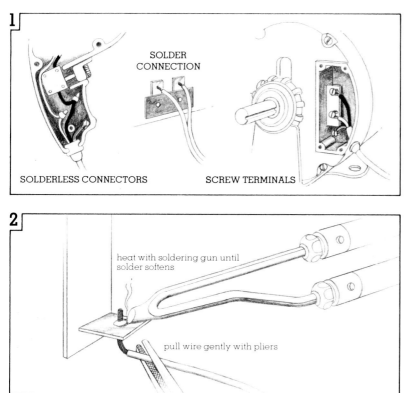

1

SOLDER CONNECTION

SOLDERLESS CONNECTORS   SCREW TERMINALS

2

heat with soldering gun until solder softens

pull wire gently with pliers

Replacing Cords

Lamp and appliance cord must be sized according to the load it will carry. For lamps, clocks, and other items that draw less than 7 amps, use No. 18 wire; 7- to 10-amp appliances need No. 16 wire; anything larger than 10 amps should have a No. 14 cord. The larger the wire number, the smaller its size.

1 You'll probably have to dismantle part of the unit to find out how its cord hooks in. Expect to find screw terminals, solder connections, or solderless connectors that screw on or crimp on.

2 Release a soldered connection as shown here. To resolder, insert the wire, heat the entire connection, including the terminal, then touch solder to it. The solder will melt and fuse the joint.

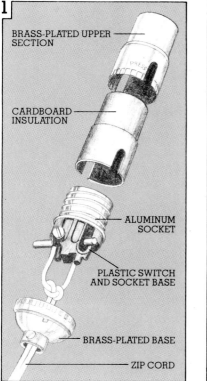

1

BRASS-PLATED UPPER SECTION

CARDBOARD INSULATION

ALUMINUM SOCKET

PLASTIC SWITCH AND SOCKET BASE

BRASS-PLATED BASE

ZIP CORD

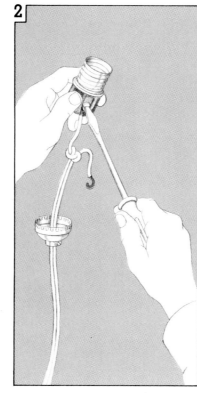

2

Replacing Lamp Sockets

When a lamp won't work and you know its bulb is OK, unplug the cord and pry up the little brass contact in the socket base. If this doesn't bring results, or if the cardboard insulation has deteriorated, replace the socket.

While you're at it, you might want to install a new cord and plug (a polarized one), too. The easiest way to thread new cord through a lamp base is to tie it to the old one with a piece of string. As you withdraw the old, the new will follow it.

1 Examine the socket shell and you'll find the word *press*. Push hard here and the unit will pull apart into the series of components illustrated.

2 Slip the new socket base onto the cord, tie it with an Underwriters knot, and attach wires to each of the terminals. Reassemble everything and the job is done.

Replacing Switches and Receptacles

Tired of pampering a balky switch or a paint-glopped receptacle that holds plugs with only the feeblest of grips? Armed with just a screwdriver, a neon test light, and the know-how explained on these two pages, you can install a new one in 15 minutes or less, and that includes time for a couple of trips to your service panel to cut and restore power. That's because all you have to do is wire the new device the way the old one was wired. To learn about some of your choices in new switches and receptacles, see pages 196 and 197.

To be safe, *always* de-energize a switch or receptacle before you touch its inner workings. To do this, you'll need to shut off your home's main circuit breaker or pull its main disconnect fuse block (see pages 140-141 for how to do this). Or deactivate only the circuit you think you'll be working on, then check the condition of the circuit with a test light, as shown here. Note, however, that to test a switch, you must have a good bulb in the fixture it controls. For more information about testing switches, turn to page 151.

Switches

1 Is the circuit live? With the switch off, touch the tester's probes to its screw terminals. If the light glows, the circuit is still hot.

2 If the tester doesn't light, remove the screws holding the switch's ears to the box and pull out the device. Now loosen the screw terminals and disconnect the wires.

3 A three-way switch has three terminals. Note which is marked or otherwise identified as the *common* before you unhook the wire. This terminal may not be in the same place on your new switch.

4 Some new switches have push-in terminals in back, as well as screws on the sides. If you use screws, wrap wires around them in a clockwise direction.

5 Now tuck the wires and switch back into the box and tighten the hold-down screws. Don't force anything; switches crack easily.

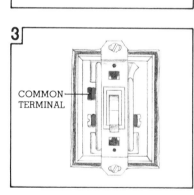

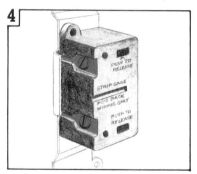

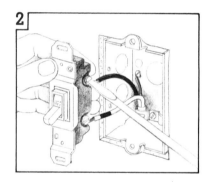

COMMON TERMINAL

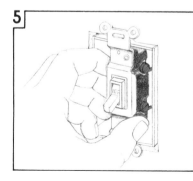

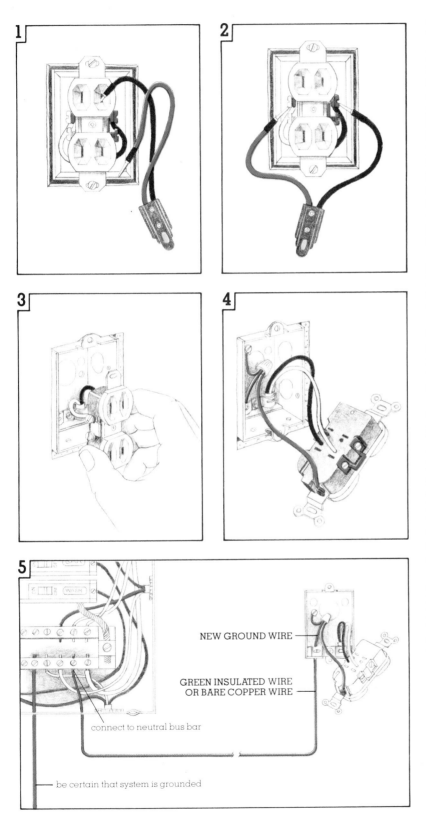

NEW GROUND WIRE

GREEN INSULATED WIRE
OR BARE COPPER WIRE

connect to neutral bus bar

be certain that system is grounded

Receptacles

1 Can you replace a two-slot, non-grounding receptacle with a safer, three-hole version? To find out, remove the wall plate, leave power on, and touch one probe of the tester to the receptacle strap or the box. Now insert the other probe into each of the slots. If either lights up the tester, the box itself is grounded and you can install a three-hole type. If not, either get a two-slot receptacle or — better yet — run a separate ground as shown in the bottom sketch on this page.

2 To learn whether a receptacle is live, touch the tester probes to screws on either side. The light will glow if there's power.

3 Remove the hold-down screws and pull out the device. Be sure to note which wires are attached to which terminals before unfastening them.

4 Newer receptacles have push-in terminals as well as screws. Whichever you use, connect white wires to silver, black to brass. If you find a bare wire inside the box, ground the receptacle's green screw to it and to the box with a couple of short green wires. If there is no bare wire but you know the box is grounded, run a jumper directly from the receptacle to the box.

5 To ground an ungrounded box, run a wire from it to the service panel or to a cold water pipe. Turn to pages 183-186 for information on how to go about fishing wires through finished space.

Troubleshooting Incandescent Fixtures

Incandescent fixtures vary widely in style, but most have some arrangement of the components illustrated in the anatomy drawing at right.

A *canopy plate* attaches to a wall or ceiling fixture box, and also supports a *bulb holder* that consists of one or more *sockets*. *Leads* connect the sockets to wiring in the box.

To get at the bulbs, you usually must remove some sort of translucent glass or plastic *diffuser*. Most manufacturers post a maximum wattage on the canopy. Bulbs of a wattage higher than the recommended rating generate too much heat, which is the main enemy of incandescent fixtures.

When a fixture shorts out, you can almost be certain that the problem lies in the fixture itself or in its electrical box. If one refuses to light, however, the switch that controls it also could be faulty.

(NOTE: Be sure to shut off power before beginning.)

1 Inspect the socket. Cracks, scorching, or melting means it should be replaced. You can find a new one at a lamp parts store.

If the socket is intact and securely mounted to the canopy plate, remove the bulb and check the contact at the socket's base. If there's corrosion, turn off the circuit — not just the switch — and scrape the contact with a screwdriver or steel wool. Also pry up the contact a bit.

2 If the problem remains, shut off the circuit again and drop the fixture from its outlet box. To do this, remove either a single nut in the center or a pair of screws located off-center. Now check for loose connections and for cut, frayed, or melted insulation. Wrap any bare wires with electrical tape.

ANATOMY OF AN INCANDESCENT CEILING FIXTURE

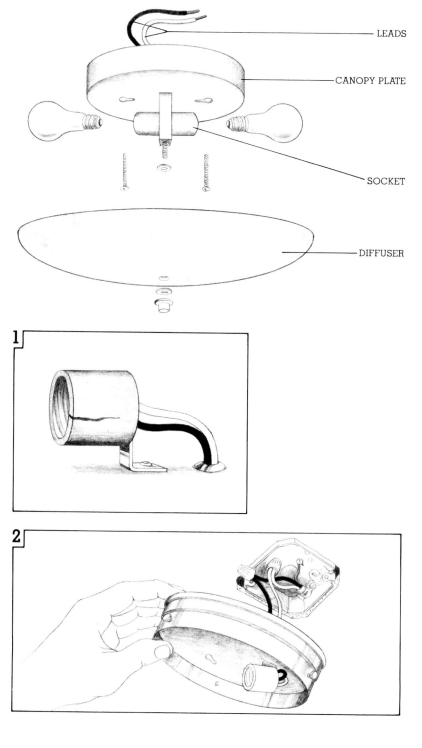

LEADS

CANOPY PLATE

SOCKET

DIFFUSER

Testing Switches

1 Internal switches on a fixture or lamp usually are connected with a pair of small pressure connectors. **To test the switch, unplug the lamp and remove the connectors holding the switch's leads.** Leave the bare wires twisted together but arrange them so the connections aren't touching each other or anything else.

Restore power to the lamp or fixture and carefully touch your tester to the connections. Now flip the switch and test again. If the tester lights, the switch is bad.

2 To test a wall switch, turn it to the "on" position, and touch the tester to the terminal screws. If the tester lights, the switch must be replaced, as shown on page 148.

3 Nervous about poking into a live switch? Then shut down its circuit and conduct your investigation with a continuity tester. In the above situations, the tester should light when the switch is on, but not when it's off. If you get a glow in both positions or no glow in either position, you need a new switch.

To check out a three-way switch such as this one, shut off the circuit and attach the tester's clip to the common terminal; it's usually identified on the switch body. Now touch the probe to one of the other terminals and flip the switch. If it's OK, the tester will light in one position or the other. Repeat this test with the other terminal.

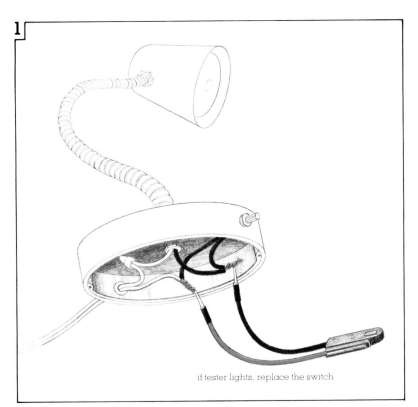

if tester lights, replace the switch

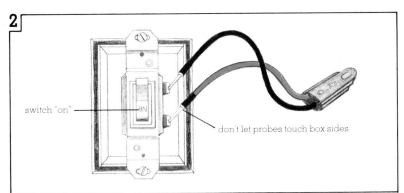

switch "on"

don't let probes touch box sides

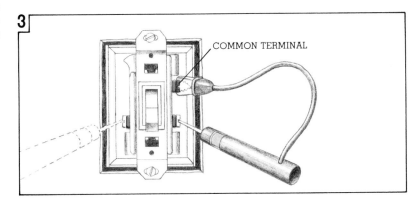

COMMON TERMINAL

Troubleshooting Fluorescent Fixtures

Switching on an ordinary light bulb charges a metal filament that literally burns with white heat. Fluorescent tubes, on the other hand, don't get nearly as hot because they operate in a different way.

Anatomically (see sketch below), the heart of a fluores-

cent fixture is its *ballast*, an electrical transformer that steps up voltage and then sends it to a pair of *lamp holders*. The current from the lamp holders excites a gas inside the tube, causing its phosphorus-coated inner surface to glow with cool, diffused light.

Because they produce far less heat, fluorescent tubes last much longer than incandescent bulbs and consume considerably less electrical energy. Problems are fewer, too. Following are the major ills you're likely to encounter with fluorescent fixtures.

ANATOMY OF A RAPID-START FLUORESCENT LIGHT

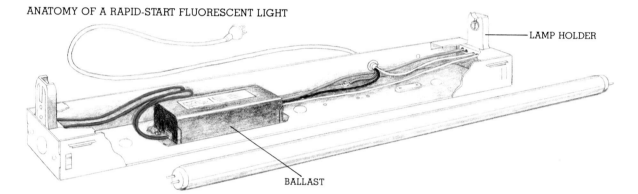

LAMP HOLDER

BALLAST

1 Rarely do fluorescent tubes burn out abruptly. When a tube won't light, try wiggling its ends to be sure they're properly seated.

If this doesn't get things glowing again and yours is a rapid-start tube like the one shown, suspect a loose or broken connection. **Start your search by turning off power to the circuit,** removing the tubes and the fixture cover, and inspecting all connections inside. Next, check the switch (see page 151).

2 As a last resort, you may have to drop the entire fixture and look for loose connections and broken or bare wires in the outlet box.

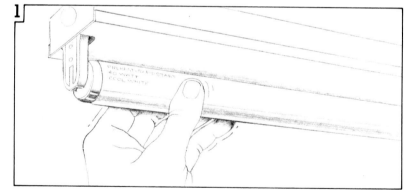

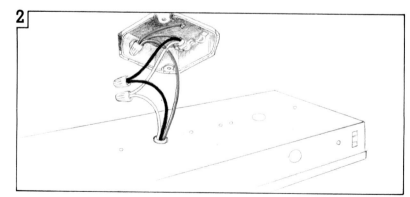

3 When a tube begins to fail, the normally grayish bands near its ends gradually blacken. Uniform dimming usually means the tube simply needs washing. When you shop for a new tube, select one of the same wattage as the old one.

4 Older, delayed-start fluorescent lights flicker momentarily as they light up. If the flickering continues, make sure the starter is seated by pushing it in and turning clockwise.

When the ends of a tube light up but its center does not, the starter probably has gone bad. To remove it, press in and turn counterclockwise.

5 Humming, an acrid odor, or tarlike goop dripping from a fixture indicates that the ballast is going bad. To replace it, follow the procedures shown below. But first compare the price of a new ballast with that of a new fixture. You may be better off replacing the entire unit.

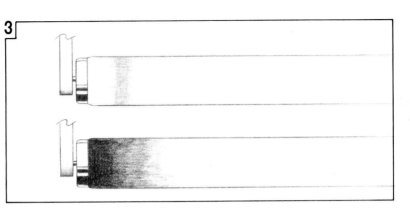

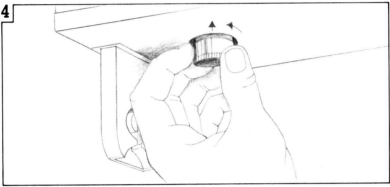

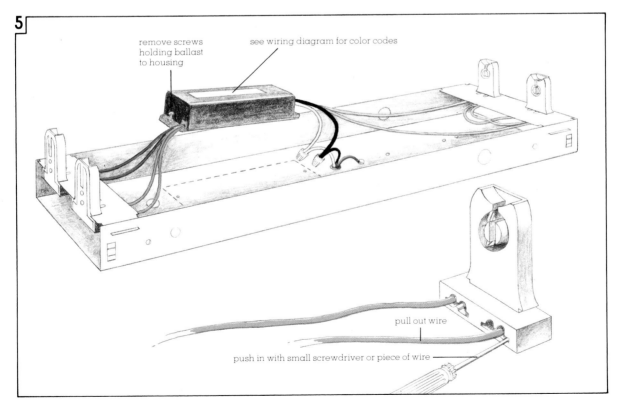

remove screws holding ballast to housing

see wiring diagram for color codes

pull out wire

push in with small screwdriver or piece of wire

Wiring Receptacles, Fixture Outlets, and Switches to Existing Circuits

Tired of hassling with a long extension cord or groping around in a dark closet to find something? You can eliminate these and other irritations by installing a new handily located receptacle or a switch-controlled light fixture.

Adding an outlet or two needn't be a big job if you can tap into an under-used circuit nearby. This page shows how to compute whether a circuit can handle additional load, and where you can tap in for power. Then the following pages take

you step by step through nine common new receptacle, light, and switch hookups.

What if you can't find a circuit with capacity to spare? Then you'll have to bring in a fresh one from the service panel, as shown on pages 166-169.

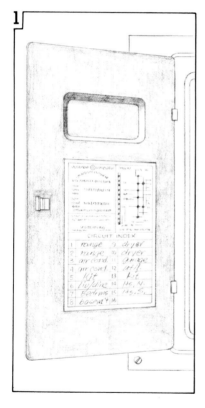

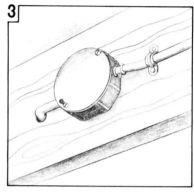

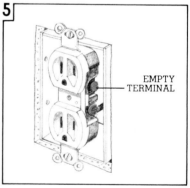

EMPTY TERMINAL

Determining the Load

1 Start by identifying the customers on a circuit. It's a process of elimination. Lights that go out and appliances that won't work when a circuit is shut down are on that circuit. Log your findings on the inside of the service panel cover.

2 Now prepare a worksheet to determine whether the circuit you plan to tap can handle the extra load. If the total amperage of its

regular customers doesn't exceed 80 percent of the circuit's rated capacity, you can add to it.

Where to Tap In

3 If your basement ceiling is open, look for a junction box near where you need the new outlet. To get a cable to it, you may have to "fish" through walls (see pages 183-186).

4 Or check the attic. Here you might find a junction box atop the joists, as shown, or buried under

insulation. Just make sure you're not tapping into the box for a ceiling fixture (a switched circuit).

5 Consider nearby receptacles, too. If you find one with a set of unused terminals, you can fish wire from here to the new location. A prime candidate might be in an adjacent room near where you want the new outlet.

A New Approach To Understanding Wiring Diagrams

One reason why ordinary wiring diagrams seem baffling at first is that they show everything already hooked up. To figure out what's going on, you have to trace each wire's path, which is like trying to understand how to tie a knot by untying one.

These drawings use another approach. Follow the sequences and you'll see circuit extensions develop a step at a time.

Adding Another Receptacle By Tapping an Existing One

Let's start with one of the simplest situations: tapping into a duplex receptacle. Remember that this will work only if the receptacle is at the end of a wiring run. If it's not, you'll find all the terminals already occupied.

(NOTE: Be sure to shut off power before beginning.)

1 Remove the screws that secure the existing receptacle to the box. If it's not a grounded type, consider replacing it with one that is (see page 149).

2 Cut an opening for the new box and fish cable from the existing outlet (see pages 183-186).

Once the cable is in place, connect it to the existing and new boxes (see page 187), and install the new box (pages 176-177). Hook up the grounds as shown.

3 Connect the black wire to the hot side of both the new and existing receptacles. Hot terminals have brass-colored screws.

4 Make the white and ground connections to the silver and green screws, and screw the receptacles to their boxes. Finally, turn on the power and test your installation (see page 149).

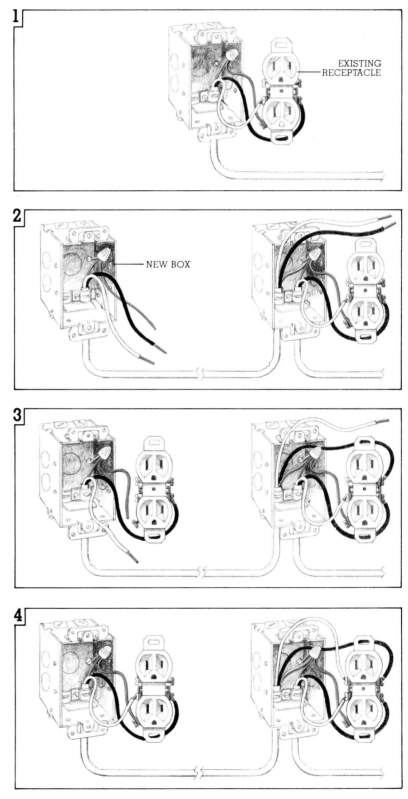

Splitting a Receptacle and Controlling It With a Switch

Examine a duplex receptacle and you'll see that the sets of terminals on either side are connected only by a small metal tab. Break this bridge and the upper and lower receptacles can function independently.

This comes in handy in several situations. In a kitchen or shop, for example, you might want to connect a heavily used outlet to two circuits. Or you might want to control half the receptacle with a switch so you can turn a living room lamp on and off from a doorway.

(NOTE: Be sure to shut off power before beginning.)

1 Disconnect the wires from the receptacle, then run two-conductor cable and install a new box, following exactly the same steps illustrated on the opposite page. Because it's almost impossible to fish cable laterally inside walls, you'll probably have to route it to the basement or attic, then bring it up or drop it down from there. Hook up ground wires.

2 Now route the circuit's hot leg to the switch, using the jumper connection shown in the existing receptacle box.

3 Wrap the white wire with black tape to show that it's hot, too, then connect it to the switch and receptacle terminals. Next, connect the remaining black wire to the receptacle as shown. Snap off the brass-colored tab with long-nose pliers to split the outlets, but leave the silver-colored tab in place.

4 Connect the white and ground wires to the receptacle, screw the devices to their boxes, turn on the power, and make your tests. Here the upper outlet will be live only when the switch is on. The lower one remains hot at all times.

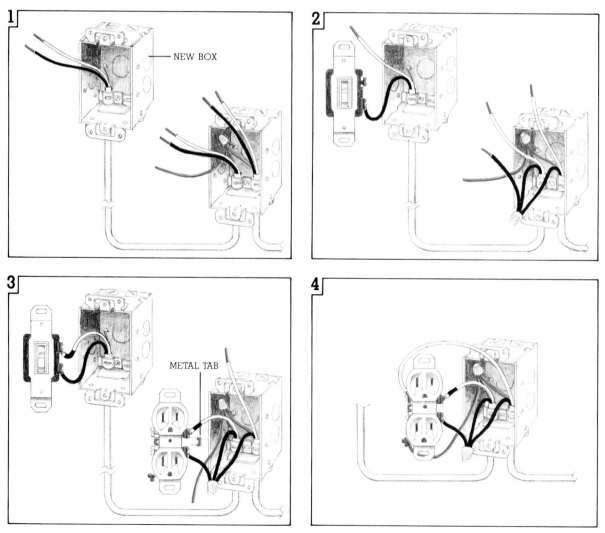

Installing a Ceiling Fixture (With Switch Beyond)

Fixture installations get a bit tricky because you wire them differently depending on where they're located in relation to the power source and the switch or switches that will control them. Will power flow through the switch to the fixture, or vice versa? Here, the switch is beyond.

(NOTE: Be sure to shut off power before beginning.)

1 Open up a junction box and you'll see something like this. You may see even more wires. If you do, locate the circuit you want by testing sets of wires one by one with a continuity tester.

2 Run cable and install the new fixture and switch boxes. Connect the ground wires as shown.

3 Connect the black wires as shown. Note how the black wire picks up power at the junction box and takes it to and through the fixture box and on to the switch.

4 Now mark the white wire running between the fixture and switch boxes with black tape. Hook one end of it to the switch.

5 Finally, connect the black-taped white wire to the black fixture lead, the untaped white wire to the white lead, and all the white wires at the junction box.

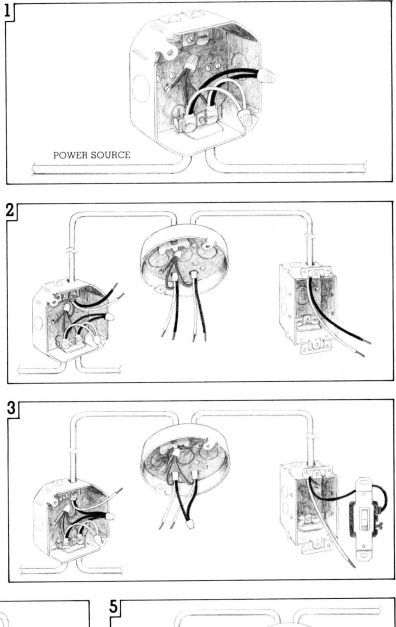

POWER SOURCE

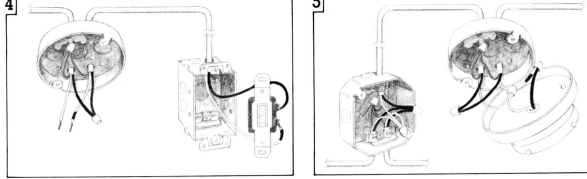

Installing Two Ceiling Fixtures Controlled By One Switch (Fixtures Beyond Switch)

In this installation, power comes to the switch first, then goes on to both of the fixtures. A single switch can control as many fixtures as you like if you extend the run from one to the next. Make sure, though, that the wattage total doesn't exceed the maximum indicated on the body of the switch. Toggle switches are rated in amps; dimmer switches list maximum wattage.
(**NOTE: Be sure to shut off power before beginning.**)

1 Fish cable, install new boxes where you want the switch and fixtures, and connect the ground wires as shown. Power can come from a junction box or receptacle with an empty set of terminals, as shown on page 155.

2 Hook the black wires to the switch's terminals. These carry current to the fixtures when the switch is on, but not when it's in the off position.

3 At the first fixture you'll have three black wires. Connect them all together as shown. At the second fixture hook its black lead to the incoming black wire.

4 Since the switch interrupts only the circuit's hot leg, you don't connect white wires to it. Attach them to each other and to the fixture's white leads as illustrated.

Note: You can control several fixtures with a switch that's beyond them, too. Just route power as was done on page 157, then back to the fixtures. If you want to operate two lights with separate switches, we'll show how that's done on the next page.

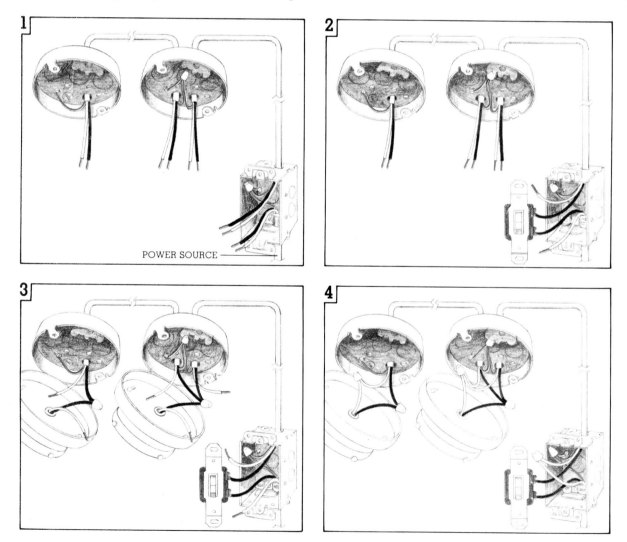

POWER SOURCE ──

Installing Two Fixtures Controlled By Separate Switches

If you're going to the trouble of installing two ceiling outlets and a wall box, you might be surprised to learn that it's only a little more work to provide individual switches for the fixtures. You simply "gang" together two boxes for the switches and connect them to the fixtures with three-wire cable.

Electricians are fond of three-conductor cable because in most instances it can do twice the work of the two-conductor version. Study this example and you'll be ready for the intricacies of three- and four-way switching that follow.

(NOTE: Be sure to shut off power before beginning.)

1 Here, three-conductor cable goes from the switch box to one fixture, then on to the next. Power comes to the fixtures first via two-conductor cable.

2 Bring power to the switches by connecting the black wires as shown. Short lengths of wire let you attach to switch terminals.

3 Now complete the switch hookup with the red and white wires. Be sure to code the whites with tape to show that they're hot.

4 Complete the circuit by connecting the red and white wires to the fixture leads as shown. If power in your installation will come first to the switches, split the incoming black wire as shown here, and run the outgoing red and black wires from the switches to the fixtures. The neutral wire, which is "shared" by both of the switch circuits, goes right on through, as shown on page 158.

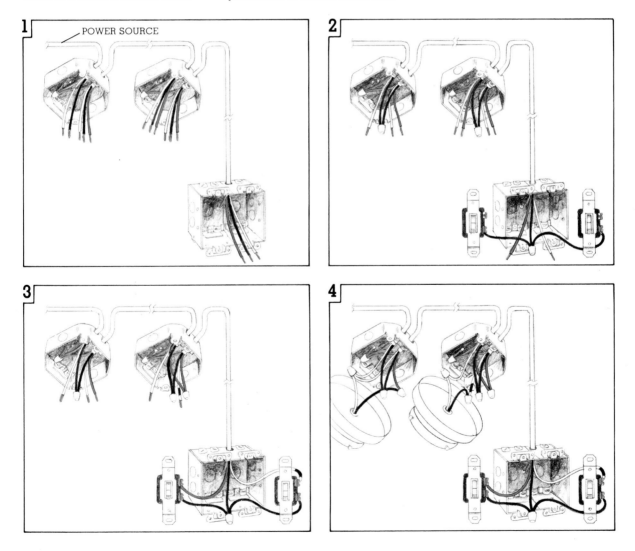

Installing Three-way Switches—Case No. 1

Prepare for numerical confusion when you deal with three-way switches. First of all, they control fixtures from two locations, not three. Secondly, they do have three terminals and need three-conductor circuits. And finally, you hook them up in one of three ways, depending on where the switches are in relation to the power source, the fixture, and each other.

(NOTE: Be sure to shut off power before beginning.)

1 In this first of three examples, power comes in through one switch, travels to the fixture, then to the second switch. (See page 162 for three-way switching.)

2 Locate the "common" terminal on each switch. It will be labeled or darker than the other two. Connect the incoming hot wire.

3 Attach "traveler" wires to the other terminals, then route them through the ceiling box to the other switch. Note that at the light, one white wire becomes hot.

4 Complete the hot leg of the circuit by connecting the black wire to the second switch's common terminal and to the fixture.

5 Run the neutral leg back to the power source. Either switch will operate the light.

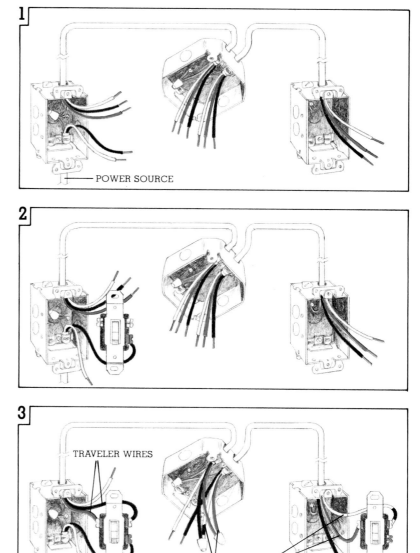

POWER SOURCE

TRAVELER WIRES

TRAVELER WIRES

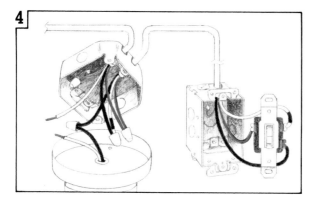

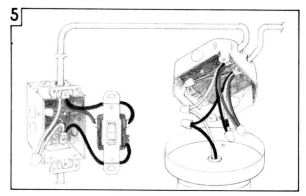

Installing Three-way Switches—Case No. 2

The preceding page shows how to wire three-way switches when the light is between the two switches. Here we show what to do when it's beyond both switches. We've included a dimmer in this example. (Remember: With most dimmers you can use only one per circuit.)

(**NOTE: Be sure to shut off power before beginning.**)

1 For this project you need to run three-conductor cable only between the switches. Power comes into the first switch and out of the second on just two wires. Connect ground wires as shown. (See page 162 for three-way switching rules.)

2 As before, connect the hot leg of the power source to the first switch's common terminal.

3 Next, connect the travelers to each of the switches. (Warning: You can burn out a three-way dimmer by hooking it up incorrectly. Professional electricians often set up the circuit with ordinary three-way switches, turn on the power and check it, then replace one with a dimmer.)

4 Connect the outgoing black wire to the dimmer's common lead and to the black fixture lead.

5 Complete the circuit by connecting the white wires as shown.

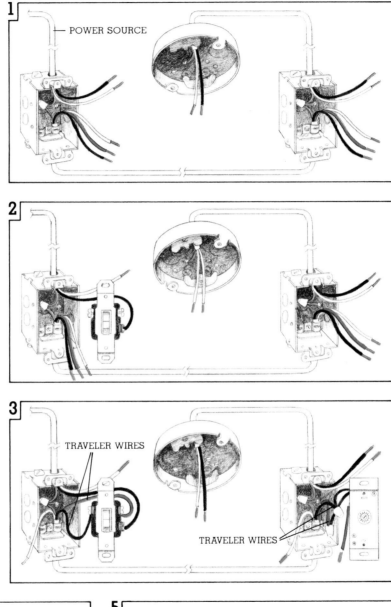

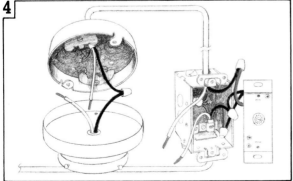

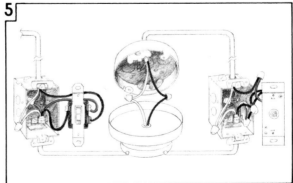

Installing Three-way Switches—Case No. 3

In this final three-way switch situation, the light fixture is ahead of both of the switches that control it.

(NOTE: Be sure to shut off power before beginning.)

1 You need three conductors only between the switches, not to and from the fixture. Connect ground wires as shown.

2 Bring the hot leg of the circuit through the ceiling outlet to the common screw of the first switch.

3 Connect the traveler wires as shown. Be sure to tape the whites.

4 Bring the hot leg back by connecting the black wire to the common terminal of the second switch and to the white wire in the first switch box. Tape it black, too.

5 Finally, connect the fixture leads as shown.

You won't get in trouble with any three-way switch installation as long as you observe these ABCs:

(A) Always attach the incoming hot (black) wire to the common terminal of one switch.

(B) Connect the traveler terminals only to each other, never to the light.

(C) Connect the common terminal of the second switch only to the black fixture lead.

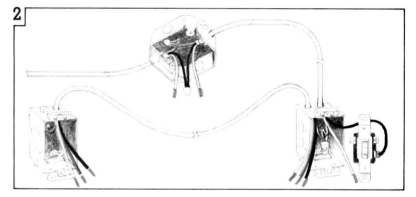

POWER SOURCE

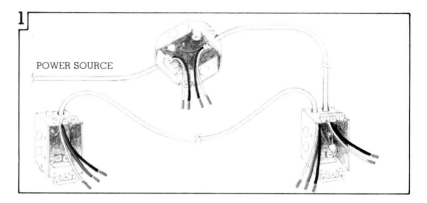

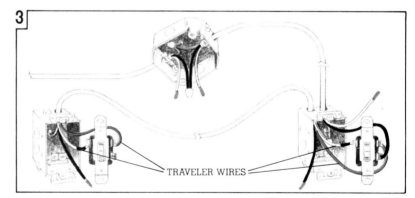

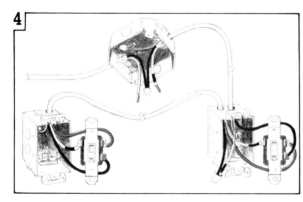

TRAVELER WIRES

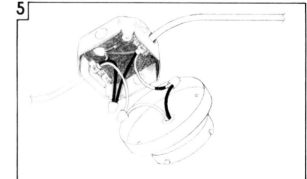

Installing Four-way Switches

And now for the final entry in our switching numbers game: the four-way switch. This one has four terminals, and you can install any number of them between a couple of three-way switches. Use four-ways when you want to control a light from three or more locations. Just remember that in four-way situations, the first and last switches must always be the three-way type.

(NOTE: Be sure to shut off power before beginning.)

1 Here, incoming power flows from switch to switch to switch to light, but it could just as easily follow one of the other routes illustrated on the preceding pages. Start by connecting the ground wires as shown. Next connect the black wire from the power source to the first switch's common terminal.

2 Now connect all the traveler wires as shown. Four-pole switches carry only travelers.

3 At the second three-way switch, link its common terminal to the fixture's black lead. This completes the circuit's hot leg.

4 Connect all the white wires back to the power source, turn on the power, and admire your switching handiwork.

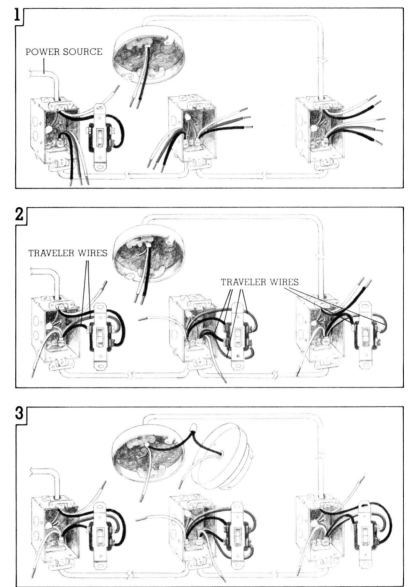

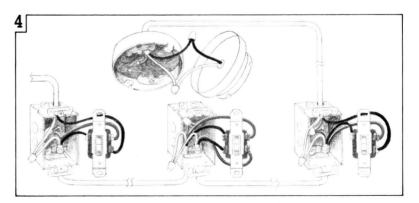

Installing a Ground Fault Circuit Interrupter

Fuses and circuit breakers protect the *wiring* in your home. Now let's meet a device that protects *you.* Called a ground fault circuit interrupter (GFCI), it senses tiny leakages of current and shuts off the power before you can say GFCI.

In most circumstances, leakage of current isn't a big problem. In properly grounded systems most of it is carried back to the service panel, and what remains would scarcely give you a tickle.

But let's say *you* happen to be well-grounded, standing on a wet lawn, for example, or touching a plumbing component. Then that tiny bit of errant current would pass through your body on its way to the earth. Depending upon the voltage, as little as 1/5 of an amp, about enough to light a 25-watt bulb, can be fatal.

Wired into both of the conductors in a circuit, a ground fault circuit interrupter continuously compares current levels flowing through the "hot" and "neutral" sides. These should always be equal. If the mechanism senses a difference of just 1/200 of an amp, it trips the circuit. Power is interrupted in 1/40 of a second or less, fast enough to prevent injury to any healthy child or adult.

Any ground fault is a potential hazard. Even if you're using a faulty tool or appliance with a grounding wire that's in good condition, you aren't completely safe from a serious shock.

This is why today's codes require GFCIs that monitor all receptacles in outdoor, bathroom, and garage locations —the places where you're most

likely to come in contact with a good ground. The National Electrical Code doesn't say anything about basement shops, laundries, or other heavy-equipment areas, but you might want to add a GFCI in these locations as well. A wet basement floor can provide a fatal ground.

If yours is an older home, chances are it doesn't have GFCI protection, and you should seriously consider providing it. These devices are fairly costly, but they're no more difficult to install than an ordinary receptacle or circuit breaker. The next page tells how.

(**NOTE: Be sure to shut off power before beginning.**)

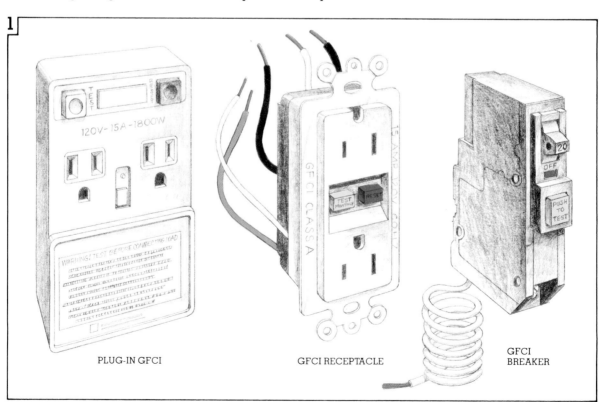

PLUG-IN GFCI GFCI RECEPTACLE GFCI BREAKER

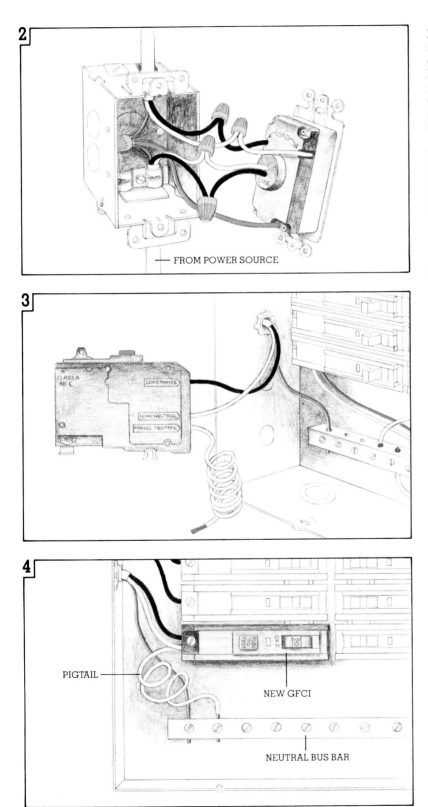

2

— FROM POWER SOURCE

3

4

PIGTAIL

NEW GFCI

NEUTRAL BUS BAR

1 GFCIs come in three different models. A *plug-in* type is the easiest to install. You just insert its blades into a receptacle, then plug a tool or appliance into its outlets. This one can only be used indoors, but it's portable, so you can easily move it to a work site.

GFCI *receptacles* replace ordinary receptacles and can be installed outdoors. Some protect only themselves. Others monitor the entire circuit. Test and reset buttons let you check the device.

GFCI *breakers* protect the entire circuit, too. These units also do the job of an ordinary breaker.

2 Hook up a GFCI receptacle as shown here. Incoming power goes to the *line* leads. *Load* leads send it to other receptacles on the circuit. If you're wiring one at the end of a line, cap off the load leads with solderless connectors, or buy a version that protects just one receptacle.

3 GFCI breakers clip into a service panel just as the ordinary breakers shown on page 169, but you wire them differently. To replace a conventional type with a GFCI, first shut off all power to the service panel, then snap out the old breaker.

You'll notice that only the circuit's "hot" side is connected to the breaker. The white wire goes to the panel's neutral bus bar. Disconnect *both* the hot and neutral wires and attach them to the GFCI as shown here.

4 Now ground the white *pigtail* by loosening a terminal screw on the bus bar, inserting the wire, and tightening the screw.

Finally, turn the power back on, set the breaker, and push the test button. This simulates a ground-fault condition and the breaker should trip. (Note: Follow the safety, procedures on pages 168 and 169 for service panel work.)

Adding Circuits to Your System

And now for the most advanced project in this book: tapping new circuits into your home's service panel. Whether you'll want to try this one yourself or hire an electrician to do all or part of the job depends as much on the situation at your service

entrance as it does on your confidence and electrical expertise.

This page and the next tell how to assess that situation. The two that follow show how to make the final connections.

Your first consideration: Are the wires to your meter bringing in enough capacity to handle the extra load? Look for an amperage rating on your home's main fuse, circuit breaker, or disconnect switch. Older 60-amp

service probably can't be stretched. Upgrading this is a job for your utility or a professional.

Newer 100-amp service may have enough reserve to handle an additional circuit or two, while 150- or 200-amp service usually can take care of all but a major addition to your home's electrical load. To find out exactly how much more you can add, go through this step-by-step analysis.

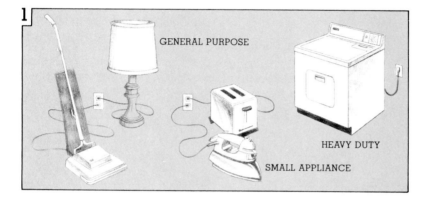

1 Begin by breaking down your home's circuits into the three categories illustrated here: general purpose, small appliance, and heavy duty.

General-purpose circuits may have about 10 light or receptacle outlets. They usually carry 15 amps, sometimes 20. Ideally you should have one general-purpose circuit for every 500 square feet of living space. Some local codes stipulate that lighting and receptacles be on separate general-purpose circuits.

Small-appliance circuits often supply 20-amp current to just two or three receptacles. Codes call for two small-appliance circuits in the kitchen, and you'll probably need others for the laundry, a shop, or a window air conditioner.

Heavy-duty circuits feed just one customer, such as a furnace, an electric dryer, or a range. You may need 240- or 120/240-volt wiring for some of these appliances.

Which of these circuits do you need, and where? The chart at left, based on requirements in the National Electrical Code, tells what you should have. Note that some circuits now must be equipped with ground fault circuit interrupters (GFCIs), as explained on pages 164 and 165.

Circuit Need Selector

Location	Circuits
Living, dining, bedrooms, hallways, finished basements	A 15-amp general-purpose circuit for each 500 square feet. For a room air conditioner, install a small-appliance circuit.
Kitchen	At least two 20-amp small-appliance circuits and a 15-amp lighting circuit. An electric range needs a 120/240-volt circuit.
Bathroom	A 15-amp general-purpose circuit with GFCI protection.
Garage	A 15- or 20-amp general-purpose circuit with GFCI protection.
Laundry	A 20-amp small-appliance circuit for the washer and a gas dryer; you'll need a 120/240-volt circuit for an electric dryer.
Workshop	A 20-amp GFCI circuit; for larger shops run two, or a separate lighting circuit.
Outdoors	One 20-amp GFCI circuit.

GENERAL PURPOSE

HEAVY DUTY

SMALL APPLIANCE

Add up the amperage ratings for all of your home's circuits and you may be alarmed to discover that their total exceeds the service rating on the main fuse or circuit breaker. Does this mean your electrical system is already overtaxed?

Probably not. Remember that few if any of the circuits ever work at full amperage capacity, and it is unlikely that you'll ever operate *all* of your home's electrical equipment at the same time.

This is why codes allow electricians to *de-rate* total household demand when they're computing how much service a home needs. The table at right goes through a typical de-rating calculation for a 2,000-square-foot house with 100-amp service, five small-appliance circuits, and two heavy-duty circuits.

In assigning wattage values, don't count the number of general-purpose circuits at all. Just use three watts per square foot of house area as a rule of thumb. Small-appliance circuits count at 1,500 watts each. Only with heavy-duty circuits do you use full wattage ratings, and if two items, such as an electric furnace and air conditioning, never run at the same time, ignore the one that draws less.

Rate only the first 10,000 watts of the total at full value, then calculate 40 percent of the remainder. The answer, 64.2 amps in this example, indicates that the system easily could accommodate several more circuits.

2 Now let's see if your panel has room for any more circuits. If it has circuit breakers like the one below, you might find a blank space or two. If not, double up by replacing an existing breaker with a pair of *skinnies* or a *tandem* device.

In a fuse box you might be lucky enough to find an unused *terminal* and *socket* that could be put to work. More likely, you'll have to add a sub-panel, as shown on page 169. *(continued)*

How to De-rate Service Capacity

Formula	Example
Add	
General-purpose circuits (square footage x 3 watts)	6,000 W
Small-appliance circuits (number x 1,500 watts)	7,500 W
Heavy-duty circuits (total of appliance name-plate ratings in watts)	10,000 W
Total:	23,500 W
Compute	
The first 10,000 watts at 100%	10,000 W
The remaining 13,500 watts at 40%	5,400 W
De-rated total:	15,400 W
Divide	
The total de-rated wattage by voltage	15,400 W
	240 V
De-rated amperage:	64.2 A

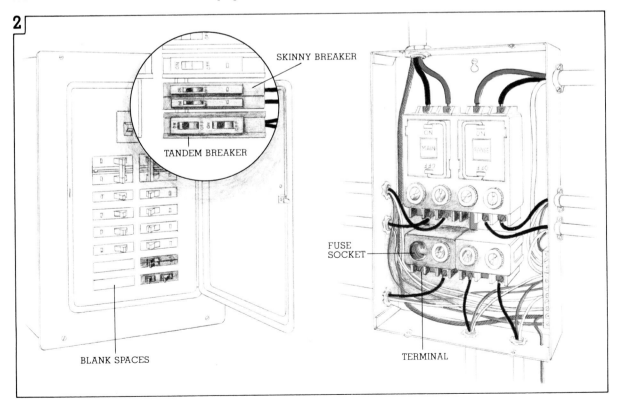

2

SKINNY BREAKER

TANDEM BREAKER

FUSE SOCKET

BLANK SPACES

TERMINAL

Adding Circuits
(continued)

3 To install a new circuit, you work backward, first mounting boxes for the new outlets, then interconnecting them with cable and bringing it back to the service panel in what the pros call a "home run." Pages 154-163 and 170-199 show what happens in the outfield and at the bases. Here's the scene at home plate.

(**NOTE: Before you even remove the cover from a service panel, make absolutely certain that no power is flowing through it or to it.**) Where is your home's main disconnect switch, fuse, or circuit breaker? It might be outside near the meter (as shown here), inside near the service panel, or in the panel.

If you have a remote disconnect, you can just flip off the switch or pull the fuse, open up the box, and test it as explained below. If, however, your main disconnect is part of the service panel, you should seek advice from an electrician, an electrical inspector, or your utility company. Turning off an integral disconnect kills power to the individual circuits, but live current will still be coming into the box. To stop the flow entirely, you may have to have the meter pulled by your utility company, or hire an electrician to make the final connections.

4 Now let's make sure the power is off. Standing on a board, rubber mat, or other insulator, and being careful not to touch electrical or plumbing fittings, remove the cover plate.

Then, identify the terminal screws for the main power cables. They'll be the biggest ones in the box and probably will be located at the top. Gently touch them with the probes of a voltmeter, as illustrated here. If you get a reading, the box is still live. Here, both lines are still carrying power to the breaker panel; at the fuse panel, both are dead.

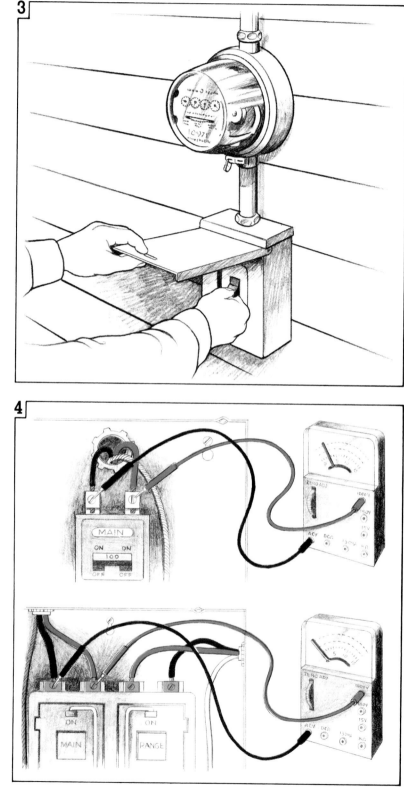

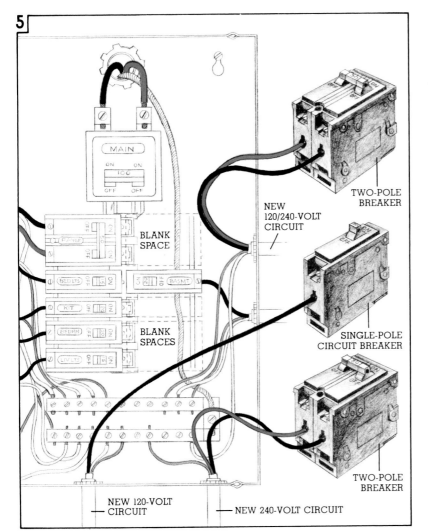

5 BLANK SPACE

NEW 120/240-VOLT CIRCUIT

TWO-POLE BREAKER

SINGLE-POLE CIRCUIT BREAKER

BLANK SPACES

TWO-POLE BREAKER

NEW 120-VOLT CIRCUIT

NEW 240-VOLT CIRCUIT

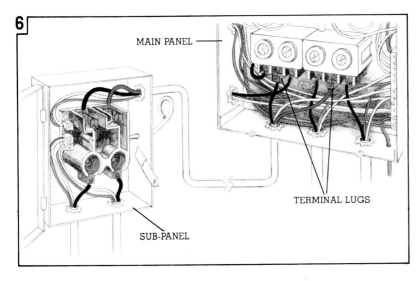

6 MAIN PANEL

TERMINAL LUGS

SUB-PANEL

5 When you're satisfied the power is off, you can make relatively quick work of the final connections. If you're hooking in several circuits, connect them one at a time so you can keep the wires straight.

Begin by punching the center from a convenient knockout. Then pry out one or more of the knockout's concentric rings to make a hole the size of the cable connector you'll be using.

Now strip back the cable covering, allowing for enough wire to reach the neutral bus bar as well as the spot you have in mind for the new breaker. Connect the cable to the box.

Inside, run the white and circuit ground wires to the neutral bus bar. For a 120-volt circuit, attach the red or black wire to the terminal of a *single-pole* breaker (see sketch). Clip the breaker onto one of the panel's hot bus bars and the job is done.

For a 240-volt circuit, which is really just two 120s, you need a *two-pole* breaker. It's twice as wide as a single-pole type. In this case, both of the circuit wires are hot and attach to the breaker as shown. Only the ground wire goes to the neutral bus bar.

Combination 120/240-volt circuits use the same two-pole breaker; connect the third, white wire to the neutral bus bar. GFCI breakers install somewhat differently, as explained on page 165.

6 A sub-panel gets you out of a crowded fuse box, and if you're adding several circuits far from the main panel, you might want to connect them to a remote sub, then make just one "home run" back to the main panel.

Besides the new panel itself and the fuses or breakers it will hold, you also need cable with three wires sized to handle the amperage the sub-panel will draw (see page 171), plus the *terminal lugs* shown.

ELECTRICAL BASICS AND PROCEDURES

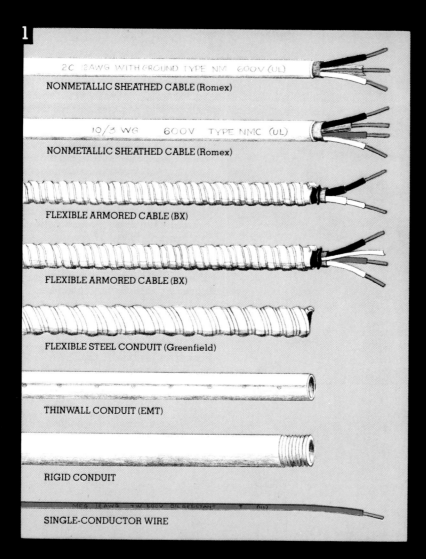

1

2C 12AWG WITH GROUND TYPE NM 600V (UL)

NONMETALLIC SHEATHED CABLE (Romex)

10/3 WG   600V   TYPE NMC (UL)

NONMETALLIC SHEATHED CABLE (Romex)

FLEXIBLE ARMORED CABLE (BX)

FLEXIBLE ARMORED CABLE (BX)

FLEXIBLE STEEL CONDUIT (Greenfield)

THINWALL CONDUIT (EMT)

RIGID CONDUIT

MEG 14AWG 3W 600V OIL RESISTANT T GN

SINGLE-CONDUCTOR WIRE

Once you've decided where you want a new outlet and how you're going to tap into an existing circuit or the service panel itself, you're faced with the task of actually getting the project done. This section gives the nuts-and-bolts know-how you need to do just that.

Electrical projects amount to little more than simple assembly work. You just fasten together a series of standardized components in equally standardized ways.

The pages that follow present the cables, boxes, fittings, and other devices you'll be using, and tell how the National Electrical Code says they are to be assembled.

Don't, however, rely solely on the national code. It is simply a series of widely accepted recommendations about how work should be done. Local codes take precedence, and these vary in some details from community to community.

Not all codes let homeowners do their own wiring. Some require that a licensed person make the final connections. Others allow you to do the work after passing a test that shows you're familiar with the basics explained here.

Selecting Cable

1 Most local codes let you use *nonmetallic sheathed cable* inside walls, floors, and other places where it can't be damaged. Information on the plastic covering tells what's inside.

Our topmost example has two No. 12 (American Wire Gauge) conductors, plus a ground. *Type NM*, also called Romex, a trade name, goes in dry locations only.

The second cable shown has three No. 10 conductors, plus a ground. *Type NMC* runs in dry or damp locations. A third type of nonmetallic cable, not shown, is *UF* (underground feeder). It's allowed in wet places, too, which means you can bury it.

Flexible armored cable, also known as BX, another trade name, has a spiral-wrapped steel cover. It can be used in dry or damp places and for short exposed runs.

Flexible steel conduit, or Greenfield, looks like armored cable without the wires. You cut it to length, thread wires through it, then install the completed pieces. With *thinwall* and *rigid conduit*, you fish wires after conduit has been run. Most codes require you to use these for exposed runs.

2 In some localities, you can save money by running *aluminum* or *copper-clad aluminum* wiring. Be warned, however, that aluminum expands and contracts considerably more than copper, causing loosening at terminals. So use only devices marked *CO/ALR* or *CU/AL* with aluminum.

3 The size of wire you must install depends on the amperage it will carry. Wire sizes are inversely proportional to their numbers. Drawings at right show the sizes you'll likely work with and some typical uses. Use one size larger with aluminum.

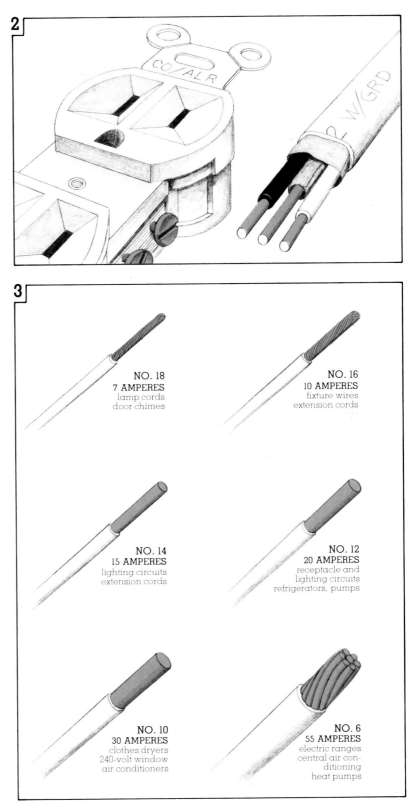

NO. 18
7 AMPERES
lamp cords
door chimes

NO. 16
10 AMPERES
fixture wires
extension cords

NO. 14
15 AMPERES
lighting circuits
extension cords

NO. 12
20 AMPERES
receptacle and
lighting circuits
refrigerators, pumps

NO. 10
30 AMPERES
clothes dryers
240-volt window
air conditioners

NO. 6
55 AMPERES
electric ranges
central air conditioning
heat pumps

Electrical Boxes, Accessories, and How to Install Them

What's Available in Boxes

Shop for electrical supplies and you won't find many cables that differ from the ones illustrated on page 170. The drawings on the opposite page, on the other hand, show only a few of the hundreds of different boxes and accessories you can choose from.

When you think about the jobs a box might be called on to do, you begin to understand why so many versions are available. Primarily, of course, any box has only one function: to house electrical connections. But those connections might be to a switch, a receptacle, the leads from a light fixture, or other sets of wires.

Codes govern how many connections you're allowed to make within a box, depending on its size. If you must make more, you have to use a bigger box. (See the chart below.)

Another major reason for the variety of boxes is convenience. If, for instance, you'll be pulling cables through a finished wall, use an *old-work* box that can be mounted from outside the wall.

To keep confusion at a minimum, let's break them down into a few broad categories.

1 *Switch/receptacle* boxes hold either device and serve as the workhorses in any electrical installation. Several of the metal ones shown here can be ganged into double, triple, or larger multiples by removing one side.

Take note of the round-cornered version shown. Called a *utility* or *handy box*, it is used with conduit in exposed locations and cannot be ganged.

Nonmetallic switch/receptacle boxes are made of plastic and are prohibited by some codes. They can't be ganged. *Weatherproof boxes* go outdoors.

2 *Fixture/junction* boxes may support lighting fixtures, or split circuits off into separate branches. These are round, octagonal, or square.

3 *Accessories*, as you can see from the sample array here, are myriad. You can easily figure out what most of these do, or check the pages to come.

Determining Which Box to Use

Overcrowd a box and you risk damaging solderless connectors, piercing insulation, or cracking a switch or receptacle, any of which could cause a short. That is why codes spell out how many wires you may install in boxes.

The table at left displays the NEC requirements. As you count, bear in mind these points:
1) Don't count fixture leads joined to wires in the box.
2) Count as one a wire that enters and leaves without a splice.
3) Count as one any number of cable clamps, hickeys, or studs.
4) Don't count external connectors, but if the box has internal clamps, do count them as one.
5) Count each receptacle or switch as one.
6) Grounding wires running into a box also count as one.
7) Don't count grounding wires that begin and end in the box.
(continued)

Choosing the Correct Box Size

Type of box	Size in inches (Height x width x depth)	Maximum number of wires			
		No. 14	No. 12	No. 10	No. 8
Switch/ Receptacle	3x2x1½	3	3	3	2
	3x2x2	5	4	4	3
	3x2x2¼	5	4	4	3
	3x2x2½	6	5	5	4
	3x2x2¾	7	6	5	4
	3x2x3½	9	8	7	6
Utility	4x2⅛x1½	5	4	4	3
	4x2⅛x1⅞	6	5	5	4
	4x2⅛x2⅛	7	6	5	4
Fixture/ junction	4x1¼ round or	6	5	5	4
	4x1½ octagonal	7	6	6	5
	4x2⅛	10	9	8	7
	4x1¼ square	9	8	7	6
	4x1½ square	10	9	8	7
	4x2⅛ square	15	13	12	10
	4¹¹/₁₆x1½ square	14	13	11	9
	4¹¹/₁₆x2⅛ square	21	18	16	14

1 SWITCH/RECEPTACLE BOXES

METALLIC

NONMETALLIC

WEATHER-PROOF

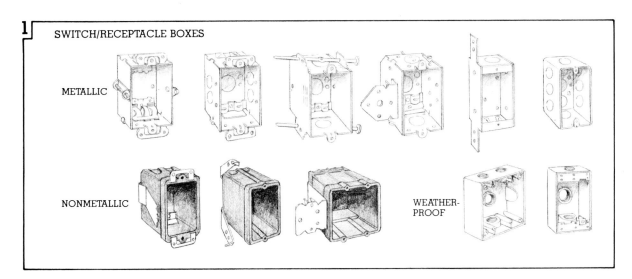

2 FIXTURE/JUNCTION BOXES

METALLIC

NONMETALLIC

WEATHER-PROOF

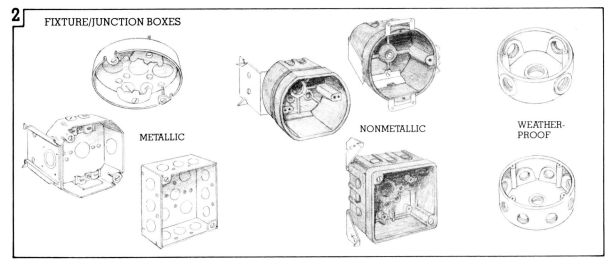

3 ACCESSORIES

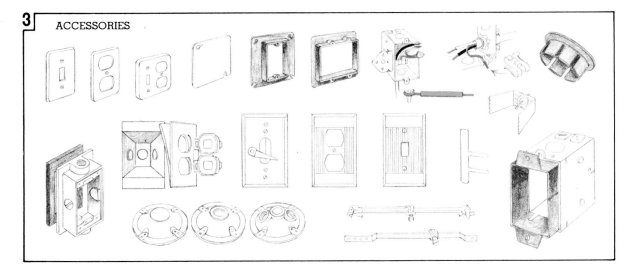

Electrical Boxes
(continued)

Installing Boxes in Unfinished Space

The order you decide to follow in doing the procedures shown here and on the next 20 pages depends largely on the state of the walls and ceilings in which you'll be adding outlets.

When electricians wire a new house, they typically fasten boxes to the framing, as illustrated here, run cable from box to box, then make home runs to the service panel. You'd do the same in a new addition, basement remodeling, or other unfinished construction project. After you've "roughed in" your wiring, you put up wall and ceiling materials, then install devices in the boxes.

But when you have to fish wires through finished walls and ceilings, matters become more complicated. Then you usually begin by making an opening where you want the new outlet and bringing cable to the opening. Only after you've fished the cable and connected it to the box do you install the box.

If you're wiring unfinished space, count yourself lucky. With the framing out in the open, you can install a box in about the time it takes to drive a couple of nails. Here's how:

1 With switch and receptacle outlets, the critical thing to keep in mind is that the box's edge must end up flush with the surface of the wall you'll be installing. New-work boxes let you compensate for the thickness of paneling or drywall in one of several ways.

Many *nail-up* and *straight-bracket* boxes have a series of *gauging notches* on their sides. You align the appropriate notch with the outer edge of the stud and nail or screw it in place. Note that the straight-bracket box shown here is only 1½ inches deep, so it can be attached to a 2x2 or 2x3 furring strip.

Some *L-bracket* boxes adjust to suit the thickness of your wall material. Others accommodate only one thickness. *Utility (handy) boxes* mount on the surface, so you needn't worry about aligning them. Run conduit first (see pages 188-191), and attach to masonry as shown on the opposite page.

Locate switches 48 to 50 inches above the floor and receptacles 12 to 16 inches above it. Check what your local code says about spacing between receptacles. The National Electrical Code requires that they be placed so that no point along any wall is more than six feet from an outlet. This means a receptacle for every 12 running feet of wall.

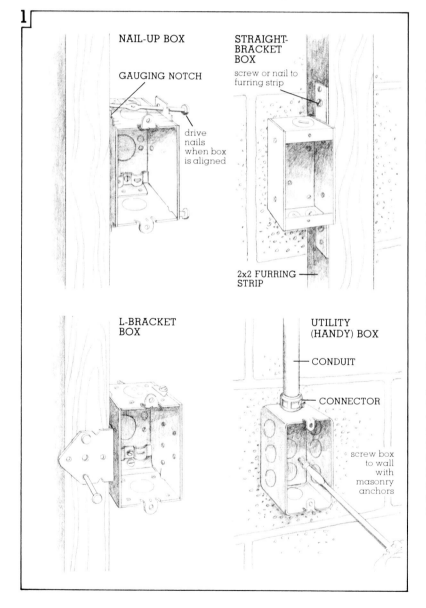

1

NAIL-UP BOX

GAUGING NOTCH

drive nails when box is aligned

STRAIGHT-BRACKET BOX

screw or nail to furring strip

2x2 FURRING STRIP

L-BRACKET BOX

UTILITY (HANDY) BOX

CONDUIT

CONNECTOR

screw box to wall with masonry anchors

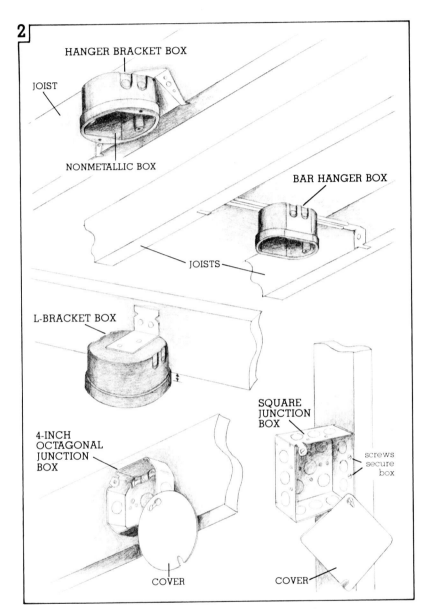

2 HANGER BRACKET BOX

JOIST

NONMETALLIC BOX

BAR HANGER BOX

JOISTS

L-BRACKET BOX

SQUARE
JUNCTION
BOX

4-INCH
OCTAGONAL
JUNCTION
BOX

screws
secure
box

COVER

COVER

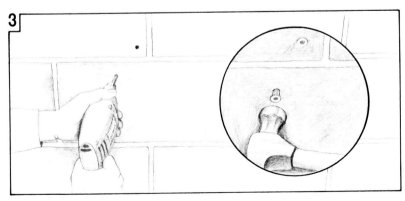

3

2 Fixture and junction boxes are equally easy to install at the framing-in stage. As with switch and receptacle outlets, all codes demand that fixture boxes be flush with the finished ceiling or wall surface. Junction boxes, on the other hand, are often covered. They go inside wall or ceiling cavities.

Is there a joist at the spot where you want a fixture? Boxes with a *hanger bracket* fasten to the joist as shown. Be sure to allow for the thickness of the ceiling material you'll be using. You can buy metal boxes with brackets similar to the one on this plastic version.

A *bar hanger* lets you locate a box between joists. This one adjusts to suit different joist spacings, and you can slide the box along the bar to situate your new outlet where you want it.

An *L-bracket* offers yet another way to go. Fixture boxes don't have gauging notches, so in an installation like this one you have to measure to compensate for the ceiling material's thickness.

Some junction boxes come with brackets. Others just nail or screw to a joist, stud, or rafter. Regardless of the type of box you're installing, always secure it with two fasteners. And if the box will be supporting a light fixture or other heavy object, make sure it's anchored well enough to carry the load.

3 Mounting a box on a masonry wall calls for a bit more work. Hold the box in position and mark the location of its two holes. Next, drill into the wall with a masonry bit and insert a couple of lead or plastic screw anchors. Finally, screw the box to the anchors. *(continued)*

Electrical Boxes
(continued)

Installing Boxes in Finished Space

The preceding two pages show the simple procedures involved in installing boxes in unfinished space. But most of us have to deal with the reality of finished walls and ceilings, a more challenging prospect.

How do you get at the framing and attach boxes to it without making big holes? In most instances, you don't want to make contact with the framing. Instead, simply make a hole the size of the box, then secure it to the surface. Special old-work boxes and accessories make the job easier than you might envision.

Before you begin, though, consider how you're going to get cable to the new location. Pages 183-186 show the routes you should explore.

1 Begin by making a small test hole, inserting a bent piece of wire into the wall, and rotating it as shown. If the wire hits something, move a few inches and try again. In some walls fireblocking stretches horizontally between the studs at a height of about 48 inches, just where you'd like to locate a switch. If this is the case, you'll have to install the box higher or notch it into the blocking.

2 Some old-work boxes come with a template to hold against the surface and trace around. Otherwise, use the box itself. Just make sure the box or template is level before you mark the outline of the opening.

3 Now carefully cut around the outline. If the surface is drywall, you can do this with a utility knife. In paneling or plaster, use a keyhole saw. With plaster you'll encounter wood or metal lath that also must be cut. Mask around the

outline with tape to prevent crumbling.

4 The wall opening serves as a hole in the ice for your cable-fishing expedition. Once you've pulled in the cable, attach it to the box (see page 187) and fit the box in place.

To secure it, you have several options. If the opening has paneling or sound lath around it, you probably can fasten the box's ears to the wood with screws.

Box support straps tie metal switch/receptacle boxes securely to drywall and plaster/metal lath walls. *Side-clamp* boxes grip the surface from behind when you tighten the screws. Some plastic boxes have a *spring clip*. Push the box into the opening up to its ears and the clip pops open inside the wall cavity.

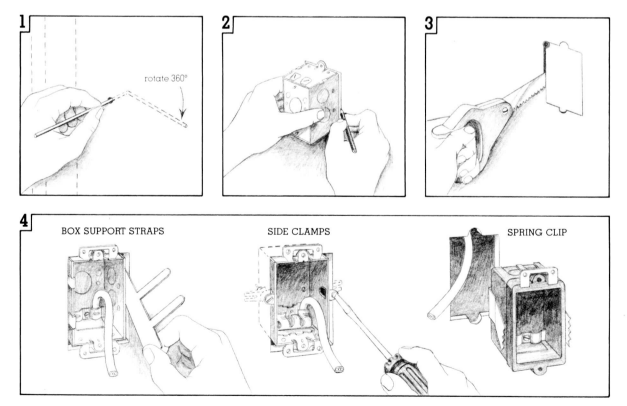

BOX SUPPORT STRAPS   SIDE CLAMPS   SPRING CLIP

5 A ceiling box has to support a fixture as well as itself, so in most cases you should fasten directly to framing. If you're fortunate enough to have attic space above, here are three ways to attach to joists.

First, mark the box's location on the ceiling and drive nails up through it to orient you upstairs. If there's a joist adjacent to the opening, nail an L-bracket box to it. If not, use a *bar hanger* or 2x4 support.

6 No access from above? Then you'll have to try one of these alternatives for your installation.

If the fixture is lightweight, such as a smoke detector, you might be able to get by with a *spring-clip* box that works just like the switch/receptacle version shown opposite. *Ceiling pan* boxes are only ½ inch deep and recess into the surface.

As a last resort, you may have to open up the ceiling and install a *bar hanger*. With drywall, cut out a rectangle. With plaster, chip a path and install an *offset hanger*.

7 After you've checked the electrical installation, patch up the ceiling opening as shown here. With drywall, you might be able to use the same piece you cut out. Make an opening for the box, nail the panel to the joists, and tape the seam with joint compound. Fill plaster with patching compound.

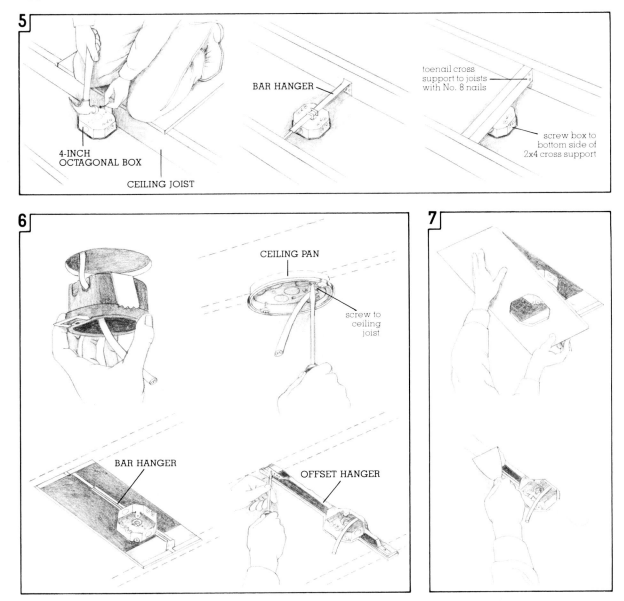

5

BAR HANGER

toenail cross support to joists with No. 8 nails

screw box to bottom side of 2x4 cross support

4-INCH OCTAGONAL BOX

CEILING JOIST

6

CEILING PAN

screw to ceiling joist

BAR HANGER

OFFSET HANGER

7

How to Work With Nonmetallic Sheathed Cable

The Paths Cable Can Travel

When is a straight line not necessarily the shortest distance between two points? Answer: When the line is an electrical cable zigzagging from one outlet to another in a circuit.

Electricity basically *wants* to zip along conductors when there's a call for its energy. Sharp turns and longer trips don't bother it. This means you can snake cable up and down walls, along or across joists, and around obstructions without worrying that you'll impede the flow.

Cable is priced by the foot, however, and extra feet can add up fast. So to be economical, you'll want to keep your runs as short as possible.

In new work, that's not too difficult. Examine the cutaway of a typical new-home installation at right, and you can see that most of the cables proceed directly to their destination.

Locating the dryer near the service panel, for instance, let the electrician minimize the amount of heavier, more costly cable needed for its 240-volt circuit, and he didn't have to bend and install much conduit to carry the wire.

Here two general-purpose circuits pop up through the *sole-plate* and take off around perimeter walls to receptacle outlets. Others follow or span floor joists. Note that a junction box such as the one shown in the foreground lets you save a considerable amount of money and effort by bringing a single three-conductor cable from the service panel to the box, then splitting off with two-wire cable where the circuits diverge.

In planning an electrical layout, especially if you'll be running more than one circuit, it helps to draw a floor plan of your home to scale, then mark in the routes cable will traverse. To estimate how much you'll need, measure the distances involved, add 10 percent for bends and unexpected detours, and another six to eight inches for each time cable will have to enter or leave a box.

If you're thinking about fishing through finished walls and ceilings, you have some detective work ahead of you, and you'll probably use more cable than you would if the framing were exposed.

Your first task is to determine exactly what's in the space you want to run cable through. Let's say, for instance, that you want to install a new appliance receptacle for an air conditioner in an exterior wall, directly above the service panel. If there's no insulation in that wall, it's easy to drop straight down to the panel. If the wall is insulated, though, the task becomes more difficult, because you'll have to work your way through the obstruction. (You'll find tricks for wiring finished spaces on pages 183-186.)

Finally, if your project will include switches, especially three-ways, brush up on switching basics (pages 156-163), and indicate on your diagram where you'll need to run three-wire cable. *(continued)*

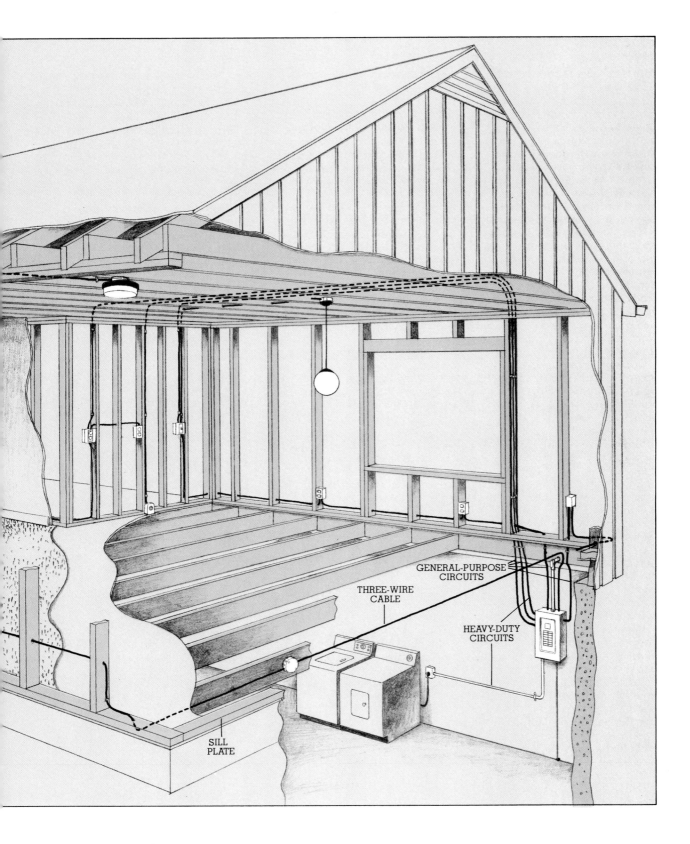

GENERAL-PURPOSE
CIRCUITS

THREE-WIRE
CABLE

HEAVY-DUTY
CIRCUITS

SILL
PLATE

Running Cable in Unfinished Space

Horizontally Through Wall Cavities

Here you have two choices: Notch the studs and run cable through the notches, as illustrated on this page, or bore holes through the studs, as shown on the opposite page.

With interior partitions you can choose either option, but you might find boring easier. On outside walls notching the studs is best. Running cables through studs would compress the insulation, reducing its effectiveness.

1 With a chisel, make a notch in each stud that's slightly larger than the cable you'll be using. At corners, two notches get you around the bend.

2 Protect cable at each notch with a 1/16-inch-thick *steel plate*. Its purpose is to ward off any nails or screws that might be driven accidentally through the wall surface, penetrate the cable, and cause a short in the circuit.

Plates like the ones shown in this sketch, which are available from electrical suppliers, have spurs top and bottom. Just drive them into the wood with a couple of hammer blows.

3 Don't try to make sharp bends with cable. Crimping it could break a conductor or damage the insulation. Instead, arc gradually around corners and up to boxes.

Secure cable with a *strap* located within 12 inches of each steel box, eight inches from nonmetallic boxes. And let six to eight inches of cable hang out so you can easily make connections in boxes later.

4 With an electric drill and a sharp spade bit, you can make holes in a hurry. Align them by eye, but be sure to bore at or near the center of each stud. Holes closer to the wall surface than 1¼

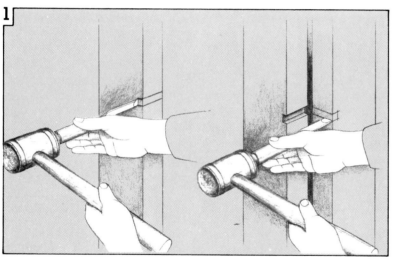

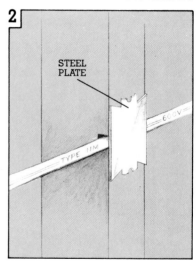

STEEL PLATE

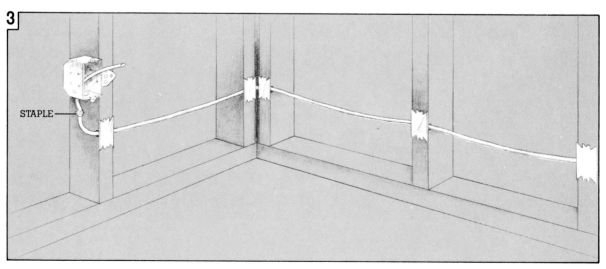

STAPLE

inches need the protection of a metal plate.

Don't holes weaken the studs? Only slightly, if at all, but to be safe use a bit just a little larger than the cable.

5 Beyond the guidelines given here, you don't need to be especially neat or exacting when running cable. Your handiwork will be covered anyway, and the current doesn't care what path it follows from one outlet to another.

Vertically Through Wall Cavities
6 Your biggest problem here is getting through the two, three, or more thicknesses of lumber at the base and/or tops of walls. A spade bit may not be long enough to do the job. If it won't penetrate, measure and bore a second hole from below or above.

Or consider investing in an electrician's bit extension, like the one shown on page 183. To use this, first bore with the spade bit alone. When you're almost to the bit's hilt, add the extension and continue. Considering the small cost of a bit extension, this is probably the best option.

A third alternative is to bore with a hand-operated brace and bit. Extensions are available for these, too.

7 On vertical runs, secure the cable with straps every 4½ feet and near changes in direction, as well as within 8 to 12 inches of boxes. You can use ordinary hammer-driven staples, too. Be careful when hammering the staples because they can damage the insulation or break a conductor. Notice here how the cable loops through the top plate to eliminate a sharp, compound bend that could conceivably cause problems. *(continued)*

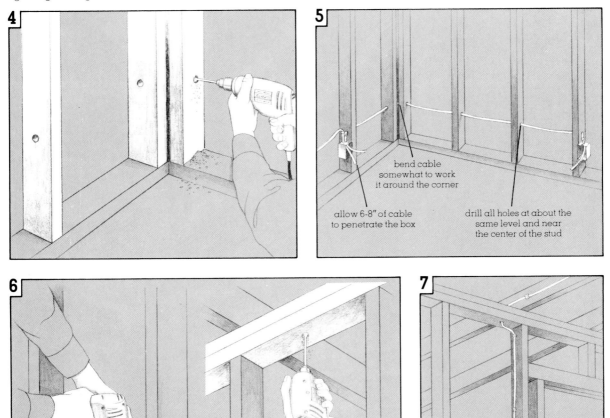

4

5
bend cable somewhat to work it around the corner

allow 6-8" of cable to penetrate the box

drill all holes at about the same level and near the center of the stud

6

7

Running Cable in Unfinished Space *(cont.)*

Through Attics and Floors

1 What you do with cable in an attic depends on how accessible and usable the attic is. If access consists of nothing more than a simple trap door in a hallway or closet ceiling, and if headroom is too limited to consider using the space for anything, you can simply staple cable to the tops of joists. If it passes within six feet of the attic opening, however, protect the cable with 1x2 *guard strips* nailed down on either side.

2 If your attic has stairs or a permanent ladder leading to it, the National Electrical Code says you must bore holes and thread cable through the joists. Do this even if you're not planning to use the attic. The next owner of your home might decide differently.

If there's flooring up there, you'll have to pull it up to install the cable or plan an alternate route along rafters and other framing. In a basement, wires should be run through conduit. (See pages 188-190 for instructions.)

3 No. 8 and larger cable, which you might use for a 240-volt appliance circuit, is too stiff to thread easily through joists, so the NEC allows you to strap it to the joists. Check your local code, however, because many require that all exposed runs be protected with conduit.

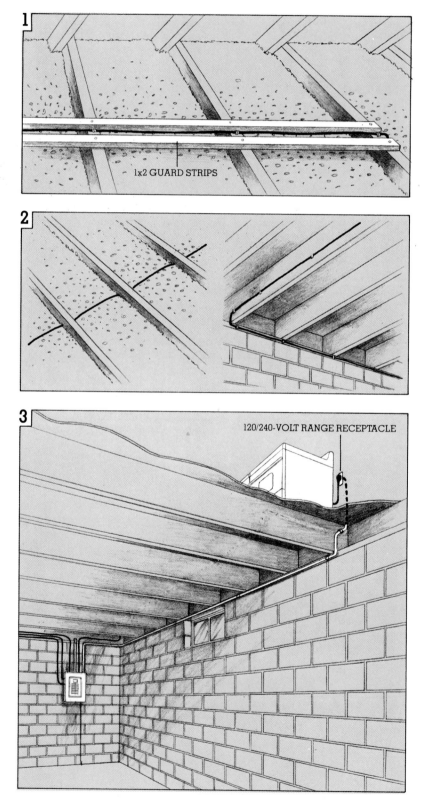

1x2 GUARD STRIPS

120/240-VOLT RANGE RECEPTACLE

Running Cable in Finished Space

Where There's Access From Above or Below

1 With most interior partitions you can simply drill through the top or bottom plates (you may need a bit extension), and feed cable up or down to the box opening. If you encounter fire blocking, see drawing No. 5.

2 In some cases you can reach the top or bottom of a wall from unfinished space, but can't get a drill at the plates. Then you have to work the other direction.

At the top of a wall make an opening as shown. At the bottom where there's only one plate, remove the baseboard and locate the cutout ¾ inch above the floor.

3 Start to bore through the corner of a plate, hitting it at about a 45-degree angle. Once the hole is started, tip the drill to a more vertical angle. After the bit is in deeply, pull out, install an extension, and continue on through.

4 Now push cable up or down to the box opening, and loop it through the plate. Pulling cable through walls is a two-person job. One tugs gently from the unfinished space, the other coils cable and feeds it through the box opening.

5 If there's blocking in the wall, locate it and make an opening that straddles the horizontal framing member. To get cable past, chisel a notch in the wood. Before you patch the hole, install a metal plate such as the ones shown on page 180.

If your walls are drywall and you've cut carefully, you can probably butter the edges of the cutouts with joint compound, plug them back into their openings, and tape the seams. In plaster walls, fill the opening with patching plaster. *(continued)*

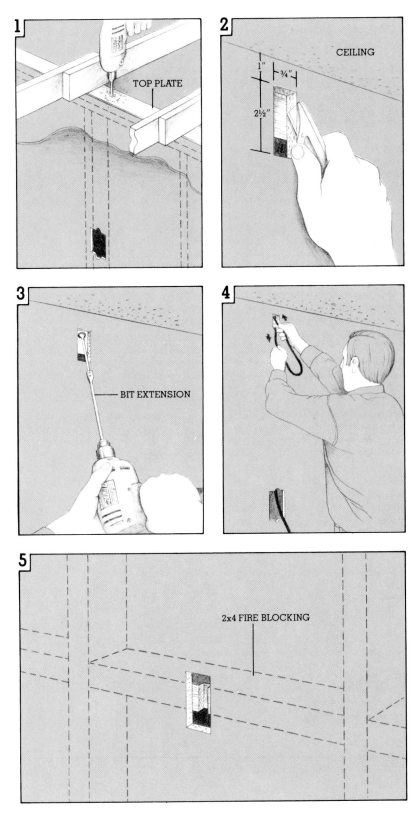

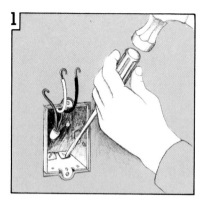

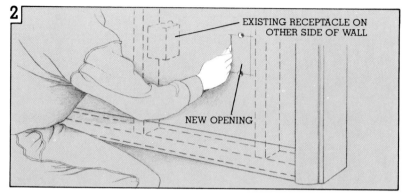

EXISTING RECEPTACLE ON
OTHER SIDE OF WALL

NEW OPENING

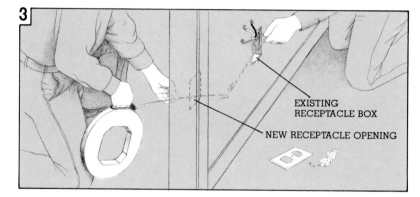

EXISTING
RECEPTACLE BOX

NEW RECEPTACLE OPENING

Running Cable in Finished Space *(continued)*

Fishing Cable from a Nearby Outlet

1 If you don't have access from un-finished space, don't despair. Power for a new outlet might be just around the corner or down the wall. First, go through the cal-culations explained on page 154 to determine whether the existing circuit can handle the new load. Next, shut off the power and check for a set of unused terminals on the receptacle you'd like to tap. If you find a pair, disconnect the device and remove a knockout, as shown here.

2 Ideally, you should situate the new outlet in the same wall cavity as the old one. If you don't, you'll have to follow a course similar to that shown on the opposite page.

3 Thread one fish tape (or a bent coat hanger) into the knockout and another through the new opening. Wiggle one or the other until you hook them together.

4 Pull the tape from the existing box though the opening and at-tach cable to it. If the new box doesn't have internal connectors, install an external type first, as explained on page 187.

5 Finally, pull cable to the old box and connect it. Install the new box and make your electrical hookups.

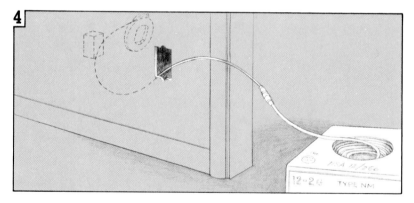

12-2 G   TYPE NM

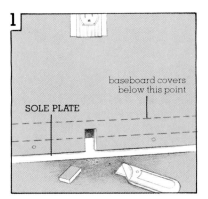

Another Way to Add Another Outlet

1 To tap an existing receptacle that's in the same room as the proposed new one, you'll have to burrow cable behind the baseboard, a job that calls mainly for patient carpentry.

The trickiest part comes first, when you have to pry trim from the wall without damaging either. Pop nails loose one at a time, wedging the wood away from the wall as you move down its length.

Once the board is free, notch wallboard or plaster beneath the outlet you'll be picking up power from. Note that when the baseboard is replaced, all scars will be covered.

2 You may find a gap at the wall's base that's big enough to accommodate the cable. If not, cut away just enough material to make a channel for it. Feed cable through a knockout in the existing box and pull it out of the wall below.

3 If your new outlet is a receptacle, you can probably just poke cable up through the wall to the opening. For a switch, you may have to fish, as shown on the opposite page.

4 To get around a door, remove its casing. Here again, there may be enough space to sneak cable through, or you may have to cut away some of the wall material. When you renail the trim, take care that you don't pierce the cable's insulation. *(continued)*

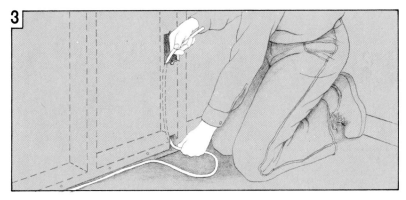

baseboard covers below this point

SOLE PLATE

Running Cable in Finished Space *(continued)*

Running Cable for a Switch-Controlled Ceiling Fixture

1 Getting cable through a finished ceiling to a new switch outlet in a finished wall calls for planning, perseverance, and a dollop of fisherman's luck.

The luck comes first when you determine which direction the ceiling joists run. That's the path your cable will have to follow. Next, cut an opening for the new outlet in line with where the switch will go, and figure out how you're going to get power to the switch. In the situation illustrated here, a receptacle is in the same wall cavity. For other possibilities, check the preceding pages.

2 At the point where the wall and ceiling meet, make ¾x4-inch openings, then chisel a channel into the plates so the cable can pass. If the room has ceiling molding, you might be able to hide your work behind it.

3 Now slowly feed fish tape to the ceiling opening. Because it's made of springy metal, the tape tends to coil up when it meets any resistance. If that happens, pull back a few feet, shake the tape, and try again. Shaking also helps locate the tape — listen carefully and you can hear it rattling.

For longer runs you might decide to use two tapes, feeding in one from either end and snagging them as shown on page 184. This part of the job can be frustrating. Keep at it, though, and sooner or later you'll bring in a catch.

4 You can probably just push the cable down through the wall. If not, work a fish tape up, and pull the cable to the switch box opening. Staple the cable into the notch in the plates before you patch up the wall and ceiling.

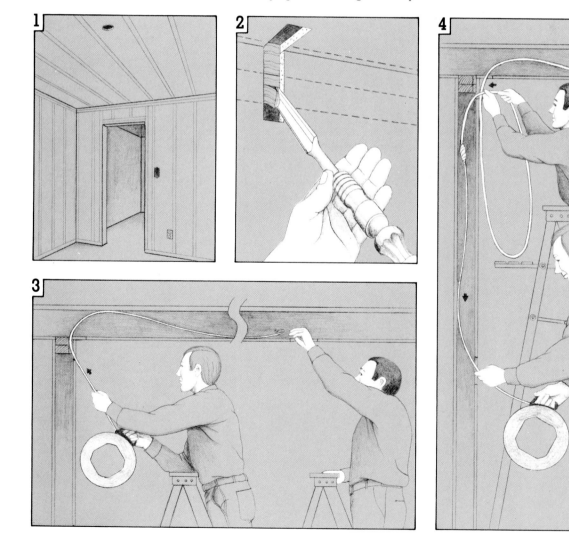

Connecting Cable to Boxes

The final step in "roughing in" an electrical installation happens when you fasten cable to the boxes. Here are the different systems you can use with Type NM wiring.

1 Slide a *clamp connector* onto the cable six to eight inches from the end and tighten its *saddle*. Then remove the *locknut*, slip the connector into a knockout, and screw the locknut back on. Finally, tighten the nut by whacking one of its lugs with a hammer and nail set.

2 A *plastic connector* is even easier to use. It snaps into the knockout, then you feed six to eight inches of cable through and secure it by turning a *capture screw*. With other types you do the same by prying up a locking wedge or squeezing the unit with a pair of pliers. A plastic connector also can be inverted and installed from inside an existing box, a big convenience in old-work situations.

3 Some boxes have internal *quick clamps*. You just pry up a spring-metal tab and slip the cable through. Codes require a connector with all metal boxes.

4 Other steel boxes for non-metallic cable come with *internal saddle clamps*. Tightening a screw grips the cable.

5 Some nonmetallic boxes have a similar internal clamp. The National Electrical Code doesn't require a clamp in a nonmetallic box, provided you secure the cable within eight inches of the box. This applies only to single boxes. You need clamps with multiple units.

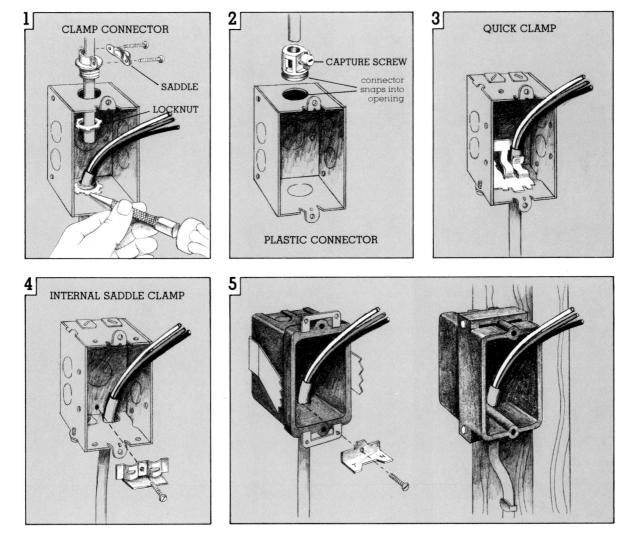

1 CLAMP CONNECTOR — SADDLE — LOCKNUT

2 CAPTURE SCREW — connector snaps into opening — PLASTIC CONNECTOR

3 QUICK CLAMP

4 INTERNAL SADDLE CLAMP

5

How to Work With Conduit

Some codes now require that conduit, not cable, be run inside the walls of a new home or addition, and almost all call for conduit in exposed locations such as unfinished garages and basements. This means that sooner or later in your electrical "career," you'll probably have to master the bending, fitting, and wire-pulling basics explained here and on pages 190-191.

Conduit has several advantages. The wires encased in the tubing can't be damaged easily. The tubing serves as a ground. And even when conduit is buried in walls, you can upgrade later by pulling new wires through.

You have to plan conduit runs carefully, however, and get the knack of bending the tubing in gentle arcs with no crimps that might impede pulling wires through.

Bending It

1 For indoor jobs, select *thinwall electrical metallic tubing* (EMT). It's sold in 10-foot sections — ½, ¾, or 1 inch in diameter — that you shape with a conduit bender.

To get conduit around a corner, first measure from the box to the top of the bend *(distance A)*, then subtract the *take-up* that will be gained by the bend *(B)*. For ½-inch conduit allow a take-up of five inches; for ¾- and 1-inch sizes, allow six and eight inches, respectively.

2 Now slip the bender onto the tubing and align it as shown.

3 With one foot on the foot piece of the bender, pull slowly and steadily on the handle. Be careful. Tugging too sharply will crimp the tubing and you'll have to start over again with another piece.

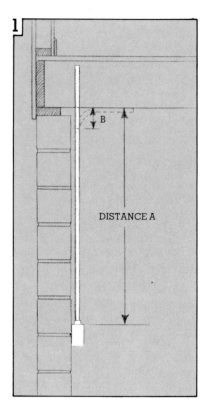

DISTANCE A

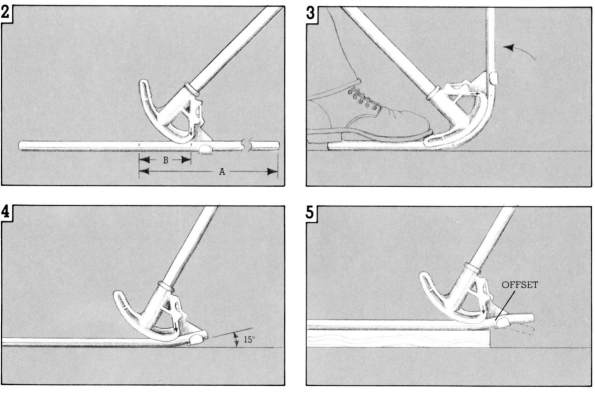

Codes don't allow crimped conduit. When the handle reaches a 45-degree angle with the floor, you've completed a 90-degree bend. Don't be surprised if your first few efforts mangle the tubing. Making smooth, crimp-free arcs takes practice.

4 If you'll be mounting conduit on a flat surface, you'll need to form *offsets* at each box. For these, first make a 15-degree bend, as shown.

5 Then flip the tubing over, move the bender a few inches farther down, and pull until the conduit is parallel with the floor. Offsets must be aligned in relation to any other bends in the tubing. With some brands, a stripe along the length of each section helps you do this.

Codes forbid a total of more than 360 degrees in bends along any run. This limits you to four 90-degree quarter-bends, three if you'll have offsets at the ends.

Changing Direction Without Bending

6 If you have more than three or four turns to negotiate, plug in a junction box. It lets you start another run. More boxes and fewer bends make wire-pulling much easier.

7 If you don't feel you want to tackle bending an offset, use an *offset connector*. These save effort, but you still must account for them in tallying up bends. Assign each a value of 45 degrees.

8 A *pulling elbow* is just the thing for negotiating corners. Its removable cover allows you to pull wires through it easily. But don't make connections inside; wires must pass through without a break.

Cutting Conduit

9 Rather than trying to compute exact take-up distances for each quarter-bend and offset, you may want to start with a section of conduit that is six or eight inches longer than the run's lineal distance, make your bends, then cut a few inches off each end.

A hacksaw makes short work of cutting conduit. To keep the tubing from rolling as you saw, hold it against a cleat, as shown. Or use a miter box, which also ensures square cuts. Hacksaw blades with 32 teeth per inch work best for cutting conduit.

10 Stick a file, reamer, or edge of a screwdriver into the cut tubing end and rotate to remove sharp burrs that could chew up insulation.

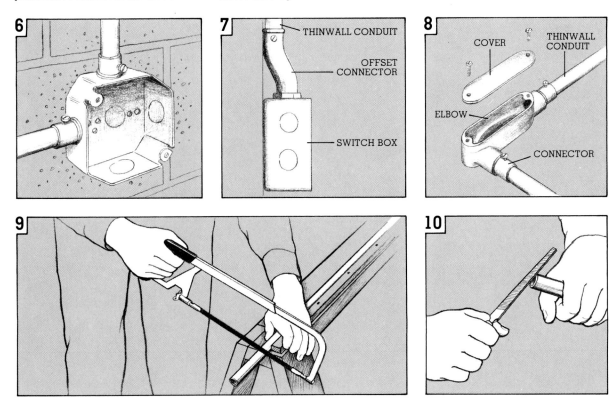

How to Work With Conduit *(continued)*

Joining and Supporting It

1 Pulling wires through conduit sometimes subjects components to stress. And because good grounding depends on secure metal-to-metal connections, you need to make sure your installation is mechanically strong. To join sections end to end, use one of the *couplings* shown here.

2 Anchor runs with a *strap* every 10 feet and within three feet of boxes. In masonry walls, use screws and plastic anchors. The barbed strap drives into framing.

To mount conduit inside walls, you can bore holes in the studs, as shown on page 180), or notch framing and protect the tubing with metal plates (see page 181). Make all connections before securing boxes to the framing.

Connecting It to Boxes

3 *Connectors* differ mainly in the way they attach to the tubing. With the *setscrew* type, you slip on the connector and tighten the screw. *Compression* connectors require a wrench; *indenters,* a special crimping tool.

All three attach to the box with the same stud and locknut arrangement used with cable connectors. You insert the stud into a knockout, turn the locknut finger-tight, then hit the nut with a hammer and nail set until its lugs bite into the box.

Another version, the *90-degree angle* connector, not surprisingly makes a 90-degree connection possible. Don't forget to count it as a quarter-bend.

A *two-piece* connector comes in handy when you need to conserve space in a box. Instead of a locknut, it has a slotted compression fitting. As you tighten the nut, the fitting squeezes the conduit.

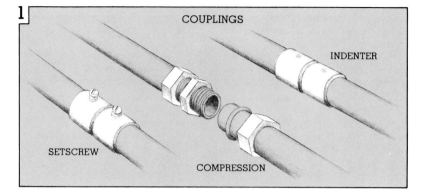

COUPLINGS

INDENTER

SETSCREW

COMPRESSION

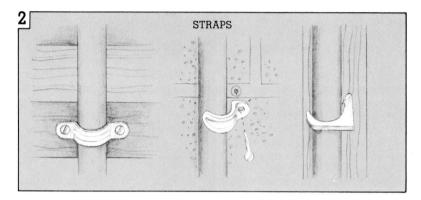

CONNECTORS

SETSCREW   COMPRESSION   INDENTER

90 DEGREE ANGLE   TWO-PIECE

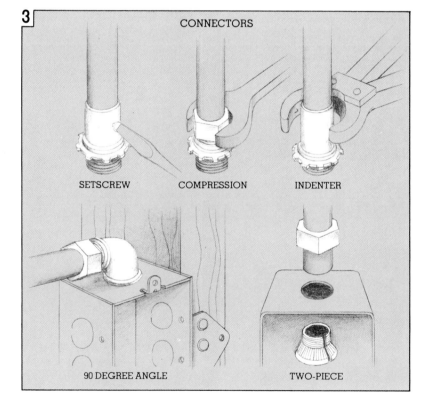

STRAPS

Pulling Wires Through Conduit

1 Now comes the moment when you realize why codes are so specific about bends, crimps, and burrs in tubing. Any hangups can lacerate insulation or even make it impossible to get wires through at all. Just how difficult your "pull" will be depends largely on how far you have to go. For a relatively short, straight run such as this, you probably can push the wires from one box to the other.

Use Type TW conductors, one black, one white, plus other colors for the hot legs of any additional circuits. Feed them carefully to protect insulation.

2 If you can't push the wires, you'll need a fish tape and a helper. Snake the tape through the conduit, then secure wires to it as shown here.

3 Now begin pulling with gentle pressure. As the wires work past bends, expect to exert more muscle. If you have lots of wires or a long pull, lubricate the wires with talcum powder or pulling grease (sold by electrical suppliers).

4 Leave six to eight inches of extra wire at each box. And never splice wires inside conduit. They must run continuously from box to box. To learn about connecting wires, see pages 196-199.

How many wires can you pull through conduit? Codes are surprisingly optimistic about this, and allow more than you can expect to stuff into a run. As a rule of thumb, you should be able to get four No. 12 wires through a short, straight section of ½-inch tubing. With bends or offsets, reduce to three or use ¾-inch conduit. Subtract one wire for each increase in wire size; add one for each increase in tubing diameter.

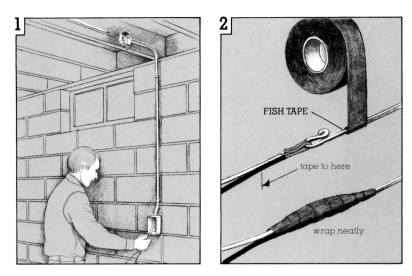

FISH TAPE

tape to here

wrap neatly

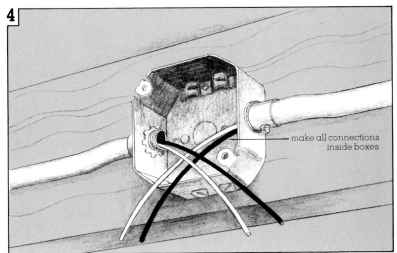

make all connections inside boxes

How to Work With Flexible Armored Cable (BX) and Flexible Metallic Conduit (Greenfield)

In many localities, armored cable and flexible conduit are orphans. You might find one or the other in an older home, but not be permitted to use it for new work. A few other communities insist that you run *only* armored, not nonmetallic cable. Check codes in your area.

Cutting Techniques

1 The first special twist you'll notice about these products is the steel covering. To get through it, hold a hacksaw at a right angle to the spirals and cut partway through the armor. With cable be especially careful not to nick insulation on the conductors inside. With Greenfield, there aren't any conductors inside.

2 Now twist the armor and it will snap free. The paper-wrapped conductors (and an aluminum *bonding strip*, if there is one) can be snipped with ordinary wire cutters. To expose the conductors for connections, cut only the sheathing at a second point about a foot away, then snap and twist off the armor.

Installation Pointers

3 and 4 Run armored cable and flexible conduit just as you would nonmetallic cable, threading it through holes or plate-protected notches in studs and other framing members. BX and Greenfield are much heavier and stiffer than NM, so you need to change directions gradually.

Like NM, armored cable usually is used only in concealed loca-tions, but you can take advantage of its flexibility in exposed runs of up to 24 inches. Furnace motors often are connected this way to compensate for vibration.

5 Support metal-clad cable with *straps* or *staples* every 4½ feet and within 12 inches of boxes. If you're fishing through existing walls or ceilings, you won't be able to do this, of course, but secure the run as best you can.

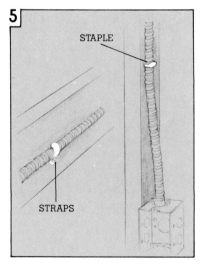

BONDING STRIP

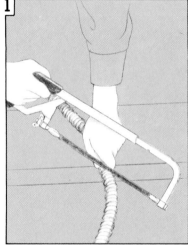

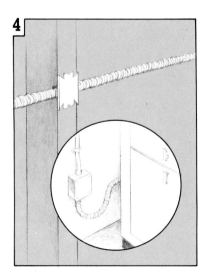

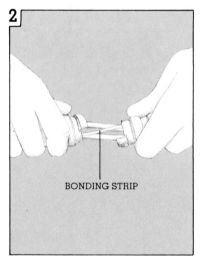

STAPLE

STRAPS

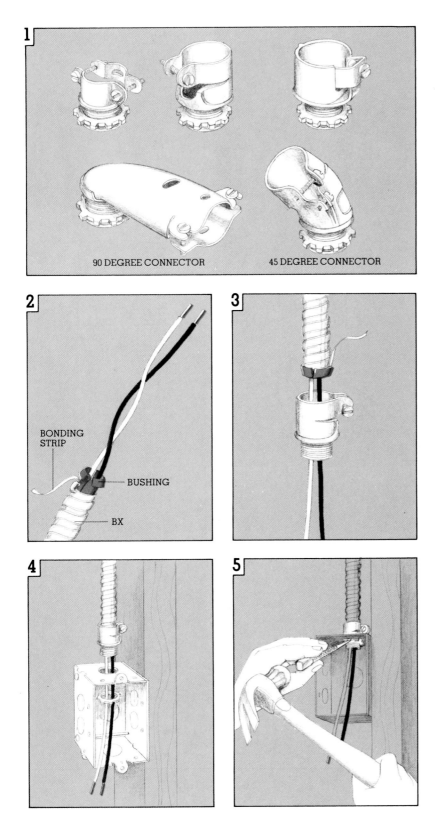

90 DEGREE CONNECTOR   45 DEGREE CONNECTOR

BONDING STRIP

BUSHING

BX

Connecting BX and Greenfield to Boxes

1 The important thing to remember when you're hooking up to armored cable or flexible metal conduit is that the wires must be protected against the armor's sharp edges.

One way to safeguard the wires is to install an *anti-short bushing*, as shown in sketch 2. With these you use peephole connectors that let inspectors verify that there's a bushing inside. If you'd rather not bother with bushings, spend a bit more and buy *insulated-throat* connectors (not shown). *Right-angle* and *45-degree* connectors come insulated and non-insulated.

2 When you pull off the brown paper that surrounds the wires in BX cable, try to rip it back an inch or so inside the armor. This leaves room to slip in a bushing. If the cable you're using has a bonding strip, fold it back as shown.

3 Now just slip on a connector and secure the bonding strip to the connector's tightening screw. Check to be sure the bushing is in place, then tighten the screw. As with rigid conduit, flexible conduit and armored cable are self-grounding. You don't need a third wire with them.

4 Slip the wires and connector into a knockout, slip on a locknut, and turn it finger-tight. As with all wiring, connections can be made only in boxes.

5 Draw the locknut snug with a hammer and nail set. Finally, tug on the cable to be sure everything is securely fastened.

Your Switch and Receptacle Options

If you've always thought that a switch is a switch and a receptacle is a receptacle, prepare for a surprise. The array illustrated here represents only a sampling of the dozens of different UL-approved devices offered by electrical equipment manufacturers.

Some of the alternatives are strictly color choices. Besides brown and ivory, most also come in white, and some in black, gray, even red, yellow, blue, and other hues, with wall plates to match.

Many of the differences are more than decorative, however. Let's take a look at them.

1 For most of your switching needs, you'll probably choose a *single-pole toggle*. Standard toggles, the ones that flip on and off with a loud snap, are all but obsolete in home wiring installations. Today's *quiet* switches operate with a scarcely audible click. And *silent* switches, some of them illuminated so you can find them in the dark, turn on and off with no noise whatsoever.

Three- and *four-*way toggle switches are available in quiet and silent versions. To learn about wiring these, see pages 160-163. *Push* switches come with one or two buttons. The single-button version is a quiet type; the two-button is silent.

Looking for something a bit more decorative? Select a *rocker*. Keep in mind, however, that you'll pay a premium for their sleekness. *Tamperproof* switches can only be operated with a key. These make special sense for shop tools and other devices you don't want kids to play with.

Dimmers let you adjust lighting levels to suit your mood and needs. The *rotary* type comes in two versions. One turns incandescent lights on or off with a push. The other does the same when you turn the control fully counterclockwise. Just a tap of your fingers operates a *touch* dimmer; holding them on the switch a little longer adjusts the brightness.

To add another switch in a single box, get a *double*. It takes up no more space than a standard receptacle.

2 Have you ever noticed that the left and right slots in a receptacle are different sizes? That's because plugs on some appliances are *polarized* so they'll be grounded through the neutral side of the circuit. Standards by Underwriters Laboratories and the National Electrical Code now require that lamp cords also be polarized.

Duplex receptacles let you plug two items into the same outlet. Many newer homes have *20-amp grounded* types. With aluminum wiring, use only *15-amp* types labeled *CO/ALR*. If your outlet boxes aren't grounded, install *15-amp ungrounded* receptacles. These are made only for replacements in existing circuits.

The switch in a combination *switch/receptacle* can be hooked up to control the receptacle it's paired with or another outlet elsewhere. A *20-amp single* makes it all but impossible to overload a critical circuit. Get a *twist-lock* version and an appliance can't be accidentally disconnected, either.

Select *240-volt* receptacles according to the appliance's amperage rating. Plugs for appliances of 15, 20, 30, and 50 amps have different blade configurations.

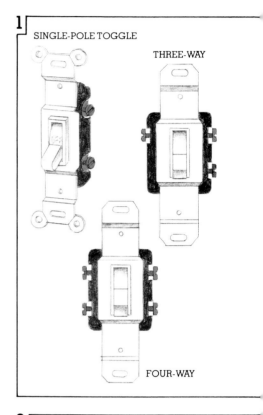

1 SINGLE-POLE TOGGLE

THREE-WAY

FOUR-WAY

2 20-A GROUNDED

15-A GROUNDED

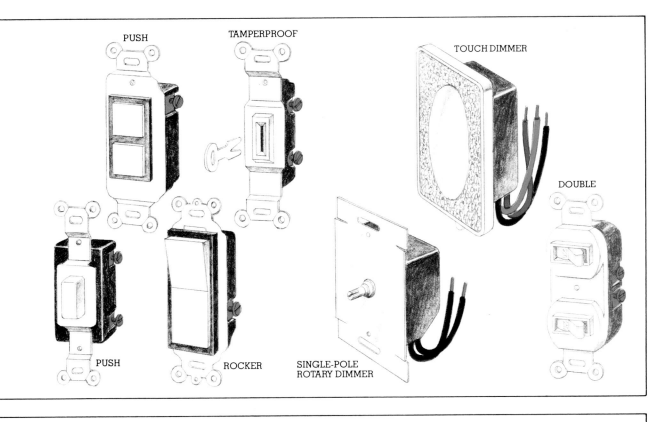

PUSH

TAMPERPROOF

TOUCH DIMMER

DOUBLE

PUSH

ROCKER

SINGLE-POLE
ROTARY DIMMER

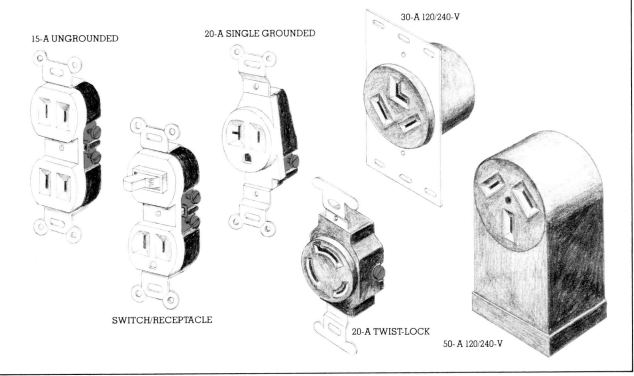

15-A UNGROUNDED

20-A SINGLE GROUNDED

30-A 120/240-V

SWITCH/RECEPTACLE

20-A TWIST-LOCK

50- A 120/240-V

Making Electrical Connections

The final (and most fun) phase of an electrical installation comes when you tie all the wires you've run to each other and to the switches, light fixtures, and receptacles they'll be supplying. Here's how to strip away insulation and make the right connections.

Stripping Cable

1 The easiest way to remove the plastic sheath from nonmetallic sheathed cable is with an inexpensive *cable ripper*. (You may find it easier to strip the cable before connecting it to the box.) Slip six to eight inches of cable into the ripper's jaws, squeeze, and pull. This slits open the sheathing without damaging insulation on the conductors inside.

2 Now peel back the sheathing and any paper or other filler material. You'll find two or three separately insulated conductors and a bare ground.

3 Cut off the insulation and paper with a utility knife. Nicking the insulation on the conductors could cause a short, so always cut away from them. Leave at least ¼ inch of sheathing inside the outlet box.

4 You can also strip sheathing with a utility knife. Make a shallow, lengthwise cut down the center, as shown. Again, take care to avoid cutting into the conductor insulation. Remove the sheathing and paper as shown in sketch 3.

To learn about removing the sheathing from armored cable, see page 192. Single-conductor wires that run inside conduit have no sheathing. With these you strip the conductors as shown in sketches 5 and 6.

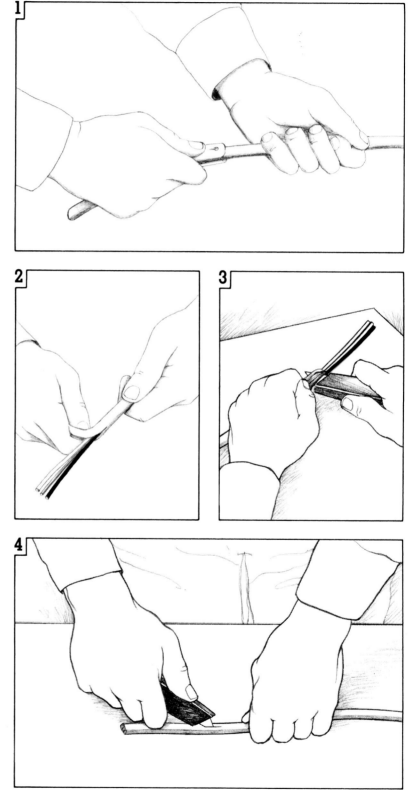

5 A *combination tool* makes short work of insulation removal. Locate the size of the wire on its jaws, clamp down, pull the tool away from you, and the covering pops off. Some cable rippers can strip in much the same way.

6 You can also remove insulation with a sharp knife. Start the cut at an angle so you don't nick the wire, then peel off the insulation. You'll have to use this technique to strip wires larger than No. 6.

Connecting Wires to Each Other

7 To splice two or more wires, a *solderless connector* is your best bet. Some screw on, others must be crimped (use the crimping jaws of your combination tool), still others have a setscrew and threaded sleeve. Check your code to learn which type is preferred in your community.

With all but the setscrew variety, hold the wires side by side, twist them together, and turn or crimp on a connector. Make sure that no bare conductors are exposed and that all wires are locked in.

Solderless connectors come in a variety of color-coded sizes to suit the gauges and numbers of wires you'll be splicing.

8 A few codes require that all splices be soldered. Others prohibit soldering house wiring. Again, you start by twisting together the wires.

9 Next, heat them with a soldering iron and melt rosin-core solder over the splice. Soldering requires some practice, but once you master the knack of flowing on just enough to do the job, it goes quickly.

10 After the solder cools, wrap the splice with electrical tape. Cover about an inch of insulation as well as the bared conductors. Some electricians also tape solderless connectors. *(continued)*

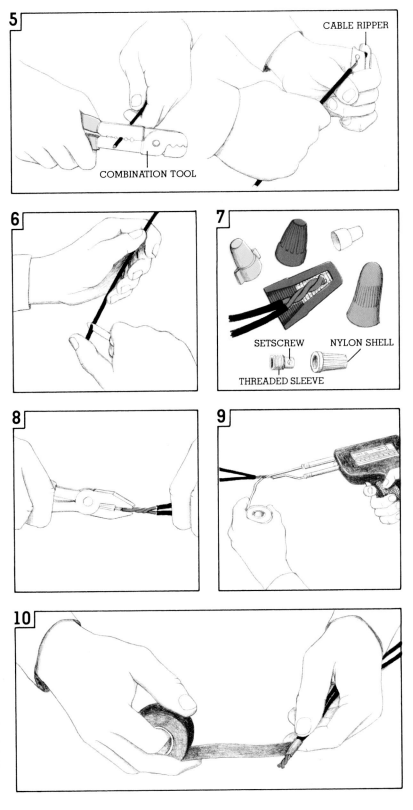

Connecting Wires to Each Other *(continued)*

11 If you attempt to splice a stranded wire to a solid conductor, as you might have to when you're hooking up a light fixture or dimmer switch, you'll discover that the more flexible stranded material bunches up when you try to screw on a connector. To make a more secure connection, first wrap the stranded wire around the solid one, as shown.

12 Then bend the solid conductor over the wrap. Finally, turn on a solderless connector and tape any wire that shows.

Connecting Wires to Switches and Receptacles

1 Many of today's receptacles and switches offer a choice of connections. You can strip wires and push them into holes in the rear of the device, or wrap the conductors around screw terminals on the sides.

   Push-ins have a slight edge in convenience. On the back of the device you'll find a *strip gauge* that indicates exactly how much insulation to remove.

2 Insert the bare wires into the holes and push until a metal spring grips them. With receptacles, holes on the neutral side will be marked *white*. Because switches connect only to hot wires, it doesn't matter which holes you use.

3 To disconnect a push-in, insert stiff wire or the blade of a small screwdriver into the slot next to the terminal. If you've inadvertently bared more wire than necessary, either release the wire and snip off the extra, or, if you'd rather, wrap the exposed section with electrical tape.

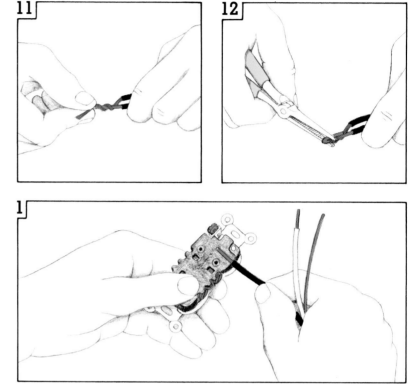

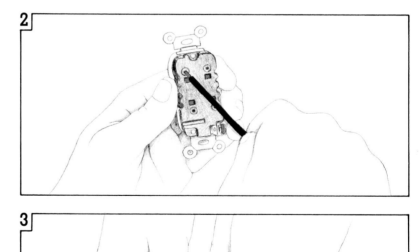

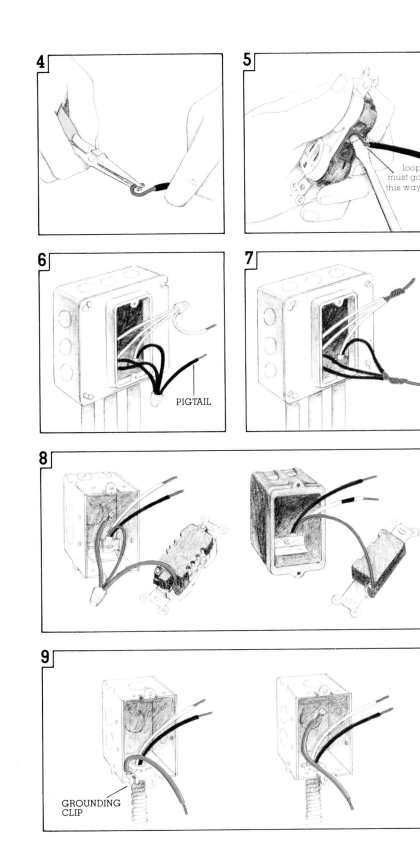

4 With screw terminal-type devices, you bare just enough wire to wrap around the terminal, then form it into a loop with long-nose pliers. It takes practice to make loops that are neither too big nor too small and that lie flat.

5 Always hook the wire clockwise around the terminal so that tightening the screw will close the loop. With receptacles, the black wires go to the brass side, white to silver. Don't overtighten the screws, because if you crack a device, you have to throw it out.

6 Never attach more than one wire to a terminal. Codes don't allow it. Instead, you can connect two or more wires with a third short one to make the *pigtail* shown here. In computing the permitted number of wires in a box (see page 172), count each pigtail as one.

7 Or you can twist the wires for this special splice. It must be soldered and taped, and also gets a value of one in your wires-in-the-box calculations.

8 How you ground receptacles and switches depends on the type of wiring you're using as well as the type of box. If you're working with nonmetallic sheathed cable and metal boxes, use the arrangement shown in the left-hand portion of the sketch. With non-metallic boxes, the cable's grounding wire connects directly to the device, as shown at right.

9 With armored cable and flexible or rigid conduit, the metal covering serves as the grounding wire. For these, just run a green or bare wire from the device's grounding screw to a screw in the box, or secure it to the box with a *grounding clip*. More about grounding on pages 137, 149, 164, 165, and 169.

BASIC PLUMBING

Probably you've always been one of those "leave plumbing to the plumbers" kind of people. Most, in fact, go that route whenever they need plumbing-repair work or a plumbing improvement in their home.

So why your sudden interest in learning how to be your own plumber? Perhaps you have a repair or two to make and can't seem to find anyone willing to do the work for a reasonable price. Or maybe you've just received a higher-than-expected bid on a bathroom or kitchen remodel-

ing. Whatever your motivation, the simple fact is that today you pay "the price" for what you can't do yourself.

The idea of doing plumbing projects yourself rather than having a professional do the work can be overwhelming at first. That's why we begin by discussing the system itself. It's here you'll realize that the whole is simply the sum of its parts and that with the proper groundwork you can attack this or that problem or tackle most plumbing improvements and come away successful.

Then, after a brief discussion of the tools of the plumbing trade you need to become familiar with, we move on to a section titled "Solving Plumbing Problems" where we discuss some common plumbing problems you are likely to have to deal with. Here you'll learn how to open clogged drains and to repair leaky and frozen pipes, faucets, toilets, and water heaters, as well as how to troubleshoot food waste disposals and to quiet noisy pipes.

The next major section of the book, "Making Plumbing Improvements," focuses on a good number of popular plumbing projects. In it you'll find step-by-step instructions and sketches showing how to install wall- and deck-mount faucets, fixture stop valves, lavatories and kitchen sinks, toilets, and several more projects. And if you have some big plumbing plans, we've included information about extending existing supply and drain lines.

Next comes "Plumbing Basics and Procedures" where we tell how to choose the right pipe materials and fittings, how to measure pipes and fittings, and how to work with the various types of pipe. References to this basics section appear at appropriate junctures throughout.

Working to Code

Your responsibilities as an amateur plumber mirror those of a licensed tradesman—to provide for a supply of pure and wholesome water, and for safe passage of liquids, solid wastes, and gases to the outside. That means you must work to code, using only those techniques and materials regarded by the codes as acceptable.

The procedures in this book represent the editors' understanding of the 1982 Uniform Plumbing Code (UPC). (Canadian residents may obtain a copy of the Canadian Plumbing Code by writing the National Research Council of Canada, Ottawa, Ontario, Canada, K1A0R6.) Local codes and ordinances take precedence; so check with local officials to make sure you are complying with their guidelines. Check also to see whether your project requires a permit and any inspections.

GETTING TO KNOW YOUR SYSTEM

Because most of your home's plumbing components are hidden behind or under finish materials, about all you see are the fixtures and an occasional pipe disappearing into a wall or floor.

But these are only the tip of the plumbing system iceberg. The anatomy sketch at right depicts the elements common to all residential plumbing networks. Note that the *supply lines* and the *drain-waste-vent lines* act independently of each other.

Water enters your house by way of a sizable pipe that connects to a municipal water line or to a private well. If you have city water, it flows through a *meter* that monitors usage.

From there, it travels to the *water heater.* Water from a private system goes to a *pressure tank* before going to the heater.

From the water heater, a pair of water lines—one hot and one cold—branch out through the house to serve the various fixtures and water-using appliances. These supply lines are under pressure. Note the *stop valves* at the meter, the water heater, and the various fixtures and appliances. These enable you to shut down part or all of the system to make repairs or improvements. (If your lines aren't equipped with stop valves, see pages 244–245.)

The drain-waste-vent portion of your plumbing system depends on gravity to help rid the house of liquids and solid wastes. These lines also serve as a passageway to the outside for foul-smelling and potentially harmful gases. Note that all of the fixtures except the toilet empty into a *trap.* Water here forms an airtight seal that prevents gases from backing up and leaking into the house.

From the trap, wastes travel through pipes sloped at no less than ¼ inch per foot to the larger *main drain,* then down and out of the house to a sanitary sewer, septic tank, or cesspool. Toilets, which are trapped internally, drain directly into the main drain.

One or more *cleanouts* in the main drain allow you to gain access for clearing clogged lines. Traps serve the same function for clearing fixture drains.

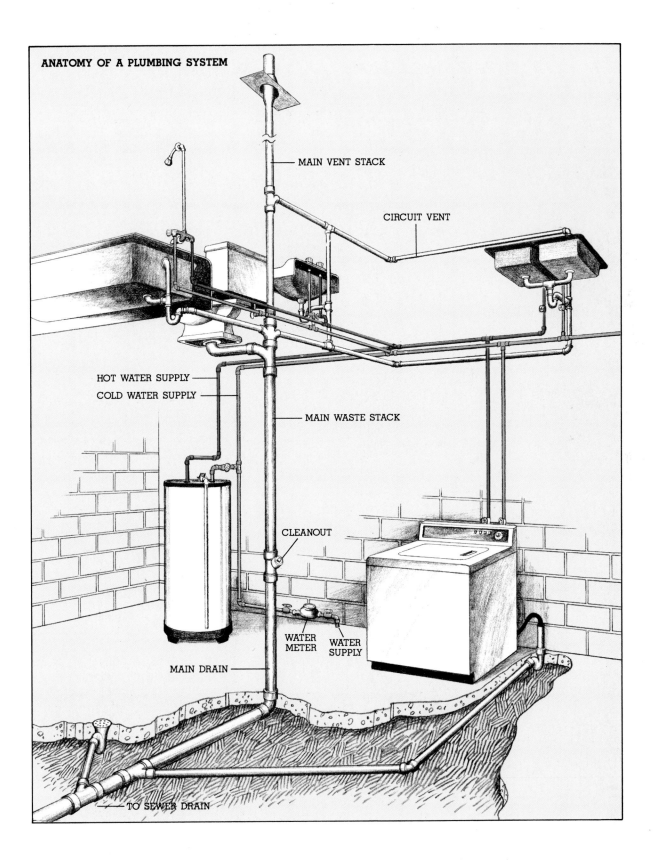

ANATOMY OF A PLUMBING SYSTEM

MAIN VENT STACK

CIRCUIT VENT

HOT WATER SUPPLY

COLD WATER SUPPLY

MAIN WASTE STACK

CLEANOUT

WATER METER

WATER SUPPLY

MAIN DRAIN

TO SEWER DRAIN

TOOLS FOR PLUMBING WORK

Ask anyone in the plumbing trade and he'll tell you that having the right tool for the job is a must. Without it, even simple tasks become difficult. The same applies to you as a do-it-yourself plumber. Fortunately, though, you probably have many of the tools shown here. Purchase the others if and when they're needed.

To clear drain lines—the most common of plumbing maladies—you'll need a *plunger* (or force cup), a *drain auger* for blockages that won't yield to plunging, and a pair of *rib-joint* or other type of *pliers* to remove the fixture's trap, if necessary. A *closet auger*, with its specially formed head, makes quick work of clearing blocked toilet traps.

For faucet and other repairs, make sure you have: *rib-joint pliers* or an *adjustable-end wrench* and a couple of *screwdrivers* (and possibly an *allen wrench*) to remove faucet han-

dles, spouts, and seat washers; a *seat cutter* to renew pitted seats; and a *seat wrench* to remove hopelessly worn-out faucet seats. You'll find a *basin wrench* handy, too, as it allows easy access to otherwise hard-to-get-at nuts. In addition to these tools, have penetrating oil on hand to loosen stubborn nuts or screws. Also have an assortment of washers and O rings to replace defective ones.

Adding to, modifying, or repairing your home's plumbing lines calls for a different set of tools. *Calipers* help you determine both inside and outside pipe diameters. *Tubing cutters* make clean cuts in copper pipe and flexible copper tubing. For limited-space situations, you'll find a *mini-cutter* the ideal tool for cutting copper.

Bending flexible copper tubing to the desired shape is

easy with a flexible *tubing bender*. And to prepare this material for a flare joint, you'll need a *flaring tool*.

The only tool required for soldering copper pipe is a *propane torch*. But to ready the pipe for soldering, you'll need emery cloth to remove oxidation, flux to allow for free flow of the solder and to aid the bonding process, and solder to seal the joint.

A *hacksaw* or a *close-quarters hacksaw* makes an easier chore of sawing through threaded or plastic pipe. And to disengage or join lengths of threaded pipe, get yourself a couple of *pipe wrenches*. Materials to have when working with threaded or plastic pipe are penetrating oil, joint compound or pipe tape, and solvent for joining plastic pipe.

And if you ever need to cut into cast-iron pipe, rent a *cutter* specially designed for this purpose. It is shown on page 256.

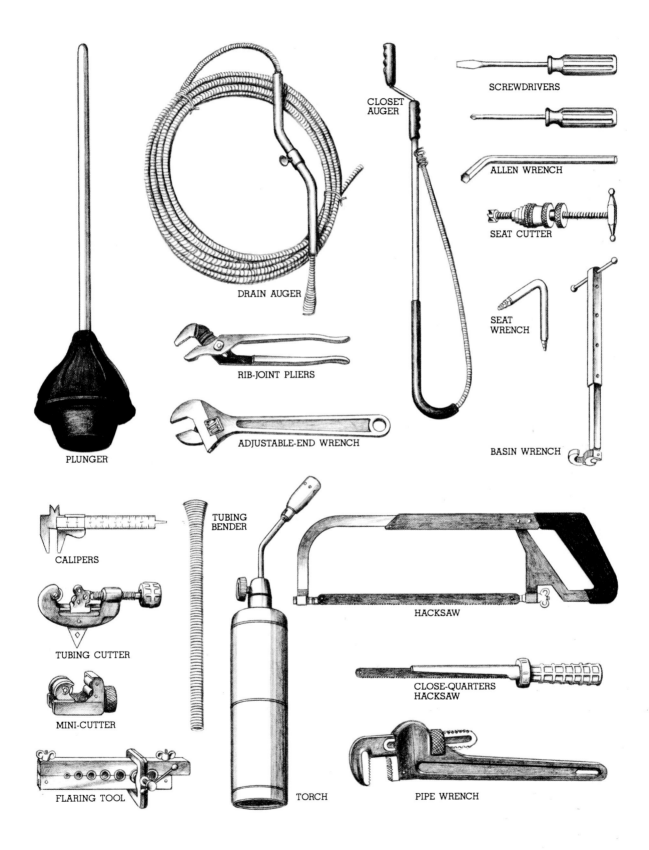

SCREWDRIVERS

ALLEN WRENCH

CLOSET AUGER

SEAT CUTTER

SEAT WRENCH

DRAIN AUGER

RIB-JOINT PLIERS

BASIN WRENCH

ADJUSTABLE-END WRENCH

PLUNGER

CALIPERS

TUBING BENDER

HACKSAW

TUBING CUTTER

CLOSE-QUARTERS HACKSAW

MINI-CUTTER

FLARING TOOL

TORCH

PIPE WRENCH

SOLVING PLUMBING PROBLEMS

Maybe you haven't been confronted yet by a stopped-up drain, a dripping faucet, or a gurgling toilet. But be assured: Sooner or later the law of plumbing averages will catch up with you.

Try to get someone to your home to fix one of these everyday nuisances, and you'll discover a second fact of contemporary life: The repair doesn't come cheap. When you have a plumbing contractor do the work for you, you're paying not only for his expertise, but also for a portion of the overhead involved in running his business. That's why it's not uncommon to pay $25 or more for even the simplest repair—one you may have been able to deal with yourself for a few cents.

With a few basic tools and elementary know-how, you often can handle many jobs yourself in fairly short order. For example, once you know of the existence of a *retrieving tool*, you can fish a ring or other item out of a drain as shown at left without the panic usually associated with these situations.

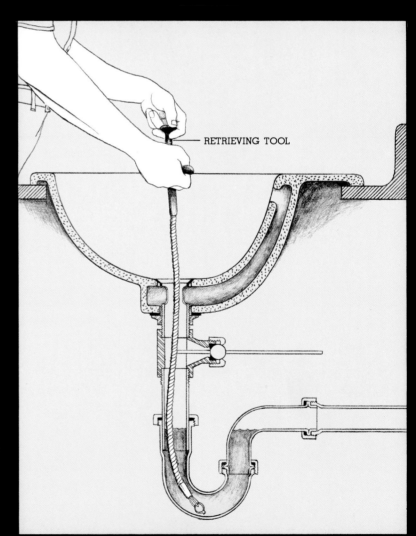

RETRIEVING TOOL

Opening Clogged Drains

When a fixture stops up, you'll naturally want to take immediate action. But before you rush at the problem with a plunger or auger, take a moment to analyze where the blockage seems to be.

Check the anatomy drawing on page 203, and note that your home has three types of drains.

Fixture drains have a trap and short sections of pipe on either side; *main drains* collect waste from all the fixture drains; and a *sewer drain* carries liquid and solid waste out of the house and to a community sewer, cesspool, or septic tank.

Nine times out of ten, the problem will be close to a fixture. To verify your suspicions, check other drains in your home. If more than one won't clear, something is stuck in a main drain. If no drains work, the problem is farther down the line, and you'll have to continue investigating.

Sinks and Lavatories

1 Clearing a sink or lavatory may involve nothing more than removing the strainer or stopper from the bowl's drain opening—a job that's generally as fast as it is easy. Bits of soap, hair, food matter, or other debris here may be the culprit.

Kitchen sink strainer baskets simply lift out. Some lavatory stoppers do, too. (See page 213 for a look at a typical lavatory.) Others require a slight turn before lifting. With a few, you must reach under the sink and remove a pivot rod.

2 A plunger uses water pressure to blast out obstructions. This means its rubber cup must seal tightly around the drain opening before you begin working the handle up and down. (Water in the bowl helps create this seal.) Stuff a rag in the overflow outlet of lavatories in order that the pressure can build and free the blocked passage.

3 If plunging doesn't work, fit an auger down the drain. Cranking its handle rotates a stiff spring that bores through a stubborn blockage. If this doesn't get results, dismantle the trap as shown on page 212, and auger the drainpipe that goes into the wall or floor.

Note: Chemical cleaners can sometimes speed up a slow-draining sink or lavatory, but don't dump them into one that's totally clogged. If they don't clear the drain, your problem is compounded by dangerously caustic water.

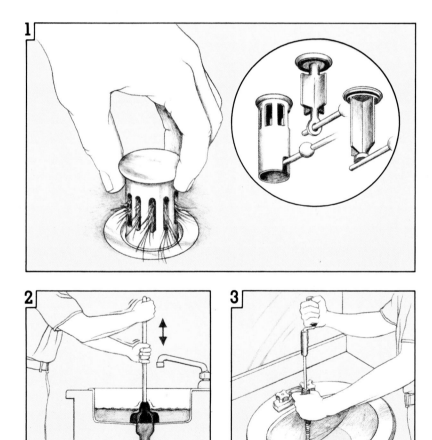

Opening Clogged Drains *(continued)*

Tubs and Showers

1 If a tub drain clogs, reach first for your plunger. If your tub has a *pop-up stopper,* you must remove it before plunging. Wiggling helps free the floppy linkage assembly.

Before you plunge, plug up the overflow, and allow an inch or so of water to accumulate in the tub (this helps seal the rubber cup around the tub outlet). As you work the plunger up and down, you will hear water surging back and forth in the drain.

2 If plunging doesn't do the trick, thread in an auger. If there's no stopper in evidence, you have a *trip-lever assembly,* like the one illustrated below, left. With this type, pry up or unscrew the *strainer* so you can insert the auger.

If you can get only a few inches of the auger into the drain and that doesn't clear it, then the problem is in the tub's trap directly below the overflow. To clear it, you'll have to follow a different route.

The best way to approach most tub traps is down through the *overflow tube.* This involves removing the pop-up or trip-lever assembly, which you do by unscrewing the overflow plate and pulling out the conglomeration of parts attached to it. (For more about pop-up and trip-lever assemblies, turn to page 213.)

Now feed the auger down through the overflow and into the trap. Cranking the auger all the way through the trap usually will clear the drain. If not, you'll have to remove the trap or a cleanout plug at its lowermost point, and auger toward the main drain. With a second-floor tub, this may involve making a hole in the ceiling below.

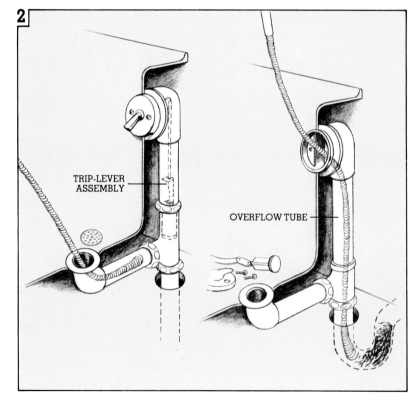

POP-UP STOPPER

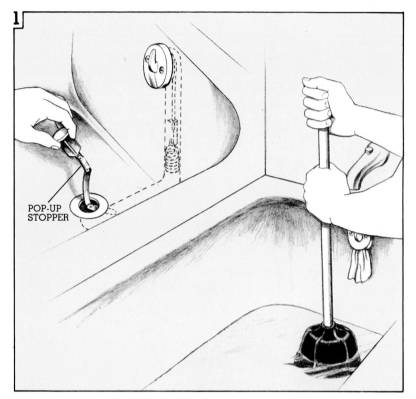

TRIP-LEVER ASSEMBLY

OVERFLOW TUBE

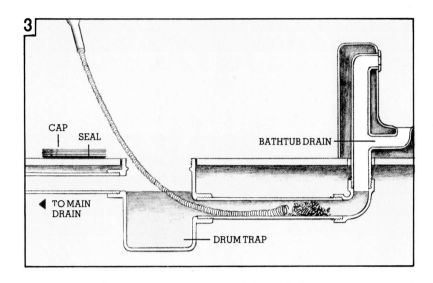

3 If there's a removable metal cap in the floor beside your tub, your tub is equipped with a *drum trap*. To free up one of these, begin by bailing out the tub; use rags or old towels to soak up any remaining water. Otherwise, the trap could flood over when you remove the cap.

Loosen it slowly, watching for water welling up around the threads. If this happens, mop up as you go. After you've removed the cap and its rubber seal, work the auger away from the tub, toward the main drain.

If, on the other hand, the trap is only partially full, as shown here, the obstruction is between the tub and trap, and you should auger toward the tub.

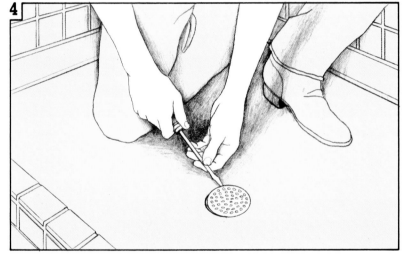

4 A clogged shower drain may respond to plunging. If not, remove its strainer, which may be secured to the drain opening by a screw in the center or snapped into place.

5 Now probe an auger down the drain and through its trap. If this doesn't work, you may be able to blast out the blockage with a hose. Pack rags around it, hold everything in place, then turn the water fully on and off a few times.

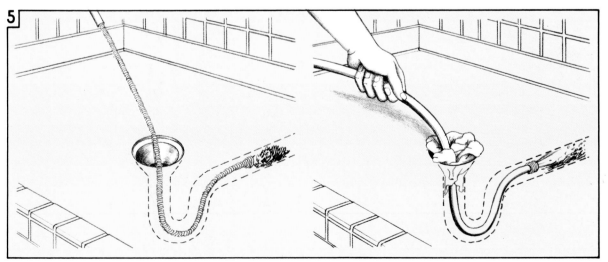

Opening Clogged Drains *(continued)*

Toilets

1 When a toilet clogs, don't flush it, or you'll also have a flood to deal with. Instead, use a bucket to carefully add or bail out water until the bowl is about half full. More than this could create a sloshy mess while you're plunging; too little, and the plunger won't make a tight seal around the bowl's outlet.

You can clear a toilet using an ordinary plunger, but the molded-cup type illustrated here generates stronger suction. Work up and down vigorously for about a dozen strokes, then yank away the plunger.

If the water disappears with a glug, you probably have succeeded. Check by pouring in more water. You may need to repeat the process several more times. If it doesn't get results, try augering, as shown in sketch 2.

Note: Never attempt to unclog a toilet with a chemical drain cleaner. Chances are, it won't do the job, and you'll be forced to plunge or auger through a strong lye solution that could burn your skin or eyes.

2 A *closet auger* makes short work of most toilet stoppages. This specialized instrument has a longer handle than the trap-and-drain version shown on the preceding pages.

To operate it, pull the spring all the way up into the handle, insert the bit into the bowl outlet, and begin cranking. If you encounter resistance, pull back slightly, wiggle the handle, and try again.

A closet auger will chew out just about anything but a solid object, such as a toy or makeup jar. If you can hear something other than the auger rattling around in there, you'll have to pull up the bowl, turn it over, and shake or poke out the item. See pages 250 and 251.

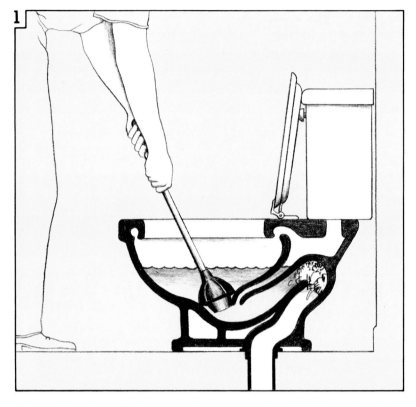

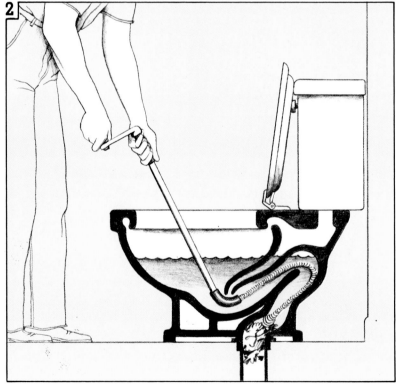

Main Drains and Sewer Lines

1 When one of these clogs, you may prefer to call in a plumber or drain-cleaning service. The work can be messy (you'll be dealing with raw sewage), and you may need a longer and stronger auger than the ones commonly used for fixture drains.

The key to getting an auger into a main drain is a Y-shaped fitting that is called a *cleanout*. You'll find one near the bottom of your home's soil stack, and there may be others higher up.

Begin by loosening the plug of that lowermost cleanout. If water oozes out, you can be sure the blockage is below somewhere. If not, try to find another cleanout above and work from there. Or climb up on the roof and auger down through the vent stack.

Before removing any cleanout, have buckets on hand to catch the waste water in the drain line.

Now thread an auger into the opening; work it back and forth a few times. Another often-successful way to clear main drains is to use a "blow bag" like the one illustrated.

2 If neither procedure works, you'll have to move downstream. Some houses have a house trap near where the drain lines leave the house. If yours does, open one of its plugs and thread an auger in. The blockage may be in the trap itself.

3 To clear a sewer line, try flushing it with a garden hose. Don't let the water run more than a minute or so, however; it could back up and cause drains to overflow. If this doesn't work, either call in a firm that specializes in opening clogged sewer lines, or rent a *power auger*. Operating one of these is a two-person job.

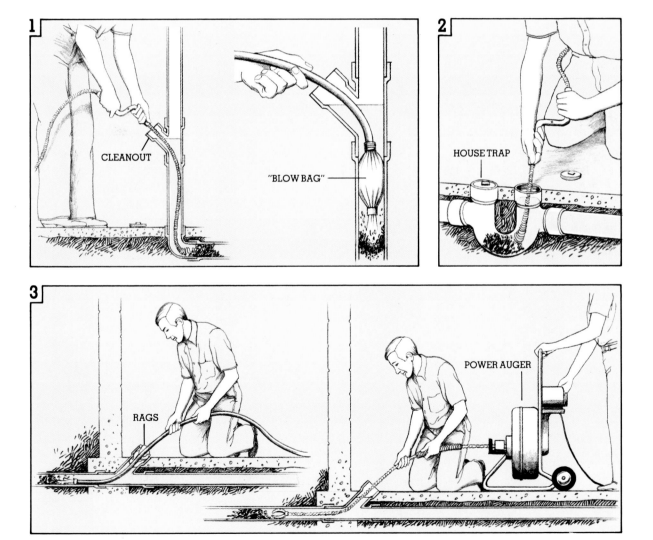

1 CLEANOUT   "BLOW BAG"

2 HOUSE TRAP

3 RAGS   POWER AUGER

Dismantling Fixture Traps

Sometimes the plunging and augering techniques shown on pages 207–209 fail to clear a drain. Or, sometimes you've dropped something down there and want it back. If either situation occurs, see whether the fixture's trap has a nutlike cleanout fitting at its bottommost point. Opening it lets you work an auger farther back toward the main drain or retrieve objects that have fallen in.

No cleanout? Don't be discouraged. It takes only a little more time and effort to remove the entire trap.

Trap configurations vary, but all include some combination of the slip-joint fittings shown below. These come apart easily, and let you reassemble components with a minimum of wrench work.

1 Before you begin, shut off water at the fixture stops (or the system shut-off) or remove faucet knobs so no one can inadvertently flood the scene down below. Position a bucket to catch water that will spill out when you remove the trap.

Now loosen any *slip nuts* securing the trap. Protect plating by wrapping tape around the jaws of your wrench or pliers. After a half-turn or so, you can unscrew the nuts by hand.

The exploded view here shows how *adjustable traps* dismantle. A *tailpiece* from the fixture slips into one end, an *elbow* connects the other end to a *drainpipe*. Most slip connections seal by compressing rubber washers; older ones may be packed instead with lampwick, which looks like string, but makes a tighter seal. Other traps (not shown here) resemble Js and Ss. They also come apart by loosening the slip nuts.

2 *Fixed traps* have slip fittings only at one end. To disconnect one of these, loosen both slip nuts, slide the tailpiece into the trap, then turn the trap loose from the drainpipe.

Before you reassemble a slip fitting, check its washer for wear or deterioration. Lampwick always should be replaced; wrap a couple turns around before you begin threading on the nut.

Be careful, too, that you don't strip or overtighten a slip nut. Turn it as far as you can by hand, then use pliers or a wrench to go an additional quarter-revolution.

To test for leaks, completely fill the fixture, then open the drain and check all connections. Slightly tighten any that leak.

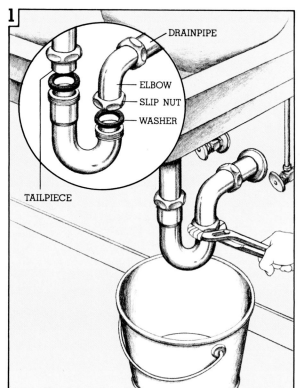

1 DRAINPIPE · ELBOW · SLIP NUT · WASHER · TAILPIECE

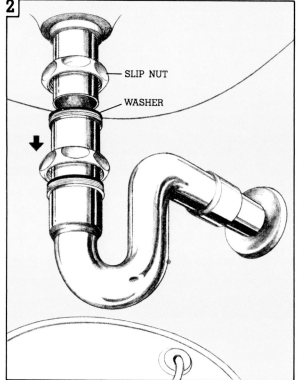

2 SLIP NUT · WASHER

Adjusting Drain Assemblies

When water in a lavatory or tub pulls a disappearing act or the fixture seems to take forever emptying itself, you can be fairly certain that a pop-up or trip-lever assembly isn't doing its job properly. With just a pair of pliers and a screwdriver, you can put a stop to either problem quickly.

1 If your tub or lavatory has a *pop-up* mechanism similar to those illustrated here, first pull out the stopper and thoroughly clean away any hair, soap, or other matter that may be keeping it from seating snugly. (See page 207 for help with removing lavatory stoppers.)

Next, check the *stopper seal.* If it's cracked or broken, pry off the rubber ring and install a new one. Look, too, for signs of wear or damage around the *flange* the stopper seats into.

Now replace the stopper and observe whether you can snug it down with the pop-up mechanism. If not, or if water is draining slowly, you need to make a simple adjustment or two.

For a lavatory, crouch under the basin and examine the position of the *pivot rod.* When the stopper is closed, this should slope slightly uphill from the *pivot* to the *clevis.* If it doesn't, loosen the *setscrew,* raise or lower the clevis on the *lift rod,* and retighten the screw.

Now the stopper may not operate as easily as it did before. This you can adjust by squeezing the *spring clip,* pulling the pivot rod out of the clevis, and reinserting it in the next higher or lower hole.

If water drips from the pivot, try tightening its *cap.* Or you may need to replace the *pivot seal* inside.

To adjust a tub pop-up, unscrew the *overflow plate,* withdraw the

entire assembly, and loosen the *adjusting nuts.* If the stopper doesn't seat tightly, move the *middle link* higher on the *striker rod;* if the tub is slow to drain, lower the link.

2 A *trip-lever* mechanism lifts and lowers a *seal plug* at the base of the overflow tube. When this drops into its *seat,* water from the tub drain can't get past. But because the plug is hollow, the overflow route is only slightly constricted.

Dismantle and adjust a trip-lever as you would a pop-up. Also check the *seal* on the bottom of the plug and replace it, if necessary.

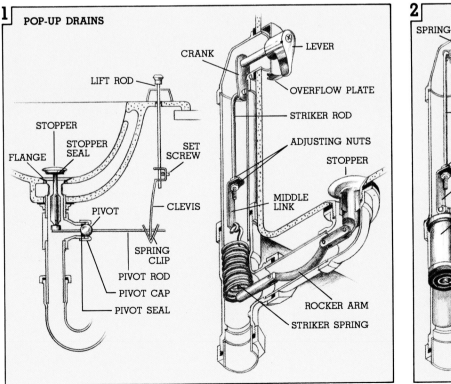

1 POP-UP DRAINS

LIFT ROD · CRANK · LEVER · OVERFLOW PLATE · STRIKER ROD · ADJUSTING NUTS · STOPPER · STOPPER · STOPPER SEAL · FLANGE · SET SCREW · MIDDLE LINK · PIVOT · CLEVIS · SPRING CLIP · PIVOT ROD · PIVOT CAP · PIVOT SEAL · ROCKER ARM · STRIKER SPRING

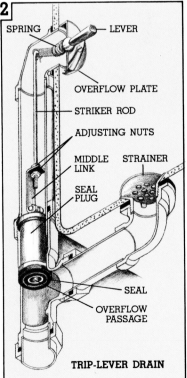

2 SPRING · LEVER · OVERFLOW PLATE · STRIKER ROD · ADJUSTING NUTS · MIDDLE LINK · STRAINER · SEAL PLUG · SEAL · OVERFLOW PASSAGE

TRIP-LEVER DRAIN

Remedies for Leaky and Frozen Pipes

If you've ever had a plumbing emergency at your house, you already know that water on the loose can wreak havoc. Even a tiny leak, left to drip day and night, will soon rot away everything in its vicinity. A pipe that freezes and bursts can cause a major flood when the thaw comes.

As soon as you spot a leak, shut off the water to take pressure off the line. Then locate exactly where the problem lies.

Water can run a considerable distance along the *outside* of a pipe, a floor joist, or the subfloor, so it may take time and a strong light to find the problem's source.

Ultimately, any leaking pipe or fitting will need replacing. Pages 260–273 tell how. Meanwhile, unless you're dealing with a gusher or the problem is buried in a wall, floor, or ceiling, the temporary measures shown here will serve until you

· can make a permanent repair.

Left unattended, any frozen pipe will turn into a leaking one, so you'll want to take immediate action when a freeze-up occurs. Again, these remedies will get you through a crisis but not necessarily prevent a recurrence. Pages 216 and 217 tell what to do about pipes that chronically freeze.

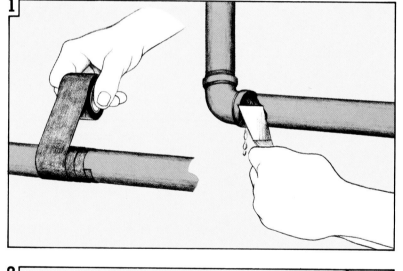

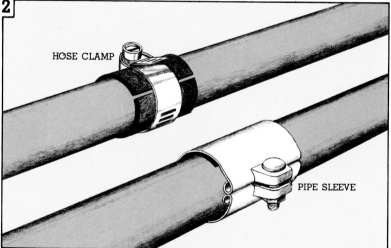

HOSE CLAMP

PIPE SLEEVE

1 For a pinhole leak, dry off the pipe and wrap it with several layers of plastic electrician's tape. Wind it about 6 inches in either direction of the hole.

At fittings, your best bet is to pack epoxy plumber's putty around the connection. This fast-setting compound makes a watertight patch.

2 An automotive *hose clamp* and a piece of rubber—both available at automobile service stations—also make an effective leak stopper. Just wrap the rubber around the pipe and tighten up the clamp.

The galvanized pipe commonly used in homes built a generation ago tends to rust from the inside out. Once a leak appears, you can expect others to follow. If the pipes at your house have begun to deteriorate, lay in a supply of *pipe sleeves* sized to fit your lines. These make semipermanent repairs that will last for several years.

If a leak seems to be more a drip than a squirt, and you can't find where it's coming from, the pipe simply may be sweating. Wrapping it with insulation, as shown on page 216, will eliminate condensation.

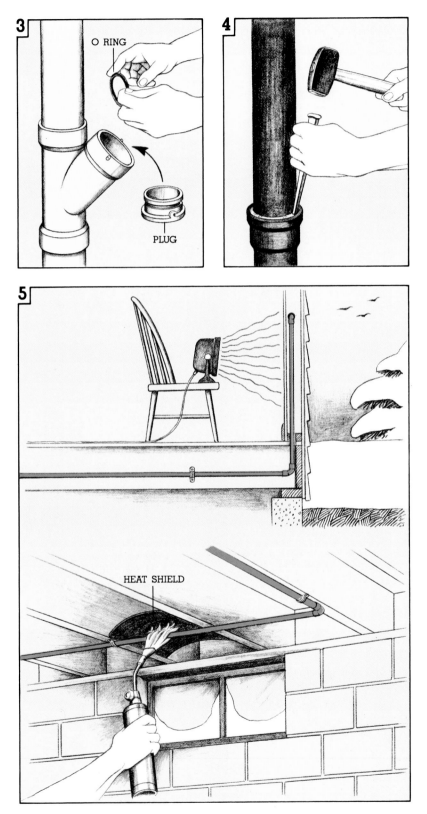

O RING

PLUG

HEAT SHIELD

3 Drain-waste-vent (DWV) lines are less leak prone. Once in a while, however, a cleanout plug may begin to ooze water.

If this happens at your house, warn everyone in the household not to use any fixtures for a few minutes, then remove the plug and reseal it. For iron plugs, wrap the threads with pipe tape or coat them with joint compound. Plastic plugs twist free. Lubricate the O ring with petroleum jelly and replace the plug.

4 Leaks at the joints of cast-iron DWV pipes are easy to deal with. If yours is the hub-and-spigot type illustrated here, tamping down the soft lead it's been sealed with usually will eliminate the problem. Don't whack the pipe too hard, though; you could crack it.

Or perhaps your home's DWV lines are connected with a no-hub clamping system, such as depicted on pages 257, 262–263 and 273. If so, simply tightening the clamp probably will stop the leak.

5 Frozen pipes obviously need to be warmed, and how you apply the heat depends to some extent upon where the pipe is. If it's concealed in a ceiling, wall, or floor, beam a heat lamp at the surface. Keep it 8 to 12 inches away so you don't risk starting a fire.

A propane torch offers the quickest (but riskiest) way to thaw exposed pipes. Every winter, homes burst into flames because precautions weren't taken when using a torch around combustible materials. Never use one near gas lines, though, and use a heat shield to protect combustible materials. Ice tends to form along the entire length of a pipe, so put a spreader tip on the torch and move it back and forth. Don't let the pipe get too hot to touch; steam pressure could explode it.

If you don't have a torch or if the pipes are in tight quarters, wrap them with towels and pour hot water over the frozen section. Or heat the pipe with a hair dryer. Regardless of how you choose to thaw out a pipe, first open the faucet it supplies so steam can escape.

Preventing Pipe Freeze-Ups

Icy-cold tap water may taste refreshing; but it's also a chilling omen that a pipe or pipes are in peril. Here are some steps you can take to protect them from the cold.

1 Electric heat tape draws only modest amounts of current. You simply wrap it around the pipe and plug one end into an outlet. A thermostat turns the tape on and off as needed. Tape won't, of course, work during power outages, the times your home most needs protection against freezing temperatures.

2 Pipe jacketing comes in standard lengths you just cut with a knife and secure with plastic electrical tape. Ordinary insulation, cut in strips and bundled around pipes, works equally well. Be sure to insulate all joints and connections, too.

   In an extremely cold wall or floor, you may be better off to pack the entire cavity with insulation. Also consider insulating long hot-water runs, especially any that pass through unheated spaces. You'll conserve water-heating energy.

3 As an emergency preventive, crack open the faucet you're concerned about and let water trickle through the line. If there's a cabinet underneath, open its doors and let room heat warm the pipes. Beaming a small lamp at the pipes also protects short runs through cold spaces during the winter's worst temperatures.

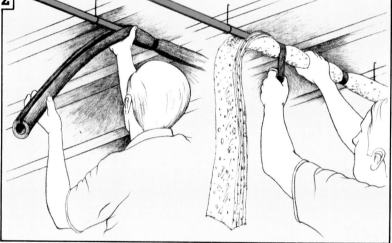

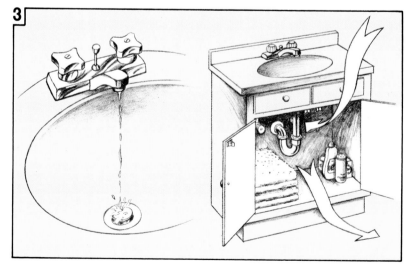

Winterizing Plumbing

Once upon a time, homeowners who were vacating a house for a month or two, or even the entire winter, simply turned down the thermostat and left enough heat to keep pipes from freezing. Today's high energy costs make that an expensive proposition.

Fortunately, you can shut down your entire plumbing system and let the furnace hibernate while you're gone.

1 Call the water department and ask them to turn off service at the valve outside your home. They may want to remove the meter, too. If not, close the valve on its supply side.

2 Now start at the top of your home's supply system and open every faucet. Shut off power to the water heater and drain it, too. At the bottom of the system, look for *stop-waste valves* near the water meter, and maybe elsewhere as well. Open the *drain cock* in each of these.

It's essential that you drain every bit of water from supply lines. If you find a low-lying pipe that doesn't have a faucet or drain cock, crack open a union. Siphon water from dish and clothes washers.

3 Empty fixture traps of water by pouring in automotive antifreeze mixed with water according to directions on the can. For a toilet, pour a gallon of antifreeze solution into the bowl to start the flushing action. Some of it will remain in the toilet's trap. Finally, if your house has a main house trap, fill it with full-strength antifreeze.

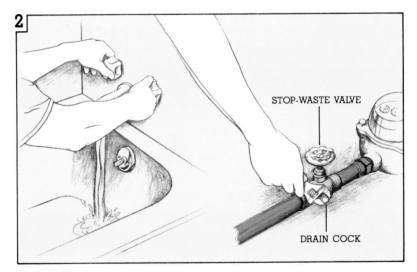

STOP-WASTE VALVE

DRAIN COCK

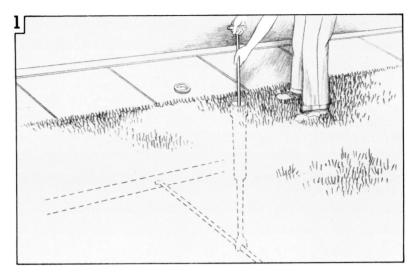

Repairing Leaky Faucets

A faucet's job is to deliver a stream of water on command, and rarely will yours fail to oblige whenever called upon. If trouble develops within, it almost invariably results in a drip, drip, drip from the spout, or an oozing from around the faucet body.

If either of these problems crops up around your house, you first must identify what type of faucet you're dealing with, then repair or replace the faulty part. Start by looking over the anatomy drawings shown here and on the following pages.

Stem Faucets

Stem faucets, such as the ones below, always have separate hot and cold controls. With many types, turning a handle twists a threaded *stem* up or down. In its off position, the stem compresses a rubberlike *washer* into a beveled *seat*, stopping the flow of water. As the washer wears, you have to apply more and more pressure to turn off the unit, and that's when dripping usually begins.

Newer versions, the so-called *washerless stem faucets*, replace the washer with a much more durable *diaphragm* or rubber *seal/spring assembly*. With this latter type, the stem rotates rather than raises and lowers to control water flow.

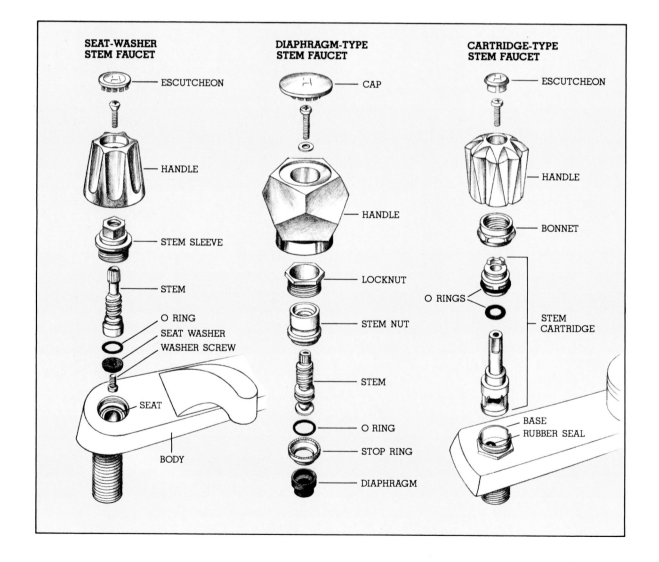

SEAT-WASHER STEM FAUCET — ESCUTCHEON, HANDLE, STEM SLEEVE, STEM, O RING, SEAT WASHER, WASHER SCREW, SEAT, BODY

DIAPHRAGM-TYPE STEM FAUCET — CAP, HANDLE, LOCKNUT, STEM NUT, STEM, O RING, STOP RING, DIAPHRAGM

CARTRIDGE-TYPE STEM FAUCET — ESCUTCHEON, HANDLE, BONNET, O RINGS, STEM CARTRIDGE, BASE, RUBBER SEAL

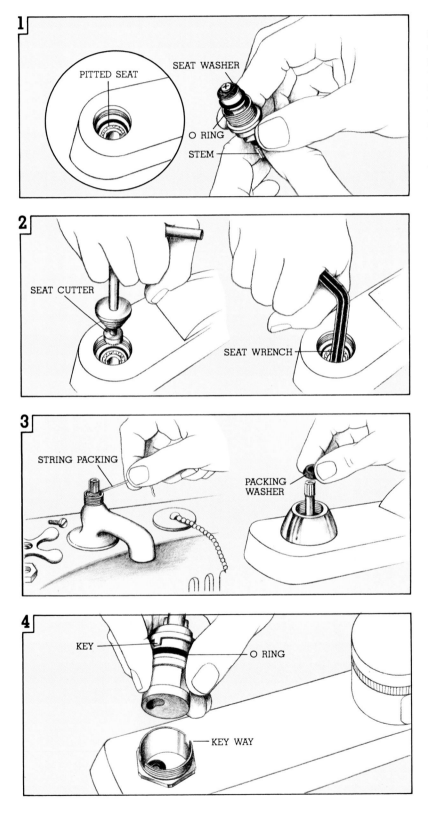

1 When the spout of a *threaded* stem faucet leaks, you can be sure that either the seat washer or the seat itself needs attention. Shut off the water supply to the faucet, then disassemble the faucet to the point where you can get a look at the washer at the base of the stem (see the anatomy drawing on the opposite page).

If the washer is cracked, grooved, or partially missing, back out the screw holding the washer to the stem and insert a new washer. Also check the O ring around the stem as well as the packing or packing washer. Replace these if needed.

Maybe the washer isn't the trouble maker. The seat at the base of the faucet body may be pitted or badly corroded.

2 Depending on its condition, the seat may require either grinding or replacement. Special tools, a *seat cutter* and a *seat wrench*, perform these tasks. If you run up against a stubborn seat, squirt on some penetrating oil to free things up.

3 You generally can trace leaks around faucet handles and from the base of the faucet to O rings or stem packing. Both wear out eventually and need replacement. Many older faucet stems came with packing that forms a tight seal under pressure. When replacing old packing, be sure to wrap the new packing clockwise around the stem. With newer faucets, a packing washer takes the place of the packing string.

4 If yours is the newer, cartridge-type stem, it's best to replace the seal and O rings whenever the faucet acts up. Remove the seal and spring with the end of a pencil. When reinserting the cartridge, be sure to align the *key* with the *key way*.

Repairing Leaky Faucets *(continued)*

Tipping-Valve Faucets

Its slim *control handle* makes a tipping-valve faucet easy to identify. This handle connects to a *control cam*, which when rotated activates the two *tipping-valve mechanisms* under the body cover. These mechanisms have several components: a *plug, gasket, stem, spring, screen,* and *seat.*

Raising the faucet handle forces the cam against the valve stems, lifting them off their seat. The farther back you throw the handle, the more water that enters the mixing chamber.

Note the handle's position in the sketch below. At left of center, it rotates the cam to tip the hot water stem, allowing only a stream of hot water to pass through. The cold water stem remains unaffected.

For the most part, tipping-valve faucet troubles—all easy to spot and correct—originate in three areas.

Leaks from the spout portend a breakdown of one or more of the valve mechanism components. Fix these by replacing the whole mechanism. If you notice leakage around the handle, the cam assembly O ring has given way. Sketch 3 on page 221 shows how to repair this. Finally, leaks around the spout mean a deteriorated spout O ring.

Though tipping-valve faucets no longer are made, you can still get the parts—sold in stores usually in kit form—necessary to remedy all of these problems. The repair kit won't include a screen; it's no longer considered needed.

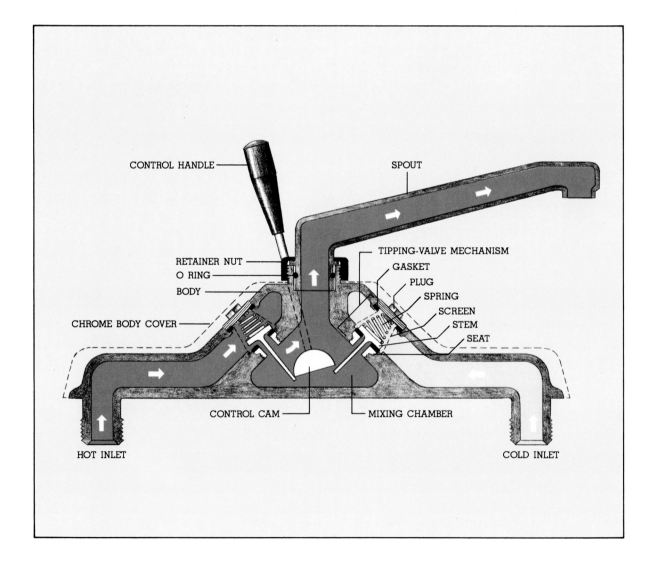

1 First things first. Shut off the water supply to the fixture and drain the water that remains at the faucet by raising the handle in its center position. To disassemble, loosen the retainer nut with a cloth-covered pair of pliers.

Next, grab hold of the spout and raise it out of the faucet body. If you spy a badly worn O ring, replace it with a new one.

2 To get at the cam assembly, you'll need to loosen the setscrew holding the handle to the cam. Then remove the rear closure concealing the cam.

Now remove the screws holding the cam in place, and pull it out of the faucet body. Set the cam aside. Lift off the body cover.

3 Using a wrench, remove the valve assembly plug, then the screen, gasket, spring, stem, and the seat. (You'll need an allen wrench or a seat wrench to remove the seat.) Replace the entire assembly with the repair parts. Do the same with the other valve.

4 After making all of the above repairs, you'll have one O ring—for the cam assembly—left. Simply remove the old O ring and replace it with the new. You would do well to lubricate the new one to make it easier to replace the cam in the faucet body.

If your faucet has a spray attachment that has been acting up, now's a good time to check on the condition of the diverter valve. It's under the spout in the faucet body and can be best removed using a screwdriver and pliers. Clean its openings with a toothbrush. If this doesn't help, buy a new one. When shopping for a diverter, be sure to take the old one with you so your local supplier can tell which type you have.

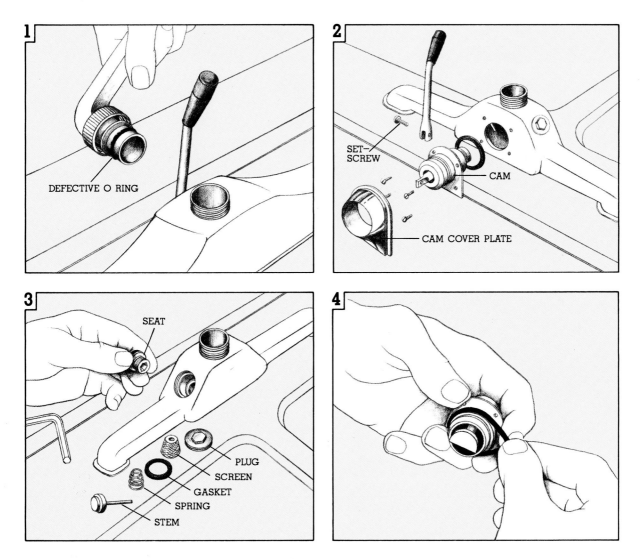

Repairing Leaky Faucets *(continued)*

Disc Faucets

As you can see by looking at the anatomy drawing below, disc faucets depend not on a washer and seat to shut off and control the flow of water, but rather on a *disc* arrangement.

Raising the faucet lever of one of these causes the upper portion of the disc assembly to slide across its lower half, allowing water to enter the *mixing chamber.* Naturally, the

higher you raise the lever, the more water enters. Conversely, lowering the lever closes off the *inlet ports.*

Moving the lever from side to side determines whether hot or cold water or a mixture of the two comes out of the spout.

The disc assembly itself, generally made of long-lasting ceramic material, rarely needs replacing. However, the inlet ports can become restricted by various mineral deposits. If this happens, simply disassemble the faucet as shown opposite and scrape away the minerals with a pocketknife.

If the faucet leaks around its base, one or more of the *inlet seals* probably needs replacing. It's a good idea to replace all of the seals, as the failure of one generally signals the impending demise of the rest.

Most plumbing supply outlets stock a supply of repair kits for this as well as other types of faucets. Before going to your supplier for a replacement kit, though, jot down the brand of faucet you have on a piece of paper (the name is on the faucet body). Or take the disc along if you already have removed it from the faucet body.

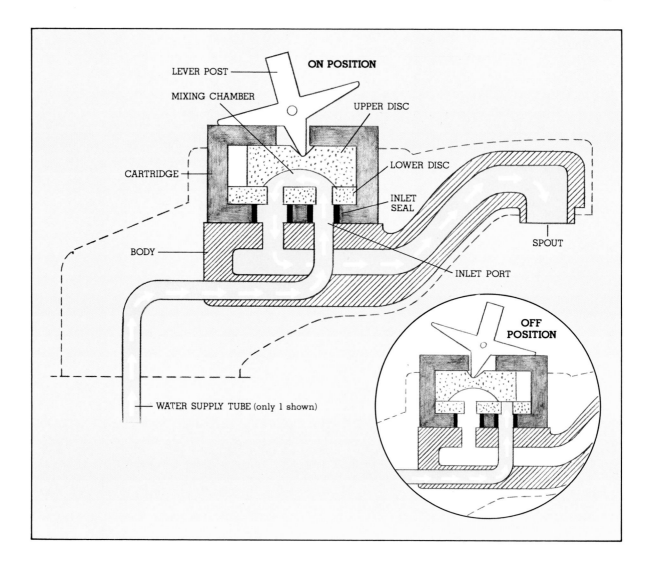

LEVER POST · **ON POSITION**

MIXING CHAMBER

UPPER DISC

LOWER DISC

CARTRIDGE

INLET SEAL

SPOUT

BODY

INLET PORT

WATER SUPPLY TUBE (only 1 shown)

OFF POSITION

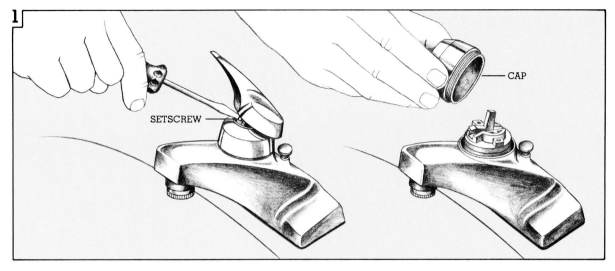

SETSCREW

CAP

1 To repair a leaky disc faucet, first shut off the water supply to the unit, then drain the lines by lifting the lever to its highest position. Look closely under the lever, and you'll see a setscrew that secures the lever to the lever post. Using an appropriately sized screwdriver, turn the setscrew counterclockwise until you can raise the lever off the post.

Next, lift off or unscrew the decorative cap concealing the cartridge. With this done, loosen the screws holding the cartridge to the faucet body, then lift out the cartridge.

2 On the underside of the cartridge you'll find a set of seals. To replace them, just pull out the old, worn-out ones and insert the new. While you're doing this, also check for sediment buildup around the inlet ports, and remove it to clear the restriction.

3 Reassemble the faucet, reversing the disassembly procedures. When inserting the cartridge, be sure to align its holes with those in the base of the faucet body.

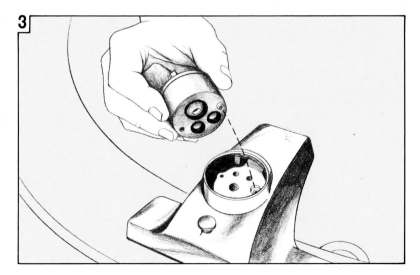

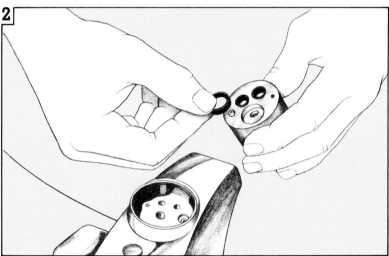

Repairing Leaky Faucets *(continued)*

Rotating-Ball Faucets

Inside every rotating-ball faucet, a slotted *ball* sits atop a pair of spring-loaded rubber *seals.* In the "off" position, this ball (held tight against the seals by the cap) effectively closes off the supply of water.

But look what happens when the faucet handle is raised (see detail drawings). The ball rotates in such a way that its openings begin to align with the supply line ports. When this happens, water can pass through the ball and on out the spout. Moving the handle to the left allows more hot water into the mixing chamber; to the right, more cold water.

Not surprisingly, usually after long use the seals and springs can give out. You'll find out how to replace these on the opposite page.

Realize, too, that these faucets can spring leaks from around the handle and, with swivel-spout models, from under the base of the spout. Handle leaks indicate either the *adjusting ring* has loosened a bit or the *seal* immediately above the ball has worn.

Under-spout leaks, on the other hand, result from O-ring failure. Inspect the rings encircling the *body* and, on units with diverter valves, the valve's O ring as well. Replace, if necessary, as shown opposite.

While you have the faucet apart, also check the ball for wear and corrosion. If it's faulty, simply replace it with a new one.

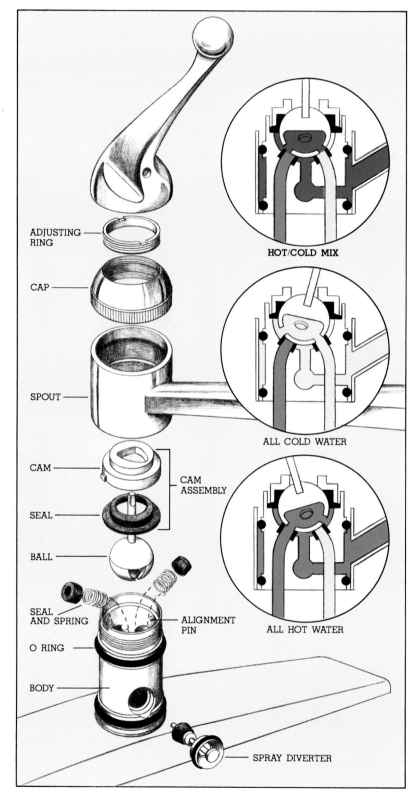

ADJUSTING RING

CAP

SPOUT

CAM

CAM ASSEMBLY

SEAL

BALL

SEAL AND SPRING

ALIGNMENT PIN

O RING

BODY

SPRAY DIVERTER

HOT/COLD MIX

ALL COLD WATER

ALL HOT WATER

1 To disassemble a rotating-ball faucet, first shut off the water supply, then drain the lines by lifting straight up on the handle. Using an allen wrench, loosen the setscrew holding the handle in place.

Next, loosen the adjusting ring (the wrench packed with repair kits is the correct tool), and unscrew the cap. You may need to apply pressure with cloth-covered adjustable pliers to budge the cap.

2 Lift out the cam assembly, ball, and, in the case of a swivel-spout faucet, the spout. The spout, being friction-fit around the body, may prove stubborn. So be prepared to apply some muscle at this point.

To remove worn seals and springs from the body, on the other hand, requires only minimal effort. Simply insert either end of a lead pencil into each seat, then withdraw the pencil. Check for restriction at the supply inlet ports, scrape away any buildup you find, then insert the new springs and seals.

3 If the faucet has a swivel-spout, pry the O rings away from the body using an awl or other sharp-pointed tool. Roll the new ones down over the body until they rest in the appropriate grooves. Replace the diverter O ring in the same manner.

4 As you reassemble the faucet, be mindful that you must align the slot in the side of the ball with the pin inside the body. Note, too, that the key on the cam assembly fits into a corresponding notch in the body.

After hand-tightening the cap, tighten the adjusting ring for a good seal between the ball and cam. If there is a leak around the handle after restoring pressure to the lines, tighten the adjusting ring further.

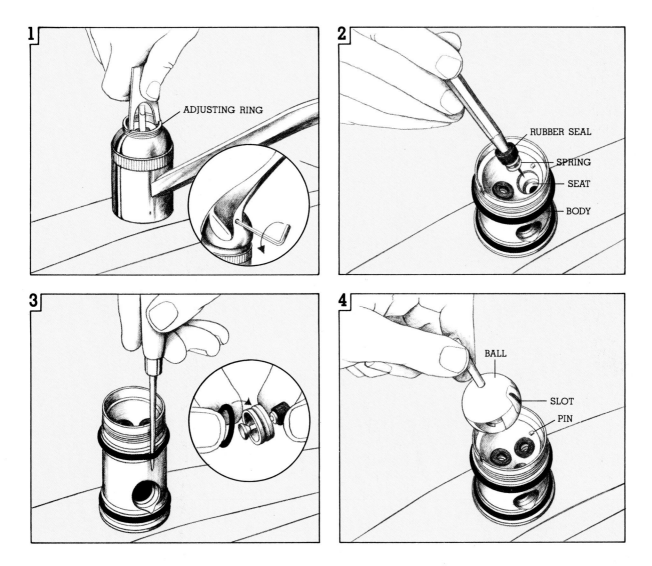

Repairing Leaky Faucets *(continued)*

Sleeve-Cartridge Faucets

Most washerless faucets rely on a combination of seals and O rings to control and direct water. Not so with the sleeve-cartridge type. Instead, the cartridge itself is ringed by a series of strategically placed O rings.

Look at the anatomy drawing below, and you can see that the O rings fit snugly against

the inside of the faucet body. This arrangement serves two purposes. The diagonally set O ring forms a seal between the hot and cold supply lines. The other O rings ensure against leaks from the spout, from under the handle, and on swivel-spout models from under the spout.

Note, too, that when the handle is raised, the stem raises also and the holes in it align with the openings in the cartridge. You control the temperature by rotating the handle either to the left (hot) or to the right (cold).

When this type of faucet acts up, you can replace either the O rings or the cartridge itself if it has corroded. And because of the faucet's simple design and few replaceable parts, repairing one generally doesn't take long. In fact, disassembling the faucet may account for the bulk of the work involved. Both of these procedures are covered on the opposite page.

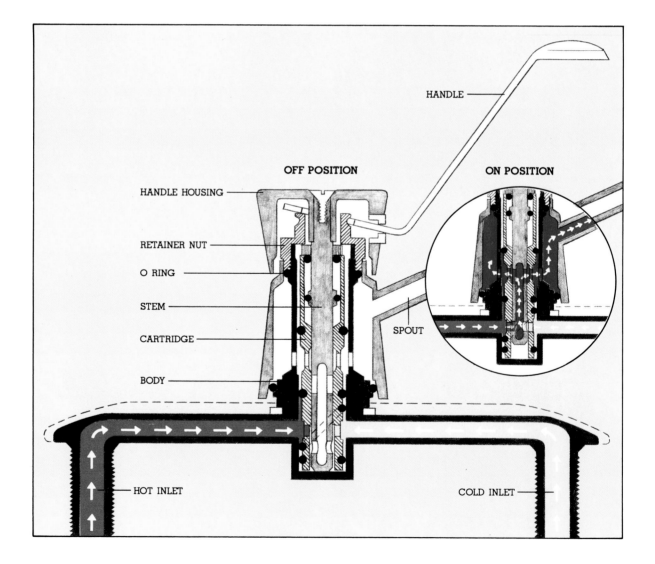

1 Sleeve-cartridge faucets vary somewhat in design from model to model, but all disassemble pretty much as follows. As always, you must shut off and drain the water lines first.

With this out of the way, pry off the decorative handle cover concealing the handle screw. Be careful you don't crack the cover in doing so; most are made of plastic.

Now remove the handle screw and lift off the handle assembly. On swivel-spout models, you'll encounter a *retainer nut*. Unscrew it, then lift off the spout.

Depending on the model you have, you may need to lift off a cylindrical sleeve to get at the cartridge. You should now be able to see the *retainer clip,* the device that holds the cartridge in place. Using long-nose pliers, remove the clip from its slot.

2 With pliers, lift the cartridge from the faucet body. Note the position of the *cartridge ears.* They face the front and back of the faucet, and it's important that when the cartridge is replaced they be in the exact same position. If a special tool is required to remove the cartridge, instructions should be included with the new cartridge.

3 Remove the O rings, install new ones, then reinsert the cartridge and retainer clip. If yours is a swivel-spout model, lubricate the O rings around the outside of the body, then force the spout down over the rings and into position.

4 Tighten down the retaining nut, using adhesive-bandaged or cloth-coated pliers to guard against marring the chrome spout. Finish the job by reinstalling the handle, restoring water pressure, and checking the faucet for leaks.

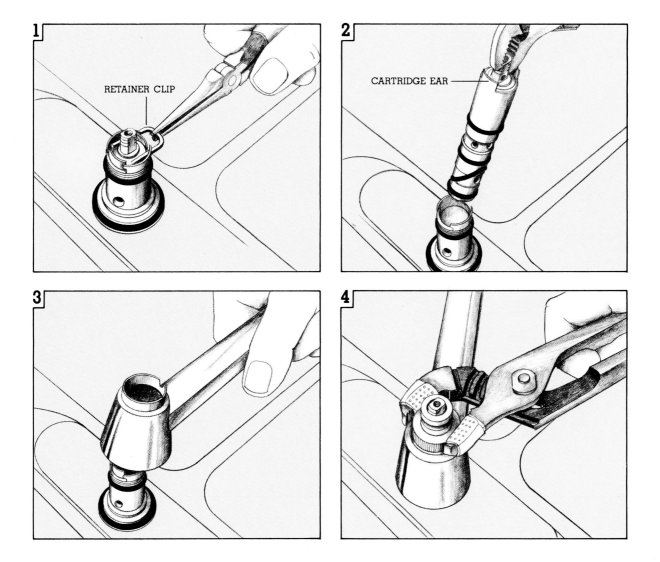

1 RETAINER CLIP

2 CARTRIDGE EAR

Repairing Leaky Faucets *(continued)*

Tub/Shower Faucets

Tub/shower faucet valve mechanisms—hidden behind the control handles—are so inconspicuous most people never give a thought to them. That's fine as long as everything works as expected.

When things go wrong, though, the faucet's sheltered position can cause you problems. A badly corroded faucet body or a leaky behind-the- wall supply connection in most instances means you'll have to perform wall surgery—a fairly involved operation—to get at and correct the problem. The text and sketches on the oppo- site page tell you how to han- dle these and other problems.

Though styled quite different- ly than faucets serving sinks and lavatories, tub/shower fau- cets function in much the same way (see the two examples below). Moving the handle of a stem faucet counterclockwise raises the stem out of its seat and allows water to pass through the faucet body. Some stem-type models have a third diverter stem that directs water to the spout or shower head, whichever you wish. Others rely on a diverter spout to ac- complish this. (See pages 230–231 for repairing diverters.)

With most single-control tub/shower faucets, activating the handle controls both the intensity and temperature of the water. Some of these have a diverter valve built into the faucet body; others depend on a diverter spout.

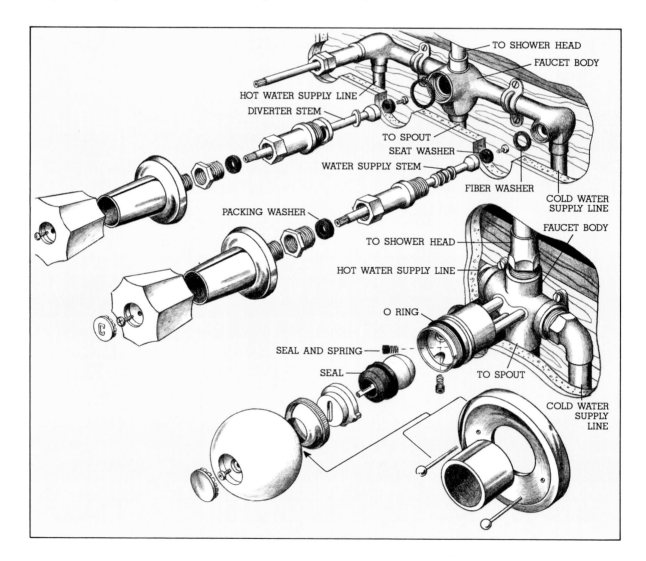

1 Spout leaks and leaks from around faucet handle(s) are just as common in tub/shower faucets as any other kind. When confronted with either of these problems, start by shutting off the water supply and draining the lines. Then, using the anatomy drawings on the opposite page as a general guide, disassemble the faucet to where you can remove the valve assembly.

Check the seat washer or the seals and springs at the base of single-control valves for wear. Note, too, the condition of the packing, packing washer, and O rings. Replace the necessary parts and reassemble the faucet.

2 Shower heads, too, sometimes need fixing. If water squirts out around the head, first try tightening the nut holding it to the arm. If it still leaks, then remove the head and check the washer for wear. Replace it if necessary.

If not enough water is coming out of the shower head, mineral deposits may be the villain. To investigate, disassemble the head, clean the orifices in it, then put everything back together again.

3 Over time, mineral deposits can choke off the flow of water through a faucet. Or maybe a connection between a supply line and the faucet

begins to leak. Both situations require that you get at the faucet body. Before making any incisions, though, look around for an access panel. (Though not common in newer construction, older homes may have them.)

If necessary, cut into the wall, shut off the water supply, drain the lines, and cut the faucet body free with a hacksaw. If necessary, replace the supply lines. Hook up the new faucet and repair the wall surface.

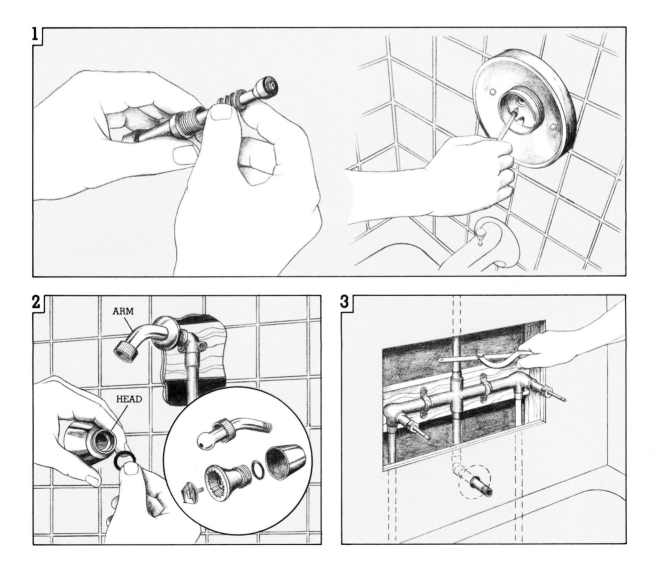

ARM

HEAD

Repairing Sink Sprays, Diverters, Aerators

As mentioned earlier, some sink and lavatory faucets have sprays and diverter valves. And most all have an aerator at the tip of the spout. With sprays, troubles can develop in the connections, gaskets, or the nozzle. Most often, you can trace diverter maladies to worn washers or O rings. And about the only troubles that crop up with aerators are leaks caused by a worn gasket or a loose housing, and "low pressure" that results from mineral deposits clogging the screen. Fortunately, however, you can troubleshoot and correct all of these problems with a minimum of hassles.

1 Though diverters vary in shape from brand to brand, all operate in much the same way as the one shown here. When water isn't flowing toward the spray outlet, the valve remains open and allows water to proceed out the spout. But notice how it reacts when you press the nozzle's lever. It closes off the passage leading to the spout.

Nothing happens when you press the lever? Check to see whether the hose is kinked. A slow stream of water coupled with some water coming from the spout may signal a stuck valve or a worn washer or O ring. (See also step 2.) To check out the diverter, disassemble the faucet (see pages 220–227 for help with this). You'll find the diverter in the faucet body under the spout or in the spout itself. Replace the faulty parts, or the diverter itself, if necessary.

2 Minerals may be restricting the flow of water through the spray. Clean the spray disc with a straight pin as shown. Check other parts of the spray for wear and tighten all connections.

3 To check out a suspect aerator, disassemble it, then brush the screen clean if necessary.

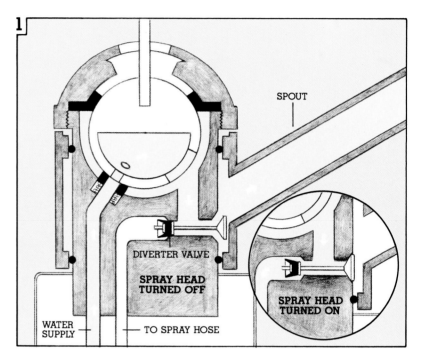

SPOUT

DIVERTER VALVE

SPRAY HEAD TURNED OFF

SPRAY HEAD TURNED ON

WATER SUPPLY

TO SPRAY HOSE

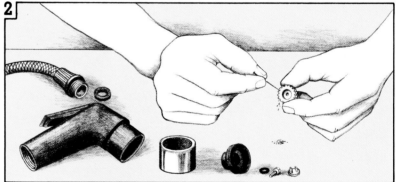

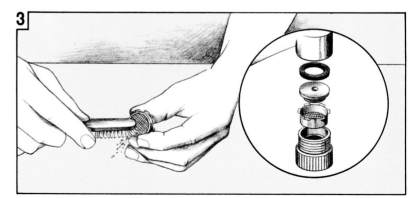

Repairing Tub/Shower Diverters

Tub/shower diverters fall into two general classifications. One group, typified by the stem type valve in the upper portion of the sketch, are housed in the faucet body and direct the flow of water from there. Tub diverter spouts, on the other hand, act independently of the faucet.

The sketch at right shows how each works. In the closed position, the diverter valve blocks off the water flow to the shower head. Opened fully, it diverts incoming water to the shower head. Here again, diverter mechanisms vary by manufacturer, but they all do the same thing.

With the tub diverter spout shown, lifting up on its knob while the water is running seals off the inlet to the spout and forces the water up to and out of the shower head. The water pressure will maintain the seal. But when the water is shut off the knob will drop back into its usual position.

When a tub diverter spout wears out, or if the lift rod attached to the knob breaks off from the plate it's attached to, you may as well replace the spout. To remove the defective one, insert a hammer handle or another suitable item into the spout and rotate it counterclockwise until it separates from the nipple it is attached to. Wrap pipe compound or tape around the nipple and install the new spout.

If a stem-type valve begins to leak or no longer will divert water properly, shut off the water supply to the faucet, drain the lines, and remove the nut holding the stem in place. Withdraw the stem, inspect the packing washer or O ring and the seat washer if your diverter has one, and replace any worn-out parts you find.

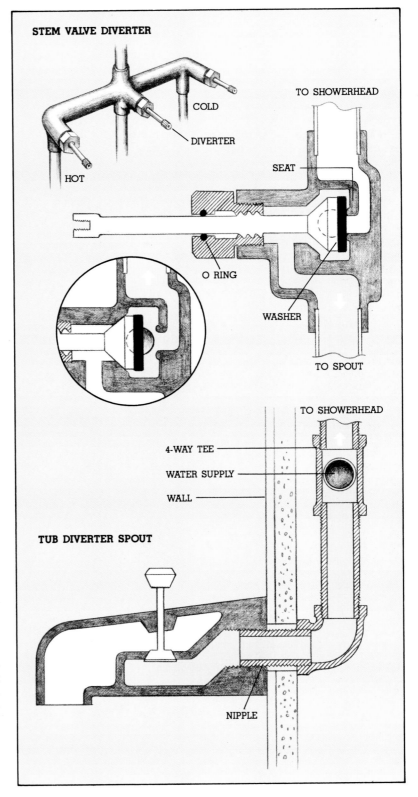

STEM VALVE DIVERTER

COLD

DIVERTER

HOT

TO SHOWERHEAD

SEAT

O RING

WASHER

TO SPOUT

TO SHOWERHEAD

4-WAY TEE

WATER SUPPLY

WALL

TUB DIVERTER SPOUT

NIPPLE

Repairing Toilets

Ever had to fiddle endlessly with the flush handle of a toilet to stop the water? Or fight with a tank ball that just refuses to rest squarely in its seat? Or peer helplessly into a toilet tank wondering what on earth is causing that incessant trickle of water? You're not alone!

Most people could care less about how toilets do what they do. But the sad fact is that some day you're going to have to make acquaintance with this necessary household unit. Let's take a behind-the-scenes look at a typical toilet and its rather simple workings.

When someone flips the *flush handle*, a chain reaction of events occurs. The *trip lever* lifts up the *tank ball* via a *lift wire/lift rod* arrangement. As the water rushes down through the *ball seat* and *flush passages* into the *bowl*, the reservoir of water and the waste in the bowl yield to gravity and pass through the toilet's *trap* out into a nearby drain line.

Inside the tank, the *float ball* rides the tide of the outrushing water until, at a predetermined level, the rod it attaches to trips the *flush valve*. (The tank ball settles back into its seat at this time, too.) This valve allows a new supply of water to enter the tank through a *fill tube* and the bowl through the *overflow tube*. When the float returns to its full position, the flush valve closes, completing the process.

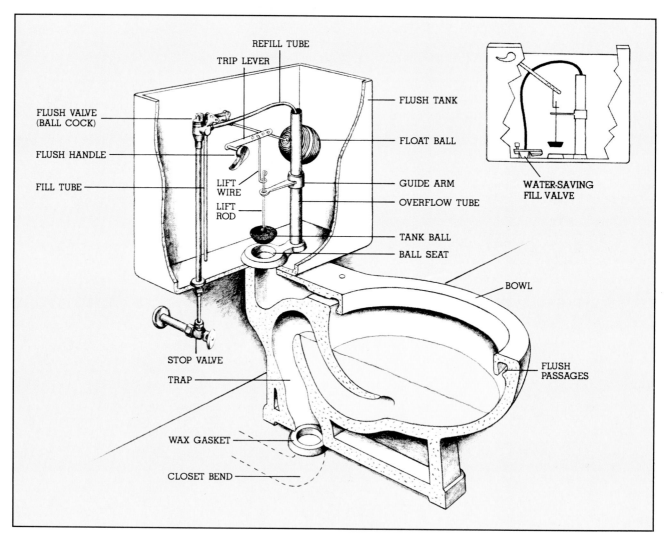

REFILL TUBE
TRIP LEVER
FLUSH VALVE (BALL COCK)
FLUSH HANDLE
FILL TUBE
LIFT WIRE
LIFT ROD
STOP VALVE
TRAP
WAX GASKET
CLOSET BEND
FLUSH TANK
FLOAT BALL
GUIDE ARM
OVERFLOW TUBE
TANK BALL
BALL SEAT
BOWL
FLUSH PASSAGES
WATER-SAVING FILL VALVE

Flush Tank Repairs

Since most of the mechanical action goes on inside the flush tank, it's not surprising that there, too, is where most problems develop. Here's a rundown of some common maladies and their solutions.

1 If you have difficulty getting the flush valve to close after a flush, the *float rod* may not be rising up high enough. Remove the tank cover, being careful not to chip it and observe if water passes into the overflow tube. Then lift the rod with your hand. If the flush valve closes, bend the rod downward slightly. This simple procedure may solve your problem.

2 It's also possible the float ball has taken on some water. When this happens, the ball won't rise high enough to close the valve. To check out this possibility agitate the ball and listen for a swishing sound. To remove a faulty ball, rotate it counterclockwise until you disengage it from the float rod. Replace the ball with a new one.

3 If the float ball passes inspection, look next at the flush valve (ballcock) assembly. **Before attempting to remove the *float rod mechanism*, though, shut off the water supply and flush the toilet.** Remove the thumbscrews holding the assembly in place, then lift it out and set it aside. (If yours is a diaphragm-type flush valve assembly, see the detail for help.)

4 Slip the blade of a screwdriver through the slot at the top of the plunger and lift it up out of the housing. Typically, you'll find a seat washer as well as one or more split washers. Remove and replace all of the washers, reassemble the flush valve assembly, and restore water pressure.

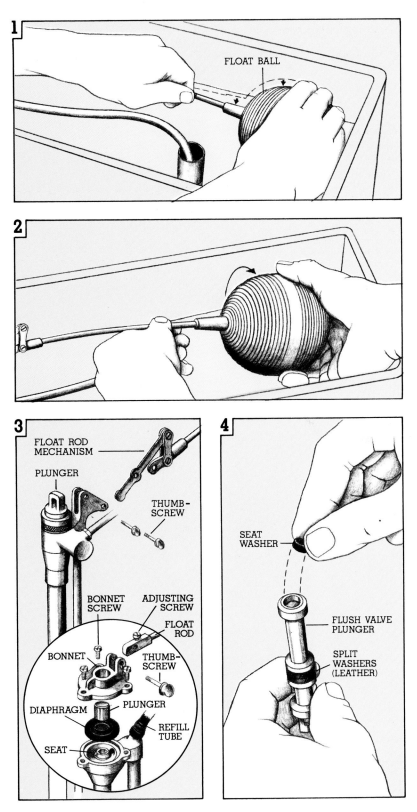

Flush Tank Repairs *(continued)*

5 Of course, if for some reason water continues to leak out of the tank, the valve controlling incoming water may never get a chance to shut off. Or it may shut off only temporarily. If either situation fits your circumstance, and the float ball and flush valve check out properly, you have *tank ball* or *ball seat* problems.

Start by observing the tank ball as the tank empties. Does it settle squarely in its seat? If not, loosen the *guide arm* and rotate it for better alignment. Also check the *lift wire/lift rod* assembly and bend either part, if necessary, so the ball seats properly.

6 If the tank ball needs replacing, unscrew it from the lift rod and install a new one. Or, to eliminate any future problems with the lift wire, lift rod, or guide arm, replace the old ball with a *flapper* and chain. To do this, disengage the lift wire from the trip arm, then loosen and lift out the guide arm. Slip the flapper down over the overflow tube and fasten the chain to the trip lever.

7 A pitted or otherwise corroded ball seat also can prevent the tank from filling properly. To check out the seat, run a finger completely around it. If you detect a problem, scour the seat with a steel wool pad.

8 Newer flush valve assemblies, such as the one shown, simplify the flushing operation. And because they're corrosion-resistant plastic, they seldom act up. Sliding the float cup up or down on the rod controls the level of water in the tank.

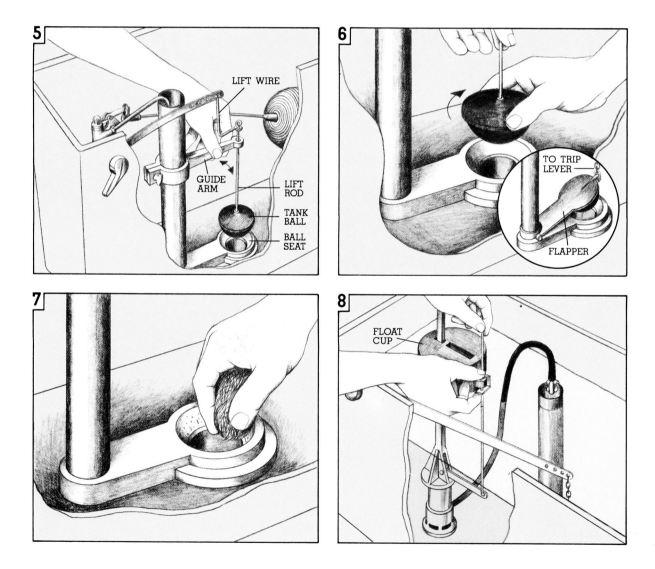

Stopping Exterior Leaks

1 As you can see, a *beveled gasket* at the base of the flushing valve shank and a *rubber washer* immediately beneath the tank (under pressure from a *locknut*) form a tight seal between the water inside the tank and the outside. Over time, however, either the locknut can work loose or the seals can give out.

If you notice a leak here, first tighten the locknut. If that doesn't work, shut off the water supply, flush the toilet, and sponge out the water that remains in the tank. Disconnect the water supply line, remove the locknut holding the flush valve as-

sembly in place, and replace the old gasket and washer with new ones. Also, check the supply line washer for wear and replace it if necessary.

2 Extended use also can cause the *tank hold-down bolts* to loosen just enough to produce a leak. Remedying this is easy. Using a long-shanked screwdriver and a wrench, snug down the bolt as shown.

3 With some older-style toilets, the tank connects to the bowl via a fitting similar to the one shown. If leaks develop at either end of the fitting, tightening the nuts should dry things up in a hurry.

4 Leaks from around the base of the bowl indicate one of three things. The *bowl hold-down bolts* may need tightening, the *wax gasket* around the bowl inlet needs replacing, or the bowl is cracked. If a new gasket is in order, turn to pages 250 and 251 for more information.

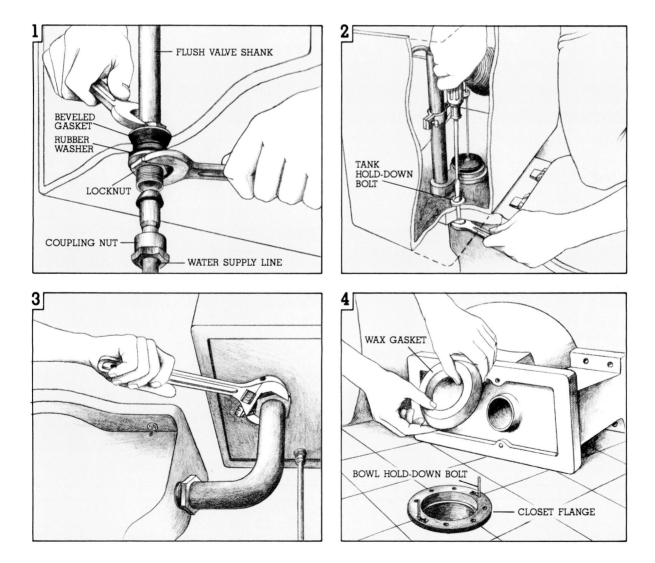

Maintaining and Repairing Water Heaters

Study the anatomy drawings at right and you will discover that water heaters are little more than giant insulated water bottles. As hot water is used, cold water enters the unit via a *dip tube.* Naturally, this lowers the water temperature inside the tank. When this happens, a *thermostat* calls for heat. With gas and oil units, *burners* beneath the water tank kick in and continue heating the liquid until the desired temperature is reached. *Heating elements* perform the same function in electric water heaters.

Harmful by-products of combustion are ushered out of gas- and oil-fired units through a *flue* running up the middle of the tank. Electric heaters, since no combustion occurs, don't require venting to the outside.

When water heater troubles develop, it's usually due to sediment buildup or rust. You can do much to thwart the effects of both by opening the *drain valve* every few months and drawing off a few gallons of water. This purges rust and other gunk from the heater.

A regular maintenance checkup, about once a year, is your best insurance against most water heater maladies.

1 Either on top or high on the side of your water heater you'll find a *relief valve* to open if temperature or pressure inside the tank gets dangerously high. To test it, pull on its handle; if water rushes out of the pipe attached to it, all is well.

If nothing happens, close the stop valve in the cold water line, turn gas valve to pilot or shut off electrical power to the unit, and drain off enough water so the level in the tank is below the relief valve outlet. Now

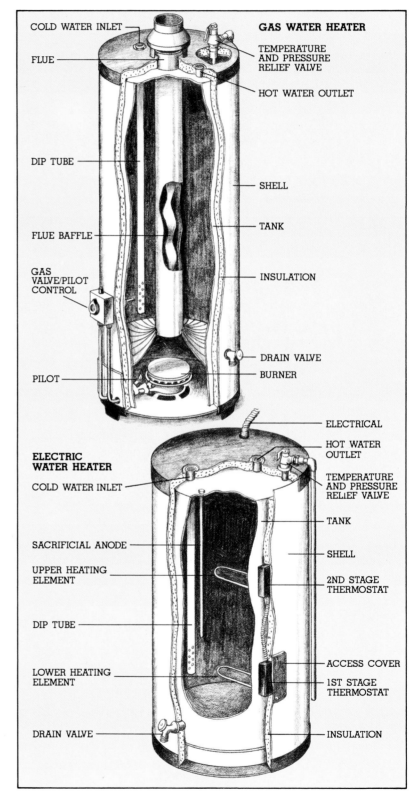

GAS WATER HEATER

COLD WATER INLET

FLUE

TEMPERATURE AND PRESSURE RELIEF VALVE

HOT WATER OUTLET

DIP TUBE

SHELL

TANK

FLUE BAFFLE

INSULATION

GAS VALVE/PILOT CONTROL

DRAIN VALVE

PILOT

BURNER

ELECTRICAL

HOT WATER OUTLET

ELECTRIC WATER HEATER

TEMPERATURE AND PRESSURE RELIEF VALVE

COLD WATER INLET

TANK

SACRIFICIAL ANODE

SHELL

UPPER HEATING ELEMENT

2ND STAGE THERMOSTAT

DIP TUBE

LOWER HEATING ELEMENT

ACCESS COVER

1ST STAGE THERMOSTAT

DRAIN VALVE

INSULATION

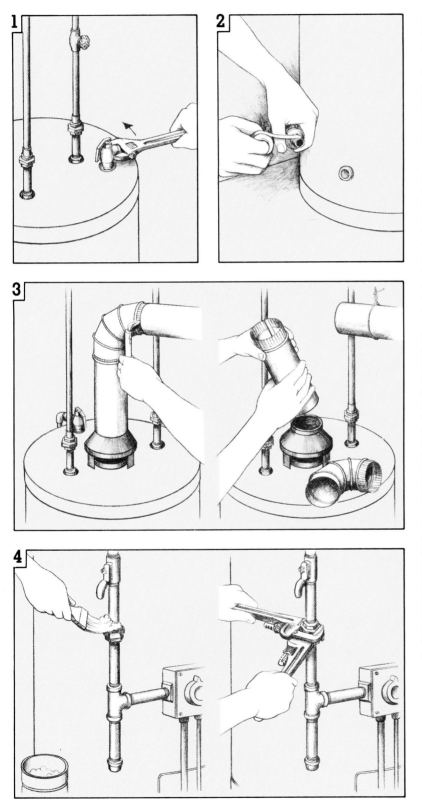

disengage the drainpipe from the valve, and the valve from the water heater.

Thread on a new valve, making sure to use pipe tape or pipe joint compound to seal the connection thoroughly. The pressure rating of the relief valve must not exceed the pressure rating of the heater. Reconnect the drain line, open the cold water stop valve, and you're all set.

2 Have a leaky water heater drain valve? To repair it, close the cold water stop valve, shut off the fuel supply, and completely drain the water heater. Screw out the faulty valve, then, after applying pipe tape or pipe joint compound to the connection's male threads, install a new assembly. Restore power to the unit, then open the stop valve and allow the tank to refill.

3 The condition of water heater flue pipes deserves careful monitoring. A rusted out or loose-fitting connection permits harmful vapors, including carbon monoxide, to enter the living area. If you suspect a leak in the water heater flue pipe, check out your suspicion by holding a candle as shown here. If the flame is drawn toward the pipe, you have a leak. This is one repair you shouldn't put off. Replace the defective section or sections immediately.

4 Water heater fuel line leaks are a serious matter, too. Generally, once a joint is sealed, you won't have any problem with it. But after making any repair to the fuel line, such as replacing a length of pipe, be sure to brush a soapy water solution on the joint. If you see new bubbles forming, there's a leak. Tighten the connection with a couple of pipe wrenches as shown in the illustration.

Troubleshooting Food Waste Disposals

A loud clanking noise, the strained buzz of an electric motor, or no action at all—each of these symptoms means you have waste disposal problems. Fortunately, though, the symptom often is worse than the illness. And if you know how to diagnose these strange goings-on, you should be able to get things going again without the expense of a plumber or a time-consuming trip to your plumbing parts supplier.

1 Disposals are pretty tough customers, but they're no match for flatware, bottle caps, and the like. If one of these undesirables falls accidentally into the grinding chamber, you'll hear the commotion right away. At best, the grinding blade will deform the item. Worse, a jam can result.

If your unit jams, shut off the power to it. Then remove the splash guard and survey the situation. Once you locate the obstruction, insert the end of a broom or mop handle into the grinding chamber and pry against

the turntable until it rotates freely. With one brand of disposal, you insert an allen wrench into a hole in the bottom of the disposal, and work the tool back and forth. Remove the obstruction from the chamber. Impossible jams require professional attention.

2 If your disposal motor shuts off while in operation, its overload protector probably sensed overheating and broke electrical contact. To reactivate the motor, wait about five minutes for it to cool, then push the reset button (it's on the bottom of the disposal).

If the unit won't start, make sure the fuse or circuit breaker controlling the flow of power to the disposal is functioning. Verify, too, that the unit is plugged in or otherwise connected to the power source.

3 Since a disposal gobbles up huge amounts of food waste, it's only to be expected that occasionally the drain line may clog. If this happens, disassemble the trap (make sure you have a pan or bucket beneath it to catch the water that will spill).

If the trap itself is clear, thread a drain auger into the drainpipe.

Caution: Do not attempt to clear a blocked drain line with chemicals of any type because if the solution doesn't work, you'll have a line filled with caustic solution.

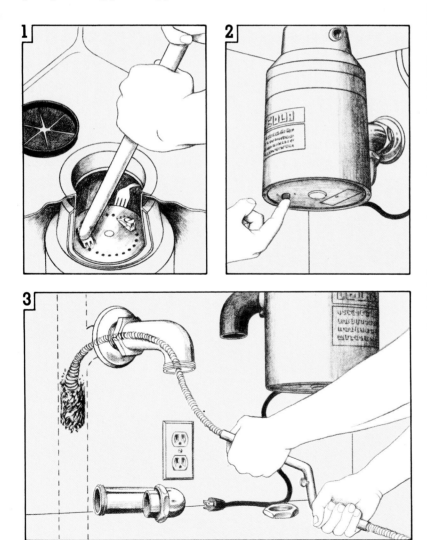

Quieting Noisy Pipes

Considering the conditions under which your home's water pipes operate, it's not surprising they make the noises they do. But that doesn't make their unexpected outbursts any less distracting. So if you've had it with that tick, tick, ticking, with the loud banging, and with all the other irritating clatter your pipes produce, read on.

Water hammer is perhaps the most common pipe noise of all. It results from a sudden stop in the flow of water, as would be the case when you turn off a fast-closing faucet.

You can generally trace *ticking* to a hot water pipe that was cool, then suddenly heated by circulating water.

Machine gun rattle, the annoying sound sometimes heard when you barely open a faucet, may indicate a seat washer is defective or loose. Air in the water lines also can be the culprit.

1 Generally, you can guess at the vicinity of a noisy pipe just by hearing it. So begin your sleuthing by going to the basement and checking to see whether one of the pipes has been knocking up against or rubbing a floor joist or subflooring. Once you've found the trouble spot, simply cushioning the pipe as shown here may be all you need to do. Short lengths of rubber pipe insulation are ideal for this.

2 The only sure way to deal effectively with water hammer is to install *water shock arrestors,* or *air chambers,* at strategic locations in your water lines. As you can see here, there are several ways to go, but the goal is always the same—namely, to provide a cushion of air for water to bang up against. Ideally, you should outfit each water supply line leading to each fixture with one of these devices. But to cut down on costs, start with those lines you know are causing problems. Installing a large air chamber between the water meter and the water heater makes good sense, too.

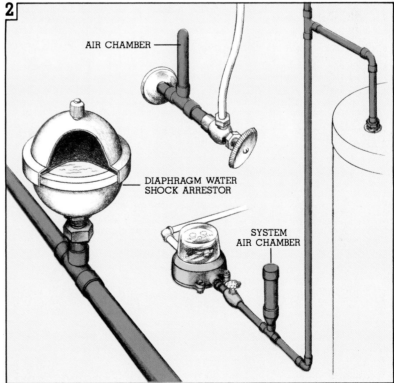

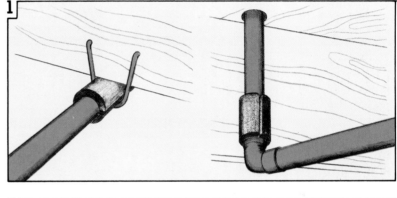

AIR CHAMBER

DIAPHRAGM WATER SHOCK ARRESTOR

SYSTEM AIR CHAMBER

MAKING PLUMBING IMPROVEMENTS

Too often people pick up their phone instead of their toolbox when it comes to installing a new toilet, sink, or even a faucet. Although usually the easy way out, there is another, less-expensive course of action. Why not tackle these and other plumbing improvements yourself? Sure, you'll take longer to make the hookups than a licensed plumber would, but think of the savings and the satisfaction you'll derive, not to mention the knowledge you'll gain about your home's plumbing system.

In the next 19 pages we have projects designed to improve your house's plumbing. You'll learn how to install faucets, sinks and lavatories, toilets, and much, much more. Naturally, some projects are more demanding than others, but you can accomplish every one of them without professional help.

Beginning on page 252, we even cover the specifics of how to extend existing plumbing lines to a new location. If this part of the project sounds as if it's too much to handle, you can always call in a licensed plumber to do the "rough-in," then take over from there yourself.

Installing Wall-Mount Faucets

Most faucets produced today are the *deck-mounted* type discussed on pages 242 and 243. But a great many *wall-mount* faucets still are in use, especially in older homes. So, many plumbing manufacturers carry a line of this type, too. Shown at right are two typical wall mounts: a newer type rotating-ball faucet and an older-style stem faucet.

Before going shopping for a new wall-mount faucet, measure the distance between the centers of the water supply pipes. Or better yet, take the old faucet with you. Doing either will enable your supplier to provide a compatible replacement.

1 Begin your installation by shutting off the water supply to the existing fixture and draining the lines. Then, loosen the nuts connecting the faucet body to the supply lines. On some newer models, you will have to remove the faucet body cover to get at the nuts. If you can't seem to budge

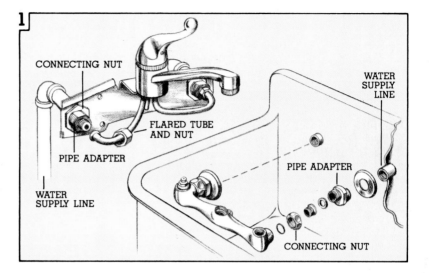

things loose, apply some penetrating oil, wait a few minutes, then try again. Set aside the old faucet body and unscrew all connecting hardware used to join the body to the supply lines.

Now follow the installation instructions that accompanied the new faucet. To ensure a leak-proof hookup, apply joint compound to or wrap pipe tape around all pipe threads.

When you've completed the installation, test for leaks by restoring water pressure. Tighten any loose connections.

2 A freezeproof wall hydrant, another wall-mount faucet, permits you to run water to an exterior wall without fear of burst pipes. To install one, first tap into a nearby cold water line using a tee fitting. Then extend the run to about 12 inches from the exterior wall and thread, solvent-weld, or solder an adapter fitting to the pipe.

3 Bore a hole through the wall, slip the hydrant into place, and join it to the adapter. Outside, screw the escutcheon to the siding.

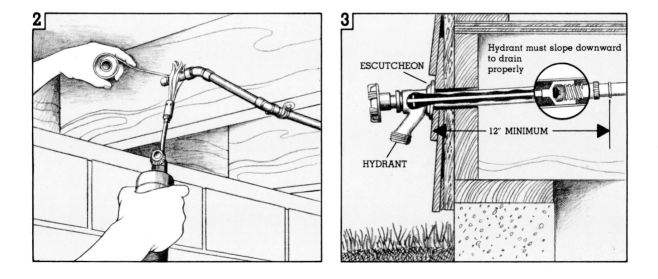

Installing Deck-Mount Faucets

The most difficult aspect of installing a new deck-mount faucet may be selecting the faucet itself. Your options are staggering, and as long as the faucet's inlet shanks align with the holes of the sink or lavatory you'll be securing it to, any style is fine. If you plan to install a sink or lavatory as well as a faucet, select the fixture first, then the faucet.

When replacing a worn-out or outdated stem faucet, ask your plumbing supplier for advice on the type faucet to purchase. Chances are he'll suggest one of the newer rotating-ball, disc, or washerless cartridge faucets because all are long-wearing and easy to repair.

For information on the correct way to install sinks and lavatories, refer to pages 246–249. And to find out more about the various types of faucets, see pages 218–227 for specifics.

1 Naturally, before installing a new faucet in an existing fixture, the old one must come out. To remove the old fixture, first shut off the water supply, then drain the lines. Work your way into the space below the sink or lavatory (this often can be quite a challenge); take a flashlight, a basin wrench, and an adjustable-end wrench with you.

Once you're in a fairly comfortable position, disengage the water supply inlet tubes from the faucet. Now, using the basin wrench, loosen and remove the locknuts holding the faucet to the deck. If your faucet is equipped with a spray attachment, remove the nuts securing the hose to the faucet body and the spray head to the deck.

After taking a well-deserved break, lift the old faucet up off the deck and set it aside.

Note: If your installation involves a sink or lavatory as well as a faucet, set the faucet and the drain assembly before positioning the fixture.

Begin installation of the new faucet by turning the faucet body upside down and slipping the *bottom plate* (smooth side down) and then the *rubber gasket* over the inlet shanks. Then set the faucet into the appropriate holes in the sink or lavatory deck.

2 Down under the fixture again, start a washer and locknut onto each inlet shank. Draw them up hand-tight, then tighten further with the basin wrench.

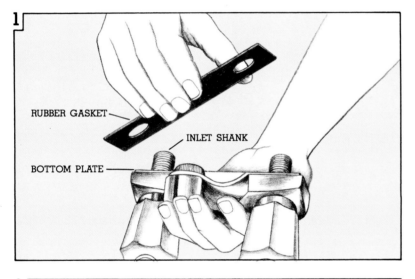

RUBBER GASKET

INLET SHANK

BOTTOM PLATE

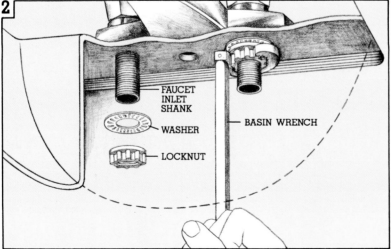

FAUCET INLET SHANK

WASHER

LOCKNUT

BASIN WRENCH

3 For faucets with spray attachments, secure the *hose guide* to the deck with the same washer/locknut arrangement used for the faucet itself. Then thread the spray hose down through the hole in the deck. Apply pipe joint compound to the threaded nipple at the end of the hose and secure it to the *spray outlet shank*.

4 To connect the water supply tubes to the faucet's inlet shanks, first fit a *compression nut, ring,* and *washer* onto each supply tube (this configuration varies from manufacturer to manufacturer). Then maneuver the tubes into the inlet shanks. Force the washer, ring, and nut up to each shank, then hand-tighten the nut. Further tighten with a wrench.

5 To complete the installation of a faucet in an existing lavatory, lower the *pop-up rod* down through the hole near the rear of the faucet spout, and through the holes at the upper end of the *linkage strap* attached to the *ball rod*. Tighten the thumbscrew to secure the rod.

With new lavatories, insert the *ball rod* into the opening in the *drain body* and secure it with the nut provided. Slip the rod through the linkage strap, then perform the procedure in the previous paragraph.

Open the water supply lines, partially fill the bowl with water, and check for leaks.

If the stopper fails to keep water in the bowl, loosen the thumbscrew and adjust the pop-up rod until the stopper provides a leakproof seal.

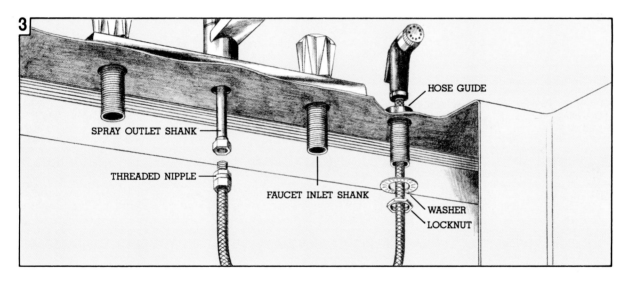

3

HOSE GUIDE

SPRAY OUTLET SHANK

THREADED NIPPLE

FAUCET INLET SHANK

WASHER

LOCKNUT

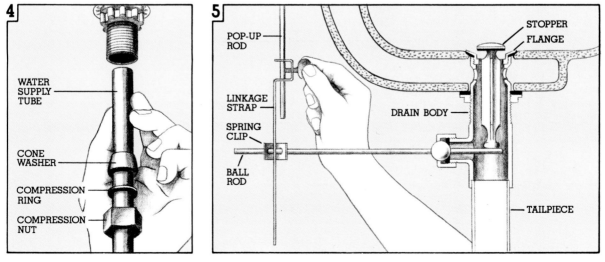

4

WATER SUPPLY TUBE

CONE WASHER

COMPRESSION RING

COMPRESSION NUT

5

POP-UP ROD

LINKAGE STRAP

SPRING CLIP

BALL ROD

STOPPER

FLANGE

DRAIN BODY

TAILPIECE

Installing Stop Valves

Like most of the other elements that make up home plumbing systems, stop valves go largely unnoticed by most people. That is until a water line suddenly bursts. Or a faucet washer goes bad and causes a leak. Or it comes time to replace an old toilet.

At times like these, do-it-yourselfers gain a keen appreciation for these handy fittings.

If your home's fixtures are outfitted with stop valves, shutting off the water supply to them won't be a hassle, nor will it necessitate shutting down the rest of the system. (Just turn the valve handle clockwise till it's fully closed, open the faucet(s) to drain the lines, then go ahead with your job.) If not, consider adding them—a not-too-difficult task.

No matter what material your water supply lines are made of, there's a stop valve made to order, in sizes ranging from ¼ inch on up. With copper lines, use brass valves. Iron and plastic pipes take iron and plastic stops respectively. *Transition fittings* (see pages 262–263) even allow you to change materials (for example, from galvanized iron to plastic). Where the valve will be in view, choose one that has a chromed finish.

Plumbing outlets and building material home centers stock all the items you'll need. At some outlets, you can buy the components in kit form.

1 To determine your stop valve needs, simply take a quick look at your home's fixtures and other water-carrying equipment. Lavatories, sinks, tubs, showers, and clothes washers should have one for both hot and cold lines. Toilets and water heaters require only one, on the cold water line, and dishwashers need one on the hot line only. Check out the water meter, too. It should have a valve beyond it.

2 When you shop for a stop valve, you may well be asked whether you want a *gate* valve or a *globe* valve. In most residential installations the globe type is better for several reasons. It not only is reliable, but also can be repaired easily, if necessary, and can control the flow of water through the line.

Gate valves, on the other hand, are better suited to controlling main water lines and pump lines. As a result, you probably won't find many uses for them.

Note that globe valves operate in much the same way as stem faucets, whereas gate types control flow with a gatelike apparatus that moves up and down. Both types are available *straight* or *angled* to adapt to various situations.

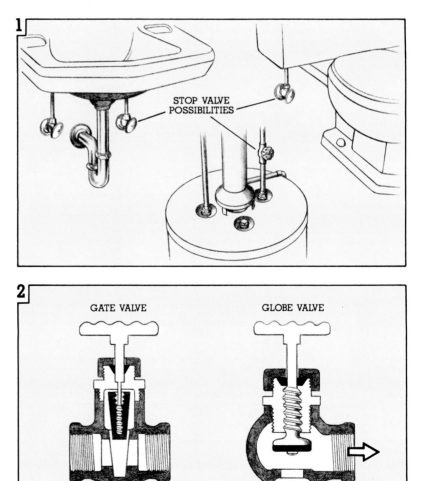

STOP VALVE POSSIBILITIES

GATE VALVE   GLOBE VALVE

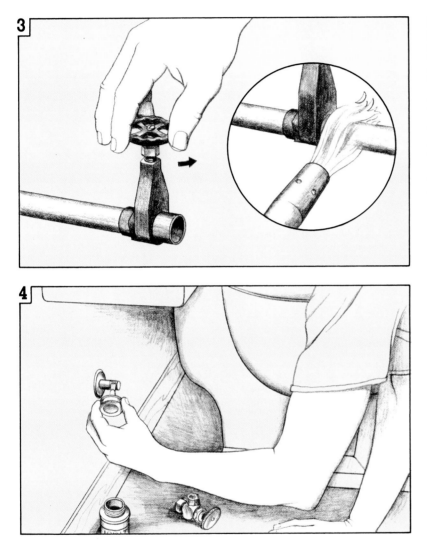

3 To install a stop valve, first shut off the water supply to the fixture and open the faucet to drain the line. Then cut into the line near the fixture. If you're dealing with copper pipe, use a tubing cutter; for iron or plastic pipe, you'll need a hacksaw.

Next, prepare the pipe to accept the fitting (see pages 266–272 for particulars). Before slipping a brass valve on a copper line, be sure to fully open the handle counterclockwise to prevent heat buildup and washer damage when heating the pipe. And when heating the connection for soldering, direct the flame at the valve, as shown, rather than at the pipe. Otherwise, the solder may seal the connection improperly.

4 If you're adding a stop to a fixture supplied by threaded pipe, simply apply a liberal coat of joint compound to the pipe's threads, then screw the fitting on till it's finger-tight. Tighten the connection further with pliers and a pipe wrench. Protect chrome-finished fittings by wrapping the jaws of the pliers with adhesive bandages or scrap material of some sort.

With the connection complete, restore water pressure to the line and test for leaks.

5 Installation of plastic stops differs only in that these you solvent-weld to the pipe. To do this, first dry-fit the stop and make alignment marks on the pipe and the valve. Remove any burrs that may be at the end of the pipe, and apply solvent to the inside of the fitting and the outside of the pipe. Working quickly, fit the stop on the pipe and give it a quarter-turn to spread the solvent. After making all hookups, turn on the water supply and test for leaks.

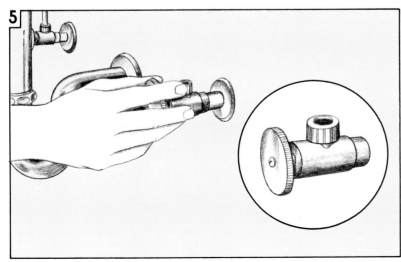

Installing Kitchen Sinks and Deck-Mount Lavatories

Ask any do-it-yourselfer who has ever completed a plumbing remodeling project and he'll tell you that the fun part comes when it's time to set the sink in place. It generally not only signals completion of the job, but also ranks as one of the easier plumbing tasks you'll undertake. See the material below and on the opposite page for all the particulars.

When shopping for a new deck-mount fixture, you won't find any shortage of products to choose from. What you will need to decide on is what material to choose—stainless or enameled steel, porcelain-covered cast iron, plastic, or vitreous china—and whether to buy a *rim-type* or *self-rimming* model (which has a rimlike flange around the bowl).

Sometimes, you can save considerable money if you're willing to do a little comparison shopping. Just make sure that in doing so you compare apples with apples. Often, look-alike fixtures resemble each other in appearance only.

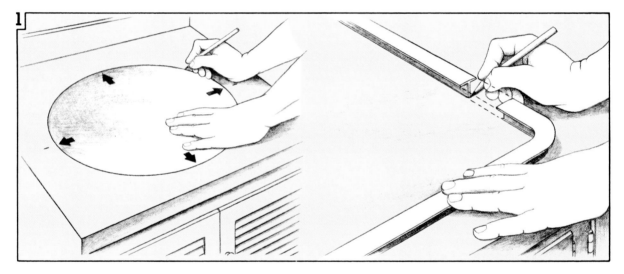

1 To replace an existing fixture, you must remove the old one. Begin by shutting off the water supply, then draining and disconnecting the water lines and the trap joining the sink or lavatory to the drainpipe. With self-rimming fixtures, you should be able to force the sink free by pushing up on it from below. Rim-type fixtures require that you first remove the lugs holding them in place. If you're removing a two-bowl cast-iron sink, you'll need help lifting it out of the opening.

To cut an opening in a counter top to accommodate a new sink or lavatory, first trace the outline of the opening. If yours is a self-rimming type fixture, use the template provid-ed. With rim-type units, position the frame squarely, then trace around the outside edge of its leg as shown. Use a saber saw to make the cut in the counter top.

2 Before lowering the sink or lavatory into the opening, it's wise to make the faucet and drain assembly hookups. For help with mounting the faucet, see pages 242–243. With lavatories, the drain assembly consists of a *basin outlet flange*, a drain body, a gasket, a locknut, and a *tailpiece*.

To assemble the components, start by running a ring of plumber's putty around the basin outlet. Then insert the flange into the outlet. Complete the hookup as shown here.

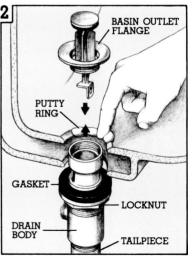

BASIN OUTLET FLANGE

PUTTY RING

GASKET

LOCKNUT

DRAIN BODY

TAILPIECE

3 Kitchen sinks, and certain other sinks, too, have basket strainers that tie the sink to the drain. To install one, lay a bead of plumber's putty around the sink outlet, then lower the basket (and a washer) into the outlet. With your free hand, slip the other washer and the locknut onto the strainer's shank. Tighten the locknut. Later, a tailpiece and trap will join the sink to the drain line.

4 To set a self-rimming fixture, apply a bead of silicone adhesive around the underside of the fixture's flange, about ¼ inch in from the edge. Then turn the fixture right side up and lower it into the opening, being care-ful to align it correctly. Press down on the fixture; some of the caulk will ooze out between it and the counter top. Smooth this excess with a slightly dampened finger.

5 To set a rim-type sink, fasten the rim to the sink, following the direc-tions that accompany the rim. Now set the sink into the opening in the counter top and secure it with lugs positioned at 6- to 8-inch intervals around the sink (see the detail). Snug up the lugs with a screwdriver.

Complete the installation by hook-ing up the water lines as shown on pages 242–243, and the drain as shown on page 212.

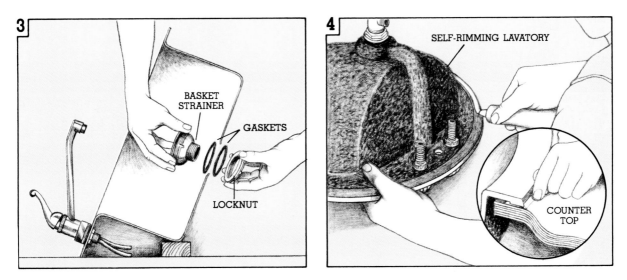

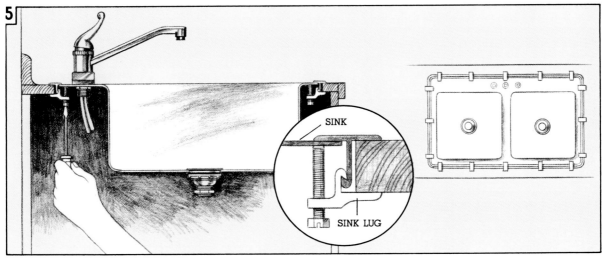

Installing Wall-Hung Lavatories

Like wall-mount faucets (see page 241), wall-hung lavatories are fading into the residential plumbing sunset. Most people prefer deck-mount fixtures like those on pages 246–247.

But plenty of wall-hung lavatories are still around. If you have one that needs replacing, or if you've had your eye on a pedestal-type lavatory at the local plumbing materials supplier, this and the following page will prove helpful to you.

As with their deck-mount cousins, wall-mount fixture prices tend to indicate the quality of the item.

1 When installing a new wall-mount, often your first job is to remove the old one. Start by shutting off the water supply; then drain and disconnect the water lines and the trap connecting the lavatory to the drainpipe. Pull straight up on the fixture and it should separate from the hanger bracket. If it doesn't, look underneath and make sure the lavatory isn't being held in place with bolts.

If yours is a new installation, running the water and drain lines comes first. For help with this part of the project, see pages 252–259. Once the lines are in, cut a 2×10 to span the distance between the studs that flank the pipes. Be careful not to drive nails into concealed pipes. Nail it between the studs. For greater strength, notch the studs to accept the 2×10 (the top of the 2×10 should be about 35 inches from the floor). Nail the 2×10 into place.

(With pedestal-type lavatories, which derive much of their support from the pedestal itself, you needn't bother with the 2×10. Special clips—supplied with the fixture—screwed firmly to the wall studs provide adequate support.)

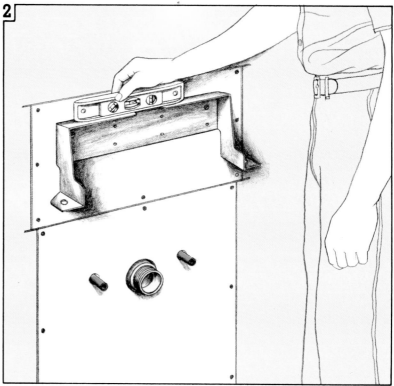

2 Now apply the finish wall material, then secure the hanger bracket to the 2×10 blocking, making sure that the bracket is level. (Refer to the instructions that accompany the fixture to find out the correct bracket height.) Use plenty of wood screws for this, as the bracket must withstand a considerable load.

3 Turn the lavatory on its side and make the faucet and drain body hookups. For help with this, see pages 242–243 and 246. Once this is out of the way, carefully lower the fixture onto the hanger bracket. The flange on the hanger bracket fits into a corresponding slot in the lavatory. With some models, toggle bolts help anchor the bracket to the fixture.

4 If the fixture you're installing came with support legs, fasten them to the lavatory, then adjust them to provide adequate support. To do this, twist the top portion of each leg. Use a torpedo level to check whether the fixture is level.

5 To complete the installation, first equip both water supply lines with a stop valve (if they don't already have them). Pages 244–245 show how to do this. Then connect the water supply inlets to the stop valves, and the trap to the drain body and the drainpipe. Restore water pressure, run water into the basin, and check for leaks. Tighten any loose connections.

(Note: Bracket-supported wall-hung lavatories will stand up well to normal everyday use, but be sure to remind everyone in the family that exerting excessive downward pressure on them can spell trouble.)

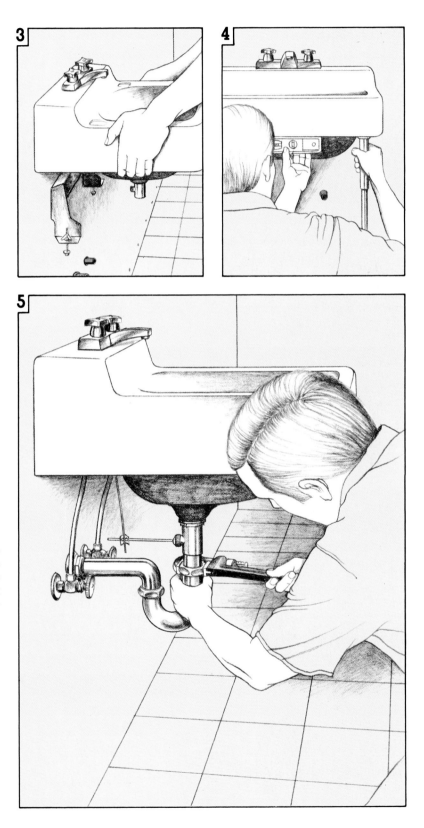

Installing a Toilet

Plumbers know it! Home builders and remodeling contractors do, too! But the average person has no idea how easy it is, under normal circumstances, to install a toilet. In fact, to replace an existing fixture or install one where the supply and drainage lines are in place, or "stubbed-in," should take you no more than a few hours to do the entire job.

Naturally, the job becomes more complex if you have to run water and drain lines to a new location. If that is your situation, refer to pages 252–259, which deal with extending existing plumbing lines. You may be best off to have a licensed plumber run the drain lines and possibly the water lines to the desired location for you.

The copy and sketches below and on the opposite page take you step-by-step from the installation of a closet flange onto a closet bend to the hookup of the water supply line.

When shopping for a toilet, you'll quickly notice the price differences between products. Most of these are attributable to quality variations. Although all toilets are molded of vitreous china clay, and baked in a high-temperature kiln, the similarity ends there.

Despite their attractive price, it's best to shy away from *washdown* toilets, as they are less efficient and noisier than the better-quality *reverse-trap* or *siphon-jet* models.

1 Unless you're replacing an existing fixture, start by installing a closet flange (be sure the bolt slots are parallel to the wall), then inserting the bowl hold-down bolts that come with the toilet. For plastic pipe, apply solvent to the outside of the *closet bend* and the inside of the *closet flange*. Fit the flange down onto the bend, then twist the flange a quarter-turn to spread the solvent. Further secure the flange by driving screws into the floor material below.

With lead pipe, cut the pipe down to floor level, fit a brass flange over the pipe, form the lead so it lies back against the flange (see the detail), clean the joint, apply flux, and solder the joint where the two materials meet (aim the torch at the flange rather than the lead). Again, fasten the flange to the floor with screws.

2 If you're replacing an old toilet with a new one, remove the old one using the techniques shown here, only in reverse order. Carefully remove the toilet from its container, then turn the bowl upside down on a cushioned surface. Run a bead of plumber's

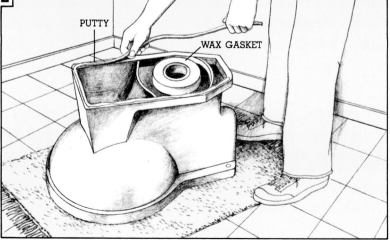

CLOSET FLANGE

CLOSET BEND

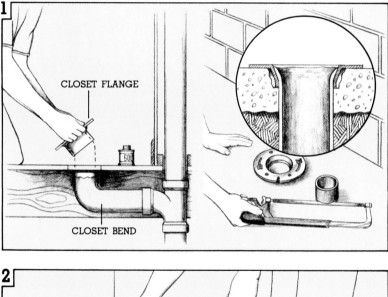

PUTTY

WAX GASKET

putty around the perimeter of the bowl's base, and fit a wax gasket (sold separately) over the outlet opening.

3 Return the bowl to its upright position, and gingerly set it in place atop the closet flange. Make sure the hold-down bolts align with the holes in the bowl's base. Slip a metal washer over each bolt, place on the nuts, and tighten snugly. Don't overtighten or you could crack the bowl and have to return to the store for another unit.

4 Now you're ready for the tank. First, lay the *spud washer,* beveled edge

down, over the bowl inlet opening. This washer forms the seal between the tank and bowl.

5 Gently lower the tank onto the bowl, being sure to align the tank's holes with those toward the rear of the bowl. Now secure the tank to the bowl with hold-down bolts, washers, and nuts provided with the new toilet. Note that the rubber washer rests inside the tank under the bolt. Once firmly in place, this washer will prevent leaking.

6 Complete the installation by hooking up the water supply line as shown here, and then fastening the

toilet seat (sold separately) to the bowl. Turn the stop valve to open, allow the tank to fill with water, then flush the toilet several times and check for leaks.

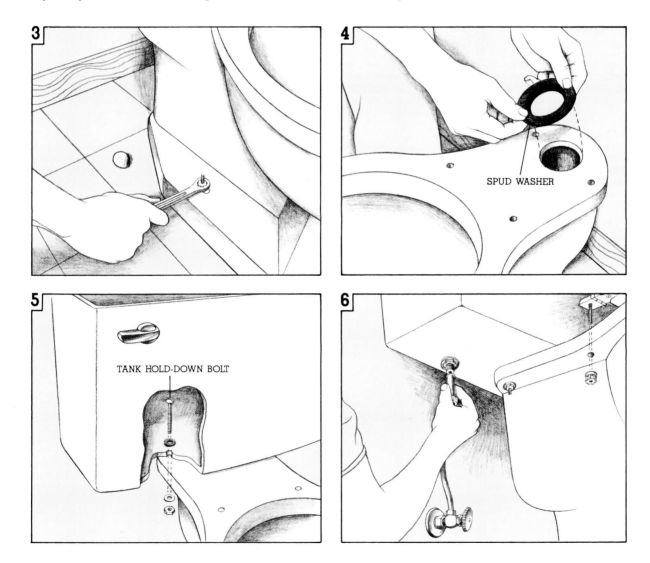

SPUD WASHER

TANK HOLD-DOWN BOLT

Tapping In for a New Fixture

The improvements shown on the preceding pages can be considered end-of-the-line jobs—you simply hook new fittings or fixtures to pipes that are more or less where you want them. Now let's look at several different ways you can run lines to a spot where you didn't have a fixture before.

With water, getting there is the easiest part of the problem. In fact, supply lines are the last item a plumber considers when he lays out a new run. Far trickier are the drain-waste-vent (DWV) lines that carry away water, waste, and potentially harmful sewer gas.

These and the pages that follow show only the easiest ways to tap in for a new fixture—and our hookups apply only to liquid-waste carriers such as lavatories, tubs, showers, and some sinks. For a toilet, kitchen sink, or the elaborate DWV lines you'd need for a new bathroom, you may want to consult a plumber.

Realize, too, that even for these relatively simple modifications, you'll probably need to apply to your local building department for a permit, and arrange with them to have the work inspected before you cover up any new pipes.

Planning Drain Lines

Before you begin to think about extending your plumbing system, map out exactly where its existing lines run. Your home probably has one or more drainage arrangements similar to the one shown here.

Notice that the existing fixtures, indicated in white, cluster near a *wet wall.* It's usually a few inches thicker than other walls to accommodate the 3- or 4-inch-diameter *stack* required in residential construction. (To find your wet wall, note where the stack is on your roof.) Hot and cold supply lines (not shown) may be in the wet wall, too.

The fixtures drain into the main stack directly or into *horizontal runs* that slope toward it at a pitch of at least ¼ inch per foot. Runs of more than a few feet also must be vented (check local codes), usually via a short *vertical run* and a *circuit vent* that returns to the stack. This piping is concealed inside normal-thickness walls and floors.

The fixtures shown in blue depict your main options. Generally, the closer to the stack you can get, the easier your job will be.

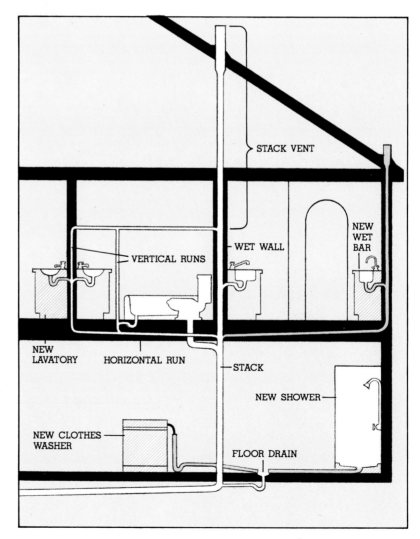

STACK VENT

WET WALL

NEW WET BAR

VERTICAL RUNS

NEW LAVATORY

HORIZONTAL RUN

STACK

NEW SHOWER

NEW CLOTHES WASHER

FLOOR DRAIN

Venting Possibilities

Think of a main stack as a two-way chimney—water and wastes go down, gases go up. Just as you wouldn't install a fireplace without a chimney, neither should you consider adding a fixture without properly venting it. Strangle a drain's air supply and you risk creating a siphoning effect that can suck water out of traps. This in turn breaks the seal that provides protection from gas backup. The flow of wastes oftentimes becomes retarded too.

Codes are very specific about how you must vent fixtures, and these requirements differ from one locality to another. So check your community's regulations for details about the five household systems illustrated below.

Unit-venting—sometimes called *common-venting*—lets two similar fixtures share the same stack fitting. With this method you can put a new fixture back to back with one that already exists, creating a Siamese arrangement on opposite sides of the wet wall. You simply open up the wall, replace the existing *sanitary tee* fitting with a *sanitary cross* and connect both traps to it. The drains of unit-vented fixtures must be at the same height.

Wet-venting lets a portion of one fixture's drain line also serve as the vent for another. Not all codes permit wet-venting, and those that do specify that the vertical drain be one pipe-size larger than the upper fixture drain; in no case can it be smaller than the lower drain.

Realize, too, that regardless of how you vent a fixture, codes limit the distance between its trap outlet and the vent. These distances depend on the size of drain line you're running. For 1¼-, 1½-, and 2-inch drain lines—the sizes you'll most likely be working with—2, 3, and 5 feet are typical figures.

Thinking about installing a new shower, sink, or washing machine in your basement? If so, codes may allow you to *indirect vent* the new fixture into a floor drain. In this situation, the open drain serves as a vent for the fixture.

In a few situations, you might also be able to tap into a *circuit vent.* The new fixture must be between the vent and the stack, though. And don't try this with anything other than a small lavatory or bar sink; existing DWV lines might not be able to handle the load from a big water-user.

As a last resort, consider a *separate vent* for a fixture placed some distance from the stack. Without a doubt, this is the most costly and time-consuming way to go, but it offers the utmost in flexibility. More about separate venting on page 259.

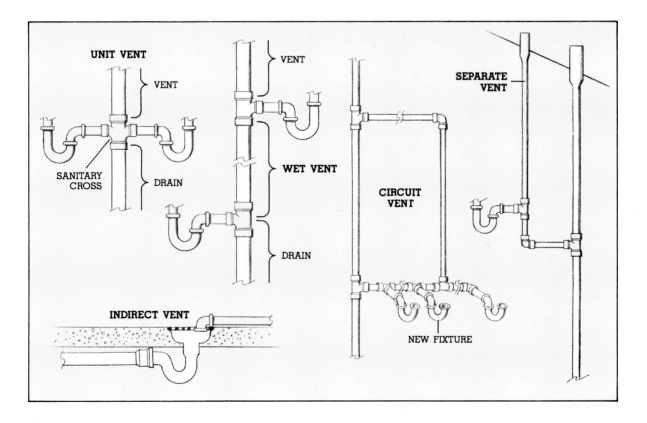

Tapping into Wet Wall Lines

Exactly how you connect a new fixture to existing drain and supply lines depends partly on what the lines are made of and partly on the materials permitted by your plumbing code.

The drawings here show the plan of attack you'd follow in a newer home that has a plastic or copper drain-waste-vent stack and supply lines. In an older house plumbed with a cast-iron stack and galvanized supply pipes, adapt the procedures shown on pages 256–259.

Before you begin, shut off your home's main water supply. Drain the lines by opening faucets at the system's lowest point. Also provide ventilation for sewer gas that escapes when you cut into the stack. Or cap the lines with duct tape.

1 Open up the wet wall to the center of the studs on either side of the stack. This gives you plenty of room to maneuver and makes it easier to patch the opening later.

A big cutout also helps you seek out supply lines, which may or may not be in the same cavity. If not, and you don't want to make another opening, bring them up from below.

Next, firmly anchor the stack, using a pair of *riser clamps* that rest on cleats above and below the point where you'll be cutting in.

2 Now it's time for some careful measuring. Mark the fixture's rough-in dimensions on the wall, making sure the location doesn't exceed the maximum code-permitted distance explained on page 253. Once you know exactly where the trap will be, draw a line that slopes from that point to the stack at the rate of ¼ inch per foot. This tells you exactly where the new fitting's inlet opening must be located.

Cut either copper or plastic with a hacksaw. Take your time when doing this: The cuts must be square. Remove a section of pipe that is about 8 inches longer than the *sanitary tee* you'll be installing.

3 Taking out a sizable section of the stack gives you enough room to fit in the tee with a couple of *spacers* cut from the leftover stack pipe. Fit the tee, spacers, and a pair of *slip couplings* into place as shown. Slide the couplings up and down to secure the spacers.

Tubs, showers, and most sinks and lavatories commonly require that you install 1½-inch drainpipe and fittings; some lavatories hook up with 1¼-inch stock.

At this point, just dry-assemble the components. Don't solder or solvent-weld them until you've cut and fit the remainder of the drainage run.

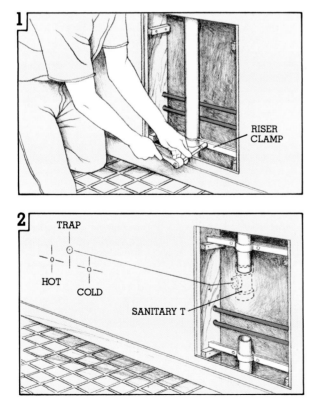

1

RISER CLAMP

2

TRAP

HOT

COLD

SANITARY T

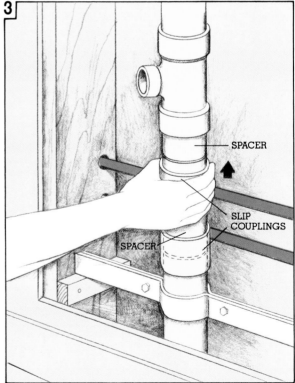

3

SPACER

SLIP COUPLINGS

SPACER

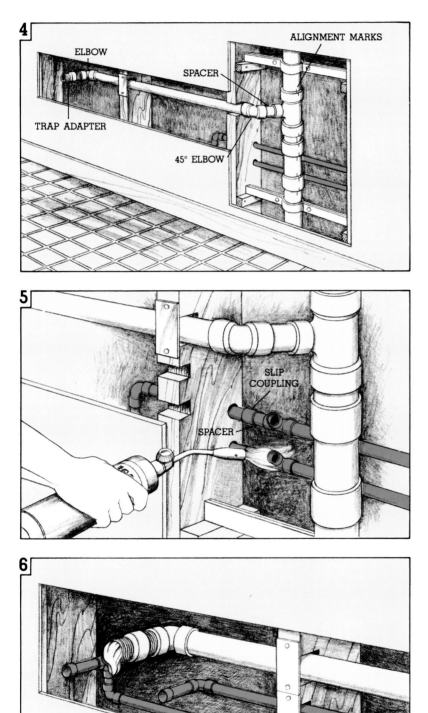

4 For concealed runs, cut out a strip of drywall and notch the studs just deeply enough to support the pipes. You can secure an exposed run to the studs, using pipe straps.

You'll probably need a *45-degree elbow* and short *spacer* to negotiate the turn at the stack, and a *90-degree elbow* and a *trap adapter* at the trap.

Once you're satisfied that everything lines up properly and falls ¼ inch per foot toward the stack, scribe each pipe and fitting with *alignment marks*, then go back and permanently solder or solvent-weld each component. To learn about soldering copper pipe, see pages 266 and 267; for plastic, turn to pages 270–272.

Concealed pipes should be protected with metal plates nailed to each stud as shown. This wards off any nails or screws that might be driven into the wall after the pipe is covered.

5 Tap rigid copper and plastic supply lines using similar spacer/slip coupling/tee setups; with flexible tubing, you can dispense with the coupling and spacer, cutting out just enough to fit in the tees.

Again, cut, dry-assemble, and check the runs before completing the connections. Supply lines should slope away slightly from the fixture so they can be drained. If you'll be soldering copper, wet down the wall cavity and have a fire extinguisher and water on hand in case nearby wood catches fire.

6 Unless you'll be connecting the new fixture right away, cap off the supply lines, turn on the water, and check for leaks. Cap the drain, too, or stuff a rag into it so sewer gas can't escape into your home. Don't close up the wall until you've tested all supply and drain connections. To learn about hooking up the fixture itself, see pages 241–251.

Tapping into Exposed Basement Lines

Many older homes originally were equipped with hub-type cast-iron drain pipes and galvanized supply lines. But that doesn't mean you have to stick with these materials when you add a new fixture. A no-hub fitting gets you into the stack with a minimum of hassle, and special adapter fittings let copper or plastic supply lines take over where the galvanized leaves off. Here's how to make the transition in a typical under-the-floor situation.

1 Kitchen sinks and branch drains from first-floor bathrooms often join the stack just below floor level. A tee fitting like this one offers an ideal spot to tap in.

Begin by securely supporting the stack above and below; cast iron is heavy, so brace it well. You may also need to add a hanger to hold up the horizontal run.

2 To cut into the stack you'll need to rent or borrow a chain-type pipe cutter. Wrap the chain around the stack, hook it, and, with the handles open, crank the chain tight with the turn screw. Then draw the handles together. This part of the job takes muscle, but the cutters at each link will eventually prevail and cause the pipe to break cleanly. Cut just beneath the pipe's hubbed end.

3 Make a second cut about 4 inches below the first, then cut the horizontal run. Have a helper on hand—the fitting may simply drop clear, or you may have to wrestle it loose from the hub above. If that doesn't work, hit the fitting with a heavy hammer, or melt the lead in its hub with a torch.

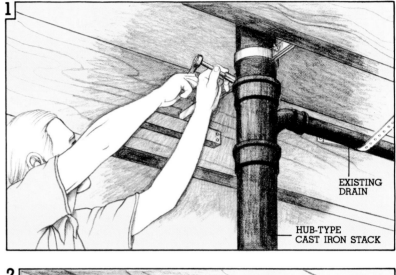

EXISTING DRAIN

HUB-TYPE CAST IRON STACK

CUTTER

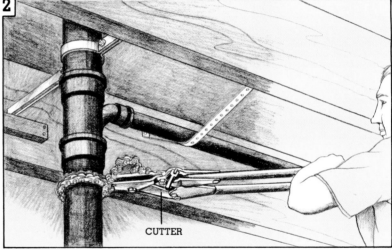

4 No-hub fittings were designed to be completely compatible with old-style cast-iron pipe. For this connection you need a *sanitary cross*, a couple of *spacers*, and *clamps* sized to suit the cross' inlets and outlets.

To assemble the connection, slip clamps over the pipe ends, insert the fitting, slide the clamps into place, and tighten them with a screwdriver. One advantage of no-hub is that you needn't be fussy about aligning fittings, as you must with plastic or copper. If a connection is out of kilter, you simply unscrew the clamps, straighten out the fitting, and retighten. For more about working with no-hub, see page 273.

5 Two more lengths of pipe, an elbow, and a sanitary tee complete the drain run. If codes permit, you may want to go with a plastic run instead. Avoid boring through the *soleplate* if you can. If you can't, center the hole and don't make it any larger than necessary. Leave at least ⅝ inch of wood around the hole. Support the run with a strap in the basement and a riser clamp that rests atop the soleplate. Check that the horizontal pipe slopes ¼ inch per foot.

6 Sometimes, the distance required for the new run exceeds code requirements. In that event, you need to run a separate vent. Here's what's involved.

Begin in the attic. Again, if you must bore through a plate, size the hole just big enough to handle the pipe's outside diameter. For a 1½-inch drain, you'll probably need only a 1¼-inch vent; check your code.

Now mark the point where you need a hole in the roof by driving a nail up through the sheathing. Remove the shingle that the nail penetrates and bore through the sheathing. If there's a rafter in the way, you can offset the vent with a couple of 45-degree elbows. *(continued)*

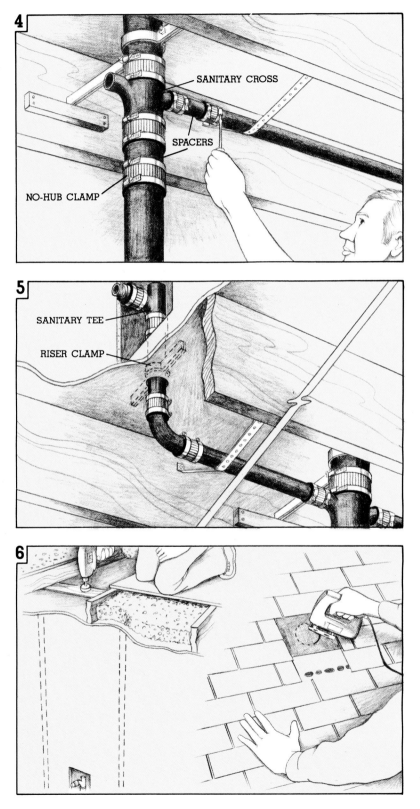

Tapping into Exposed Basement Lines *(continued)*

7 If you've used no-hub pipe to this point, you may want to consider switching to copper or plastic for the vent stack. These materials weigh much less, and the longer lengths you'll need will be easier to maneuver and set into place.

Make the switch with a *hubless adapter* at the sanitary tee. One end of this fitting accommodates no-hub clamps, the other has a socket for copper or plastic pipe.

8 Regardless of the material you decide to use for a vent, be sure to anchor it with a riser clamp to wood structural members in the attic.

In colder climates, codes generally call for an *increaser* up top where piping penetrates the roof. This prevents freeze-ups that could clog the vent. It typically measures at least 2 inches in diameter, but check your code for specifics. Also find out how high the vent must extend above the roof. One foot is typical.

Cap off your installation, using a *vent flashing* that slips over the increaser. Tuck its flange under shingles on the up-roof side and seal all around with roofing cement.

9 With the DWV system complete, all that remains is to extend supply lines to the new location. If you find a couple of convenient unions in an existing run, crack these open and dismantle them back to the nearest fittings. Otherwise, cut each supply line pipe back to the nearest fitting and turn out the pieces.

To go from galvanized to plastic or copper, use a threaded *adapter* like the one shown here. Never hook copper pipe directly to galvanized. Electrolytic action will corrode the connection.

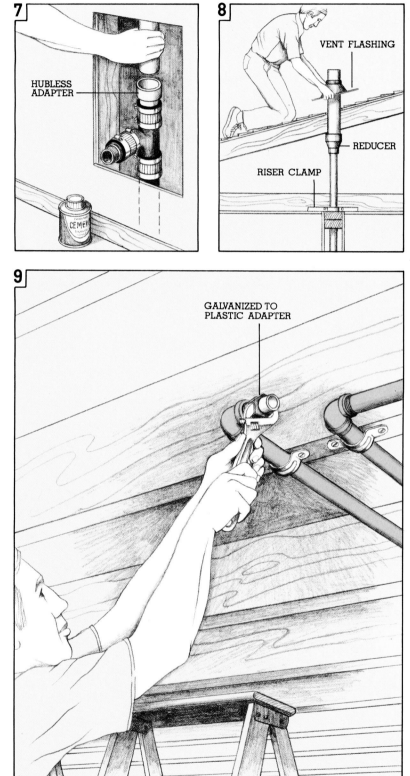

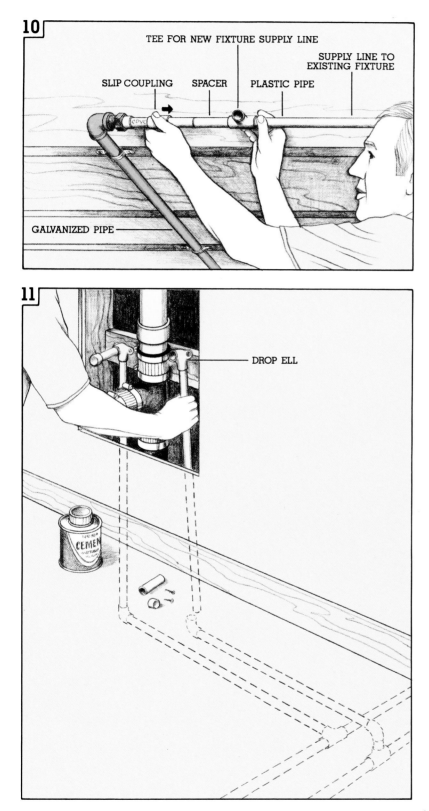

10 Now replace the run you've removed with copper or plastic pipe and a tee fitting. Splice in with a slip coupling and spacer. Don't solder or solvent-weld the connections until you've assembled the remainder of the supply line and checked to be sure everything fits properly.

Supply lines should fall slightly away from fixtures so the system can be drained easily from its lowest point. You needn't slope them as drastically as you did the drain line; just slightly off-level is adequate.

11 A pair of *drop ells* at the fixture location offers a way to both support pipes and get them around the bend. Attach them to a cleat toenailed into studs on either side of the wall cavity.

You may need to add an extra elbow to either the hot or cold supply line to space them apart the 6 or 8 inches typically required in fixture roughs.

After all dry-assembled runs check out, you can solder or solvent-weld all of its fittings, as shown on pages 266–267 and 270–272. Before you solder, open every faucet on the run. Heat from the torch can burn out washers and other parts, and built-up steam could rupture a fitting or pipe wall.

Remember, too, that plastic lines, especially those that handle hot water, need room for expansion and contraction. Enlarged holes in framing members allow for this.

The moment of truth comes, of course, when you cap off the supply lines, turn on the water, and look for leaks. Some codes require two plumbing inspections—one before you patch up the wall and install the fixture, the other when all work is completed.

PLUMBING BASICS AND PROCEDURES

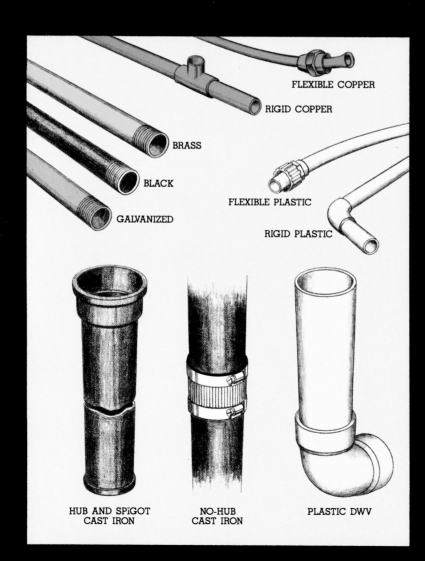

FLEXIBLE COPPER

RIGID COPPER

BRASS

BLACK

GALVANIZED

FLEXIBLE PLASTIC

RIGID PLASTIC

HUB AND SPIGOT
CAST IRON

NO-HUB
CAST IRON

PLASTIC DWV

This section delves into the largely hidden elements of your home's plumbing system—its pipes and the fittings that join them together.

Check the drawing at left and the chart on the opposite page and you'll find you have a multitude of choices here. That's because piping materials and the systems used for assembling them have undergone a dramatic evolution in the past 40 years.

Before World War II, most homes had galvanized steel, brass, or bronze supply lines, and cast-iron drain-waste-vent (DWV) systems. After the war, copper became the favored material for supply lines, and sometimes for DWV runs as well. More recently, plastic has appeared on both the supply and DWV scenes, and no-hub clamps have made cast iron much easier to deal with.

Which you choose for a project depends partly on the job you want it to do, and partly on the materials local codes do and don't permit. You needn't, however, be limited by the existing pipes in your home. Special adapter fittings make it easy to interconnect new materials with old.

Choosing the Right Pipe Materials

Material	Type	Uses	Features and Joining Techniques
Copper	Rigid	Hot and cold supply lines; DWV*	The most widely used, although more costly than other types. Lightweight and highly durable. Sold in 20-foot (and sometimes shorter) lengths. Solder it together.
	Flexible	Hot and cold supply lines	Comes in easily bent 60- and 100-foot coils. Solder or connect with special, mechanical fittings.
Threaded	Galvanized steel	Hot and cold water lines; DWV* (not for gas)	Because it's cumbersome to work with and tends to build up lime deposits that constrict water flow, galvanized isn't widely used anymore. Standard-length pipe must be cut, threaded, and screwed into fittings, but you can buy shorter precut sections that are already threaded.
	Black steel	Gas and heating lines; vent piping	The main difference between this and galvanized is that "black pipe" rusts readily and isn't used as a carrier for household water.
	Brass and bronze	Hot and cold water lines	Again, you cut and thread. Very durable but also very costly.
Plastic	ABS	DWV* only	Black in color. Lightweight and easy to work with, it can be cut with an ordinary saw, and cemented together with a special solvent. Not all local codes permit its use.
	PVC	Cold water and DWV*	Cream-colored, blue-gray, or white. PVC has the same properties as does ABS, but you can't interchange these materials or their solvents.
	CPVC	Hot and cold supply lines	White, gray, or cream-colored. Same properties as ABS and PVC.
	Flexible polybutylene (PB)	Hot and cold water lines	White or cream-colored. Goes together with special fittings. Costly and not widely used.
	Flexible polyethylene (PE)	Cold water and gas	Black. This material has the same properties as polybutylene. Used mainly for sprinkler systems.
Cast iron	Hub and spigot	DWV* only	Joints are packed with oakum, then sealed with molten lead. Some plumbers use a special compression-type rubber gasket.
	No-hub	DWV* only	Joins with gaskets and clamps.

*DWV is the plumbing industry abbreviation for drain-waste-vent lines.

Choosing the Right Fitting

The parts bins at a plumbing supply house contain hundreds of fittings that let you interconnect any pipe material in an almost unimaginable number of ways. To know what to ask for, though, you have to master a plumber's vocabulary that's largely alphabetical. Here are the ABCs of ells (Ls), tees (Ts), and wyes (Ys).

1 As you might guess, *supply (or pressure) fittings* can be used only in *supply lines*. You can see why by looking at the details here. A drainpipe and fitting join and form a smooth inner surface to ensure passage of solid wastes. But with supply pipes and fittings, you'll note a restriction where pipe and fitting meet.

When changing directions in a supply run, you'll need an *elbow* (ell). Most make 90- or 45-degree turns. A *street ell* has male and female connections to allow for insertion into another fitting. A *reducing ell* joins one size pipe to another.

When you order fittings, give the size first, then the material, and finally the type you want. You might, for example, ask for a "½-inch galvanized 90-degree ell." With reducing fittings, give the larger size first, then the smaller.

Tees are used wherever two runs intersect. *Reducing tees* let you connect pipes of different diameters, as you would in taking a ½-inch branch off a ¾-inch main supply line.

A *coupling* connects pipes end to end. *Reducers* let you step down from one pipe diameter to a smaller one. *Slip couplings* (not shown) get you into an existing copper or plastic line, as shown on pages 256–259.

Adapters let you go from male to female or vice versa. Special adapters, sometimes called *transition fittings*, permit you to change from one pipe material to another.

In any run of threaded pipe, you'll need a *union* somewhere. This fitting compensates for the frustrating fact that you can't simultaneously turn pipe into fittings at either end.

Caps and *plugs* close off the ends of pipes and fittings. A *bushing* lets you thread a pipe into a larger-diameter fitting.

Nipples—lengths of pipe that are less than 12 inches long—are sold in standard sizes because short pieces are difficult to cut and thread. A *close nipple* is threaded from one end to the other to join female connections.

2 Examine *drainage fittings* and note how they're designed to keep waste water always flowing downhill. Sometimes called *sanitary fittings*, they have gentle curves rather than sharp angles, where waste might get hung up.

Choose ¼ *bends* for 90-degree turns, ⅕ bends for 72-degree angles, ⅙ for 60 degrees, and ⅛ for 45 degrees.

Sanitary branches such as the *tee, wye,* and *cross* shown here come in a variety of configurations that suit situations where two or more lines converge. These can be tricky to order, so make a sketch of your proposed drainage lines, identifying all pipe sizes, and take it to your supplier when you order.

Toilet hookups require a *closet bend*, which connects to the main drain, and a *closet flange*, which fits over the bend and anchors the bowl.

Your drainage system probably has at least one *cleanout*, but consider installing another to get an auger into a drain that chronically clogs.

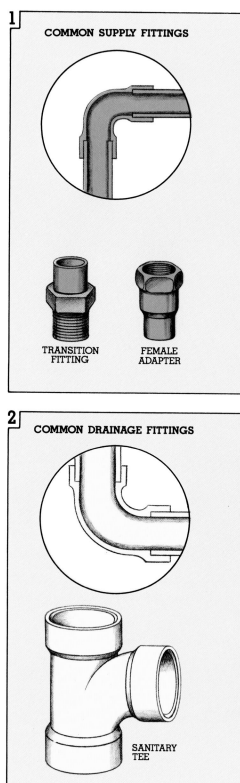

1 COMMON SUPPLY FITTINGS

TRANSITION FITTING

FEMALE ADAPTER

2 COMMON DRAINAGE FITTINGS

SANITARY TEE

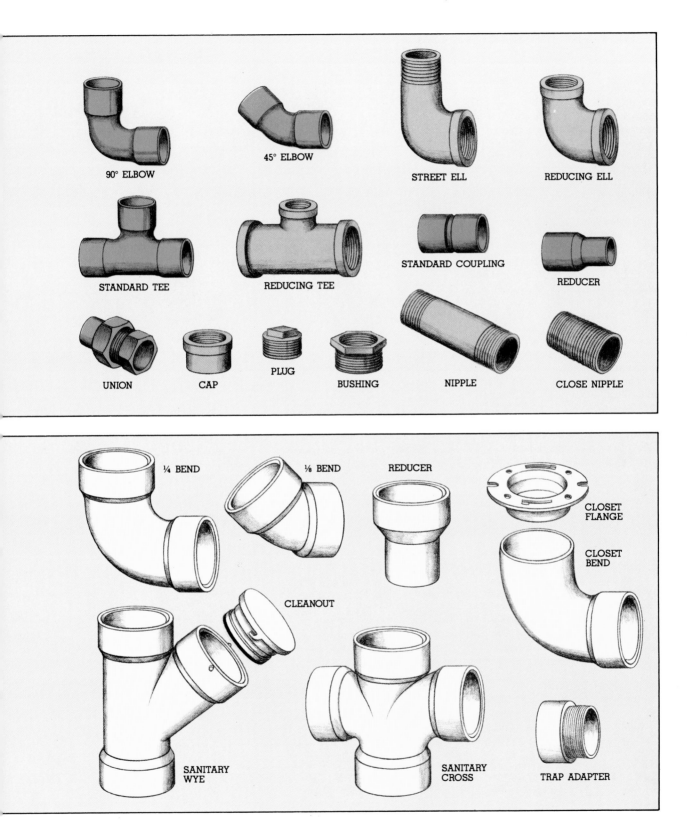

90° ELBOW

45° ELBOW

STREET ELL

REDUCING ELL

STANDARD TEE

REDUCING TEE

STANDARD COUPLING

REDUCER

UNION

CAP

PLUG

BUSHING

NIPPLE

CLOSE NIPPLE

¼ BEND

⅛ BEND

REDUCER

CLOSET FLANGE

CLOSET BEND

CLEANOUT

SANITARY WYE

SANITARY CROSS

TRAP ADAPTER

Measuring Pipes and Fittings

One of the most frustrating things that can happen in a plumbing project is to shut off the water, break into a line, then discover you haven't bought the right-size pipe or fittings to put things back together again.

Errors in measuring are easy to make, too, because plumbing dimensions aren't always what they appear to be. Holding a rule to the outside of a steel pipe, for example, might seem to indicate that you're dealing with ¾-inch material. But pipes are always sized according to their *inside diameters,* as illustrated in sketch 1. Since the wall thickness of steel pipe adds another ¼ inch or so, the true size of that "¾-inch" line is actually ½ inch. This—known as the *nominal dimension*—is what you'd ask for at a plumbing supplier.

Sizing up fittings can be just as confusing. Their inside diameters must be large enough to fit over the pipe's outside diameter, so what is known as a ½-inch fitting (because it's used with ½-inch pipe) has openings that are about ¾ inch in diameter.

The third mathematical pitfall for amateur plumbers occurs when you need to compute the length of pipe necessary to get from one fitting to the next. Here you must account for the depth of each fitting's socket, as well as the distance between them.

To keep straight these critical ins and outs of plumbing measurements, study the drawings on these pages and refer to the dimensions chart for specific guidelines.

1 Measure a pipe's inside diameter if possible. This may vary from standard pipe size, depending on wall thickness. To get the nomimal dimension, round off to the nearest ⅛ inch.

It's not practical to open up a pipe in an existing run just to measure it. It's much better to examine the fittings. Some manufacturers indicate on the fitting itself the size pipe it's intended for.

2 Calipers or dividers offer the most accurate way to measure outside diameters. To convert from outside to inside dimensions, see the chart opposite.

3 To figure the length of a pipe, first measure from face to face, as shown. Next, check the chart for the socket depth of the material you're working with. Since pipes have fittings on both ends, multiply by two, then add the face-to-face length.

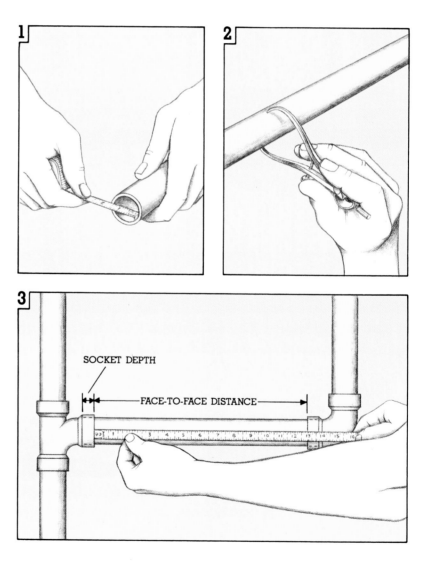

SOCKET DEPTH

FACE-TO-FACE DISTANCE

4 Pipes must engage fully in fixture sockets. Otherwise, the joint could leak. Socket depths vary from one pipe size and material to another. Only with no-hub cast-iron pipe do you not have to factor in the sockets.

When you're buying fittings, invest in a handful of different size caps. They're available in copper, plastic, and threaded. Then if you've misread a dimension—as even experienced plumbers do occasionally—you can cap off the line and turn the water on again before heading off to the plumbing supplier.

Refer to the chart below when you want to determine a pipe's nominal size by measuring its outside diameter, and when you need to factor in socket depths in computing lengths.

As a rule of thumb, the outside diameter (OD) of copper is ⅛ inch greater than its inside diameter (ID) nominal size; for threaded and cast iron, the figure is ¼ inch; and for plastic pipe, figure ⅜ inch to account for the wall thickness.

Copper, cast-iron, and smaller threaded fittings have standardized socket depths. With sizes ½ inch and larger, variations in tapping and threading equipment may add or subtract 1/16 inch or so from our dimensions. If you're planning a run with more than just a few fittings, double-check by measuring a pipe,

twisting a fitting onto it, and measuring again.

Socket depths for plastic pipe vary somewhat, too, depending on the brand and whether you're dealing with ABS, PVC, or CPVC. Just place a measuring tape into the sockets of larger-diameter plastic fittings. With smaller sizes, measure the pipe, apply cement, push on a fitting, and measure again. Don't just dry-fit the connection—the pipe won't seat completely in the socket until you soften it with the cement.

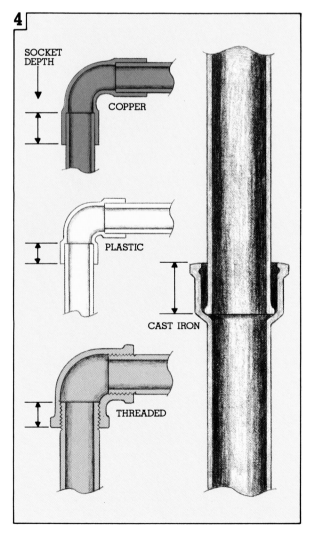

Sizing Up Pipe Dimensions

Material	Nominal Size (approx. inside diameter)	Approx. Outside Diameter	Approx. Socket Depth
Copper	¼ in.	⅜ in.	5/16 in.
	⅜ in.	½ in.	⅜ in.
	½ in.	⅝ in.	½ in.
	¾ in.	⅞ in.	¾ in.
	1 in.	1⅛ in.	15/16 in.
	1¼ in.	1⅜ in.	1 in.
	1½ in.	1⅝ in.	1⅛ in.
Threaded	⅛ in.	⅜ in.	¼ in.
	¼ in.	½ in.	⅜ in.
	⅜ in.	⅝ in.	⅜ in.
	½ in.	¾ in.	½ in.
	¾ in.	1 in.	9/16 in.
	1 in.	1¼ in.	11/16 in.
	1¼ in.	1½ in.	11/16 in.
	1½ in.	1¾ in.	11/16 in.
	2 in.	2¼ in.	¾ in.
Plastic	½ in.	⅞ in.	½ in.
	¾ in.	1⅛ in.	⅝ in.
	1 in.	1⅜ in.	¾ in.
	1¼ in.	1⅝ in.	11/16 in.
	1½ in.	1⅞ in.	11/16 in.
	2 in.	2⅜ in.	¾ in.
	3 in.	3⅜ in.	1½ in.
	4 in.	3⅜ in.	1¾ in.
Cast iron	2 in.	2¼ in.	2½ in.
	3 in.	3¼ in.	2¾ in.
	4 in.	4¼ in.	3 in.
	5 in.	5¼ in.	3 in.
	6 in.	6¼ in.	3 in.

Working with Rigid Copper Pipe

Soldering or "sweating" together rigid copper plumbing lines isn't nearly as hot and exhausting a procedure as it may sound. It's the pipes and fittings, not the installer, that do the sweating.

The term refers to a process called *capillary action,* which occurs when you heat up a joint and touch solder to it. Just as an ink blotter soaks up ink, a soldered joint absorbs molten metal, making a watertight bond that's as strong or stronger than the pipe itself.

To solder copper you need a spool of 50 percent tin/50 per-cent lead solder, a pastelike *flux* that both cleans the copper and helps solder flow more readily, and a propane torch.

When you shop for pipe and fittings for your first copper plumbing run, buy a few extra fittings and use them to practice the techniques shown here. Doing this greatly increases your chances of getting leak-proof joints. Leaks that show up when you fill the lines with water mean you have to drain and completely dry out the line before you can resolder the joint. More about this on the next page.

1 Cut copper pipe, using an inexpensive tubing cutter, like the one shown here, or a hacksaw. With a cutter, simply clamp the device onto the tubing, rotate a few revolutions, tighten, and rotate some more.

The *cutting wheel* makes a neat, square cut, but leaves a liplike burr inside that could restrict water flow. Remove this by inserting the *reaming blade* and twisting.

Make hacksaw cuts in a miter box and use a file to remove any burrs. Take care that you don't nick the metal, which could cause the connection to leak.

2 Now polish the outside of the pipe and the inside of the fitting with sändpaper or steel wool. This removes grease, dirt, and oxidation that could impede the flow of solder. Do a thorough job, but stop polishing when the metal is shiny. Avoid touching polished surfaces; oil from your fingers could interfere with the capillary action when you apply solder to join the pieces.

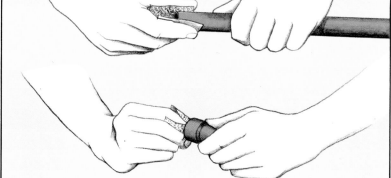

CUTTING WHEEL

REAMING BLADE

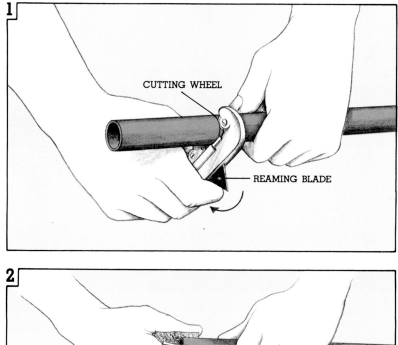

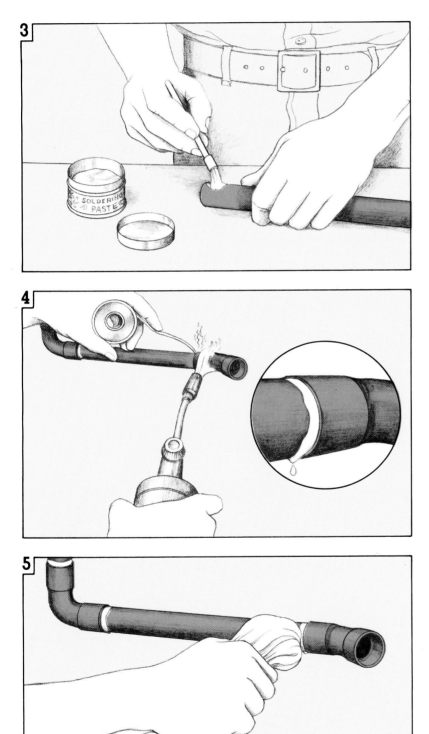

3 Apply a light, even coating of flux to both surfaces to retard oxidation when you heat the copper. As solder flows into the joint, the flux burns away. Use rosin- (not acid-) type flux for plumbing work.

4 Assemble the connection and heat the joint, using the inner cone of the torch's flame. Test for temperature by touching the joint—but not the flame—with solder as shown.

If it melts, apply more. Capillary action will pull solder around the pipe and into the joint. When molten metal drips from the bottom, remove the flame and inspect your work. A well-soldered joint has an even bead around its entire circumference. Any gaps probably will leak water.

As you practice soldering, aim to apply only enough heat to melt the solder, and only enough solder to fill the joint. Too much of either will melt all the flux and weaken the bond.

If you do have to resolder a connection, your biggest problem is to get rid of any moisture that remains inside the line. Plumbers sometimes do this by stuffing in a piece of bread (but not the crust) just upstream from the connection. This flushes easily from the system when pressure is restored and a faucet turned on. You also can buy waxy capsules that plug up the line while you work. Later, just apply heat to the point where the capsule has lodged and the capsule melts away.

5 For a tidy, professional look, lightly brush the joint, using a damp rag. Take care that you don't burn your fingers.

Most pros lay out an entire run of copper, first cutting and dry-fitting all of its components. After dry-fitting, they go back to clean, flux, and solder each joint. Support copper pipe at 6-foot intervals.

Working with Flexible Copper Tubing

Flexible copper tubing—also known as "soft copper"—is pliable enough to negotiate without elbows all but the sharpest bends. And that's good news for you. This means you don't have to install a fitting every time a run makes a change of direction, as you must when working with rigid pipe.

And though flexible accepts the same soldered fittings used with rigid, you can also make connections using the compression and flare fittings shown on this and the following page. Realize, though, that these specialized devices cost quite a bit more than standard fittings, and they aren't quite as strong, either. For economy and durability, use solder connections that will never need to be broken; save compression and flare fittings for semipermanent hookups and for those tight-quarter situations where a torch might start a fire.

Because flexible tubing isn't as damage-resistant as rigid, don't use it for long runs across open basement ceilings or in other exposed locations. For fixture connections you can buy short lengths of chrome-plated soft copper tubing.

This method is not acceptable for gas supply piping, due to the corrosive effect of natural gas. Copper tubing should not be used with gas clothes dryers.

1 Cut flexible, using a hacksaw or tubing cutter, and remove any burrs as explained on page 266. When you're cutting, take care that you don't flatten out the tube ends; watertight connections demand that they be perfectly round.

Because this material is soft, always handle it gently. Uncoil tubing by straightening it out every few inches, and bend it in gradual, sweeping arcs. Otherwise, flexible will kink and you'll have to throw it away. Kinks, which impede water flow, are almost impossible to reshape.

A *spring bender*, like the one shown here, reinforces tubing walls and minimizes kinking. To use one of these, you slip the spring over the tubing and bend at several points along the arc's radius. Filling the tubing with sand also helps avoid kinking when bending it.

2 Compression fittings assemble without special tools. You just slide a *compression nut* and *ring* onto the tubing, insert the tubing and ring into the fitting, and thread on the nut.

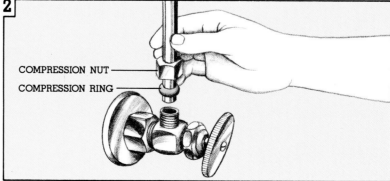

SPRING BENDER

KINKED TUBING

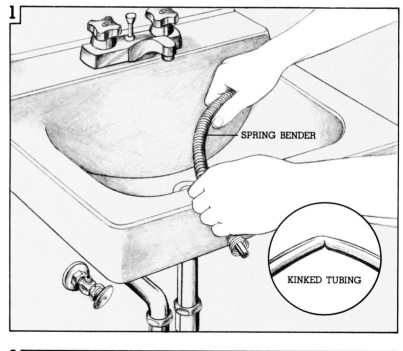

COMPRESSION NUT

COMPRESSION RING

3 Tightening the compression nut forces the ring down onto the tubing to secure and seal the connection. Be careful, though, that you don't over-tighten, which could crush the tubing and cause a leak. Go just about a quarter-turn with a wrench. If the joint leaks when you turn on the water, further tighten the nut a quarter-turn at a time.

4 For a flare fitting, you need to shape the tubing end, using either the flaring tool shown here or a tapered device that you drive into the tubing with a hammer.

The trick with both of these is to remember that you must always slip on a flaring nut before you flare the end of the tubing. With a flaring tool, you then clamp the tubing into a *block* with beveled holes sized to hold several typical pipe diameters. Align the *compression cone* in the tubing end and tighten the screw. As you turn the cone into the tubing, it flares the end. Inspect your work carefully after removing the tubing from the block. If you notice that the end has split, cut off the flared portion and repeat the process.

5 As with compression fittings, don't over-tighten a flared joint. For starters, hand-tighten, then go just a quarter-turn with a wrench. If water drips from the fitting, tighten it only until the leaking stops.

When a compression or flare fitting leaks, and gentle wrench work won't solve the problem, dismantle the joint. Was the pipe cut squarely? Were the fitting's threads meshing properly? If any parts are damaged, you'll have to start over again.

Protect compression and flare connections from strain by supporting pipe runs on either side. Since flexible tubing tends to sag when it's full of water, support horizontal lines at 4-foot intervals.

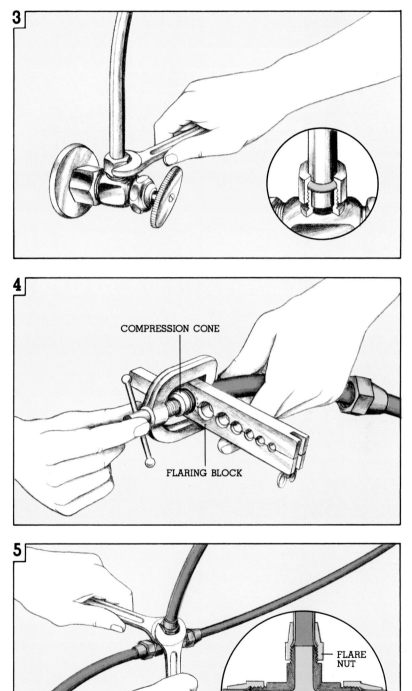

Working with Rigid Plastic Pipe

Plastic plumbing components may be the greatest thing that's happened to amateur plumbers since the invention of running water. This material cuts with an ordinary handsaw, and when it's time to assemble a run, you can forget about a torch, solder, or wrenches—everything simply cements together like the parts of a model airplane.

Not all codes allow plastic, though, and those that do spec-ify which types you can use for drainage and for cold and hot water lines. For drainage lines, your code may specify ABS only, PVC only, or either; it'll certainly require CPVC for hot water runs.

Bear in mind, too, that you can't mix these materials. Each expands at a different rate, and there's even a specially formulated cement for each.

Expansion can cause an improperly installed run of plastic pipe to creak, squeak, groan, and maybe even leak every time you turn on the water. To prevent this from happening allow lots of clearance between fittings and framing, and be sure to make oversize holes wherever pipes pass through a wall or floor.

Rigid plastic pipe, not surprisingly, isn't quite as stiff as its metal counterparts. Be sure to support horizontal runs every 4 to 5 feet.

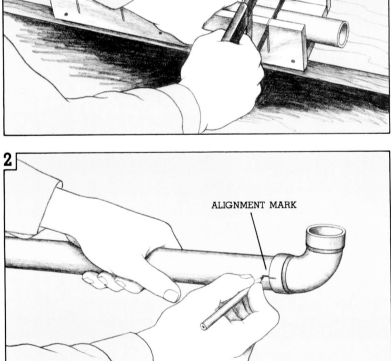

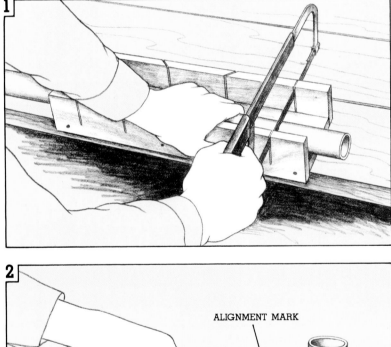

ALIGNMENT MARK

1 You can make cuts, using just about any fine-tooth saw, but use a miter box to keep them square. Diagonal cuts reduce the bonding area at the fitting's shoulder—the most critical part of the joint.

After you've made the cut, use a knife or file to remove any burrs from the inside or outside of the cut end. Burrs can scrape away cement and weaken the bond. Use a clean rag to wipe both the pipe and fitting.

2 Now dry-fit the connection by inserting the pipe into the fitting. You should be able to push it in at least one-third of the way. If the pipe bottoms out and feels loose, try another fitting. Unlike copper components, plastic systems are designed for a snug "interference fit." Tapered walls on the inside of the socket should make contact well before the pipe reaches the socket's shoulder.

Plastic pipe cement sets up in about a minute, which doesn't give you much time to make adjustments. Scoring the pipe and fitting with an *alignment mark* like this saves twisting the connection back and forth after you've applied the cement.

3 With PVC and CPVC plastics, coat the inside of the socket and outside of the pipe with a special primer before applying the cement. This begins the softening-up process. ABS doesn't require a primer.

Immediately after you've primed, brush a smooth coating of cement first onto the pipe end, then into the fitting socket, and again onto the pipe. Use the cement that's right for the material you're working with, and don't let it puddle in the fitting.

4 Now push the two together with enough force to bottom out the pipe end in the fitting socket. Twisting about a quarter-turn as you push helps spread the cement evenly. Hold the pipe and fitting together a minute or two while they fuse into a single piece. You should end up with a smooth, even fillet all the way around the joint. Wipe off any excess cement.

5 If you misalign a connection, saw it off, making sure to cut squarely; then install a new fitting with a *spacer* and *slip coupling* as shown. Solvent-welded joints are strong enough to handle within 15 minutes, but don't run water through the line for about 2 hours, if possible.

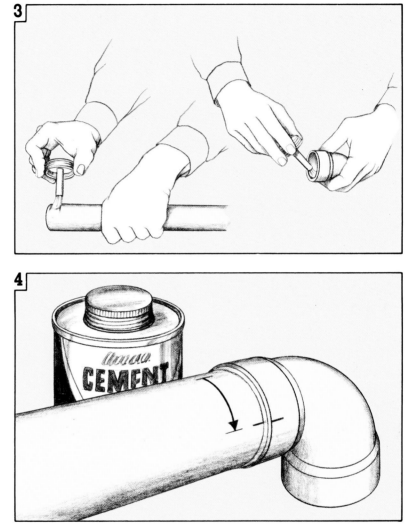

CEMENT

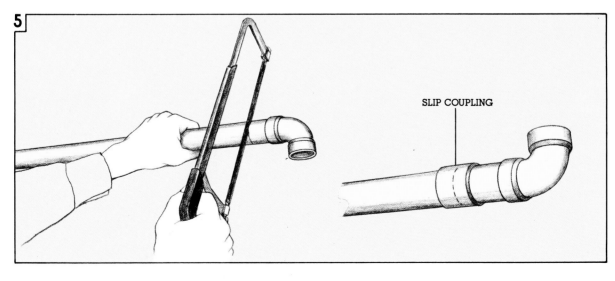

SLIP COUPLING

Working with Flexible Plastic Tubing

Think of this one as a hybrid between soft copper tubing and rigid plastic pipe. Like its copper cousin, flexible plastic comes in long coils that you can snake through tight spots without using fittings; as with rigid plastic, you have to choose the proper type for the application you have in mind, and codes in your area may disallow the material entirely.

Type PE carries cold water only, and in many communities you can use it only underground—for wells, sprinkler systems, and natural gas—where its flexibility withstands freezing and ground heaving.

Indoors, install type PB flexible plastic for hot and cold supply lines. Unlike the less expensive type PE, it's not affected by heat.

Both types are quite easy to work with. You cut them with a knife, and join sections, using fittings like the ones shown below. You also can interconnect flexible plastic with other piping materials via transition fittings that compensate for differing rates of expansion and contraction.

Though slightly more crush-resistant than soft copper, you shouldn't use PE or PB for long, out-in-the-open runs, and it should be supported every 32 inches. Be sure to clamp it loosely so the material has sufficient room to move.

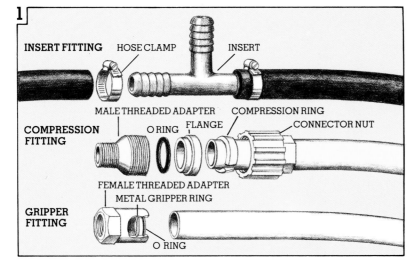

INSERT FITTING   HOSE CLAMP   INSERT

MALE THREADED ADAPTER   COMPRESSION RING

COMPRESSION FITTING   O RING   FLANGE   CONNECTOR NUT

FEMALE THREADED ADAPTER
METAL GRIPPER RING

GRIPPER FITTING   O RING

1 PE connects with plastic *insert fittings,* or you can flare the material and use the same brass fittings illustrated on page 269. With an insert fitting, slip *hose clamps* over the tubing ends, shove the tubing onto the *insert,* and tighten the clamps. Just make sure the serrations are fully inserted and the clamp is positioned squarely over top of them.

With PB, select either a *compression* or a *gripper* fitting. The ones shown connect to female and male threaded stock. You also can buy tees, ells, and other typical supply fittings.

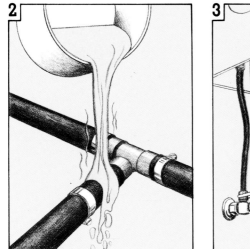

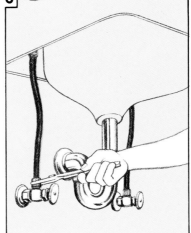

2 Sometimes it takes lots of muscle to shove PE tubing over an insert fitting. Dousing with hot water softens the tubing so it will slip on effortlessly. Use the same technique to dismantle a stubborn connection.

3 PB makes an excellent choice for stop-to-fixture hookups. It's not quite as prone to kinking as copper is, but don't overbend. You also can buy plastic stop valves for PB and CPVC.

Working with Cast-Iron Pipe

Cast iron easily wins the heavyweight title among plumbing components. Not only is it far heftier than most materials, it also lasts longer.

You'll appreciate just how tough iron is when you first begin to wrestle with it. A 5-foot length of 3-inch pipe can weigh as much as 50 pounds. It's not easy to cut cast iron, either. And unless you go with the no-hub clamp system shown below, joining sections and installing fittings can be tricky work.

For these reasons, you may prefer to contract a plumber for a major project such as a new soil stack. He'll have the tools and know-how to do the job quickly and safely.

If you're a moderately ambitious amateur—and local codes permit no-hub—you can install smaller 1½- and 2-inch cast-iron lines yourself. Plan runs that have a minimum of bends and that pitch back to the soil stack at a rate of ¼ inch per foot.

One of the joys of working with no-hub pipe is that it's compatible with the other cast-iron systems. This means that you can use it to tap into existing cast-iron lines, as shown on pages 256–259.

Does your home have cast-iron drain-waste-vent pipes? If so, they're joined in one of the three ways depicted at right. *Hub-and-spigot* piping has a bell-shaped *hub* at one end, a ridged *spigot* at the other. After inserting the spigot into the hub, a plumber packs the joint with *oakum*—a hemp saturated with pitch—then ladles in molten *lead*. Hub-and-spigot work is tricky, so leave it for the pros. You can easily break one open, though. Just chip away the lead, using a hammer and chisel, then pull the spigot free.

Piping designed for *compression* joints has hubs, but no spigots. Instead of lead and oakum, they're sealed with a special *neoprene gasket*, which is lubricated, and inserted into the hub. The spigot then is forced into place. This can be done with either a spade or a special pulling tool. Use this system to mate plastic and cast-iron piping.

No-hub joints are the easiest of all to make, and the only ones an amateur should consider. You slip a *neoprene sleeve* onto one pipe end, a *stainless steel band* onto the other, butt the pipe ends against a ridge inside the sleeve, then tighten the band's two *clamps*. No-hub pipes have the same outside diameters as those used for the other systems, so you can interconnect them easily.

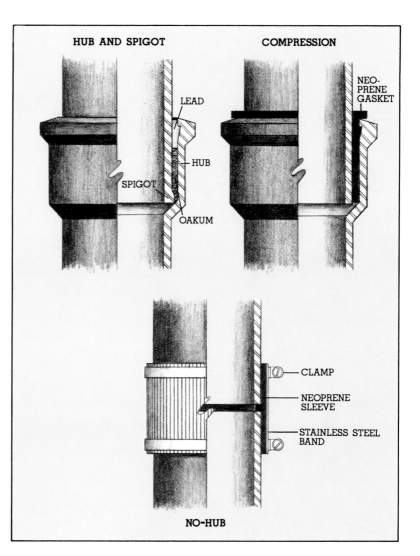

HUB AND SPIGOT

LEAD

HUB

SPIGOT

OAKUM

COMPRESSION

NEO-PRENE GASKET

NO-HUB

CLAMP

NEOPRENE SLEEVE

STAINLESS STEEL BAND

HOUSEHOLD REPAIRS

There are many joys associated with being a home-owner: pride of ownership, financial security, and simple peace of mind to name just a few. But as you know, nothing is perfect, and you'll have ample proof of this as a homeowner. Things often break, malfunction, and wear out, and someone has to do the fixing or replacing.

Why roll up your sleeves when you could just as easily call a repairman? For one thing, it's not all that easy anymore. The simpler your repair, the less likely you are to find a repairman who's willing to make the trip to your house. If you do find one, you're almost certain to pay a premium price for his time and trouble. (It's not at all uncommon to have to pay $20 to $25 per hour for household repair work.)

Once you complete that first household repair— the one you were secretly worried about because you'd never done anything like it before—you'll realize a benefit that ranks right alongside convenience and cost. You'll know the satisfaction that comes with success at something you've done yourself. And as you become successful with more and more repairs, you may even start to feel more comfortable in your home because you'll be more in control of it.

If cost savings, convenience, or self-satisfaction is important to you, you're reading the right book. We've examined houses from top to bottom and inside out to come up with a sizable list of repair problems that most homeowners must deal with at some point. Then we conveniently grouped them into four sections to help you quickly find the repair information you need. Basic electrical and plumbing repairs were handled earlier in this book.

Our first two sections deal with "Walls and Ceilings" and "Floors and Stairs." If something around your house needs a cosmetic repair, you'll probably find it explained here. Whether it's patching nail holes in walls, quieting a squeaky stair tread, or replacing a tile in a ceramic tile floor, we show you how in step-by-step detail.

For more "functional" household repairs, check into the "Windows" and "Doors" chapters that follow. You'll find help for torn screens and broken glass, windows that won't open (or won't stay that way), and doors—all kinds of them—that squeak, bind, or cause other trouble.

WALLS AND CEILINGS

If you'll look around with a critical eye at the walls and ceilings of your house, you'll be likely to spot at least a few surfaces in need of a face-lift. Maybe your problems are as minor as nail holes left behind after a mirror or some pictures were relocated, or as intimidating as a sagging lath-and-plaster ceiling. No matter what problems you find via your visual inspection, the next nine pages of this book will leave you with no more excuses for letting them remain unfixed.

As you will find out on the following three pages, refurbishing drywall and plaster surfaces isn't nearly as demanding as you may have thought. We take you step by step through the nuances of patching cracks, blemishes, and small and large holes in both drywall and lath-and-plaster surfaces. Then, because the repair must be made to blend in with the surrounding area, we show you how to retexture the surface so professionally that only you will know where the problem used to be.

Concluding this section are how-to instructions for replacing moldings and for repairing damaged ceiling or wall tiles.

Repairing Drywall Surfaces

Setting Popped Nails

1 When you spot a popped nail, drive a 1½-inch ring-shank nail about 1½ inches above it, pressing in on the drywall panel as you do. Then create a "dimple" with your last hammer blow to set the nail just below the surface (but don't break through the drywall's thick paper facing). Now either remove the popped nail or sink it well into the surface with a nail set.

2 Fill the dimple and the old nail hole with joint compound, feathering it into the surrounding surface with a taping knife. Apply as many coats as necessary to make the surface smooth. Let the compound dry between coats. Finish and retexture the repair following the instructions on page 12.

Mending Cracks and Bubbled Tape

1 You can repair minor cracks simply by filling the voids with compound. But if the joint tape curls up from the drywall surface, first use a utility knife to remove all loose tape. Be careful you don't remove the sound-fitting tape.

2 Cut a piece of joint tape to fit. Apply a bed of joint compound to the wall or ceiling, press the tape in place, and apply another coat of compound. Let dry, then add another layer of compound, then another if necessary. Feather each coat into the surrounding surface to help hide the seam. When the surface is smooth, finish the repair as instructed on page 280.

(continued)

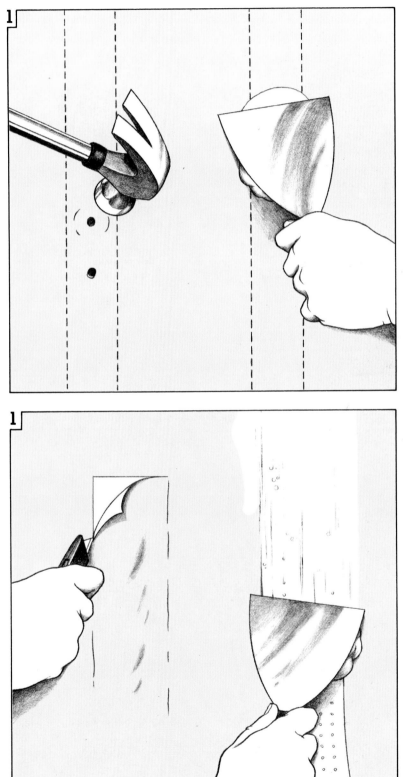

Patching Small Holes

1 Filling nail-size holes rates by far as the easiest drywall repair you can make. Use a putty knife to fill the hole with spackling compound, allowing some excess to "mound" above the surface. When the compound dries, lightly sand away the excess to leave a smooth surface.

An even easier procedure, although it is somewhat unorthodox, is to dispense with the spackling compound and the sanding, and simply fill small holes with white toothpaste. Believe it or not, it really works.

Patching Medium-Size Holes

1 Mending medium-size holes requires that you provide backing to which the joint compound can adhere. Fashion this backing from a scrap of perforated hardboard cut slightly larger than the hole, but small enough that you can maneuver it through the wall. To hold the scrap firmly against the back side of the wall, run a length of thin wire through a couple of the perforations as shown. Now, using joint compound, butter the perimeter of the backing as shown.

2 Insert the hardboard backing into the hole and center it behind

the opening. When dry, the joint compound will help the backing cling to the back of the drywall. To hold the backing in place during the interim, bridge the opening with a pencil and twist the wire ends together until the wire is taut. When the compound dries, clip the wire and remove it.

3 Now it's simply a matter of filling the recess with joint compound. Because the compound shrinks as it dries, you'll have to apply several coats to achieve satisfactory results. Let each coat dry before adding the next. Once you've completely filled in the void and don't see any

hairline cracks in the compound, sand the patch lightly and retexture its surface, following the instructions on page 280.

If you don't have any perforated hardboard around the house, try this alternative which uses a scrap of 1/4- or 1/2-inch plywood. Cut the plywood backing as you would the hardboard. Drill two holes in the center of the piece to run the wire through. Now follow through with the remaining steps as they are described above.

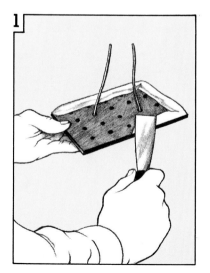

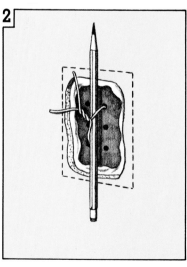

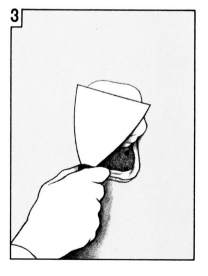

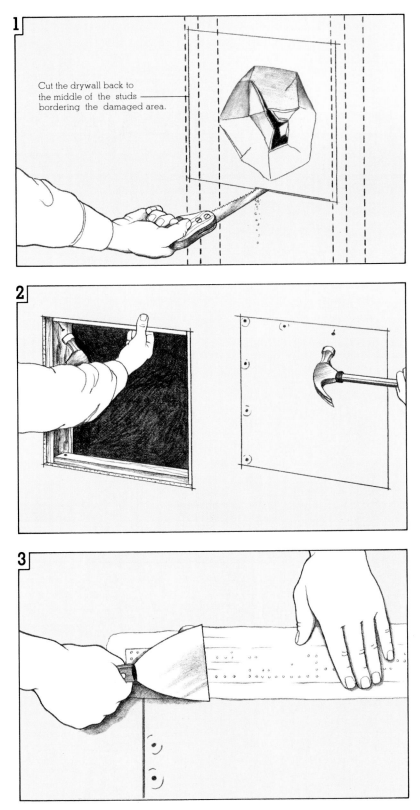

Cut the drywall back to the middle of the studs bordering the damaged area.

Patching Large Holes

1 After squaring off the area to be repaired, cut and remove the damaged drywall. Use a keyhole saw to make the horizontal cuts between the studs, and a sharp utility knife guided by a straightedge for the vertical cuts along the stud centers.

2 Fashion a like-size drywall patch from scrap drywall. Then cut two lengths of 2x2 to serve as backing supports for the top and bottom edges of the patch. Toenail the 2x2s in place, making sure they're flush with the edge of the studs. (Make this installation easier by first drilling angled starter holes for the nails.) Now fit the drywall patch into the opening and secure it with 1½-inch drywall nails spaced at least ⅜ inch in from the edges. "Dimple" each nailhead.

3 Lay down a bed coat of joint compound around the perimeter of the patch with a 4-inch taping knife held at a 45-degree angle to the wall. Avoid creating too much of a mound. Immediately center an appropriate length of drywall tape over each seam, using your hands to press it in place. Then with the taping knife, embed the tape further into the bed coat, holding one end of the tape secure with your other hand. Follow this with one or more coats of compound, feathering each coat into the surrounding surface and letting it dry thoroughly before applying the next. When the last coat has dried, finish and retexture the patch, following the steps on page 280. *(continued)*

Finishing and Retexturing the Surface

1 With enough care and patience, you can finish your drywall repairs so they'll be all but invisible.

Begin by smoothing the surface of the repair with either 80- or 100-grit coated abrasive or dampened sponge. (If you use an abrasive and the repair requires lots of sanding, be sure you wear a painter's mask to avoid inhaling too much gypsum dust. Also be careful not to sand all the way through the compound and into the tape. After sanding the area, wipe the dust off the surface with a dust cloth.)

2 Most drywall surfaces are not glassy smooth. Instead, they have a texture designed to conceal seams, nails, and minor defects in the drywall surface. You can closely duplicate most textures, each in a slightly different way. (It is a good idea to practice on a piece of scrap drywall before attempting to retexture the actual patch.)

You can approximate an "orange peel" texture by watering down some premixed joint compound and dabbing it over your repair with a sponge.

To blend a patch into a sand-textured surface, roll on some texture paint with a carpet-napped paint roller cover. To match an existing texture, apply a layer of drywall compound. Then, using a whisk broom or other stiff-bristled brush, replicate the pattern. If you're dealing with a travertine finish like the one shown, apply one layer of compound and let it set up slightly. Then, flick more compound onto the surface by using a paintbrush and knock off the high spots by lightly troweling the surface.

Beaded polystyrene and vermiculite textures on ceilings are hard to match. Although you can rent texturing equipment, your best solution may be to call in professional help to identify the type of finish you have and to duplicate its coarseness.

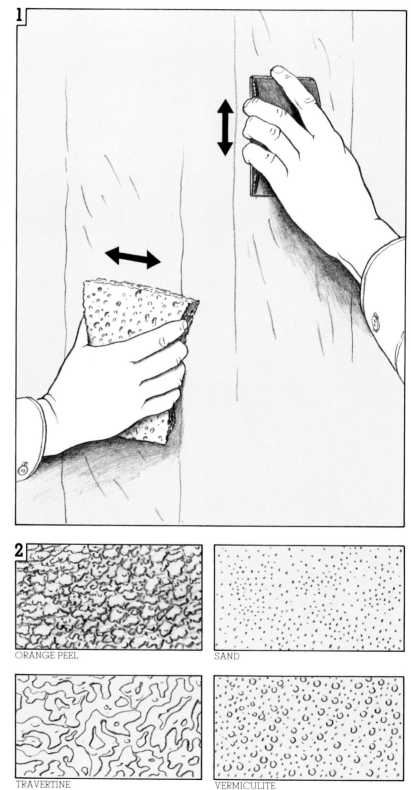

ORANGE PEEL

SAND

TRAVERTINE

VERMICULITE

Repairing Cracks and Holes in Plaster

Professional plasterers are scarce these days, but fortunately, with a little practice, you can handle most common plaster repairs yourself. Choose premixed spackling compound for small repairs such as hairline cracks and nail holes. For larger cracks and holes, however, mix powdered patching plaster with water—it's stronger than spackling compound and less prone to shrink.

Make plaster-patching a regular part of your prep work whenever you repaint. And be sure to correct any moisture leaks that might be responsible for your problems.

1 To prepare hairline cracks for patching, widen the fissures to about 1/8 inch with a screwdriver, then blow out any dust and debris that remain.

A hammer and cold chisel make short work of removing loose plaster from holes. To ensure a successful repair, work out in all directions until you reach sound plaster. Also knock the plaster from between the laths and undercut the edges as shown in the detail to help lock in the patching material.

2 If moisture has rotted the laths behind the loose plaster, cut the plaster back to at least the center of the studs adjacent to the damaged area. Remove the laths (if using a circular saw, adjust the blade to the proper depth) and nail up new wood or metal mesh-type laths.

3 To prevent the water in the plaster patching material from being drawn into surrounding surfaces and thereby weakening the patch, moisten the area shortly before making repairs. You can do this with either a spray bottle or a damp sponge. *(continued)*

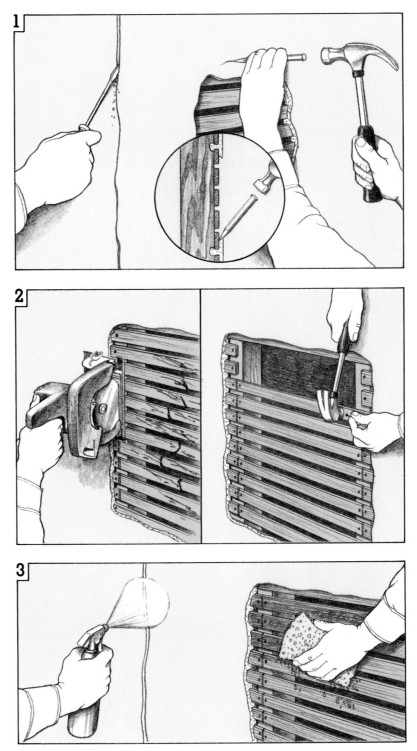

Repairing Cracks and Holes *(continued)*

4 Fill in hairline cracks by forcing spackling compound into the void with a putty knife. Let the compound dry, then apply another coat, if necessary, to bring the filler material flush with the surrounding surface.

When dealing with larger repairs, mix a batch of patching plaster according to the manufacturer's directions on the package. Starting at the edges and using a 6-inch-wide taping knife, work the plaster into the undercuts, then fill in the center. (Make sure you apply enough pressure to the patch material so that some of it fills the spaces between the laths. This is known as *keying* [or tying] the plaster to its backing.)

Because patching plaster shrinks as it dries, be prepared to lay on two or more coats of material. Let each coat dry completely before applying the next. To achieve the best possible bond between coats, wet the surface of each base coat before laying on more plaster.

5 After the top coat of plaster has had sufficient drying time (at least 24 hours), it is ready for sanding. Using a medium-grade abrasive (80- or 100-grit) wrapped around a sanding block, sand the surface with light circular strokes. Focus a portable work light on the repair area to help detect slight surface irregularities you might otherwise overlook.

6 Never try to paint a plaster repair without first priming it. If you do, the new plaster will absorb paint more readily than the surrounding surface and your patch will show through.

Before you begin priming, however, make sure your new plaster has had sufficient time to cure and set up. To be safe, wait another 24 hours after you finish sanding.

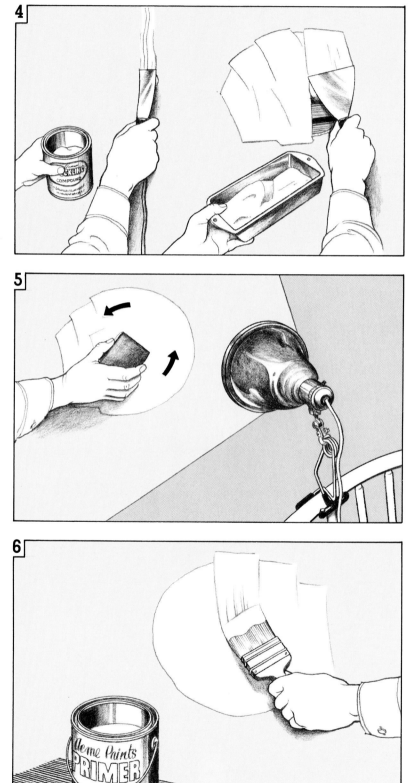

Replacing Damaged Moldings

Moldings, especially base-board, base shoe, and door casing, take quite a beating in some homes. Perhaps you have accidentally broken a length of molding while trying to remove it. Maybe temperature and humidity changes in your home have dried out some of the moldings and caused them to split. Whatever the reason for undertaking a molding repair, you'll be relieved to know you're dealing with a relatively quick and easy task in most instances.

Finding an exact match for your damaged molding could very well turn out to be the hardest part of the job. Most lumberyards and home centers stock many of the popular molding profiles, but if you can't find one that matches what you have, seek out a supplier who can mill moldings to your specifications. With older-style moldings this is often your only alternative.

1 To remove a section of base shoe, first drive all finish nails deep within or through the molding. A nail set performs this task best. Then use a pry bar to work the molding up from the floor and away from the wall. Work carefully so you don't snap the molding.

To remove other types of molding, maneuver a pry bar behind the molding, using a wood scrap to protect the wall. Apply enough leverage to loosen the finish nails that hold the molding in place. Force the molding back against the wall. If the nailheads appear, pull them with the pry bar. If not, apply more leverage against the back side of the molding and pull the molding loose. Remove any nails that remain as shown in the detail.

2 When preparing to cut a replacement molding to size, lay the new piece over the old to get an accurate measurement. When cutting the replacement to fit, place crown and cove moldings in the miter box upside down; for all others, match the position the molding will take when in place.

Stain or paint your cut-to-size molding before you install it. Then attach it to your wall's framing members as shown with appropriately sized finish nails (don't nail only to plaster or drywall). You may need an inexpensive stud finder to locate studs behind your wall. Finish by setting the nailheads and filling the voids by thumbing in putty.

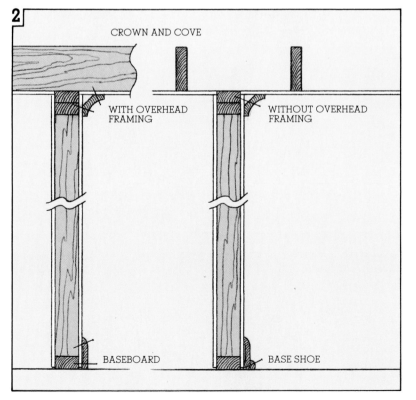

CROWN AND COVE

WITH OVERHEAD FRAMING

WITHOUT OVERHEAD FRAMING

BASEBOARD

BASE SHOE

Replacing Damaged Ceramic and Plastic Wall Tiles

Normally, ceramic and plastic wall tiles stand up remarkably well for long periods. But sometimes one comes unglued or gets bumped and breaks. Occasionally you have to remove one or more tiles to correct another problem such as a leaky tub/shower valve.

Regluing a loose tile is the simplest of these situations to handle. Just purchase the adhesive designed for this job, apply some of it to the tile with a notched trowel, and press the tile into place. Regrout the joints as suggested in caption 4.

For help with the other two situations cited above, refer to the text and sketches that follow. (Note: If you don't have replacement tiles on hand, take a sample to your local tile dealer and hope you can find a close match.)

1 To replace a cracked tile, first remove the surrounding grout using an old screwdriver. For plastic tiles grouted with elastic joint filler, use a razor blade. Be careful not to chip or mar adjacent tiles.

2 Free the tile by prying it loose with a screwdriver inserted into a hole you've drilled with a carbide-tipped bit. If that fails, use a hammer and cold chisel. Then scrape or chip off (or remove chemically) the old adhesive and grout.

3 If a replacement ceramic tile must be cut, a glass cutter and straightedge work well. To trim tiles to irregular shapes, score the surface, then make the break with tile nippers or pliers. A coping saw works best for cutting plastic tiles.

To affix the new tile, spread adhesive on its back with a serrated trowel and press the tile in place.

4 Force grout into the joint spaces with a sponge or a rubber-faced trowel, and after 10 to 15 minutes, tool the joints with a rounded toothbrush handle or a moistened finger. Scrub off excess grout with a wet sponge, repeatedly rinsing it and wringing it out.

To grout plastic tiles, squeeze elastic filler into the joints, then smooth it with your finger.

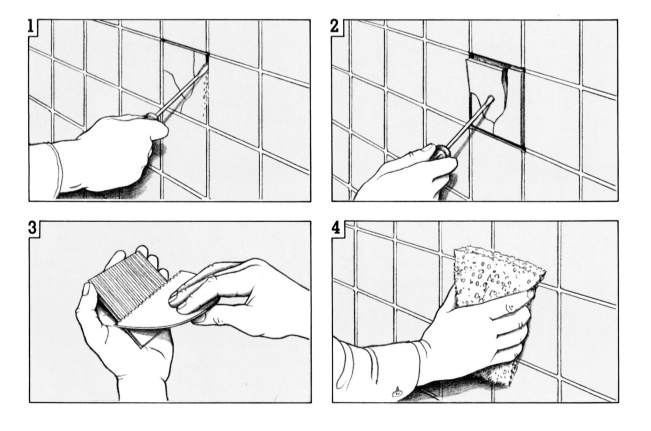

Repairing Damaged Ceiling Tiles

If you're stuck with dingy or water-damaged tiles overhead, apply a primer or clear sealer over the entire surface, then roll on new interior latex paint. (Note: Painting the tiles will reduce the sound absorbency of the ceiling.)

Dented tiles, however, should be replaced. Take a sample tile with you when you shop for replacements.

1 To remove a damaged tile, slice along its edges with a utility knife to cut through the flanges holding it in place. You may have to exert slight downward pressure with a pry bar or other tool to pop the tile free (see the detail). After removing the tile, pull out any remaining staples, tile material, or adhesive.

2 To insert a new tile, first cut off the tongue from one of its edges using a utility knife guided by a firmly held straightedge.

3 After you've applied panel adhesive to the furring strips, fit the tile into the groove of an adjacent tile. Press it flush with adjacent tiles and hold it until the adhesive has had a chance to set, or hold it with finish nails in each corner.

4 When replacing several adjoining tiles, secure most of them to the furring strips by stapling through the flanges of the tiles. Read over steps 1 through 3 in order to place the last tile.

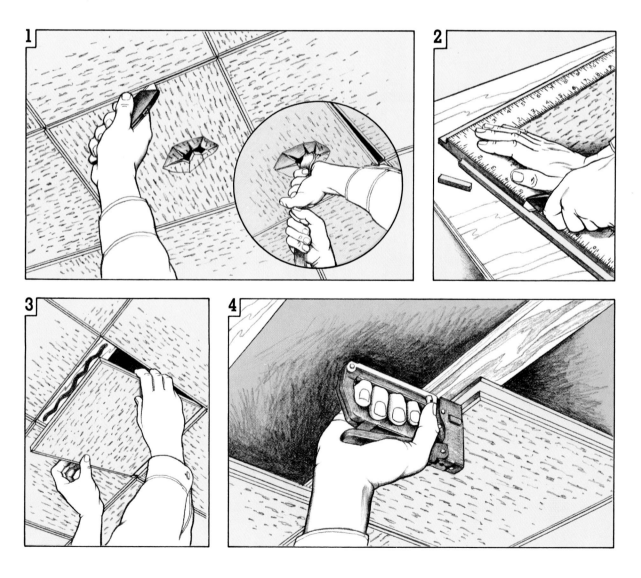

FLOORS AND STAIRS

When you stop to consider all of the weight and traffic borne by floors and stairs, it's really not surprising that they develop occasional problems that need attention. A stair tread can loosen and acquire an annoying squeak, and wood floors can become furniture-scuffed and need spot refinishing. Not even a tile floor is immune to accidents and the ordinary wear and tear that can leave you with tiles that need replacement.

This section may surprise you by pointing out the number of these jobs you can do yourself. On the next 11 pages we show you how to silence squeaks in wood floors and stairs, as well as how to touch up blemishes and replace damaged floorboards or parquet tiles. Those of you with resilient flooring, carpeting, or hard-surface materials underfoot will find help, too. We cover everything from removing stains to patching damaged areas. And where appropriate, we talk diagnosing the problem before launching into the repair steps involved. On top of this you also will find out what common household tools best suit the job at hand.

Silencing Floor and Stair Squeaks

Every house has at least one: a floorboard or stair tread that groans and creaks every time it's stepped on—and always the loudest when you go to make a midnight raid on the refrigerator.

Quieting those annoying squeaks is mainly a matter of locating them, then securing boards or stair components that have loosened and are rubbing against each other. If you're lucky, you'll have access to these trouble spots from below. If not, don't worry; we'll show you how to tackle them from above, too.

Silencing Floors From Above

1 With hardwood floors, drill angled pilot holes wherever needed, then drive spiral-shanked flooring nails into the subflooring. Set the nailheads and fill the recesses with color-matched wood putty.

2 For carpeted floors, pull back the carpeting and pad, then drive ring-shank nails into the floor joists beneath the squeaky floor.

Silencing Stairs From Above

1 To fasten down the front edges of a tread, drive spiral-shanked flooring nails at an angle into pre-drilled holes as shown. If you can round up a helper, have him or her stand on the tread as you nail. Next, set the nails and conceal the holes with wood putty.

To eliminate squeaks at the back edge of a tread, drive one or more wedges of scrap wood coated with glue into the gap between the treads and risers. Later, trim away the protruding wood.

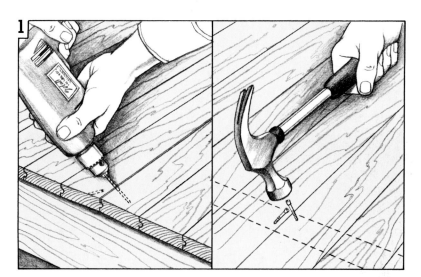

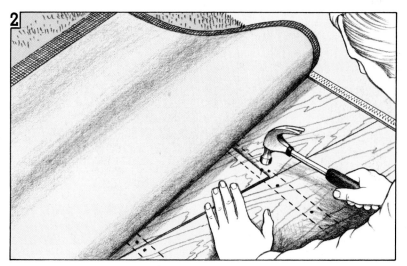

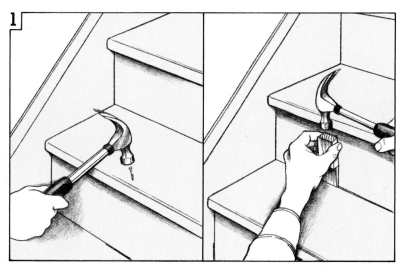

Silencing Floors From Below

1 Enlist a helper to walk on the finished floor above while you look for movement of the floor joists and of the subfloor from below. When you locate the problem area, first check to make sure that diagonal bridging between your floor joists (if any is nearby) is firm. Snugging it up may solve the problem.

    If the noise comes from between the joists, drive a tight-fitting piece of solid bridging up between the joists until it makes contact with the subfloor, then end-nail it in place.

2 To silence a subfloor that has worked away from the joists, drive glue-coated shims into the gaps between the subfloor and the joists.

Silencing Stairs From Below

1 Squeaky stair treads that have parted company with their risers respond quite well to treatments from below.

    First drill pilot holes through the small blocks of 2x2 for the wood screws that will attach to both the tread and the riser. Then coat the contacting surfaces of the blocks with wood glue and drive the screws in both directions.

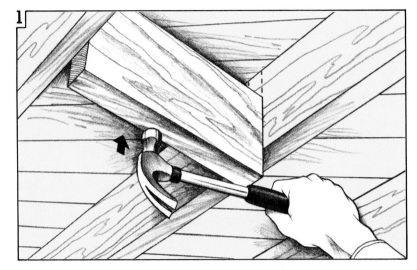

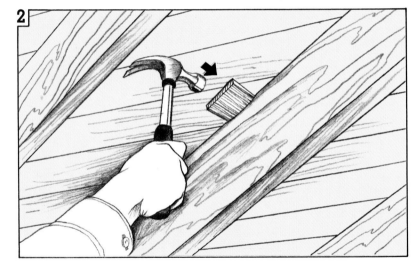

Other Wood Floor Repairs

On the previous two pages you learned how to silence your wood floors. Now we'll show you ways to restore their natural good looks—whether that involves smoothing away annoying scratches or replacing whole sections of damaged boards or tiles.

In both cases your success depends on how well you match your repair to the surrounding floor. So be sure to exercise all due care when removing the damaged flooring and when selecting stains and replacement boards or tiles. When purchasing new wood flooring, take a sample of what you have now so the salesperson can provide you with an exact match.

Hiding Scratches

1 To hide minor imperfections on waxed or varnished floors, first try rubbing the scratched areas with a rag moistened with stain that approximates the stain on your floor.

For surface cuts that don't "disappear" when you treat the surface with stains, use steel wool and a solvent such as cleaning fluid. Realize, however, that if you apply solvent, you'll need to rinse, then refinish, the treated area.

2 You can lift off most food stains and heel and caster marks by buffing the surface with the grain, using fine steel wool moistened with mineral spirits. This technique works especially well for oil-finished wood floors. With acrylic finishes, you'll also need to refinish the area you've abraded.

Replacing Damaged Wood Flooring

1 To remove one damaged floorboard, make several cuts down the center of the board with a circular saw. Adjust the cutting *(continued)*

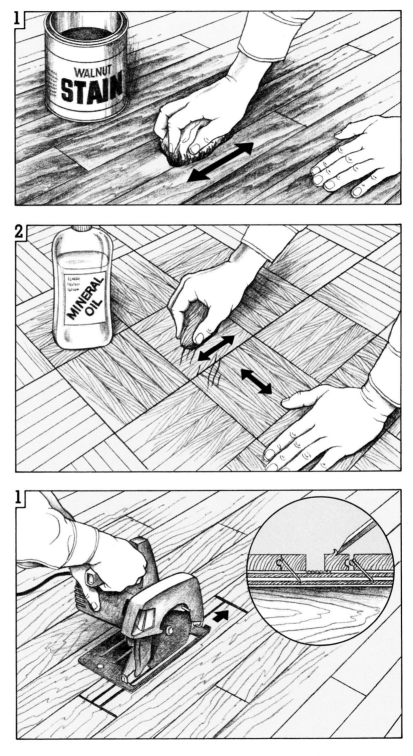

Replacing Damaged Wood Flooring *(Cont.)*

depth to the thickness of the flooring (usually $3/8$ to $3/4$ inch) so you won't damage the subfloor. Work from the center toward the ends to avoid overcutting.

Now chisel out the board, starting with the kerfed midsection and finishing with the sides. Be careful not to damage the groove of the adjacent board.

2 When you're dealing with more than one damaged board, begin by outlining the perimeter of the area to be replaced using a framing square. Go only as far as the edges of the nearest sound boards.

Now, with your circular saw adjusted to the proper cutting depth, cut along the ends of your outline (across the boards, not along their length). Again, cut from the center to the edges. Then make a series of cuts along the length of the damaged area, as was done for the single-board replacement described at the bottom of the previous page.

3 To remove the boards, wedge or drive a pry bar between a couple of the lengthwise cuts as shown, then work it back and forth until you're able to lift one of the boards. Continue prying boards loose one by one.

If you're working with parquet flooring, dispense with sawing and simply nibble away at individual tiles, relying on a hammer and wood chisel to do the job.

4 Secure replacement boards with finish nails blind-nailed through their tongues at about a 50-degree angle. To fit the last board, you'll have to chisel off the bottom of its groove, as shown. Now apply floor adhesive to the subfloor, to the tongue, and to the half-groove of the board, then tap it in place.

Glue replacement parquet tiles with wood tile floor adhesive.

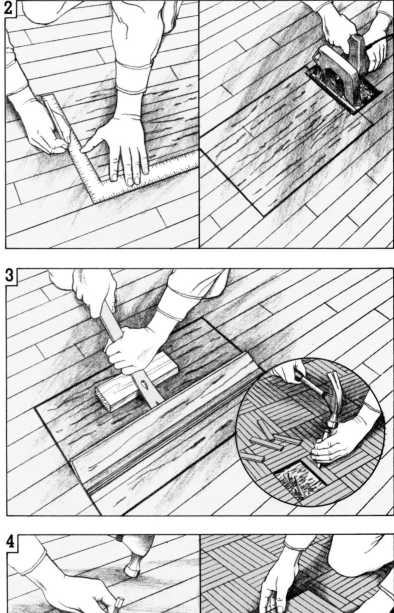

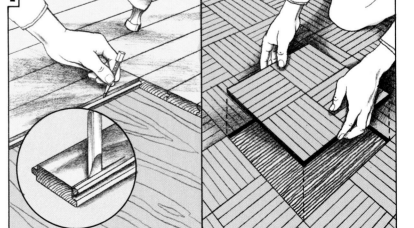

Repairing Resilient Goods

Other than giving a resilient surface floor an occasional buffing with wax or vinyl brightener to help hide minor scratches and renew the original luster, most people assume there's not much a do-it-yourselfer can do with this type of flooring material if problems develop. Not true! Provided that you can lay your hands on matching tiles or sheet goods, you shouldn't have any major difficulties, procedurally, at least, replacing a damaged tile or section of sheet goods and making your floor look almost new again. (Note: The older and more worn the goods, the harder it will be to make the repair unobtrusive.)

Replacing Tiles

1 Begin by covering over the damaged tile with a dampened cloth. Now run a warm iron back and forth across the damaged tile to soften both the tile and the underlying adhesive. (Also use this technique when you simply need to dab more adhesive under a good tile whose corner has curled.)

If you don't have an iron handy, a propane torch works just as well. With this, however, take care that you do not scorch any of the surrounding tile.

2 Score the perimeter of the tile with a utility knife and straightedge. Then, using a stiff-bladed putty knife, pry up the softened tile. If this doesn't do the job, use a hammer and chisel, working out from the tile's center.

3 Scrape away the old tile adhesive and apply new adhesive with a notched trowel. *(continued)*

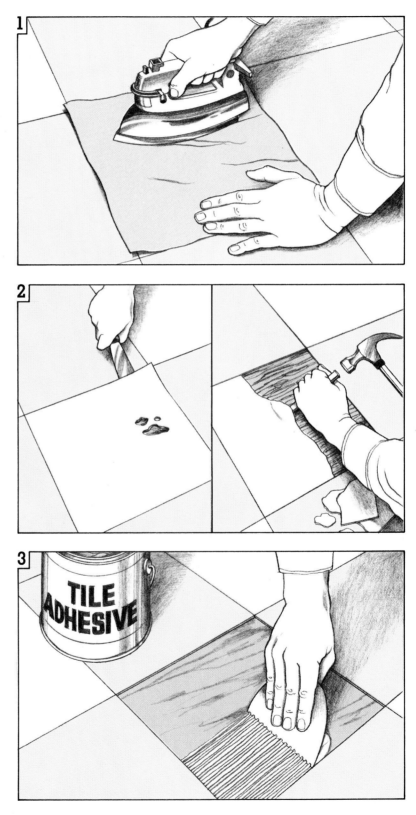

Replacing Tiles *(cont.)*

4 Before laying the replacement tile, warm it slightly under a damp cloth and iron to make it more flexible. Then align one edge with adjoining tile and press (don't slide) it in place.

Immediately clean up any excess adhesive and weight down the new tile with a heavy object.

Patching Sheet Goods

Repairing a damaged area in sheet flooring is essentially like replacing a damaged floor tile: You lay in a "tile patch" that you've cut from a piece of matching sheet goods. But unlike working with tiles, patching sheet goods demands a bit more attention to correctly sizing the patch and carefully matching its pattern to that of the existing floor.

1 Start by positioning the patch material over the damaged area, taking care to align it so the pattern matches the flooring exactly. Secure the patch to the floor with masking tape.

2 Cut through the overlay and the damaged flooring, using a utility knife guided by a straightedge. Make sure your cuts remain outside the damaged area. Cutting along pattern lines helps to conceal the patch.

Remove the old flooring just as if it were a tile (see the sketches opposite and above). Before you apply new adhesive for your patch, trial-fit the patch into the cleaned out opening. You may need to lightly sand the patch's edges for a perfect fit. Finish by placing a weight on the patch.

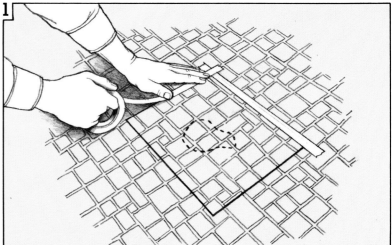

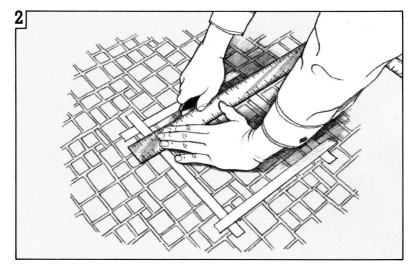

Carpeting Repairs

Removing Stains

Whatever the carpet stain, your first concern should be the same: Treat it as quickly as you can. To remove one of the stains listed in the chart at right, follow the suggested procedure. For other stains and for those you can't identify, use the technique described below.

With still-wet liquid stains, first blot the soiled area with a clean dry cloth. Then use a spoon to remove any solids you can, if there are any. Now treat the stain with dry-cleaning fluid, followed by a detergent-vinegar solution (1 teaspoon of each in a quart of warm water). Blot again, then let the area dry. If needed, reapply whichever cleaner seems to work best, dry again, and brush gently to restore the pile.

Replacing Damaged Sections

Don't attempt to patch-repair a section of carpeting that already shows noticeable wear: Your new-looking patch will probably stand out more than the original damage. Take care to install patches with the pile running in the same direction as the surrounding carpet. With rubber-backed (or other glued-down) carpet, simply glue in your cut-to-size patch. For jute-backed carpet installed with tack strips, follow these steps:

1 Start by piercing the carpet near a wall with an awl and pull the goods up off its tack strips until you have access to the back side of the damaged area. Jot down the exact dimensions of your outline. *(cont.)*

Treating Common Carpet Stains

Stain or Problem	Treatment	Notes
Wax, Grease, Tar, and Chewing Gum	Remove as much of the solid as you can by gently scraping with a dull knife or a spoon. Treat the stain with dry-cleaning fluid.	For chewing gum, apply ice cubes in a plastic bag to harden the gum before scraping.
Cigarette Burns	Snip off the darkened ends of carpet fibers and gently blot the area with a detergent-vinegar solution.	This procedure masks burn damage. For complete repair, patching is necessary.
Lipstick	Gently blot the stain with dry-cleaning fluid, then with detergent-vinegar solution. Rinse with a solution of 1 tablespoon of ammonia in a cup of water.	
Animal Stains, Fruit Juices	If the stain is still wet or fresh, repeatedly sponge it with lukewarm water. Blot dry and treat with detergent-vinegar solution. Wait 15 minutes, blot again, and sponge the area with clean water.	Stains that have caused your carpet to change color often cannot be removed.
Paint	Treat oil-based paints with turpentine, water-based paints with warm water.	
Ink	Treat ball point pen ink by blotting just the ink stain with denatured alcohol.	Permanent ink is just what its name implies. Minimize stain by blotting at once with water.

Replacing Damaged Sections *(continued)*

2 After using your framing square and a utility knife to cut out the damaged area, outline a patch of the same dimensions on the back side of your patch. Note the direction in which the patch's pile will need to run when laying out the outline, then cut the patch with a framing square and utility knife.

3 Lay the carpeting back down over the tack strips and carefully insert your patch (check pile direction). Make sure none of the carpet fibers get folded over.

Now carefully fold back the carpeting, lay seam tape (adhesive side down) along the perimeter of the patch, and heat the tape with an iron until the adhesive melts. (Don't forget to clean your iron while it's still warm.)

4 Weight the taped seams with a heavy object to help ensure a good bond. Don't disturb the patch for at least 15 minutes.

5 To re-stretch the carpet and fasten it to the tack strips, you'll need a special carpet-laying tool called a *knee kicker*, which you can rent from any rental outlet.

Position the head of the kicker about ¾ inch from the wall and kick its butt end with your knee. Work from each end toward the corner of the room.

Mending Torn or Damaged Seams

Seam splits much longer than three feet or so are best repaired by a carpet layer. But short seams, such as the kind found in hallways, respond well to the do-it-yourself repair we explain here. This technique is intended for jute-backed carpet only. To mend

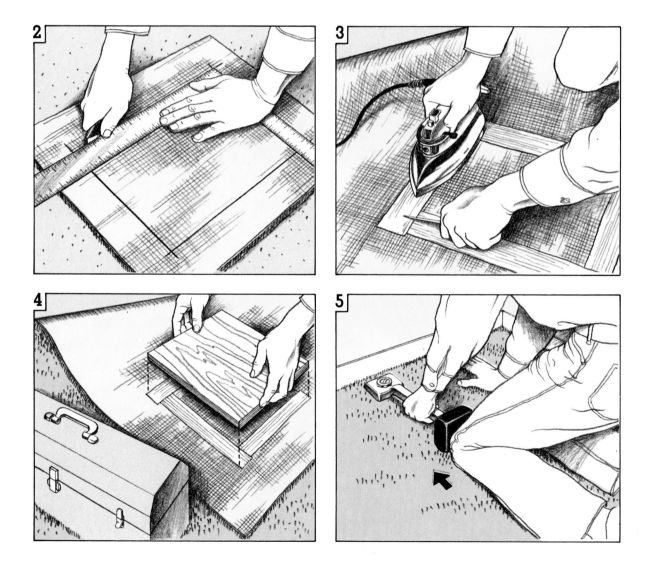

seams in rubber-backed goods or any other carpet that is glued to the floor, apply a bead of seam adhesive to both edges, join the pieces, and place a weight on them for several hours.

1 Split the seam along its entire length (be careful not to cut any carpet fibers) and roll back both pieces of carpet. Because new seam tape won't adhere to the old, remove the existing tape by softening its adhesive with a hot iron.

2 If necessary, stretch the carpet with a knee kicker so the edges of the two pieces meet but don't overlap. Secure the carpet in its correct position by driving a row of nails a short distance back from the seam line. Center new seam tape along the seam line (adhesive side up) and melt its adhesive with a hot iron. Lay both edges onto the tape, being careful not to overlap them. Weight the seam for 15 minutes.

Getting Rid of Bubbles

Carpet that is constantly exposed to moisture or that wasn't stretched tightly enough in the first place can develop bubbles. To get rid of these unsightly and potentially dangerous problem areas, use this tightening technique.

1 Pull the carpet (in the affected area) off its tack strips, and re-stretch it as shown in sketch 5 on page 294. (In large rooms you will need to rent a so-called *power stretcher* to apply adequate tension.) Once you've pulled the carpet tight, run a wide-blade chisel along the wall-floor line to crease the carpet and further push it onto the tack strips.

2 Trim the excess carpet slightly above the crease using a sharp utility knife.

3 Finally, use an awl to tuck the raw edge behind the tack strips.

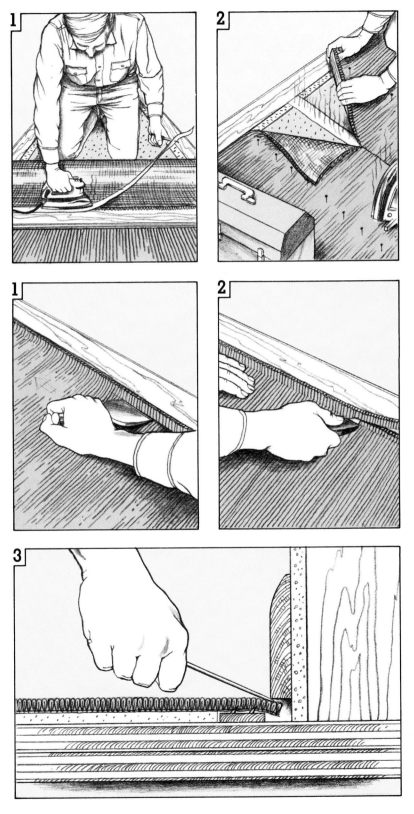

Hard-Surface Flooring Repairs

Part of the beauty of hard-surface floors like tile, brick, and slate is that they require little maintenance. But occasionally you'll still need to remove stains and (less frequently) patch a crack or replace a damaged tile. After reading this and the facing page, you'll have the know-how to handle any such problem you may encounter.

Removing Common Stains

Regardless of the type of stain you need to remove from your hard-surface floor, the sooner you do it, the better. Always wear rubber gloves when working with harsh chemicals, and never use flammable solvents around an open flame.

The chart at right lists cures for common stains on ceramic and quarry tiles, slate, and brick, as well as on grout and concrete. For stains of an unknown nature, consult a flooring dealer for advice.

Filling Cracks and Voids in Concrete

1 Prepare the damaged area by chipping away and brushing out all loose concrete. Then use a hammer and cold chisel to undercut its edges to "lock in" the patch.

2 Now fill the void with latex or epoxy patching material, packing it in with a taping knife or a rectangular trowel. Check the manufacturer's instructions on whether to dampen or otherwise treat the area before filling.

Treating Common Hard-Surface Flooring Stains

Material	Stain	Treatment
Ceramic Tile	Soap Film	Scrub with vinegar; rinse.
	Grease	Keep wet 1 hour with a 1:4 lye-water solution, then rinse and dry.
	Gum, Tar, Wax	Scrape off solids; treat remainder with a rag soaked in kerosene; dry.
	Inks, Dyes	Keep stain wet with household bleach. Warm-water rinse and dry.
	Food Stains	Scrub with trisodium phosphate solution (or bleach); rinse and dry.
	Paint	Soften and remove with acetone.
Brick Pavers, Concrete, Grout	Efflorescence	Scrub with a 1:15 (for light bricks) or 1:10 (for dark bricks) solution of muriatic acid and water. Let stand, then rinse. (Don't apply acids to colored concrete or grout.)
	Grease	Absorb what you can with sawdust or powdered cement, dissolve remaining with a degreaser. Lighten with bleach.
	Paint	For wet paint, use the appropriate solvent. For dried paint, use a remover.
	Rust	Scrub in bleach, let stand, then rinse.
	Soot	Scrub in scouring powder, then rinse.
Slate Quarry Tile		Blot all spills at once and scrub with detergent. Spills that penetrate these porous materials become permanent stains. To prevent stains, apply a sealer.

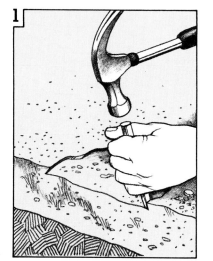

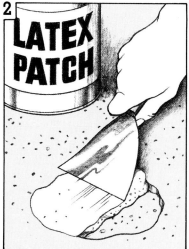

Replacing and Regrouting Tile

1 When a single tile in a field of hard-surface flooring is damaged and needs replacement, here is how to proceed. (To replace loose or deteriorated grout, omit steps 3 and 4.)

Begin by chipping out the old grout with a hammer and a cold chisel held at an angle. As you work, be careful not to damage sound adjacent tiles.

2 When all of the old grout has been loosened, clean out the joints surrounding the tile with a stiff-bristled whisk broom.

3 With the joint spaces cleaned, you now have room to chip away at the damaged tile. Using a hammer and cold chisel, begin chipping at the center of the tile and work toward the edges. Always wear eye protection when working with a cold chisel.

4 To set the replacement tile, use a notched trowel to apply adhesive evenly to the tile's back. (Ask your tile supplier which type of notched trowel—there are many—best suits the kind of adhesive and flooring you intend to use.) When overlaying a wood or resilient floor, use an epoxy cement. For concrete surfaces, dealers recommend thin-set mortar. Carefully center the tile and press (don't slide) it in place.

5 After the adhesive has had at least 24 hours to dry, fill the joint spaces with mortar, using a household sponge. You can add pigment to the new grout to match the existing joints if necessary. Wipe off the excess grout with a clean, dampened sponge.

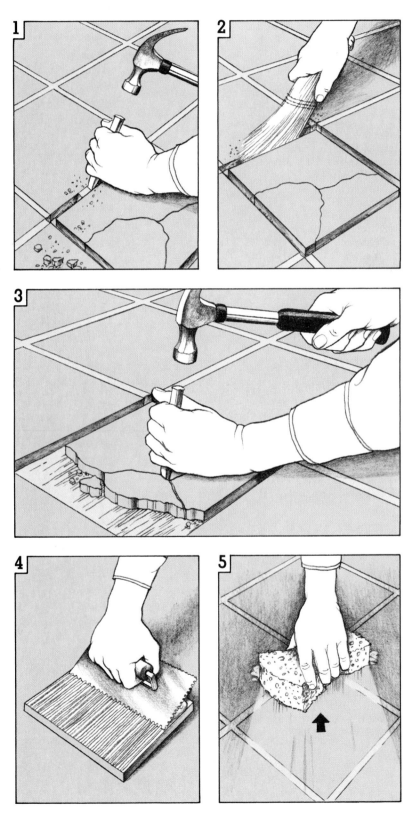

WINDOWS

Because we use windows to brighten the inside of our homes with sunshine and provide us with a view of our outdoor surroundings, we seldom notice them. But occasionally, when an errant baseball finds its way through a glass pane, or when a sash absolutely refuses to budge, or when a screen needs repairing or replacing, windows make their presence known. This chapter was written for those occasions.

Realize, however, that with proper maintenance you can do a great deal to prevent some window problems. To keep windowsills from rotting, for example, make sure they always have a protective coat of paint. Check them each spring and fall. To keep movable sashes working, occasionally clean the channels they ride in. You will be amazed at how smoothly you can make crank-operated windows perform with a squeeze of powdered graphite or a drop of penetrating oil in and around the crank mechanism periodically.

On the next nine pages you'll find the solutions to a host of window problems, including damaged screening, broken panes, balky sashes, and many others. No longer will you have to go to the expense of hiring a repairman, or worse, ignore the repair completely.

Repairing Screening

Holes and tears in screens are among the most put-off repairs around most homes. That's probably because they're not as urgent as a leaky faucet or a binding door or some of the other must-do repair jobs. But you can only procrastinate so long because eventually you won't be able to get fresh air in the house without allowing a horde of pesky flies or mosquitoes in with it.

So if you have one or more screens in need of attention, there's no better time than now to take corrective action. On this and the next two pages, we show you how to repair both small tears and gaping holes in screening as well as how to replace screening in both wood and metal frames.

The tools and materials for screen work are, with a few exceptions, as common home workshop tools as you can find. For mending, you'll need silicone glue or tin snips and a small amount of aluminum or fiber glass. To replace a wood-framed screen, you'll need a putty knife, a screwdriver, a staple gun, some scrap wood strips for stretching the replacement screening, a hammer and brads, and a utility knife. For work on metal sashes, you also may need a length of replacement plastic spline. To make screening replacement work easier still, consider investing in a special screening tool.

Mending Small Holes

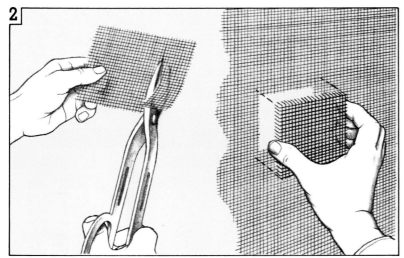

1 Very small tears in metal or fiberglass screening respond well to mending with clear silicone glue. If necessary, dab it on in successive layers until the tear is completely filled.

You can "darn" small holes in metal screening. Unravel a strand or two from a piece of scrap screening and sew the hole shut, weaving the strands into the sound fabric with a needle.

Patching Large Holes

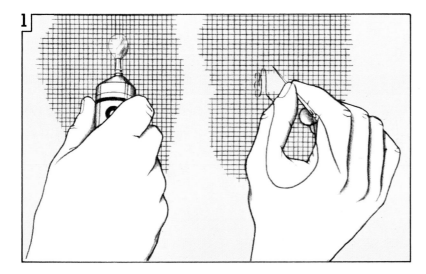

2 To repair large holes in metal screening, start by neatly trimming the damage to a ravel-free square or rectangle using tin snips. Now cut a piece of patch screening that is about two inches larger (overall) than the damaged area.

Unravel a couple of the patch's strands on each side and bend them over at a 90-degree angle. Position the patch over the opening and thread the bent wires through the sound fabric. Then bend the wires over to hold the patch in place.

The technique is even simpler for fiber-glass screening. Cut a patch of similar material with scissors and affix it with transparent-silicone glue.

Replacing Wood-Framed Screening

1 To remove the damaged screening from the frame, pry up on the wood molding strips with a putty knife. Start with the frame's center rail, if it has one, and work from the centers of the strips to their edges. Now remove all of the staples you have exposed and lift out the screening.

To cut your replacement screening to the correct size, unroll a length of it and cut a piece that is several inches wider and at least a foot longer than the frame. Fold over the top edge of the screening about ½ inch and staple this hemmed double layer as shown here, working from the center to the edges.

2 Before stapling the remaining edges of the screening in place, you'll need to make an improvised "stretcher" from a pair of 1x2s. Nail the bottom 1x2 to the floor or a bench, then position the bottom of the frame an inch or two away from the 1x2, with the excess screen lying over it. Now nail the second 1x2 atop the first so the screening is sandwiched between them.

3 Insert two wedges (made by cutting a 1x4 diagonally) between the 1x2 cleats and the bottom of the frame. Now tap the wedges with a hammer until the screening becomes taut. (Tap the wedges gently, alternating sides and being careful to avoid overstretching the screening.)

4 Now staple the bottom edge in place, followed by the sides (pull on the fabric to tighten it before stapling), and finally the center rail, if there is one. Again, begin stapling at the centers, and smooth the mesh as you work out toward the edges.

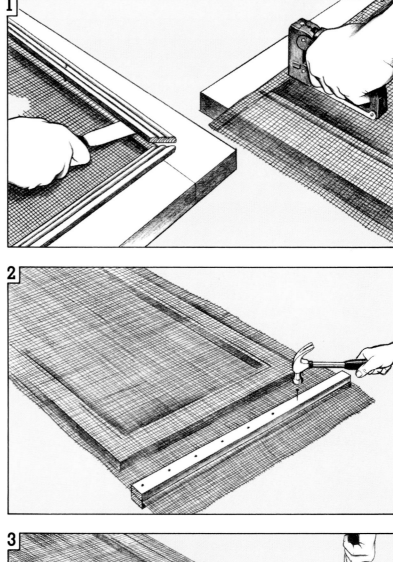

Finish the installation by trimming away the excess from the frame sides and bottom with a utility knife. Refit the screen molding with countersunk brads. Fill the recesses with wood filler.

Replacing Metal-Framed Screening

1 Unlike screens in wood frames, metal-framed screens are held in place by a spline that's friction-fit into a channel around the perimeter of the frame. Removing a damaged screen is simply a matter of prying loose this spline with the blade of a screwdriver.

2 Cut your replacement screen to the same size as the frame's outer dimensions, trimming the corners at 45-degree angles (to make them easier to tuck in). Now use a putty knife to bend an edge of the screen into the channel along one side.

3 Secure this edge by driving a spline (the original or a replacement) into the channel with a hammer and wooden block. Have a helper pull the opposite edges taut, then pull the other two taut as you tap in the remaining splines. Trim away the excess screening with a utility knife. Note in the detail the special screening tool that makes this task even easier.

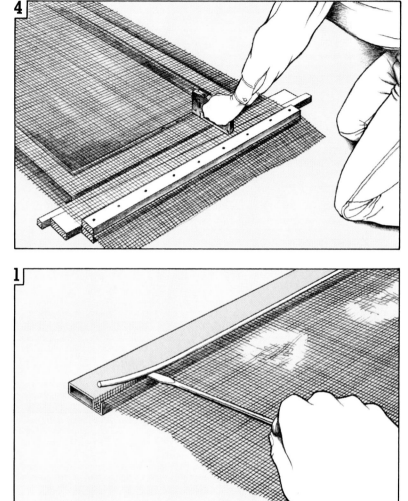

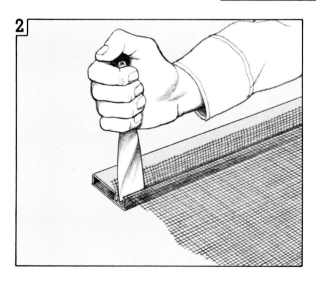

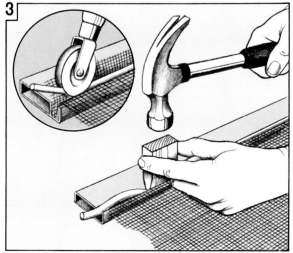

Replacing Broken Windows

Expect to pay dearly if a repairman comes to your house to replace a broken window. Most won't even take on small jobs such as this, and the few who do are forced to charge what may appear to be an exorbitant amount. All the more reason to do the job yourself. The techniques for repairing wood- and metal-framed sashes differ considerably, but neither is difficult. Just be sure to wear heavy gloves whenever you work with glass panes.

Reglazing Wood-Framed Windows

1 Start by removing any loose shards of broken glass, then use an old wood chisel to pry up the glazing compound that holds the pane in place. (Soften the compound with a propane torch if necessary.) Remove the old glazier's points which hold the pane in place.

2 Determine the size replacement pane needed by measuring the cleaned-out opening. Subtract $\frac{1}{16}$ inch from each dimension ($\frac{1}{8}$ inch for acrylic panes).

3 Have a glass supplier cut your replacement pane to size or cut your own. To cut your own, make a single score along each cutoff line with a glass cutter guided by a framing square.
   Then place the score over the dowel or the edge of a table and snap off the scrap piece. Trim any rough edges with pliers.

4 Prime the rabbeted area of the frame in which the pane will rest with linseed oil, wait 20 minutes, then lay on a $\frac{1}{16}$-inch bed coat of glazing compound.

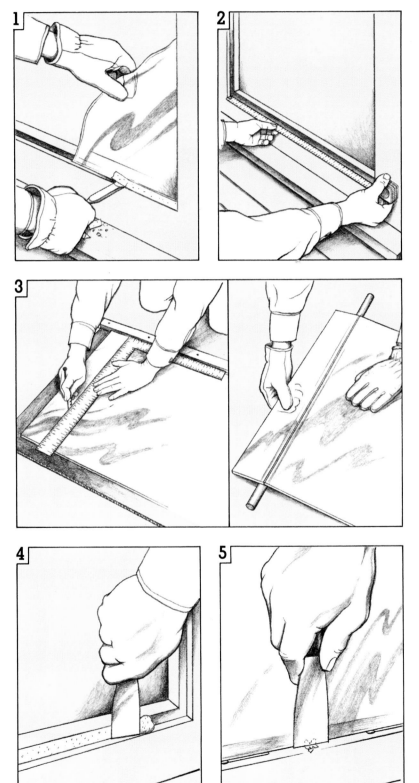

5 Position the glass pane, insert matchsticks around the perimeter to center the glass in the opening, and press into the glazing compound. Install two metal glazier's points per side as shown.

6 To complete the installation, roll some glazing compound into a ¼-inch "rope" and press it around the sash edges.

7 Bevel the compound with a putty knife held at a 30- to 40-degree angle. Allow a week for the compound to dry, then paint around the installation, overlapping the glass about ¹⁄₁₆ inch for a tight weather seal. Don't clean the window until the paint has dried.

Reglazing Metal-Framed Windows

1 Metal sashes come in a variety of configurations. Some are of one-piece construction in which glass is held in place by removable metal clips (augmented by glazing compound) or a flexible spline. Other sashes, the kind glaziers refer to as "knock-aparts," have frames that disassemble for reglazing. With the exception of some of the one-piece spring-clip types, you should remove all metal sashes from their frames when working on them.

Like wood sashes, the *one-piece steel sashes* (the kind often found in basement windows) hold glass in place with glazing compound. But underneath it, metal spring clips take the place of glazier's points. *One-piece aluminum frames* use a vinyl or rubber spline, which you can pry out with a screwdriver and re-install with a putty knife.

In the *"knock-apart"* category, many sliding sashes are held together with edge-driven screws at their corners. Once removed, you simply pull the frame members away from the glass. Some pin-type aluminum frames have internal L-brackets "dimpled" in place at their corners. To release them, drill out the dimples. To reassemble, make new dimples with an awl to hold the L-bracket in place.

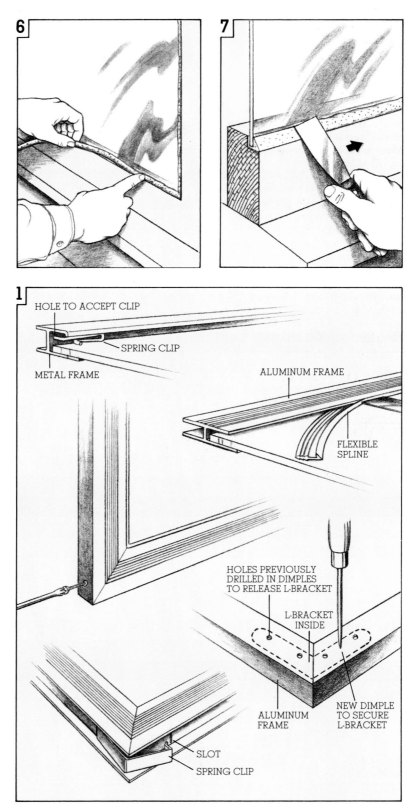

HOLE TO ACCEPT CLIP
SPRING CLIP
METAL FRAME
ALUMINUM FRAME
FLEXIBLE SPLINE
HOLES PREVIOUSLY DRILLED IN DIMPLES TO RELEASE L-BRACKET
L-BRACKET INSIDE
NEW DIMPLE TO SECURE L-BRACKET
ALUMINUM FRAME
SLOT
SPRING CLIP

Repairing Double-Hung Windows

Freeing a Balky Sash

Few things can make you feel more helpless, not to mention more frustrated, than trying to raise or lower a window sash that refuses to cooperate. Below we show and discuss several strategies that should help you free up that bind and keep your blood pressure at a manageable level.

1 If your sash barely moves, dirt may have accumulated in its channels. Try cleaning the channels, then lubricating them with a bar of soap or a paraffin block.

2 If a sash won't move at all, and you haven't used the window since you painted last, the paint may have sealed it shut. To break such a seal, first try wedging an old broad-bladed putty knife between the sash and the stops adjoining it. Gently tap the knife with a hammer, then work it back and forth. Do this along the entire length of the sash and on both sides.

3 No luck? Then grab a pry bar. Working from the outside of the house, force the bar between the sill and the bottom rail and apply upward pressure. Repeat this procedure at several different points along the sill if necessary.

4 To free a sash that has swollen because of moisture, you have a couple of options. You can drive a block of wood that's about $1/16$ inch wider than the sash channel up and down the channel to "spread" the stops enough to allow free movement of the sash. If this doesn't get things moving, sand the base of each of the sash channels as well as the inside edges of the stops to provide a bit more clearance for the sash.

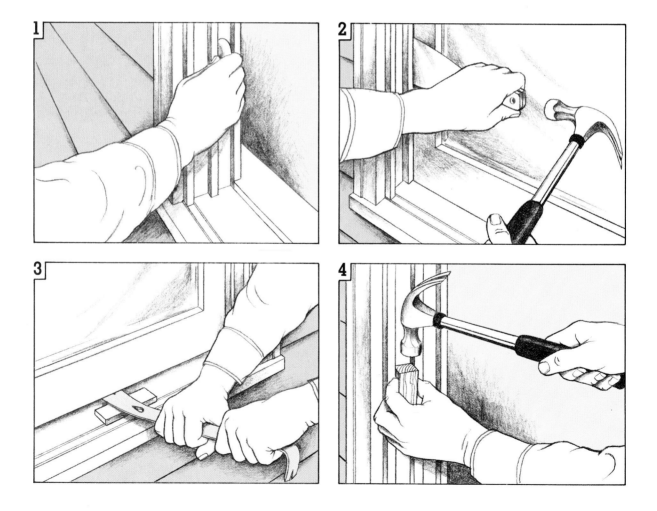

Replacing Sash Cords

Many double-hung windows are outfitted with a set of counterbalances that allow you to open the window to any height. Some manufacturers use a pair of *sash weights* and *sash cords* on each side of the window as the lifting mechanism. As long as proper balance is maintained, the window will work. But as with anything mechanical, adjustment is sometimes needed.

If your windows are the sash cord and weight type like the one shown here, and if they just stay open or cause other trouble, you can bet that one or more sash cords have broken. Here's how to solve that problem quickly.

1 Pry the inside stop molding away from the frame in several spots with a wide-bladed putty knife. (Replace an upper-sash cord by removing the parting strip.)

2 To free the sash, lift it enough to clear the stool and swing it out.

3 Remove the sash cord from its keyed slot in the side of the sash.

4 Unscrew the access panel on the jamb and take out the sash weight.

5 Feed the replacement cord (or sash chain) over the pulley and watch for it to appear at the access panel. (This is also a good time to lubricate the pulley if needed.)

6 Tie the new cord to the sash weight, return the weight to its rightful place, and knot the free end to the sash, permitting the weight to hang three inches above the sill when the sash is fully raised (or the upper sash is lowered). Replace the window and all stops.

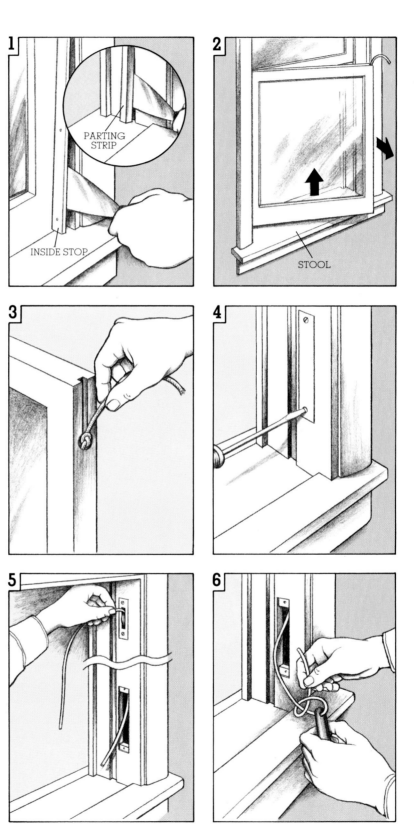

Repairing Crank-Operated Windows

The convenience of crank-operated casement, awning, and jalousie windows is a luxury akin to having power windows on your car. Unfortunately, both can bedevil you with problems. Not surprisingly, most of these difficulties center around the crank operator itself or the linkage and track mechanisms.

Before attempting any of the repairs shown here, study the drawings below. They should give you a general knowledge of how your windows open and close as well as familiarize you with window terminology. (Note: With jalousie windows, except for routine repairs, call in a professional because much of the gear and lever mechanism is hidden from view.)

For help with repairing broken glass or screens, refer to pages 299-303. And if you need to plane off a high spot on a sash that is binding, see page 309 and follow the same general approach as that prescribed for binding doors.

Getting Balky Operator Mechanisms Operating Again

1 Start by opening the window far enough to disengage the arm from the track in which the arm slides. Clean both the track and the portion of the arm that connects to the

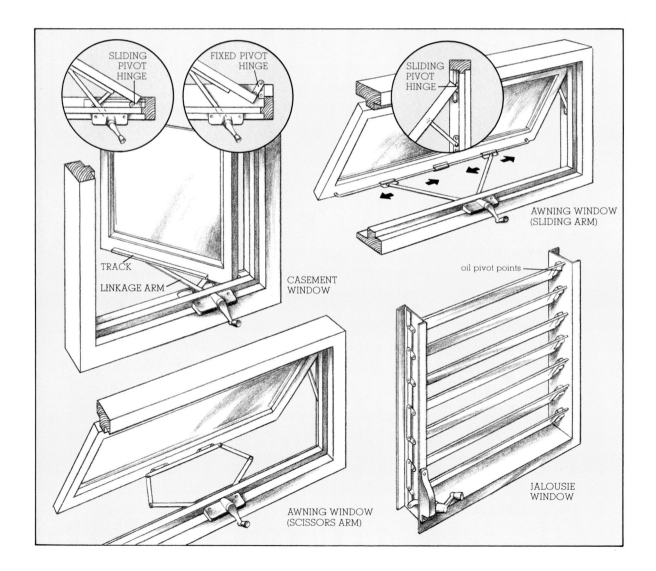

SLIDING PIVOT HINGE

FIXED PIVOT HINGE

SLIDING PIVOT HINGE

AWNING WINDOW (SLIDING ARM)

TRACK

LINKAGE ARM

CASEMENT WINDOW

oil pivot points

AWNING WINDOW (SCISSORS ARM)

JALOUSIE WINDOW

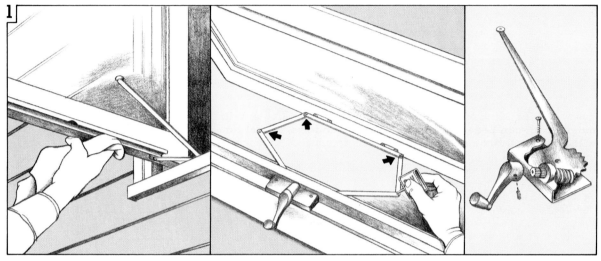

track with a rag or a cotton swab soaked in alcohol or in some cleaning liquid. Lubricate with a light grease or petroleum jelly.

Next, squeeze a penetrating oil into all pivot points and work the parts back and forth until things loosen up. Wipe up any excess oil.

The final step is to remove the operator itself, if possible, and coat the gears with a liberal amount of light grease. Replace the operator mechanism and see whether your effort has paid off.

Replacing an Operator

2 If no amount of cleaning or lubrication can make the window work smoothly, you may elect to replace the entire mechanism. To do this, open the window to the point where you can disengage the linkage arm from its track. Remove the screws holding the crank mechanism to the window frame, then slide out the entire assembly. Buy a replacement operator and install it, reversing the steps shown here.

Snugging Up a Sash

3 After lots of use, many crank-operated windows lose their ability to close tightly. Remedy this problem in either of the ways shown here. Installing weatherstripping is the easiest solution, but shimming works equally well.

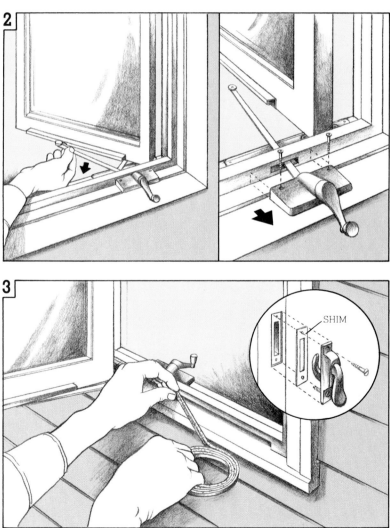

SHIM

DOORS

When a conscientious carpenter hangs doors during construction, he takes special care to ensure that they are plumb and square in their openings. Once the jambs are set and the doorknob and latch set have been installed, he verifies that the door opens and closes as it should and that the latch engages the strike plate correctly.

But that's at construction time. As time passes, the house settles, both the jamb and door itself expand and contract at different rates, and the door is opened and closed countless times. All of these factors (and others) eventually cause problems such as binding doors and loose hinges.

Although it is easy to put off door repairs until "next weekend," consider this: Like a lot of household repairs, door problems usually have a way of growing worse with neglect. Left to run their course, they can be vexing as well as serious compromises to the security and energy efficiency of your home.

In this chapter we show you how to solve several common hinged-door problems. Then we conclude with help for balky garage doors—including tips for heading off problems before they start.

Repairing Hinged Doors

When a hinged door at your house starts to act up, don't immediately pull it off its hinges and whittle away its edges with a sanding block or a plane. Instead, with the door closed, inspect its perimeter and analyze what's causing the problem. Often you can make the repair with the door in place by adjusting the hinges, stops, or strike plate.

Freeing a Binding Door

1 If your door is binding near the top or bottom of the latch edge, first make sure that the hinge leaves on the door or jamb aren't loose (turn to page 310 for help with loose hinges). No problem there? Then you may be able to solve your problem by shimming out one of the hinges. Note: Shim the top hinge to cure a bind near the bottom, and shim the bottom hinge for binds near the top.

To shim out a hinge, open the door and insert a wedge beneath the latch edge for support. Then remove the screws that hold the hinge to the door jamb. Trim a piece of thin cardboard to fit the rectangular mortise on the door jamb, and insert the shim between the jamb and the hinge leaf.

2 If shimming takes care of the bind on the latch edge but causes the door to bind at the top or bottom, or if your only problem is binding at the top or bottom, pinpoint the location of the trouble spot while opening and closing the door. Scribe a line along the door's face to denote where you want to remove wood. If the bind is along the top edge, partially open the door, drive a wedge under its latch edge, and use a block plane to remove the high spot. Work from the end toward the center to avoid splintering the end grain.

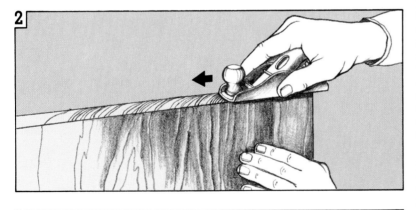

3 If the high spot is on the door's bottom edge or along the hinge edge, take the door off its hinges for planing. With a hammer and a pry bar, tap up on the head of the hinge pins as shown.

Anchor the door in a floor-standing work vise. Hold it firm by wedging one end in a corner or by straddling it, and plane high spots. Then, for side planing, work a jack plane in the direction of the grain, holding it at a slight angle to the door. If you're planing end grain at the door's bottom edge, use a block plane and shave from the door's ends toward the center.

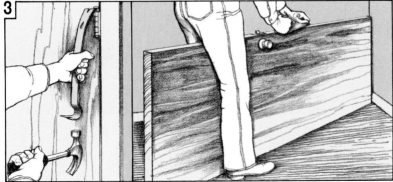

Dealing with Loose and Squeaky Hinges

1 Doors that sag or bind because of hinge-leaf screws that over time have worked loose in their holes and lost their grip are relatively easy to fix, and you needn't remove the door to do it. You should, however, open the door fully and tap a wedge of wood under the bottom of the latch edge with a hammer. This allows you to remove one hinge leaf without putting undue stress on the other hinge(s).

Now remove the loose hinge-leaf screws and determine whether the leaf will accept larger-diameter screws. If it will, install them and retighten the hinge.

If it won't, you can reuse the original screws if you provide a sound foundation in which to drive them. To do this, drill out the enlarged screw holes with a ¼-inch bit and hammer in lengths of glue-coated ¼-inch dowel. Then reposition the hinge leaf and secure it by driving the screws into the dowels.

2 If your hinges are tight but noisy, here's how to eliminate annoying squeaks and reduce the unnecessary hinge wear that corrosion can cause. First, pry up the hinge pin ¼ inch or so and squirt a few drops of light oil down into the barrel portion of the hinge. Have a rag handy to catch excess oil. Swing the door back and forth several times.

If the hinge continues to squeak, open the door fully, drive a wood wedge under the hinge side, and remove the pin. Clean any rust from the pin with steel wool, and from the barrel portion of the hinge using a stiff, pipecleaner-type wire brush. Apply a light coat of oil to the pin and replace it. (Don't drive the head of the pin all the way onto the hinge; leave a little space under it for easier removal next time.)

Curing Strike and Latch Problems

When your door closes but won't latch, it's a safe bet that your latch and strike plate aren't seeing eye to eye. Since it's impractical to tamper with the location of the latch in the door, you must make adjustments at the *strike plate* in the jamb.

1 If your latch and strike plate aren't engaging, examine the latch as the door closes to see which edge of the plate opening is causing it to hang up. (Scratches on the plate may already tell you.) If the two are off by no more than $\frac{1}{8}$ inch, remove the strike plate, anchor it in a vise, and file down the appropriate edge with a flat metal file. You also may need to chisel a larger opening in the door jamb to provide clearance for the latch.

2 If the latch and plate are off by more than $\frac{1}{8}$ inch, adjust the location of the plate in the jamb. Do this by extending the mortise in the proper direction.

To do this, score the edges of the extension to the proper depth with a sharp wood chisel and a hammer. Hold the chisel perpendicular to the jamb, with its bevel toward the mortise. Now reverse the direction of the bevel and work from inside the mortise to remove the rest of the wood, holding the chisel at about a 30-degree angle.

When a latch doesn't extend far enough into the strike plate, shim out the plate using the technique shown in sketch 1 on page 309.

3 Here's what to do when your door doesn't close far enough for the latch to engage. (This technique can also tighten the fit of a door that rattles in its frame.) Pry off the stop molding, allow the door to latch, and draw a line on the jamb to indicate where the stop molding needs to be. Reinstall the stop molding along this line. Finish the repair by painting or staining the bare wood you've uncovered.

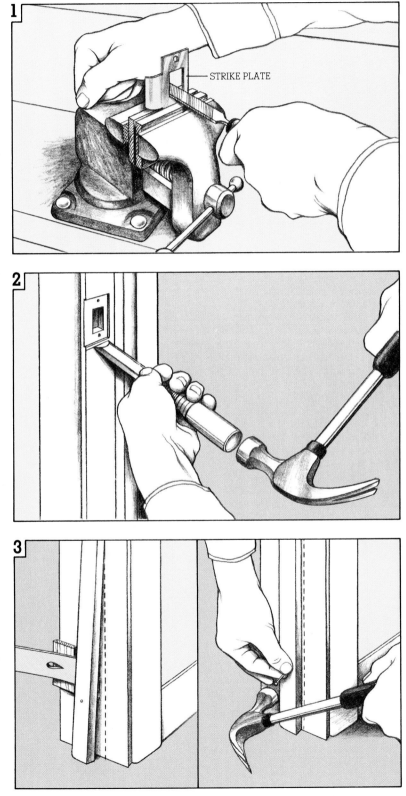

STRIKE PLATE

Repairing Garage Doors

A smoothly operating garage door is something we too often take for granted. At no time is this more evident than the morning it suddenly refuses to open.

When garage door problems do occur, they usually result from damage caused by moisture or lack of proper maintenance. Moisture—some of it unavoidable—may have warped the door, rusted its hardware, or even rotted away an entire section of framing members that hold it in alignment. Or maybe you've allowed the door's brackets to loosen or its tracks to become clogged with dirt and grime.

A periodic maintenance routine is your best insurance against garage door difficulties. This consists of nothing more than keeping the track clean, keeping the hardware lubricated, and tightening any nuts or hold-down bolts that may have worked loose. You might be surprised at how these measures head off most overhead door problems.

1 When your garage door binds as it travels on its track, it may be because the track brackets have loosened and the tracks are no longer parallel to each other. You can easily check this by measuring the distance between them with a tape measure at several points. If the tracks are out of alignment, loosen the appropriate track brackets, tap the tracks back into parallel alignment with a couple of good hammer blows (making sure that the vertical tracks are plumb), and retighten the brackets.

2 If your door binds just as it starts to open or tries to close completely and its tracks are tight and parallel, check to see whether the edges are rubbing on the inside surface of the trim molding. Sometimes abrasions at the edges of the door's face will indicate this. One way to correct this problem is to remove the outside trim molding and reinstall it slightly farther from the door to provide more clearance.

Another (often easier) way is to relocate the vertical tracks farther from the trim molding. If the bracket isn't adjustable, remove the lag screws holding the track brackets in place and reinstall the brackets with wood-block shims inserted between the brackets and the framing members. If yours are adjustable, simply loosen the bolts and make the needed adjustment.

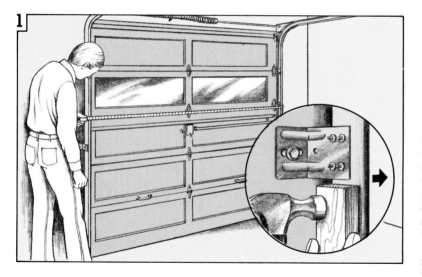

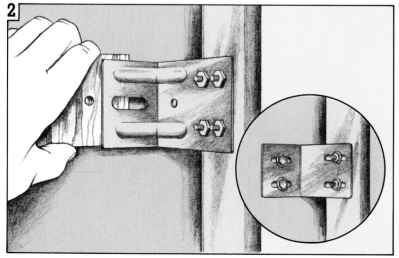

3 Perhaps the simplest garage door adjustment you can make is correcting a bar lock that fails to key into the track. You can easily move the bar lock guides up or down in their slide mounts to bring the bar into alignment.

4 Even a garage door that operates smoothly may need rebalancing from time to time. Indications of this are when the door opens or closes too easily or won't stay in its opened position. A properly balanced garage door should stay open when it's about three feet off the driveway. Above that point it should slowly rise to its fully opened position; below that point it should slowly close.

If your garage door fails to open in the way mentioned here, the springs that pull the door open probably have lost tension and need tightening. These springs are fully stretched when the door is closed, and under the least tension when it's fully open. So when you make the following adjustments, open the door fully to relax the springs, and secure there.

With some *spring tension* mechanisms, one end of the spring attaches to one of the holes in a bracket attached to the door jamb. You can increase spring tension by hooking the spring into a higher hole (you may need to remove the cable from the other end of the spring to do this). Adjust the spring on each side of the door equally to keep balanced tension.

With other spring tension mechanisms, you can add stretch to the spring by taking up slack in the cable that holds the spring's pulley connector. Take up cable slack (on both sides) about an inch at a time until you achieve the right balance.

Yet a third mechanism is known as a *torsion spring*. Unless you've had prior experience adjusting this type of door, call in a qualified serviceman to balance it for you. The torsion spring is under tremendous pressure, and is potentially dangerous if improperly handled.

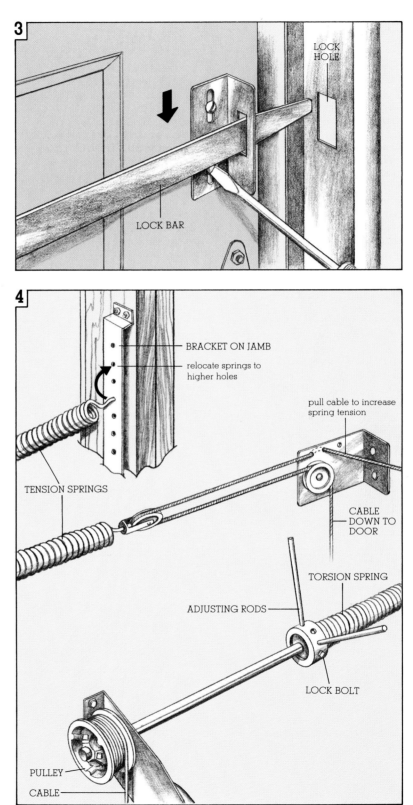

Index

**If you would like to order any
additional copies of our books,
call 1-800-678-2802 or check with
your local bookstore.**